T0205445

THE TURING TEST

STUDIES IN COGNITIVE SYSTEMS

VOLUME 30

EDITOR

James H. Fetzer, *University of Minnesota, Duluth*

ADVISORY EDITORIAL BOARD

Fred Dretske, *Stanford University*

Charles E. M. Dunlop, *University of Michigan, Flint*

Ellery Eells, *Univeristy of Wisconsin, Madison*

Alick Elithorn, *Royal Free Hospital, London*

Jerry Fodor, *Rutgers University*

Alvin Goldman, *University of Arizona*

Jaakko Hintikka, *Boston University*

Frank Keil, *Cornell University*

William Rapaport, *State University of New York at Buffalo*

Barry Richards, *Imperial College, London*

Stephen Stich, *Rutgers University*

Lucia Vaina, *Boston University*

Terry Winograd, *Stanford University*

THE TURING TEST

The Elusive Standard of Artificial Intelligence

Edited by

JAMES H. MOOR

Dartmouth College, Hanover, U.S.A.

KLUWER ACADEMIC PUBLISHERS
DORDRECHT / BOSTON / LONDON

A C.I.P. Catalogue record for this book is available from the Library of Congress.

ISBN 1-4020-1204-7 (HB)
ISBN 1-4020-1205-5 (PB)

Published by Kluwer Academic Publishers,
P.O. Box 17, 3300 AA Dordrecht, The Netherlands.

Sold and distributed in North, Central and South America
by Kluwer Academic Publishers,
101 Philip Drive, Norwell, MA 02061, U.S.A.

In all other countries, sold and distributed
by Kluwer Academic Publishers,
P.O. Box 322, 3300 AH Dordrecht, The Netherlands.

Photograph of "The Universal Electronic computer", reproduced by kind permission of
P.N. Furbank, Alan Turing's executor.

Printed on acid-free paper

Printed in the Netherlands.

CONTENTS

CONTENTS

4. DEFENSE

5. ALTERNATIVES

ORIGINS OF THE ARTICLES

Selmer Bringsjord, Paul Bello, David Ferrucci: Creativity, the Turing Test, and the (Better) Lovelace Test, in: *Minds and Machines* 11(1): 3-27; Feb 2001

B. Jack Copeland: The Turing Test, in: *Minds and Machines* 10(4): 519-539; Nov 2000

Bruce Edmonds: The Constructibility of Artificial Intelligence (as Defined by the Turing Test), in: *Journal of Logic, Language and Information* 9(4): 419-424; Oct 2000

Gerald J. Erion: The Cartesian Test for Automatism, in: *Minds and Machines* 11(1): 29-39; Feb 2001

S. Harnad: Minds, Machines and Turing, in: *Journal of Logic, Language and Information* 9(4): 425-445; Oct 2000

Larry Hauser: Look Who's Moving the Goal Posts Now, in: *Minds and Machines* 11(1): 41-51; Feb 2001

James H. Moor: The Status and Future of the Turing Test, in: *Minds and Machines* 11(1): 77-93; Feb 2001

Gualtiero Piccinini: Turing's Rules for the Imitation Game, in: *Minds and Machines* 10(4): 573-582; Nov 2000

William J. Rapaport: How to Pass a Turing Test, in: *Journal of Logic, Language and Information* 9(4): 467-490; Oct 2000

Edmund M.A. Ronald: Intelligence is not Enough: On the Socialization of Talking Machines, in: *Minds and Machines* 11(4): 567-576; Nov 2001

Ayse Pinar Saygin, Ilyas Cicekli, Varol Akman: Turing Test: 50 Years Later, in: *Minds and Machines* 10(4): 463-518; Nov 2000

Susan G. Sterrett: Turing's Two Tests for Intelligence, in: *Minds and Machines* 10(4): 541-559; Nov 2000

Saul Traiger: Making the Right Identification in the Turing Test, in: *Minds and Machines* 10(4): 561-572; Nov 2000

Sean Zdenek: Passing Loebner's Turing Test: A Case of Conflicting Discourse Functions, in: *Minds and Machines* 11(1): 53-76; Feb 2001

THE UNIVERSAL ELECTRONIC COMPUTER
installed at Manchester University by Ferranti Limited,
who are manufacturing under licence from the Corporation.

Alan Standing.

PREFACE

In 1950 Alan Turing (1912-1954) published his famous article, "Computing Machinery and Intelligence" in the journal *Mind*. This article is arguably the most influential and widely read article in the philosophy of artificial intelligence. Indeed, most of the debate in the philosophy of artificial intelligence over the last fifty years concerns issues that were raised and discussed by Turing. Turing's genius was not only in developing the theory of computability but also in understanding the impact, both practical and philosophical, that computing machinery would have. Turing believed that computers, if properly designed and educated, could exhibit intelligent behavior, even behavior that would be indistinguishable from human intelligent behavior. His vision of the possibility of machine intelligence has been highly inspiring and extremely controversial.

In this classic article Turing presented his well known imitation game and predicted that about the year 2000 "an average interrogator will not have more than 70 per cent chance of making the right identification after five minutes of questioning" in the imitation game. Based on the results of the Loebner 2000 contest and the accomplishments in the field of AI, as impressive as they are, Turing's prediction remains unfulfilled. Therefore, this is an appropriate time to reassess the Turing test. How should the Turing test be understood in light of recently published materials by Turing? What is the status of traditional criticisms of the test? Can the Turing test be defended against such criticisms? What are new criticisms of the test? Are there superior tests that might replace the Turing test? What is the significance of the Loebner contests? Does the Turing test have a future in AI or has it outworn its usefulness?

For fifty years the Turing test has been the elusive standard in artificial intelligence. Should it be a standard in artificial intelligence at all? Why hasn't it been passed? And what conclusions should we draw if it were passed? This book contains insightful papers that address the basic issues about the nature and viability of the Turing test. The book has the most recent scholarship on the subject and yet provides an overview of the last half century debate about the merits of test. The book should serve as an aid to scholars and a guide to students. Of course, it is also intended as a tribute to Alan Turing, a mathematician and philosopher much ahead of his time.

James H. Moor

The Turing Test*

B. JACK COPELAND
*The Turing Archive for the History of Computing, University of Canterbury, Private Bag 4800,
Christchurch, New Zealand and Dibner Institute for the History of Science and Technology,
Massachusetts Institute of Technology, Cambridge MA 02139, USA;
E-mail: bjcopeland@canterbury.ac.nz*

Abstract. Turing's test has been much misunderstood. Recently unpublished material by Turing casts fresh light on his thinking and dispels a number of philosophical myths concerning the Turing test. Properly understood, the Turing test withstands objections that are popularly believed to be fatal.

1. Introduction: The State of Machine Intelligence Circa 1950

The birth of Artificial Intelligence is usually placed at approximately 1956, the year in which a program written by Newell, Simon, and Shaw – later named the Logic Theorist – successfully proved theorems from Whitehead and Russell's *Principia Mathematica*, and also the year of John McCarthy's *Dartmouth Summer Research Project on Artificial Intelligence*, the conference which gave the emerging field its name. However, this received view of the matter is not historically accurate. By 1956, computer intelligence had been actively pursued for some 10 years in Britain – under the name *machine intelligence* – and the earliest AI programs to run were written there in 1951–52. That the earliest work in the field was done in Britain is in part a reflection of the fact that the first electronic stored-program digital computers to function were built in that country (at Manchester University (the MUC, 1948) and Cambridge University (the EDSAC, 1949)). Another significant factor was the influence of Turing on the first generation of computer programmers.

Turing was thinking about machine intelligence at least as early as 1941 (D. Michie, personal communication, 1998). He is known to have circulated a typewritten paper on machine intelligence among his wartime colleagues at the Government Code and Cypher School, Bletchley Park. Now lost, this was undoubtedly the earliest paper in the field. It probably concerned machine learning and heuristic problem-solving. Both were topics that Turing discussed extensively during the war years at GC & CS, as was mechanical chess. In 1945, Turing expressed the view that a computer 'could probably be made to play very good chess' (1945: 41).

Turing's 'Proposal for Development in the Mathematics Division of an Automatic Computing Engine (ACE)' (Turing, 1945), which was written at the National Physical Laboratory, London, between October and December 1945, was the first relatively complete specification of an electronic stored-program general-purpose digital computer. The slightly earlier – and better known – 'First Draft of a Report on the EDVAC' contained little engineering detail, in particular concerning electronic hardware (composed by von Neumann on the basis of discussions with other members of the Moore School group at the University of Pennsylvania, the 'First Draft' was in circulation from May 1945). In contrast, Turing's 'Proposal' contained detailed circuit designs and detailed specifications of hardware units, specimen programs in machine code, and even an estimate of the cost of building the machine (£11,200). Artificial intelligence was not far from Turing's thoughts: he described himself as 'building a brain' (D. Bayley, personal communication, 1997) and he remarked in a letter to W. Ross Ashby that, in working on the ACE, he was 'more interested in the possibility of producing models of the action of the brain than in the practical applications to computing'.

In London in 1947 Turing gave what was, so far as is known, the earliest public lecture to mention computer intelligence, saying 'What we want is a machine that can learn from experience' and '[t]he possibility of letting the machine alter its own instructions provides the mechanism for this' (Turing, 1947: 123). In 1948 he wrote a report for the National Physical Laboratory entitled 'Intelligent Machinery'. This was the first manifesto of AI and in it Turing brilliantly introduced many of the concepts that were later to become central to the field, in some cases after reinvention by others. These included the *theorem-proving* approach to problem-solving, the hypothesis that 'intellectual activity consists mainly of various kinds of search' (1948: 23), the concept of a *genetic algorithm*, and, anticipating connectionism, the proposal that networks of artificial neurons be 'trained' (Turing's word) to perform specific tasks (see further Copeland and Proudfoot, 1996, 1999a). The major part of the report consists of an exquisite discussion of machine learning. Turing describes some experiments concerning the modification of an initially 'unorganised machine', by a process akin to teaching by reward and punishment (1948: 17–21). He subsequently referred to this unorganised machine as a 'child-machine' (1950a: 457), saying that he had 'succeeded in teaching it a few things, but the teaching method was too unorthodox for the experiment to be considered really successful' (ibid.: 457). The report ends with a description of a restricted form of what Turing was later to call the 'imitation game':

> It is possible to do a little experiment ... even at the present stage of knowledge. It is not difficult to devise a paper machine which will play a not very bad game of chess. Now get three men as subjects for the experiment, A, B, and C. A and C are to be rather poor chess players. B is the operator who works the paper machine. (In order that he should be able to work it fairly fast it is advisable that he be both mathematician and chess player.) Two rooms are used with some arrangement for communicating moves, and a game is played between C and either A or the paper machine. C may find it quite difficult to tell which he is playing. (This is a rather idealized form of an experiment I have actually done.) (1948: 23)

In 1951, Turing gave a lecture on machine intelligence on British radio (Turing, 1951a), part of which is reproduced in Section 6 below. One of Turing's listeners was Christopher Strachey. To Strachey belongs the honor of having written the

2

earliest AI program, a checkers (or draughts) player which first ran successfully in Turing's Computing Machine Laboratory at Manchester University. At the time Strachey was a schoolmaster at Harrow; he later became Director of the Programming Research Group at Oxford University, where with Dana Scott he did the work on the semantics of programming languages for which he is best known. Strachey initially coded his checkers program in May 1951 for the Pilot Model of the ACE at the National Physical Laboratory. This version of the program did not run successfully; Strachey's efforts were defeated first by coding errors and subsequently by a hardware change that rendered his program obsolete. Strachey transferred his allegiance to the Manchester laboratory, which in February 1952 took delivery of a Ferranti Mark I computer; built by the Manchester firm of Ferranti, in close collaboration with the Computing Machine Laboratory, the Mark I was the world's first commercially available electronic stored-program computer. This machine had more memory than the Pilot ACE and was better suited to Strachey's purposes. With Turing's encouragement, and using Turing's recently completed *Programmers' Handbook* for the Ferranti machine (Turing, 1950b), Strachey finally got his program working. By the summer of 1952 the program could play a complete game of checkers at a reasonable speed. Strachey's program used simple heuristics and looked ahead 3–4 turns of play. The state of the board was represented on the face of a cathode ray tube – one of the earliest uses of computer graphics.

In 1952, Strachey described his checkers program at a computing conference in North America. Arthur Samuel of IBM took over the essentials of Strachey's program and coded a checkers player for the IBM 701. This was the first AI program to function in the U.S. In 1955 Samuel added learning to the program.

Strachey himself was thinking about machine learning at the time of writing his checkers player, devising a simple rote-learning scheme that he envisaged being implemented in a NIM-playing program. Strachey wrote at length concerning machine learning in a letter to Turing that he composed on the evening of Turing's radio broadcast. The following is a short extract from this letter:

> I have just been listening to your talk on the Third Programme. Most stimulating ... [i]n paricular your remark ... that the programme for making a machine think would probably have great similarities with the process of teaching; this seems to me absolutely fundamental. ... I am convinced that the crux of the problem of learning is recognizing relationships and being able to use them. ... There are, I think, three main stages in learning from a teacher. The first is the exhibition of a few special cases of the rule to be learned. The second is the process of generalisation – i.e. the underlining of the important features that these cases have in common. The third is that of verifying the rule in further special cases and asking questions about it. I have omitted any mention of 'understanding' the rule, because this is not appropriate at the moment to the action of a machine. I think, as a matter of fact, that the process of understanding a rule is connected with finding relationships between it and other rules – i.e. second (or higher) order relations between relations and this might well become

important for a machine later. ... I think it might well be possible to programme the Manchester machine to do all of these stages, though how much it would be able to learn in this way before the storage became inadequate remains to be seen. ... (Strachey to Turing, 15 May 1951)

However, Strachey missed the opportunity to be the first to achieve a functioning program that incorporated learning. The earliest such programs were written by Anthony Oettinger, at the University of Cambridge Mathematical Laboratory, home of the EDSAC. Oettinger was considerably influenced by Turing's views on machine learning. Oettinger's 'response-learning programme,' details of which were published in 1952, could be taught to respond appropriately to given stimuli, by means of expressions of 'approval' or 'disapproval' by the teacher. As training proceeded, errors became less frequent, and the learned response would be initiated by a progressively weaker stimulus. Oettinger described the response-learning program as 'operating at a level roughly corresponding to that of conditioned reflexes,' remarking that the 'behaviour pattern of the response-learning ... machine is sufficiently complex to provide a difficult task for an observer required to discover the mechanism by which the behaviour of the ... machine is determined.'

Oettinger's 'shopping machine', also reported in 1952, incorporated rote-learning. Adopting Turing's terminology, Oettinger described this program as a 'child machine.' The shopping machine's simulated world was a mall of eight shops. When sent out to purchase an item, Shopper would if necessary search for it, visiting shops at random until the item was found. While searching, Shopper would memorise a few of the items stocked in each shop that it visited. Next time Shopper was sent out for the same item, or for some other item that it had already located, it would go to the right shop straight away.

Oettinger was the first programmer to claim a program capable of passing a restricted Turing test. Shopper, he said, could successfully play a version of Turing's imitation game in which

the questions are restricted to ... the form 'In what shop may article j be found?'

2. Did Turing Offer a Definition of 'Thinking' (or 'Intelligence')?

In his classic paper on the Turing test, Moor (1976) wrote:

[T]he proponents and critics of the imitation game have misunderstood its significance. The real value of the imitation game lies not in treating it as the basis for an operational definition but in considering it as a potential source of good inductive evidence for the hypothesis that machines think. (1976: 249; see also Moor, 1987)

Twenty-five years later, the lesson has still not been learned that there is no *definition* to be found in Turing's paper of 1950. Commentator after commentator states that Turing's intention was to offer a definition of 'thinking' or 'intelligence'. French, a prominent critic of the Turing test, asserts:

The Turing Test [was] originally proposed as a simple operational definition of intelligence. (French, 2000: 115)

Perhaps the publication of the little-known remarks by Turing that appear in Section 3, below, will scupper this misunderstanding once and for all.

Unfortunately, Turing's biographer, Andrew Hodges, endorsed the claim that Turing's intention was to provide a definition. Hodges' statement that Turing

introduced ... an operational definition of 'thinking' or 'intelligence' ... by means of a sexual guessing game (1992: 415)

has no doubt misled many.

It is difficult to reconcile the suggestion that Turing intended to propose a definition of 'thinking' or 'intelligence' with his explicit statement in the 1950 paper that machines may

carry out something which ought to be described as thinking but which is very different from what a man does. (1950a: 435)

Nevertheless, some commentators who notice this remark persist in the claim that Turing put forward a definition. Block writes as follows:

An especially influential behaviorist definition of intelligence was put forward by Turing [1950a]. ... Turing's version of behaviorism formulates the issue of whether machines could think or be intelligent in terms of whether they could pass the following test ... The computer is intelligent *if and only if* the judge cannot tell the difference between the computer and the person. (Osherson and Lasnik, 1990: 248, my italics)

Then, in a footnote, in which he mentions the statement by Turing just quoted, Block remarks that Turing

jettisoned the claim that being able to pass the Turing test is a necessary condition of intelligence, weakening his claim to: passing the Turing test is a sufficient condition for intelligence. (ibid.: 249–250)

However, Turing never claimed in the first place that the ability to pass the Turing test is a necessary condition for intelligence; it is entirely misleading to describe him as *jettisoning* this necessary condition and *weakening* his claim. (Sadly, these misleading claims appear in a widely-read textbook.)

In fact, as we shall see, Turing explicitly denies that he is proposing a definition. The material by Turing presented in Section 3 may also assist in the eradication of another myth, namely that Turing did not intend to propose a *test*. Whitby complains about

the change from the label 'imitation game' to 'Turing test' by commentators,

and he says that the

suggestion that the [imitation game] might be some sort of test involves an important extension of Turing's claims. (1996: 54)

Similarly, Narayanan writes:

Turing did not originally intend his imitation game to be a test as such. (1996: 66)

Turing did indeed intend his game to be a test.

3. Turing's 1952 Presentation of the Imitation Game

The following is an extract from the typewritten script of a BBC radio broadcast entitled 'Can Automatic Calculating Machines Be Said To Think', recorded in January 1952.[1] In response to the introductory remarks

> We're here today to discuss whether calculating machines can be said to think in any proper sense of the word. ... Turing, ... [h]ave you a mechanical definition?,

Turing replies:

> I don't want to give a definition of thinking, but if I had to I should probably be unable to say anything more about it than that it was a sort of buzzing that went on inside my head. But I don't really see that we need to agree on a definition at all. The important thing is to try to draw a line between the properties of a brain, or of a man, that we want to discuss, and those that we don't. To take an extreme case, we are not interested in the fact that the brain has the consistency of cold porridge. We don't want to say 'This machine's quite hard, so it isn't a brain, and so it can't think.' I would like to suggest a particular kind of *test* that one might apply to a machine. You might call it a test to see whether the machine thinks, but it would be better to avoid begging the question, and say that the machines that pass are (let's say) 'Grade A' machines. The idea of the test is that the machine has to try and pretend to be a man, by answering questions put to it, and it will only pass if the pretence is reasonably convincing. A considerable proportion of a jury, who should not be expert about machines, must be taken in by the pretence. They aren't allowed to see the machine itself – that would make it too easy. So the machine is kept in a far away room and the jury are allowed to ask it questions, which are transmitted through to it: it sends back a typewritten answer. ... [The questions can concern] anything. And the questions don't really have to be questions, any more than questions in a law court are really questions. You know the sort of thing. 'I put it to you that you are only pretending to be a man' would be quite in order. Likewise the machine would be permitted all sorts of tricks so as to appear more man-like, such as waiting a bit before giving the answer, or making spelling mistakes, but it can't make smudges on the paper, any more than one can send smudges by telegraph. We bad better suppose that each jury has to judge quite a number of times, and that sometimes they really are dealing with a man and not a machine. That will prevent them saying 'It must be a machine' every time without proper consideration.

Well, that's my test. Of course I am not saying at present either that machines really could pass the test, or that they couldn't. My suggestion is just that this is the question we should discuss. It's not the same as 'Do machines think,' but it seems near enough for our present purpose, and raises much the same difficulties.

The 1952 exposition significantly modifies the arrangements described by Turing in 1950. According to the earlier formulation, the Turing test is a three-party game involving the parallel interrogation by a human of a computer and a human foil. According to the 1952 formulation, members of a jury question a series of contestants one by one, some of the contestants being machines and some humans. (The arrangements adopted in the Loebner series of Turing tests, sometimes condemned as improper, in fact conform to Turing's 1952 formulation of his test.) The later formulation abandons the condition, implicit in the earlier, that each interrogator shall know that one of each pair of contestants is a human and one a machine. It appears that the 1950 formulation is superior, since the test as formulated in 1952 is open to a biassing effect, which disfavours the machine. Results of the Loebner series of competitions reveal a strong propensity among jurors to classify human respondents as machines. In the Loebner competition held at Dartmouth College in January 2000, human respondents were mistaken for computers on 10 occasions, a computer for a human on none. The same effect was present in similarly structured tests performed with Colby's program Parry (Heiser, Colby et al., 1980). In a total of 10 interviews there were five misidentifications; in four of these a human respondent was mistaken for a computer. Presumably this phenomenon is the result of a determination on the part of the jurors not to be fooled by a program. This lengthening of the odds against the machine cannot occur in the three-player form of the test.

It is interesting that, in the 1952 formulation, Turing specifically excludes computer scientists from the jury. This is certainly in the same spirit as his remark in 1948, quoted above, that jurors in the chess-player version of the test should be 'rather poor' at chess. It is often pointed out (for instance by Douglas Lenat in a paper presented at Turing 2000) that certain characteristic weaknesses in human reasoning – for example, a willingness in certain circumstances to assign a lower probability to a conjunct than to the conjunction, or the tendency to fail to take notice of certain disconfirming instances of conditional statements (weaknesses which are easily detectable by Wason tests and the like) – could be used to unmask any computer not specifically programmed to reproduce these human foibles. However, it is likely that had Turing been writing after the relevant empirical discoveries by Wason, Johnson-Laird, Taversky, Kahnemann, and others, that he would have excluded from the jury not only those who are 'expert about machines' but also those who are expert about the human mind.

In the 1950 formulation, Turing introduces his test by first describing an imitation game involving an interrogator and two subjects, one male (A) and one female (B). The interrogator must determine, by question and answer, which of A and B is the man (A's object in the game being to try to cause the interrogator to make the wrong identification). Turing then asks 'What will happen when a machine takes the part of A in this game?' (1950a: 434). However, later in the paper he describes matters a little differently, saying that the part of A is taken by a machine and 'the part of B ... by a man' (1950a: 442). Sterrett (this volume) distinguishes between what she calls the 'original imitation game test', or 'OIG test', and what she calls the 'standard Turing test', which she says is described in the second of these passages. In the 'OIG test', the computer attempts to impersonate a woman, and its degree of success is compared with a male player's degree of success at impersonating a woman. If one sees the tests that Sterrett distinguishes as different, one may wonder which Turing intended to advocate (perhaps both). Traiger (this volume) argues that Turing was advocating the OIG test. However, in the 1952 formulation, Turing says simply that '[t]he idea of the test is that the machine has to try and pretend to be a man ... and it will pass only if the pretence is reasonably convincing.' Indeed, in the little-known material concerning the test contained in Section 6 below, which dates from 1951, Turing presents matters in a starkly un-gendered form: the point of the test is to determine whether or not a computer can 'imitate the brain'. It seems unlikely, therefore, that Turing's intention in 1950 was to endorse only the female-impersonator form of the test, or that he saw himself as describing different tests in the passages in question.

There is another minor tension in the 1950 paper. Turing says both that

> [t]he original question, 'Can machines think?' I believe to be too meaningless to deserve discussion (1950a: 442)

and that

> [w]e cannot altogether abandon the original form of the problem [viz. 'Can machines think?'], for opinions will differ as to the appropriateness of the substitution and we must at least listen to what has to be said in this connexion (ibid.).

Turing was no doubt overstating his case in the first of these quotations. In the 1952 material, Turing's attitude to the question 'Can machines think?' is much milder; and likewise in the material appearing in Section 6, where Turing makes liberal use of such phrases as 'programm[ing] a machine ... to think' and 'the attempt to make a thinking machine'.

4. The 1950 and 1952 Predictions

In 1950 Turing predicted that

> in about fifty years' time it will be possible to programme computers ... to make them play the imitation game so well that an average interrogator will not have more than 70 per cent chance of making the right identification after five minutes of questioning. (1950a: 442)

It has been said that the outcome of the 2000 Loebner Turing test shows Turing's prediction to have been in error. But far from it. 'About fifty years' does not mean 'exactly fifty years'. Moreover, Turing's prediction is a fairly modest one: 3 out of 10 average interrogators are to make a wrong identification on the basis of no more than five minutes questioning. (Turing's prediction is sometimes mis-reported (e.g. by Whitby 1996: 61) as being the claim that, by the end of the 20th century, computers would succeed in deceiving the interrogator 70 percent of the time.) The qualification 'average' presumably indicates that the interrogators are not to be computer scientists, psychologists, or others whose knowledge or training is likely to render them more skilled at the task than an average member of the population.

In 1952, in an exchange with another contributor to the same BBC broadcast, the Cambridge mathematician Max Newman,[2] Turing offered a prediction that is interestingly different from the above:

Newman: I should like to be there when your match between a man and a machine takes place, and perhaps to try my hand at making up some of the questions. But that will be a long time from now, if the machine is to stand any chance with no questions barred?

Turing: Oh yes, at least 100 years, I should say.

This prediction perhaps concerns success of a more substantial nature than that envisaged in the much-quoted 1950 prediction. Possibly Turing would have endorsed the result of precising the 1952 prediction in the way proposed in the 1950 paper:

> We now ask the question, "What will happen when a machine takes the part of A in this [man-imitates-woman] game?" Will the interrogator decide wrongly as often when the game is played like this as he does when the game is played between a man and a woman? (1950a: 434)

Reformulating the 1952 prediction in this fashion produces: It will be at least 100 years (2052) before a computer is able to play the imitation game sufficiently well so that judges will decide wrongly as often in man-imitates-woman imitation games as in machine-imitates-man (or human) imitation games, in each case no questions being barred.

5. De Cordemoy's Anticipation of the Turing Test in 1668

Descartes famously declared that it is

> not conceivable that ... a machine should produce different arrangements of words so as to give an appropriately meaningful answer to whatever is said in its presence, as the dullest of men can do.[3]

The Cartesian Géraud de Cordemoy wrote at some length on the matter of distinguishing between that which thinks and that which does not. The following extracts are from his *A Philosophicall Discourse Concerning Speech* of 1668.

9

> To speak is not to repeat the same words, which have struck the ear, but to utter others to their purpose and suitable to them. ... [N]one of the bodies that make echoes do think, though I hear them repeat my words ... I should by the same reason judge that parrets do not think neither. ... But not to examine any further, how it is with parrets, and so many other bodies, whose figure is very different from mine, I shall continue the inquiry ... [Concerning those] who resemble me so perfectly *without* ... I think I may ... establish for a Principle, that ... if I finde by all the experiments I am capable to make, that they use speech as I do, ... I have infallible reason to believe that they have a soul as I. (1668: 13–14)

I dub the following *de Cordemoy's Principle*: If all the experiments that we are capable of making show that x uses speech as we do, then x has a soul (i.e. thinks).

De Cordemoy himself assumed, not surprisingly, that a machine would always be easily unmasked.

> I do very well conceive, that a meer Engin might utter some words, yet I understand at the same time, that if the organs, which should distribute the wind, or open the pipes, whence those voices should issue, had a certain settled order among them, they could never change it, so that when the first voice were heard, those that were wont to follow it, would needs be heard also, provided the wind were not wanting to the Engin; whereas the words which I hear uttered by bodies made like mine have almost never the same sequel. (ibid.: 6)

Of course, even this Engin might on some occasions be mistaken for a thinking thing by 17th century folk untutored in the ways of machinery. However, experiments involving more discriminating judges (or even further experiments involving the same judges) would easily reveal that in fact the Engin does not use speech as we do. By insisting that x perform satisfactorily in all experiments, de Cordemoy's principle allows for the fact that the results of some may be misleading. In modern terms, a machine that happens to pass one Turing test, or even a series of them, might be shown by subsequent tests to be a relatively poor player of the imitation game.

In a trenchant critique of the Turing test, Shieber imputes to Turing the view that

> any agent that can be mistaken by virtue of its conversational behavior [for] a human must be intelligent. (1994: 70)

This view, supposedly embodied in the Turing test, has been the target of much criticism. The fact that a program has been mistaken for a human by a particular set of interrogators may tell only of the gullibility of those interrogators; or, indeed, the program may by good luck have given a thoroughly atypical performance, in the fashion of a first-season football star whose performance subsequently regresses to the mean. Therefore, it is argued, a positive outcome of the Turing test cannot be sufficient for the claim that the successful machine thinks. However, there is no reason to believe that Turing is any more vulnerable to this objection than is de Cordemoy. Turing's position as described by Turing is entirely consistent with the

Cordemoy-like view that the result of any given experiment is defeasible and may be disregarded in the light of other experiments.

6. Turing's Remarks on the Foundation of the Turing Test

The following is an extract from Turing's lecture 'Can Digital Computers Think?', which was broadcast on BBC radio in May 1951.[4] Turing's was the second in a series of lectures with the general title 'Automatic Calculating Machines.' Other speakers in the series included Newman, Hartree, Wilkes, and F.C. Williams. (The extract is from Turing's own typescript.)

> I believe that [digital computers] could be used in such a manner that they could appropriately be described as brains. ... This ... statement needs some explanation. ... In order to arrange for our computer to imitate a given machine it is only necessary to programme the computer to calculate what the machine in question would do under given circumstances ... If now some particular machine can be described as a brain we have only to programme our digital computer to imitate it and it will also be a brain. If it is accepted that real brains, as found in animals, and in particular in men, are a sort of machine it will follow that our digital computer suitably programmed will behave like a brain. This argument involves [the assumption] which can quite reasonably be challenged ... that this machine should be of the sort whose behaviour is in principle predictable by calculation. ...

> [A]lthough [digital computers] might be programmed to behave like brains, we do not at present know how this should be done. ... [A]s to whether we will or will not eventually succeed in finding such a programme ... I, personally, am inclined to believe that such a programme will be found. I think it is probable for instance that at the end of the century it will be possible to programme a machine to answer questions in such a way that it will be extremely difficult to guess whether the answers are being given by a man or by the machine. I am imagining something like a viva-voce examination, but with the questions and answers all typewritten in order that we need not consider such irrelevant matters as the faithfulness with which the human voice can be imitated. ...

> [O]ur main problem [is] how to programme a machine to imitate the brain, or as we might say more briefly, if less accurately, to think. ... The fact is that we know very little about [how to do this]. ... The whole thinking process is still rather mysterious to us, but I believe that the attempt to make a thinking machine will help us greatly in finding out how we think ourselves.

I dub the following *Turing's Principle*: A machine that by means of calculation imitates – or, better, 'emulates,' for Turing is concerned with faithful imitation[5] – the intellectual behaviour of a human brain can itself appropriately be described as a brain, or as thinking. (Only the intellectual behaviour of the brain need be

11

emulated: 'we are not interested in the fact that the brain has the consistency of cold porridge'.)

It is often claimed that Turing was insufficiently specific in his description of his test. What are the specifications of a *definitive* test? How long? How many judges? What number of correct identifications is to be tolerated? However, these demands appear to miss the point. Whether a given machine is able to emulate the brain is not the sort of matter that can be settled conclusively by a test of brief duration. A machine emulates the brain if it plays the imitation game successfully come what may, with no field of human endeavour barred, and for any length of time commensurate with the human lifespan. Consider two time-unlimited imitation games, a man-woman game and a machine-human game, each employing the same diversity of judges that one might encounter, say, on the New York subway. If, in the long run, the machine is identified correctly no more often than is the man in the man-woman game, then the machine is emulating the brain. Any test short enough to be practicable is but a sampling of this ongoing situation. After some amount of sampling, we may become convinced that, in the long run, the machine will play as well as the man, but only because we believe that our samples of the machine's performance are representative, and we may always change our opinion on the basis of further rounds of the game.

Turing's position appears to consist of essentially three components: (1) Turing's Principle; (2) the claim that the method of question and answer provides a suitable means for determining whether or not a machine is able to emulate human intellectual behaviour; and further (3) that the imitation game, in its specific provisions, is suitable for this purpose. How might Turing have defended these individual propositions?

Turing speaks elsewhere of the need to give 'fair play' to machines (e.g. Turing, 1947: 123). It is perhaps in some such terms that Turing would seek to defend his claim that whatever emulates the brain can appropriately be described as thinking. As for the second claim, Turing offers an explicit justification: the 'question and answer method'

> draw[s] a fairly sharp line between the physical and the intellectual capacities of a man

and

> seems to be suitable for introducing almost any one of the fields of human endeavour that we wish to include. (1950a: 434–435)

No explicit justification of the third claim is given. Some doubts about the truth of the claim – for example, that the outcome of the test is a function of the gullibility of the jury – can be allayed as above, by pointing out that (there is no reason to think Turing would have denied that) the upshot of any given round of play of the imitation game may be disregarded in the light of further rounds.

Turing's phraseology in the 1950 and 1952 presentations sometimes calls to mind his proposal (Turing, 1936) that such questions as "Is there an effective method for solving such-and-such a mathematical problem?" be replaced by the clear and unambiguous "Is there a Turing machine for solving the problem in question?" (a proposal now known as the Church-Turing thesis):

> I shall replace the question ['Can machines think?'] by another, which is closely related to it and is expressed in relatively unambiguous words. (1950a: 433)

Some pages later Turing describes this proposal as a *tentative suggestion*:

> It was suggested tentatively that the question 'Can machines think?' should be replaced by 'Are there imaginable digital computers which would do well in the imitation game?' (1950a: 442)

What in 1936 was also something of a tentative suggestion had found widespread support by the time of Turing's paper of 1948 (and since that date, of course, even more logico-mathematical evidence has amassed in favour of the suggestion):[6]

> It is found in practice that LCMs ['logical computing machines' – Turing's expression for (what Church called) Turing machines] can do anything that could be described as 'rule of thumb' or 'purely mechanical.' This is sufficiently well established that it is now agreed amongst logicians that 'calculable by means of an LCM' is the correct accurate rendering of such phrases. (Turing, 1948: 7)

Certainly no such consensus has yet arrived in the case of Turing's later suggestion. But nor, despite 50 years of vigorous and sometimes highly ingenious criticism, has there been a successful attempt to refute it.

One obvious objection to Turing's proposal is that it involves an anthropocentric bias. As Turing himself puts the objection:

> The game may perhaps be criticised on the ground that the odds are weighted too heavily against the machine. ... May not machines carry out something which ought to be described as thinking but which is very different from what a man does? (1950a: 435)

It is important to keep in mind that Turing's proposal concerns the – as it were, existentially quantified – question 'Can machines think?'. Moreover, Turing advanced the proposal in the belief that computers will play the imitation game successfully. There might indeed be questions of the form 'Can machine M think?' which could not be settled by the imitation game. Turing's opinion is presumably that any question of this form that cannot be so settled is insufficiently clear in meaning to admit of an unambiguous answer: only where the replacement by 'Can machine M do well in the imitation game?' is appropriate does the question 'deserve discussion'. At best, the objection shows only that if no successful player of the imitation game were to emerge, the question 'Can machines think?' might remain unsettled. Turing cheerfully sets aside this possibility:

> [The] objection is a very strong one, but at least we can say that if, nevertheless, a machine can be constructed to play the imitation game satisfactorily, we need not be troubled by this objection. (ibid.)

7. Attempts to Discredit the Turing Test

These have, of course, been many and varied. I select three that are especially prominent. (Shieber, for example, singles these out, describing them as 'strong' (1994: 74).)

7.1 BLOCKHEADS

A 'blockhead' (after Block, 1981) is a hypothetical program able to play the imitation game successfully, for any fixed length of time, by virtue of incorporating a large, but finite, 'lookup' table containing all the exchanges with the interrogator that could occur during the length of time in question. Such a program emulates the intellectual behaviour of the brain but (it is assumed) does not think, in contradiction to Turing's Principle. I will call this the 'lookup table objection'. Although usually credited to Block, this objection to the Turing test has occurred to a number of writers. The earliest known presentation of the objection was by Shannon and McCarthy in 1956:

> The problem of giving a precise definition to the concept of 'thinking' and of deciding whether or not a given machine is capable of thinking has aroused a great deal of heated discussion. One interesting definition has been proposed by A.M. Turing: a machine is termed capable of thinking if it can, under certain prescribed conditions, imitate a human being by answering questions sufficiently well to deceive a human questioner for a reasonable period of time. A definition of this type has the advantages of being operational, or, in the psychologists' term, behavioristic. ... A disadvantage of the Turing definition of thinking is that it is possible, in principle, to design a machine with a complete set of arbitrarily chosen responses to all possible input stimuli ... Such a machine, in a sense, for any given input situation (including past history) merely looks up in a 'dictionary' the appropriate response. With a suitable dictionary such a machine would surely satisfy Turing's definition but does not reflect our usual intuitive concept of thinking. This suggests that a more fundamental definition must involve something relating to the manner in which the machine arrives at its responses – something which corresponds to differentiating between a person who solves a problem by thinking it out and one who has previously memorized the answer. (1956: v–vi)

The formal point on which the objection rests – essentially that if the timespan of the imitation game is (finite and) bounded, and if the rate at which characters can be typed is likewise bounded, then all possible interchanges can be inscribed on a finite segment of the tape of a Turing machine – would have been obvious to Turing. In the 1950 paper, he points out that the behaviour of any discrete system with a finite number of configurations can be represented by a finite lookup table, and that a computer can mimic the system if supplied with the table:

discrete state machines ... can be described by such tables provided they have only a finite number of possible states. ... Given the table corresponding to a discrete state machine ... [and provided the calculation] could be carried out sufficiently quickly the digital computer could mimic the behaviour of [the] discrete state machine. The imitation game could then be played with the machine in question (as B) and the mimicking digital computer (as A) and the interrogator would be unable to distinguish them. Of course the digital computer must have an adequate storage capacity as well as working sufficiently fast. (1950a: 440–441)

What Turing might have said in response to Shannon and McCarthy may perhaps be inferred from his caveats concerning storage capacity and speed, especially if those remarks are taken in conjunction with the following (from the broadcast 'Can Automatic Calculating Machines Be Said to Think?'):

Newman: It is all very well to say that a machine could ... be made to do this or that, but, to take only one practical point, what about the time it would take to do it? It would only take hour or two to make up a routine to make our Manchester machine analyse all possible variations of the game of chess right out, and find the best move that way – *if* you didn't mind its taking thousands of millions of years to run through the routine. Solving a problem on the machine doesn't mean finding a way to do it between now and eternity, but within a reasonable time. ...

Turing: To my mind this time factor is the one question which will involve all the real technical difficulty. If one didn't know already that these things can be done by brains within a reasonable time one might think it hopeless to try with a machine. The fact that a brain *can* do it seems to suggest that the difficulties may not really be so bad as they now seem.

The answer to Shannon, McCarthy, Block et al, that these remarks suggest is this: firstly, the proposed recipe for building a brain-emulator cannot work, given practical limitations on storage capacity; and secondly, even if this point is set aside and we suppose that such a machine were actually to be constructed, it would *not* emulate the brain, since what the brain can do in minutes would take this machine 'thousands of millions of years.'

If Turing had been proposing a definition of 'thinking' – a logically necessary and sufficient condition – or even merely a logically sufficient condition, then the lookup table objection would indeed count against the proposal, since the objection establishes that 'if x plays the imitation game satisfactorily, then x thinks' is false in some possible world very different from the actual world. However, there is no reason to believe that Turing was claiming anything more than that his principle is actually true. The other-worldly possibility of a lookup-table machine that is fast enough to emulate the brain has no tendency at all to show that Turing's principle is *actually* false. (Likewise, it is no challenge to the actual truth of the Church-Turing thesis that a human rote-worker who occupies a possible world in which the human memory is unlimited can be in the process of writing down a number that is not computable by any Turing machine (see Turing, 1936: 231, 249–252).)

7.2. THE CHINESE ROOM

As is well-known, Searle (1980) considers the case of a human clerk – call him or her Clerk – who 'handworks' a computer program that is capable of passing the Turing test in Chinese. Clerk is a monolingual English speaker. The program is presented to Clerk in English in the form of a set of rule-books. Clerk works in a room concealed from the interrogator's view; he and the interrogator communicate by passing sheets of paper through a slot. To the interrogator, the verbal behaviour of the Room – the system that includes the rule-books, Clerk, the erasable paper memory, Clerk's pencils and rubbers, the input and output provisions, and any clock, random number generator, or other equipment that Clerk may need in order to execute the program in question – is by hypothesis indistinguishable from that of a native Chinese speaker.

Here is Searle's argument:

> [Clerk] do[es] not understand a word of the Chinese ... [Clerk] ha[s] inputs and outputs that are indistinguishable from the native Chinese speaker, and [Clerk] can have any formal program you like, but [Clerk] still understand[s] nothing. [A] computer for the same reasons understands nothing ... [W]hatever purely formal principles you put into the computer will not be sufficient for understanding, since a human will be able to follow the formal principles without understanding ... (1980: 418)

> [Clerk] can pass the Turing test; [Clerk] can fool native Chinese speakers. ... The example shows that there could be two 'systems', both of which pass the Turing test, but only one of which understands ... (ibid.: 419)

The flaw is a simple one: Searle's argument is *not logically valid*. The proposition that the formal operations carried out by Clerk do not enable Clerk to understand the Chinese inputs and outputs by no means entails the quite different proposition that the formal operations carried out by Clerk do not enable the Room to understand the Chinese inputs and outputs. One might as well claim that the statement 'The organisation of which Clerk is a part has no taxable assets in Japan' follows logically from the statement 'Clerk has no taxable assets in Japan'. Searle's example does not show, therefore, that there could be a system which passes the Turing test but which does not understand (think).

It is important to distinguish this, *the logical reply* to the Chinese room argument (Copeland, 2001, 1993), from what Searle calls the *systems reply*. The systems reply is the following claim:

> While it is true that the individual person who is locked in the room does not understand the story, the fact is that he is merely part of a whole system and the system does understand the story. (ibid.: 419)

As Searle correctly points out, the systems reply is worthless, since it 'simply begs the question by insisting without argument that the system must understand Chinese' (ibid.). The logical reply, on the other hand, is a point about entailment.

16

The logical reply involves no claim about the truth – or falsity – of the statement that the Room can understand Chinese.

7.3. FRENCH: ASSOCIATIVE PRIMING AND RATING GAMES

As already mentioned, French (1990, 2000) is among those who mistakenly interpret Turing as offering a definition of intelligence. French, moreover, takes Turing to be offering a definition of 'intelligence in general.' French argues against Turing's supposed 'operational definition of intelligence,' objecting that

> the Test provides a guarantee not of intelligence but of culturally-oriented *human* intelligence ... [T]he Turing Test [is] a test for *human* intelligence, not intelligence in general. (1990: 12)[7]

Here French is simply missing the point. Far from Turing's offering the imitation game as a test for 'intelligence in general,' Turing did intend it precisely as a means for determining whether or not a given machine emulates the human brain.

More interestingly, French also 'take[s] issue with Turing's ... claim ... that in the not-too-distant future it [will] in fact be possible actually to build ... a machine' that plays the imitation game successfully. French believes that the imitation game's 'very strength becomes a weakness': since the 'game ... provides a very powerful means of probing humanlike cognition,' only 'a machine capable of experiencing the world in a manner indistinguishable from a human being' is likely to enjoy success in the game (ibid.: 15, 25). French illustrates his claim with ingenious examples.

7.3.1. Associative Priming

Empirical studies show that in word/non-word recognition tasks, subjects take less time to determine that an item is a word if presentation of the item is preceded by presentation of an associated word (e.g. prior presentation of 'bread' facilitates recognition that 'butter' is a word). French writes:

> The Turing Test interrogator makes use of this phenomenon as follows. The day before the Test, she selects a set of words (and non-words), runs the lexical decision task on the interviewees and records average recognition times. She then comes to the Test armed with the results ... [and] identifies as the human being the candidate whose results more closely resemble the average results produced by her sample population of interviewees. The machine would invariably fail this type of test because there is no a priori way of determining associative strengths ... Virtually the only way a machine could determine, even on average, all of the associative strengths between human concepts is to have experienced the world as the human candidate and the interviewers had. (1990: 17)

French's proposal is illegitimate. The specifications of the Turing test are clear: the interrogator is allowed only to put questions. There is no provision for the use of the timing mechanisms necessary for administering the lexical decision task and for measuring the contestants' reaction times. One might as well allow the introduction of apparatus for measuring the contestants' magnetic fields or energy dissipation.

7.3.2. Rating Games[8]

The following are examples of questions that could be asked in the course of what French calls a 'rating game': on a scale of 0 (completely implausible) to 10 (completely plausible), rate ' "Flugbloggs" as a name Kellogg's would give to a new breakfast cereal', rate ' "Flugly" as the surname of a glamorous female movie star', 'rate banana splits as medicine' (ibid.: 18, 21).

French believes that questions like these will enable an interrogator to identify the computer. However, such questions may be of no assistance at all, since the computer is at liberty to attempt to pass itself off as a member of a foreign culture (e.g. as a tourist from rural Japan on his or her first trip overseas). Conveniently, French claims to discern 'an assumption tacit in Turing's article', namely that the computer must pass itself off as a member of the interrogator's own culture (ibid.: 15). French leaves it a mystery why Turing would have wished to impose a restriction which makes the test harder for the computer to pass and yet offers no conceptual gain. In fact, Turing says explicitly in the 1952 presentation that the computer is to 'be permitted all sorts of tricks so as to appear more man-like'. (Likewise the human foil need not be drawn from the same culture as the interrogator.)

French terms his rating game questions 'subcognitive', meaning that they probe the candidates' 'subconscious associative network ... that consists of highly over-lapping activatable representations of experience' (ibid.: 16). This description of the questions is driven by connectionist theory, of course. An AI researcher might say with some justice that in so far as French's sample questions ('rate dry leaves as hiding places', 'rate pens as weapons', 'rate jackets as blankets', and so forth (ibid.: 20–21)) have any one thing in common, it is that the majority of them probe the candidates on their common-sense knowledge of the world. Viewed in this light, French's rating games fail, for the most part, to provide any new challenge. Nor can French assume that only connectionist devices will perform satisfactorily in these games: it remains to be seen how high a score can be obtained by a conventional computer equipped with a massive store of common sense knowledge, such as Lenat's presently incomplete CYC.

Turing himself envisaged that the process of constructing the machine that is to 'imitate an adult human mind' may involve subjecting a 'child machine' to 'an appropriate course of education', which would possibly include allowing the machine 'to roam the countryside' equipped with 'the best sense organs that money can buy' (1950a: 455, 456, 457, 460; 1948: 13). Turing canvasses the possibility that the 'child machine' should consist of an initially unorganised network of neuron-like elements (1948: 14–16). One might reasonably conjecture that the resulting adult machine would do rather well in the Turing test. In the end, French's case against Turing's predictions of success in the imitation game rests on French's claim that unless a machine 'resembled us *precisely* in *all* physical respects', its experiences of the world would differ from ours in a way 'detectabl[e] by the Turing Test' (ibid.: 22, 23; my italics). However, French offers no argument whatsoever for this claim.

8. Prognosis

In 1953 Maurice Wilkes, head of the Cambridge University Mathematical Laboratory and designer of the EDSAC, wrote:

> If ever a machine is made to pass [Turing's] test it will be hailed as one of the crowning achievements of technical progress, and rightly so. (1953: 1231)

I agree entirely. A recent volume on Turing's work suggests that the Turing test be '[c]onsigned to history' (Millican and Clark, eds, 1996: 53). It will not be, of course. Perhaps Turing's modest prediction – a machine that is misidentified by 3 out of 10 average judges during five minutes of questioning – will indeed come to pass in the near future. As for Turing's predictions of more substantial success, one can only keep an open mind.[9]

Notes

* This paper formed the philosophy keynote address at *Turing 2000: The Dartmouth Conference on the Future of the Turing Test.*

[1] The complete script is published for the first time in Copeland (1999).

[2] Max Newman played an important part in Turing's intellectual life over many years. Newman brought Hilbert's ideas from Göttingen to Cambridge. In 1935, Turing attended lectures in which Newman discussed Hilbert's Entscheidungsproblem. In these lectures Newman introduced the concept that led Turing to his 'computing machines' (Turing, 1936): Newman defined a 'constructive process' as one that a *machine* can carry out (Newman in interview with Christopher Evans, 'The Pioneers of Computing: An Oral History of Computing', London: Science Museum (1976)). During the war Newman and Turing both worked at GC & CS, where the two cooperated closely. It was Newman who initiated the electronic decryption project that culminated in the construction of Colossus, the first large-scale electronic digital computing machine (designed by the engineer T.H. Flowers). At the end of the war Newman established the Royal Society Computing Machine Laboratory at Manchester University. Here he introduced the engineers F.C. Williams and T. Kilburn to Turing's idea of a universal computing machine, and under Newman's guidance Williams and Kilburn built the first stored-program electronic digital computer (see further Copeland 1999: 455–457). It was Newman who, in 1948, appointed Turing as Deputy Director (there being no Director) of the Manchester Computing Machine Laboratory.

[3] Cottingham et al. (1985: 140).

[4] The full text of the lecture is published for the first time in Copeland (1999).

[5] Elsewhere Turing uses the verb 'simulate': 'My contention is that machines can be constructed which will simulate the behaviour of the human mind very closely' (Turing, 1951b).

[6] See further Copeland (1996).

[7] Page references are to the reprinting of French's article in Millican and Clark (1996).

[8] This subsection is indebted to Diane Proudfoot. See further Copeland and Proudfoot (1999b).
[9] Research on which this article draws was supported in part by University of Canterbury Research Grant no. U6271. Special thanks to Diane Proudfoot for her comments on a draft.

References

Block, N. (1981), 'Psychologism and Behaviourism', *Philosophical Review* 90, pp. 5–43.

Carpenter, B.E., Doran, R.W., eds, (1986), *A.M. Turing's ACE Report of 1946 and Other Papers*, Cambridge, Mass.: MIT Press.

Copeland, B.J. (1993), *Artificial Intelligence: a Philosophical Introduction*, Oxford: Blackwell.

Copeland, B.J. (1996), 'The Church-Turing Thesis', in E. Zalta, ed., *The Stanford Encyclopaedia of Philosophy* [http://plato.stanford.edu].

Copeland, B.J. (ed.) (1999), 'A Lecture and Two Radio Broadcasts by Alan Turing', in K. Furukawa, D. Michie and S. Muggleton, eds, *Machine Intelligence* 15, Oxford University Press.

Copeland, B.J. (2001), 'The Chinese Room from a Logical Point of View', in J. Preston and M. Bishop, eds, *Views into the Chinese Room*, Oxford University Press.

Copeland, B.J. and Proudfoot, D. (1996), 'On Alan Turing's Anticipation of Connectionism', *Synthese* 108, pp. 361–377.

Copeland, B.J. and Proudfoot, D. (1999a), 'Alan Turing's Forgotten Ideas in Computer Science', *Scientific American* 280 (April), pp. 76–81.

Copeland, B.J. and Proudfoot, D. 1999b, 'The Legacy of Alan Turing', *Mind* 108, pp. 187–195.

Cottingham, J., Stoothoff, R. and Murdoch, D. (eds) (1985), *The Philosophical Writings of Descartes*, Vol. 1, Cambridge University Press.

de Cordemoy, G. (1668), *A Philosophicall Discourse Concerning Speech*, John Martin: London (repr. by Scholars' Facsimiles & Reprints, New York, 1972).

French, R. (1990), 'Subcognition and the Limits of the Turing Test', *Mind* 99, pp. 53–65 (repr. in Millican and Clark 1996).

French, R. (2000), 'The Turing Test: the First 50 Years', *Trends in Cognitive Sciences* 4, pp. 115–122.

Heiser, J.F., Colby, K.M., Faught, W.S. and Parkison, R.C. (1980), 'Can Psychiatrists Distinguish a Computer Simulation of Paranoia from the Real Thing?', *Journal of Psychiatric Research* 15, pp. 149–162.

Hodges, A. (1992), *Alan Turing: The Enigma*, London: Vintage.

Millican, P. and Clark, A. (eds) (1996), *Machines and Thought: The Legacy of Alan Turing*, Oxford University Press.

Moor, J.H. (1976), 'An Analysis of the Turing Test', *Philosophical Studies* 30, pp. 249–257.

Moor, J.H. (1987), 'Turing Test', in S.C. Shapiro, ed., *Encyclopedia of Artificial Intelligence*, Vol. 2, New York: Wiley.

Narayanan, A. (1996), 'The Intentional Stance and the Imitation Game', in Millican and Clark (1996).

Osherson, D.N. and Lasnik, H. (eds) (1990), *An Invitation to Cognitive Science*, Vol. 3, Cambridge, Mass.: MIT Press.

Searle, J. (1980), 'Minds, Brains, and Programs', *Behavioural and Brain Sciences* 3, pp. 417–424.

Shannon, C.E. and McCarthy, J. (eds) (1956), *Automata Studies*, Princeton University Press.

Shieber, S.M. (1994), 'Lessons from a Restricted Turing Test', *Communications of the ACM* 37, pp. 70–78.

Turing, A.M. (1936), 'On Computable Numbers, with an Application to the Entscheidungsproblem', *Proceedings of the London Mathematical Society*, Series 2, 42 (1936–37), pp. 230–265.

Turing, A.M. (1945), 'Proposal for Development in the Mathematics Division of an Automatic Computing Engine (ACE)', in Carpenter and Doran (1986).

Turing, A.M. (1947), 'Lecture to the London Mathematical Society on 20 February 1947', in Carpenter and Doran (1986).

Turing, A.M. (1948), 'Intelligent Machinery', National Physical Laboratory Report, in B. Meltzer and D. Michie, eds, *Machine Intelligence 5*, Edinburgh University Press (1969).

Turing, A.M. (1950a), 'Computing Machinery and Intelligence', *Mind* 59, pp. 433–460.

Turing, A.M. (1950b), *Programmers' Handbook for Manchester Electronic Computer*, Royal Society Computing Machine Laboratory, University of Manchester.

Turing, A.M. (1951a), 'Can Digital Computers Think?', in Copeland (1999).

Turing, A.M. (1951b), 'Intelligent Machinery, A Heretical Theory', in Copeland (1999).

Turing, A.M. (1952), 'Can Automatic Calculating Machines Be Said To Think?, in Copeland (1999).

Von Neumann, J. (ed.) (1945), 'First Draft of a Report on the EDVAC', Moore School of Electrical Engineering, University of Pennsylvania.

Whitby, B. (1996), 'The Turing Test: AI's Biggest Blind Alley', in Millican and Clark (1996).

Wilkes, M.V. (1953), 'Can Machines Think?', *Proceedings of the Institute of Radio Engineers* 41, pp. 1230–1234.

Turing Test: 50 Years Later

AYSE PINAR SAYGIN[1], ILYAS CICEKLI[2] & VAROL AKMAN[2]

[1]*Department of Cognitive Science, University of California, San Diego, La Jolla, CA 92093-0515, USA; E-mail: saygin@crl.ucsd.edu;* [2]*Department of Computer Engineering, Bilkent University, Bilkent, 06533 Ankara, Turkey; E-mail: ilyas@cs.bilkent.edu.tr; akman@cs.bilkent.edu.tr*

Abstract. The Turing Test is one of the most disputed topics in artificial intelligence, philosophy of mind, and cognitive science. This paper is a review of the past 50 years of the Turing Test. Philosophical debates, practical developments and repercussions in related disciplines are all covered. We discuss Turing's ideas in detail and present the important comments that have been made on them. Within this context, behaviorism, consciousness, the 'other minds' problem, and similar topics in philosophy of mind are discussed. We also cover the sociological and psychological aspects of the Turing Test. Finally, we look at the current situation and analyze programs that have been developed with the aim of passing the Turing Test. We conclude that the Turing Test has been, and will continue to be, an influential and controversial topic.

Key words: chatbots, Chinese Room, consciousness, Imitation Game, intelligence, Loebner Contest, philosophy of mind, Turing Test

1. Introduction

This is the story of the Turing Test: a modest attempt to summarize its 50 years of existence.

The British mathematician Alan Turing[1] proposed the Turing Test (TT) as a replacement for the question "Can machines think?" in his 1950 *Mind* article 'Computing Machinery and Intelligence' (Turing, 1950). Since then, Turing's ideas have been widely discussed, attacked, and defended over and over. At one extreme, Turing's paper has been considered to represent the "beginning" of artificial intelligence (AI) and the TT has been considered its ultimate goal. At the other extreme, the TT has been called useless, even harmful. In between are arguments on consciousness, behaviorism, the 'other minds' problem, operational definitions of intelligence, necessary and sufficient conditions for intelligence-granting, and so on.

The aim of this paper is to present an overview of the debate that followed Turing's paper, as well as the developments that have taken place in the past 50 years. We have tried to make this survey as comprehensive and multi-disciplinary as possible. Familiarity with special terms and concepts is not assumed. The reader is directed to further references where they are available. While the review is not strictly chronological, we have tried to present related works in the order they appeared.

Minds and Machines **10**: 463–518, 2000.
© 2001 *Kluwer Academic Publishers. Printed in the Netherlands.*

In our attempt to make this survey complete, we have explored a large number of references. However, this does not mean that we comment on each paper that mentions the TT. We devote separate sections to certain papers, discuss some others briefly, and merely cite the remaining. Some papers are explained in detail because they are representative of important ideas. From this it should not be understood that the papers for which we spare less space are less important or interesting. In fact, we sometimes devote more space to papers that are not discussed in detail elsewhere.[2]

The rest of the paper is organized as follows. Section 2 introduces the TT and analyzes 'Computing Machinery and Intelligence' (Turing, 1950). In this section, we also attempt to develop new ideas and probe side issues. Section 3 describes and explains some of the earlier comments on the TT (those from the 60's and the 70's). In Section 4, we analyze the arguments that are more recent. We study the repercussions of the TT in the social sciences separately in Section 5. Similarly, in Section 6, we give an overview of the concrete, computational studies directed towards passing the TT. Some natural language conversation systems and the annual Loebner Prize contests are discussed in this section. Finally, Section 7 concludes our survey.

2. Turing's 'Computing Machinery and Intelligence'

It makes sense to look at Turing's landmark paper 'Computing Machinery and Intelligence' (Turing, 1950) before we begin to consider certain arguments defending, attacking or discussing the TT. Turing (1950) is a very well-known work and has been cited and quoted copiously. Although what follows will provide an introduction to the TT, it is a good idea to read Turing's original rendering of the issues at hand. In analyzing the 50 years of the TT, it is important to distinguish what was originally proposed by Turing himself and what has been added on afterwards. We do not mean that the TT is (or should remain as) what Turing proposed in 'Computing Machinery and Intelligence'. Like any other concept, it has changed throughout the 50 years it has been around. In fact, one of the purposes of this paper is to trace the stepsin this evolution. Thus, it is only natural that we are interested in the original version.

In Section 2.1, we analyze Turing's original proposal. We summarize Turing's replies to certain objections to his ideas in Section 2.2. Turing's opinions on learning machines are briefly discussed in Section 2.3. Finally, we list some of Turing's predictions in Section 2.4.

2.1. THE IMITATION GAME

Turing's aim is to provide a method to assess whether or not a machine can think. He states at the beginning of his paper that the question "Can machines think?" is a highly ambiguous one. He attempts to transform this into a more concrete form

Figure 1. The Imitation Game: Stage 1.

by proposing what is called the Imitation Game (IG). The game is played with a man (A), a woman (B) and an interrogator (C) whose gender is unimportant. The interrogator stays in a room apart from A and B. The objective of the interrogator is to determine which of the other two is the woman while the objective of both the man and the woman is to convince the interrogator that he/she is the woman and the other is not. This situation is depicted in Figure 1.

The means through which the decision, the convincing, and the deception are to take place is a teletype connection. Thus, the interrogator asks questions in written natural language and receives answers in written natural language. Questions can be on any subject imaginable, from mathematics to poetry, from the weather to chess.

According to Turing, the new agenda to be discussed, instead of the equivocal "Can machines think?", can be 'What will happen when a machine takes the part of A in this game? Will the interrogator decide wrongly as often when the game is played like this as he does when the game is played between a man and a woman?' (Turing, 1950, p. 434). Figure 2 depicts the new situation.

At one point in the paper Turing replaces the question "Can machines think?" by the following:

'Let us fix our attention to one particular digital computer *C*. Is it true that by modifying this computer to have an adequate storage, suitably increasing its speed of action and providing it with an appropriate programme, *C* can be made to play satisfactorily the part of *A* in the imitation game, *the part of B being taken by a man?*' (Turing, 1950, p. 442, emphasis added).

Notice that the woman has disappeared altogether. But the objectives of *A*, *B*, and the interrogator remain unaltered; at least Turing does not explicitly state any change. Figure 3 shows this situation.

There seems to be an ambiguity in the paper; it is unclear which of the scenarios depicted in Figure 2 and Figure 3 is to be used. In any case, as it is now generally understood, what the TT really tries to assess is the machine's ability to imitate a human being, rather than its ability to simulate a woman. Most subsequent remarks on the TT ignore the gender issue and assume that the game is played between a machine (A), a human (B), and an interrogator (C). In this version, C's aim is to

Figure 2. The Imitation Game: Stage 2, Version 1.

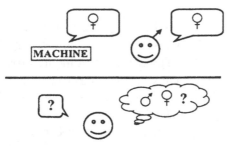

Figure 3. The Imitation Game: Stage 2, Version 2.

determine which one of the two entities he/she is conversing with is the human (Figure 4).

One may ask why Turing designed the IG in such a peculiar manner. Why the fuss about the woman, the man, and the replacement? This does not make the paper easier to understand. He could have introduced the IG exactly as he did with the woman-man issue replaced by the human-machine issue and it obviously would not be any more confusing. The main reason that the decision concerning machine thought is to be based on imitating a woman in the game is probably not that Turing believed the ultimate intellectual challenge to be the capacity to act like a woman (although it may be comforting to entertain the thought). Conversely, it may be concluded that Turing believes that women can be imitated by machines while men cannot. The fact that Turing stipulated the man to be replaced by the machine (when he might just as easily have required the woman to be replaced by the machine or added a remark that the choice was inconsequential) raises such questions, but let us not digress.

Here is our explanation of Turing's design: The crucial point seems to be that the notion of *imitation* figures more prominently in Turing's paper than is commonly acknowledged. For one thing, the game is inherently about deception. The man is allowed to say anything at all in order to cause the interrogator to make the wrong identification, while the woman is actually required to aid the interrogator.[3] In the machine vs. woman version, the situation remains the same. The machine tries to convince the interrogator that it is the woman. What is really judging the machine's competence is not the woman it is playing against. Turing's seemingly

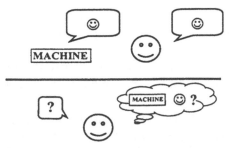

Figure 4. The Imitation Game as it is generally interpreted (The Turing Test).

frivolous requirements may actually have very sound premises. Neither the man in the gender-based IG nor any kind of machine is a woman. On close examination, it can be seen that what Turing proposes is to compare the machine's success against that of the man, *not* to look at whether it 'beats' the woman in the IG.[4] The man and the machine are measured in terms of their respective performances against real women. In Figure 3, we see that the woman has disappeared from the game, but the objective for both the machine and the man is still imitating a woman. Again, their performance is comparable because they are both simulating something which they are not.

The quirks of the IG may well be concealing a methodological fairness beyond that explicitly stated by Turing. We hold that the IG, even though it is regarded as obscure by many, is a carefully planned proposal. It provides a fair basis for comparison: the woman (either as a participant in the game or as a concept) acts as a neutral point so that the two imposters can be assessed in how well they "fake".

Turing could have defined the game to be played with two people, too; one being an interrogator, as in the original, and the other being either a man or a woman. The interrogator would then have to decide whether the subject is a man or a woman. Alternatively, the TT for machine intelligence can be re-interpreted as a test to assess a machine'sability to pass for a human being. This issue may seem immaterial at first. However, the interrogator's decision is sure to be affected by the availability (or lack) of comparison. Whether the machine's task will be easier or more difficult in this latter case is another question. We think that Turing implies that some comparison should be available; otherwise, he would have opted for the two-person version of the game. Once again, we believe that the most sensible reason behind the three-person game is to have a neutral party so as to allow the assessment of the impersonating parties with respect to each other.

In any case, as was mentioned before, the TT concept has evolved through time. Turing's original IG and its conditions do not put serious constraints on current discussions about the test. It is generally agreed that the gender issue and the number of participants are not to be followed strictly in attempts to pass, criticize or defend the TT. Even Turing himself, in the subsequent sections of 'Computing Machinery and Intelligence', sometimes ignores these issues and focuses on the question:

27

"Can machines communicate in natural language in a manner indistinguishable from that of a human being?". This is manifested in the example conversation he gives in Turing (1950, p. 434), which contains questions about poetry, mathematics, and chess – topics that one would not typically ask about in order to determine someone's gender. This may be a hint that the gender issue in the IG is indeed for purposes of fair comparison.

After defining the IG, Turing defends the choice of replacing the question "Can machines think?" with "Can machines play the imitation game?". The new problem focuses on intellectual capacities and does not let physical aspects interfere with granting intelligence to an entity. Nor does it limit thinking to specific tasks like playing chess or solving puzzles, since the question-and-answer method is suitable to introduce any topic imaginable.

An issue that is open to discussion is what Turing implies about *how* machines should be built or programmed to play the IG successfully. He seems to believe that if a machine can be constructed to play the game successfully, it does not really matter whether or not what it does to that end is similar to what a human does. Turing even considers the possibility that a machine which successfully plays the IG cannot be explained by its creators because it had been built by experimental methods. However, he explicitly states that 'it will be assumed that the best strategy is to try to provide answers that would naturally be given by a man' (Turing, 1950, p. 435). It may be concluded that Turing does not put any limitations on how to model human cognitive processes, but seems to discourage any approach that deviates too much from the "human ways", possibly because he feels it is unlikely that satisfactory solutions can be obtained in this manner. On the other hand, by not committing himself to any extreme viewpoint on the issue, he accepts the possibility that machines not mimicking human cognitive processes at all can also pass the test.

Some people interpret the TT as a setting in which you can "cheat". The game has no rules constraining the design of the machines. At some places in the paper, Turing describes how machines could be "rigged" to overcome certain obstacles proposed by opponents of the idea that machines can think. A very obvious example is about machines making mistakes. When the machine is faced with an arithmetical operation, in order not to give away its identity by being fast and accurate, it can pause for about 30 seconds before responding and occasionally give a wrong answer. Being able to carry out arithmetical calculations fast and accurately is generally considered intelligent behavior.[5] However, Turing wishes to sacrifice this at the expense of human-ness. Some commentators think this is "cheating". The machine is resorting to certain "tricks" in its operations rather than imitating the human ways. However, arithmetic is a highly specific domain. Modifying the programs in this manner cannot hurt: If a machine can pass the test, it can then be re-programmed not to cheat at arithmetic. If it does not resort to this, the interrogator can ask a difficult arithmetical problem as his/her first question and decide that he/she is dealing with a machine right then and there. We believe the best way to think about this issue is considering this as "deception", rather than as "cheating". After all, in a sense, the game is all about deception.

It can be seen that Turing considers it possible that a sufficiently human-like machine (i.e., a machine that is sufficiently good at playing the IG) is bound to make such mistakes as we attribute to humans, without such explicit tricks encoded by its constructors. This idea may seem extravagant, but considering the high level of sophistication required from a machine for passing the TT, it should not be dismissed as impossible. A striking example can be given from the inductive learning domain: No learning algorithm guarantees correct results on unseen data. Moreover, in some cases a computer errs in ways that cannot be foreseen, or even understood by its programmer. This can be distressing for machine learning researchers who are after a minimal number of mistakes, but proves the subtle point that machines can make mistakes without explicitly being shown *how to*.[6]

Turing's approach towards deception seems similar to Adam Smith's "invisible hand" from economics. Maybe Turing's conformity has its roots in his belief that one cannot go too far by such attempts: He may regard tricks as a last retouch, something to smooth out the machine-ness of the resulting programs that otherwise handle the more important aspects of human cognition. If a program that has its very bases in what some have called "cheating" can pass the TT, maybe we would have to revise some notions about the human intellect. It is not possible to say what Turing was thinking and claim to be absolutely correct. It seems as if he would be content with a machine that plays the IG successfully no matter what the inner mechanisms are.

2.2. CONTRARY VIEWS AND TURING'S REPLIES

Turing was aware that some of his ideas would be opposed at the time he wrote 'Computing Machinery and Intelligence' (Turing, 1950) and he responded to some objections that he believed his work would be confronted with. In fact, he discusses some of these earlier in Turing (1969).[7] We direct the reader to Turing (1950) for the answers to the *theological objection*, and the *argument from extra-sensory perception* for these are rather irrelevant to the current work. However, the remaining objections are worth commenting on.

The *'heads in the sand' objection*, although mostly in disguised forms, is manifested in some subsequent comments on the TT. This is, in its basic form, an aversion to the issue of thinking machines because the consequences of this would be dreadful (Turing, 1950, p. 444). Most people like to believe that humans are "special" and thinking is considered to be one of the most important traits that make us so. To some, the idea of sharing such a "human" ability with machines is not a pleasant thought. This outlook was probably more widespread in Turing's time than it is now. Turing believes that this argument is not even worth refutation, and with a little sarcasm, he states that consolation (perhaps in the transmigration of souls) is more appropriate (Turing, 1950, p. 444).

There are some theorems showing that the powers of discrete-state machines are limited. The most famous of these is probably Gödel's Theorem which shows that in consistent logical systems of sufficient power, we can formulate statements that cannot be proved or disproved within the system. An application of this result to the IG is outlined in Turing (1950, p. 445) and the reader is referred to Lucas (1961) and Lucas (1996) for more on the implications of Gödel's Theorem for machine thought.

Turing studies such results under the title the *mathematical objection*. He states that 'although it is established that there are limitations to the powers of any particular machine, it has only been stated, without any sort of proof, that no such limitations apply to the human intellect' (Turing, 1950, p. 445). Elsewhere, he notes that those arguments that rest on Gödel's and similar theorems are taking it for granted that the machine to be granted intelligence must not make mistakes, and that he does not believe this should be a requirement for intelligence (Turing, 1969).

Perhaps the most important objection is the *argument from consciousness*. Some people believe that machines should be conscious (e.g., aware of their accomplishments, feel pleasure at success, get upset at failure, etc.) in order to have minds. At the extreme of this view, we find *solipsism*. The only way to *really* know whether a machine is thinking or not is to *be* that machine. However, according to this view, the only way to know another human being is thinking (or is conscious, happy, etc.) is to be that human being. This is usually called the *other minds problem* and will show up several times in the discussions of the TT. 'Instead of arguing continually over this point it is usual to have the polite convention that everyone thinks' (Turing, 1950, p. 446). Turing's response to the argument from consciousness is simple, but powerful: The alternative to the IG (or similar behavioral assessments) would be solipsism and we do not practice this against other humans. It is only fair that in dealing with machine thought, we abandon the consciousness argument rather than concede to solipsism.

Turing believes that the IG setting can be used to determine whether 'someone really understands something or has learnt it parrot fashion' as is manifested in the sample conversation he gives in Turing (1950, p. 446). It should also be noted that Turing states that he does not assume consciousness to be a trivial or impertinent issue; he merely believes that we do not necessarily need to solve its mysteries before we can answer questions about thinking, and in particular, machine thought (Turing, 1950, p. 447).

The *arguments from various disabilities* are of the sort "machines can never do X", where X can be any human trait such as having a sense of humor, being creative, falling in love, or enjoying strawberries. As Turing also notes (Turing, 1950, p. 449), such criticisms are sometimes disguised forms of the argument from consciousness. Turing argues against some of these X's such as the ability to make mistakes, enjoy strawberries and cream, be the subject of its own thought, etc. in Turing (1950, pp. 448–450).

Lady Lovelace's objection is similar; it states that machines cannot originate anything, can never do anything new, can never surprise us. Turing replies by confessing that machines do take him by surprise quite often. Proponents of Lady Lovelace's objection can say that 'such surprises are due to some creative mental act on [Turing's] part, and reflect no credit on the machine' (Turing, 1950, p. 451). Turing's answer to this is similar to the one he gives to the argument from consciousness: 'The appreciation of something as surprising requires as much of a 'creative mental act' whether the surprising event originates from a man, a book, a machine or anything else' (Turing, 1950, p. 451).

Turing also considers the *argument from continuity in the nervous system.* As the name suggests, this objection states that it is impossible to model the behavior of the nervous system on a discrete-state machine because the former is continuous. However, Turing believes that the activity of a continuous machine can be "discretized" in a manner that the interrogator cannot notice during the 1G.

Finally, there is the *argument from informality of behavior.* Intuitively, it seems that it is not possible to come up with a set of rules that describe what a person would do in every situation imaginable. In very simple terms, some people believe the following: 'If each man had a definite set of rules of conduct by which he regulated his life, he would be no better than a machine. But there are no such rules, so men cannot be machines' (Turing, 1950, p. 452). First, Turing notes that there might be a confusion between 'rules of conduct' and 'laws of behavior'. By the former he means actions that one can perform and be aware of (like, 'If you see a red light, stop') and by the latter he means laws of nature that apply to a man's body (such as 'If you throw a dart at him, he will duck'). Now it is not evident that a complete set of laws of behavior do not exist. We can find some of these by scientific observation but there will not come a time when we can be confident that we have searched enough and there are no such rules. Another point Turing makes is that it may not always be possible to predict the future behavior of a discrete-state machine by observing its actions. In fact, he is so confident about a certain program that he set up on the Manchester computer that he 'def[ies] anyone to learn from [its] replies sufficient about the programme to be able to predict any replies to untried values' (Turing, 1950, p. 453).

2.3. LEARNING MACHINES

Turing devotes some space to the idea of *education of machinery* in 'Computing Machinery and Intelligence' (Turing, 1950). He also discusses the issue in his earlier work 'Intelligent Machinery' (Turing, 1969).

According to Turing, in trying to imitate an adult human mind, we should consider three issues: the initial state of the mind, the education it has been subject to, and other experience it has been subject to (that cannot be described as education). Then we might try to model a child's mind and "educate" it to obtain the model of the adult brain. Since 'presumably the child-brain is something like a notebook as one buys it from the stationers; rather little mechanism and lots of blank sheets' (Turing, 1950, p. 456), developing a program that simulates it is bound to be easier.[8] Of course, the education is another issue. Turing proposes some methods of education for the child-machines (such as a reward/punishment based approach) in Turing (1950, pp. 456–460) and Turing (1969, pp. 17–23).

Turing's opinions on learning machines are rather interesting, especially considering he wrote these more than 50 years ago. In most places when he discusses education of machines, there is a noticeable change in Turing's style. He seems to believe that the way to success in developing a program that plays the IG well is probably to follow the human model as closely as possible. As was mentioned in Section 2.1, he does not put any constraints on how to design the IG-playing machine, but the fact that he describes learning machines in substantial detail seems to suggest that he may prefer such an approach.

In any case, Turing believes '*if* we are trying to produce an intelligent machine, and are *following the human model as closely as we can*' (Turing, 1969, p. 14, emphasis added) a good (and fair) approach would be to allow the machine to learn just like humans.

2.4. TURING'S PREDICTIONS

Turing's paper (Turing, 1950) contains some very bold statements on the prospects for machine intelligence. Most of these probably seemed like science fiction at the time. Even now, some of us would consider these far-fetched. This section provides a sample of Turing's predictions.

It is well known that Turing believes computers to be capable of performing many "intelligent" tasks. He also thinks that they will be able to do so in a "human" way.

> The reader must accept it as a fact that digital computers can be constructed, and indeed have been constructed, according to the principles we have described, and that they can in fact mimic the actions of a human computer very closely (Turing, 1950, p. 438).

As can be seen from the following quotation, Turing believes that the difficulties in designing thinking machines are not insurmountable.

> As I have explained, the problem is mainly one of programming. Advances in engineering will have to be made too, but it seems unlikely that these will not be adequate for the requirements (Turing, 1950, p. 455).

While trying to convince the reader that the ideas he proposes are of the sort that can be realized in the foreseeable future, Turing mentions some concrete achievements he expects from computers. Those that are related to machine learning were outlined in Section 2.3. Here is another example, this time pertaining to automated software engineering:

[The machine] may be used to help in making up its own programmes, or to predict the effect of alterations in its own structure.

. . .

These are possibilities of the near future, rather than Utopian dreams (Turing, 1950, p. 449).

The game of chess has been at the center of some of the most well-known achievements in AI. Today, computer programs play against world champions and sometimes even beat them. Spectacular advances have more recently been made in computer understanding and generation of speech. Although to what extent currently available speech processing systems are intelligent is a debatable issue, they (like chess playing programs) have become part of modern life:

We may hope that machines will eventually compete with men in all purely intellectual fields. But which are the best ones to start with? Even this is a difficult question. Many people think that a very abstract activity, like the playing of chess, would be best. It can also be maintained that it is best to provide the machine with the best sense organs that money can buy, and then teach it to understand and speak English.

. . .

Again, I do not know what the right answer is, but I think both approaches should be tried (Turing, 1950, p. 460).

Take a look at computer technology at the turn of the century: What was unimaginable in 1950, in terms of memory and speed, is now reality. What Turing predicted about the IG, however, is still a challenge.

I believe that in about fifty years' time, it will be possible to programme computers with a storage capacity of about 10^9, to make them play the imitation game so well that an average interrogator will not have more than 70 percent chance of making the right identification after five minutes of questioning (Turing, 1950, p. 442).

3. From the Imitation Game to the Turing Test: The 60's and the 70's

Earlier remarks on the TT, with the exception of Colby et al. (1971), Colby et al. (1972) and Weizenbaum (1966), were mostly of the philosophical sort. This is hardly surprising because 'Computing Machinery and Intelligence' was published in a philosophy journal, *Mind*.[9] Many discussions on the IG were published in the 60's and the 70's, many of the important contributions once again accommodated by *Mind*. In this section we will take a look at these philosophical papers, leaving the more practical work described in Colby et al. (1971), Colby et al. (1972), Weizenbaum (1966) to other, more appropriate sections. Readers interested in earlier comments on the TT and machine intelligence that are not discussed in this section can consult Pinksy (1951), Mays (1952) and Reader (1969).

Keith Gunderson's comments on the IG are summarized in Section 3.1. Section 3.2 presents an approach stating that developing a TT-passing program is not going to be possible in the foreseeable future. The anthropomorphism in the TT is briefly discussed in Section 3.3, to be taken up later on. An inductive interpretation of the TT is described in Section 3.4.

3.1. ROCKS THAT IMITATE AND ALL-PURPOSE VACUUM CLEANERS

One of the earlier comments on Turing's IG came from Keith Gunderson in his 1964 *Mind* article. In this paper, titled 'The Imitation Game', Gunderson points out some important issues pertaining to Turing's replacement for the question "Can machines think?".

Gunderson develops certain objections to Turing's 'Computing Machinery and Intelligence' (Turing, 1950) by focusing on the IG. He emphasizes two points: First, he believes that playing the IG successfully is an *end* that can be achieved through different means, in particular, without possessing intelligence. Secondly, he holds that thinking is a general concept and playing the IG is but *one* example of the things that intelligent entities do. Evidently, both claims are critical of the validity of the IG as a measure of intelligence.

Gunderson makes his point by an entertaining analogy. He asks the question "Can rocks imitate?" and proceeds to describe the "toe-stepping game" (Gunderson, 1964, p. 236) in a way that is identical to the way Turing described his IG in Turing (1950). Once again, the game is played between a man (A), a woman (B), and an interrogator (C). The interrogator's aim is to distinguish between the man and the woman by the way his/her toe is stepped on. C stays in a room apart from the other two and cannot see or hear the toe-stepping counterparts. There is a small opening in the wall through which C can place his/her foot. The interrogator has to determine which one of the other two is the woman by the way in which his/her toe is stepped on. Analogously, the new form of the question "Can rocks imitate?" becomes the following: 'What will happen when a rock box is constructed with an electric eye which operates across the opening in the wall so that it releases a rock which descends upon C's toe whenever C puts his foot through A's side of the opening, and thus comes to take the part of A in this game? ... Will the interrogator decide wrongly as often as when the game is played between a man and a woman?' (Gunderson, 1964, pp. 236–237).

Gunderson believes that even if rock boxes play the toe-stepping game successfully, there would still be no reason to accept that they are imitating. The only conclusion that we can make from this would be that a rock box can be rigged in such a way that it can replace a human being in the toe-stepping game. According to Gunderson, this is because 'part of what things do is how they do it' (Gunderson, 1964, p. 238). As we will expand upon in Section 4.1, this is similar to Ned Block's argument for *psychologism* against behaviorism (Block, 1981).

Gunderson states that thinking is not something that can be decided upon by just one example. He demonstrates his belief that a computer's success in the IG is not sufficient reason to call it a thinking machine by another analogy: Imagine a vacuum cleaner salesman trying to sell a product. First, he advertises the vacuum cleaner *Swish 600* as being "all-purpose". Then, he demonstrates how it can suck up bits of dust. The customer asks what else the machine can do. Astonished, the salesman says that vacuum cleaners are for sucking up dust and that Swish 600 does precisely that. The customer answers, "I thought it was all-purpose. Doesn't it suck up bits of paper or straw or mud? I thought sucking up bits of dust was an example of what it does". The salesman says "It is an example of what it does. What it does is suck up pieces of dust" (Gunderson, 1964, p. 241).

The salesman has trouble making his sale by calling Swish 600 all-purpose and being unable to show more than one example of what it does. According to Gunderson, Turing also has the same problem because the term "thinking" is used to refer to more than one capability, just as the term "all-purpose" implies that the vacuum cleaner has functions other than just sucking up bits of dust. He concludes:

> In the end the steam drill outlasted John Henry as a digger of railway tunnels, but that didn't prove the machine had muscles; it proved that muscles were not needed for digging railway tunnels (Gunderson, 1964, p. 254).

John G. Stevenson, in his paper 'On the Imitation Game' (Stevenson, 1976) raises some arguments against Gunderson. One of these is the objection that Gunderson was expecting, namely the claim that being able to play the IG is not just *one* example; a machine that is good at the IG is capable of various things. Gunderson does not give a direct response to such objections. He mentions a reply can be formulated along the lines of showing that even combining all those things such a machine can do gives us a narrow range of abilities (Gunderson, 1964, p. 243). Stevenson doubts whether such a reply would be adequate (Stevenson, 1976, p. 132). Even if it does not exhaust everything that is related to human thinking, he believes the list of things that a computer that plays the IG can do would be quite impressive. Stevenson states that Gunderson is ignoring the specific character of the IG and that he proposes defective arguments.

3.2. THE TT AS SCIENCE FICTION

Richard Purtill, in his 1971 *Mind* paper also discusses some issues concerning the IG. Purtill criticizes some ideas in Turing's paper 'mainly as a philosopher, but also as a person who has done a certain amount of computer programming' (Purtill, 1971, p. 290). He believes that the game is interesting, but as a piece of science fiction. He finds it unimaginable that a computer playing the IG will be built in the foreseeable future.

Overall, Purtill believes the IG to be a computer man's dream. He even promises to 'eat his computer library' if anyone has a notion of the principles on which a machine that can play the game is to be built (Purtill, 1971, p. 293). He states that if computers, some day, behave like the computers in works of science fiction, he would grant them thought. But since all computer outputs can be explained as a result of a program written by humans, even if the program's outputs are guided by certain random elements, computers are not likely to play the IG successfully with the currently imaginable programming techniques. This, he believes, is because the behavior of thinking beings is not deterministic and cannot be explained in purely mechanistic terms.

Purtill believes that the game is 'just a battle of wits between the questioner and the programmer: the computer is non-essential' (Purtill, 1971, p. 291). Although the former part of the claim may be reasonable to an extent, his latter argument about the computer being non-essential is not very sound. To eliminate the computer from the picture, Purtill proposes "purely mechanical" alternatives: machines made of levers and wheels that can do the same task. We think it is unclear why this should count as an argument against the IG because, evidently, the material or structure on which the IG-playing "program" works is irrelevant. Purtill also states, anticipating the objection that the human mind might also be a highly complex collection of such mechanical processes, that if this were the case, it would mean 'human beings do not in fact think rather than that computers do think' (Purtill, 1971, p. 292), but does not attempt to justify this bold claim.

In his short paper 'In Defence of Turing' (Sampson, 1973), Geoffrey Sampson attacks Purtill's arguments briefly. First of all, he believesmost of the limitations pertaining to the realization of IG-playing computers which Purtill lists are practical difficulties that may be overcome in the (presumably not so distant) future. Secondly, he states that it is only natural that computer behavior is deterministic and that human behavior is not so easy to explain. The reasons for this are simple: computers are designed by humans; they have mechanisms that explicitly allow us to study their behavior; humans are much more complex in terms of both internal states and possible inputs than any contemporary computer (Sampson, 1973, p. 593). Sampson also rejects Purtill's opinion that the consequence of the claim that human thinking is an extremely complex, yet computer-like, mechanical process is that men do not think. He holds that thinking, by definition, is something human beings do.

3.3. ANTHROPOMORPHISM AND THE TT

In a short paper that appeared in *Mind* in 1973, P.H. Millar raises some important issues which will show up in later works. He first discusses some vices and virtues of the IG and states that it is irrelevant whether or how the computers or the human beings involved in the game are "programmed". Then, he introduces the question of whether the IG is a right setting to measure the intelligence of machines. Millar notes that the game forces us to "anthropomorphize" machines by ascribing them human aims and cultural backgrounds. Millar asserts that the IG measures not whether machines have intelligence, but whether they have *human* intelligence.

He believes that we should be open-minded enough to allow each being, be it a Martian or a machine, to exhibit intelligence 'by means of behavior which is well-adapted for achieving its own specific aims' (Millar, 1973, p. 597). We will return to this issue later on, especially in Section 4.5.

3.4. THE TT INTERPRETED INDUCTIVELY

In his important paper 'An Analysis of the Turing Test' (Moor, 1976), James Moor attempts to emphasize the significance of the imitation game. As can be seen from the title, the term "Turing Test" was already being used to refer to the IG by 1976. Moor's main assertion is that 'the Turing Test is a significant test for computer thought if it is interpreted inductively' (Moor, 1976, p. 256).

Moor disagrees with the idea that the TT is an operational definition of intelligence.[10] Rather, he proposes, it should be regarded as a source of inductive evidence for the hypothesis that machines can think. Moreover, Moor does not agree with the claim that even if the TT is not an operational definition, it should at least be a necessary condition for granting computers intelligence. According to him, there could be other evidence based on the computer's behavior that leads to inferences about the computer's thinking abilities. However, he believes that the test provides a sufficient condition for intelligence-granting to computers. But his view is not "absolute"; he accepts that it is possible to revise a positive inference about a computer's possession of thought based on a TT, if other evidence is acquired afterwards.

Moor lists two arguments that support the TT as a good format for collecting inductive evidence. 'First, the Turing Test permits direct or indirect testing of virtually all of the activities one would count as evidence for thinking ... Secondly, the Turing Test encourages severe testing' (Moor, 1976, pp. 251–252). By the latter, Moor means the test's requirements are not too easy to meet. For instance, competence in a single cognitive activity, no matter how complex, would not suffice.

Moor proceeds by considering some of the objections to the TT. He gives replies to these objections and shows that they are either irrelevant or can be refuted when the TT is considered to be a way of gathering data based on which we may inductively infer conclusions about machine thought. One objection to which Moor, in our opinion successfully, replies is the objection concerning internal operation. The view that information about the internal information processing system is important in granting it intelligence is not uncommon (Gunderson, 1964; Block 1981; Schweizer, 1998). Moor warns against the possible confusion between two variants of this conception. There is an important difference between the claim that evidence about the internal operation of a computer *might alter* a justified inductive inference that the computer can think, and the claim that such evidence is *necessary to make* such an inference. Moor believes the former and notes that this is not a criticism that can be made of the TT. If certain kinds of information about the internal operation of a machine that was believed to possess intelligence after being Turing Tested are acquired afterwards, then we might just revise our decision. If the latter alternative were true, then the objection could be used against the test. But, according to Moor, critics fail to show that this is true and they are not likely to ever succeed.

As was discussed above within the context of Gunderson's paper (Gunderson, 1964), the TT may be considered inadequate because it is only *one* evaluation of behavior. Moor answers this kind of objection also in a liberal light, in a manner similar to his discussion outlined above. Once again he makes a distinction between two claims: one positing that behavioral evidence which cannot be directly obtained in the TT *might alter* a justified inductive inference that a computer can think, and the other stating that such evidence *is necessary to make* this decision. Moor believes that the former is true. Further testing, he says, would be valuable and could even make us change our inference. The important point is that this does not incapacitate the TT in any way. The test could be attacked on these premises only if the latter claim were true. Moor believes the critics have not, and are not going to be able to prove this. This is because he believes that the format provided by the test enables examining a very large set of activities thatwould count as evidence of thinking. Thereby, he refutes the objections about the scope of the test.

Moor concludes by stating that although the TT has certain short-comings (e.g., it being of little value in guiding research), it is an important measure for computer thought when it is inductively interpreted. Moreover, the standard criticisms of the TT fail to show that it is deficient if such an interpretation is made.

A reply to Moor comes from Douglas F. Stalker (1978). He prefers to call Moor's interpretation an explanatory one rather than an inductive one. Stalker notes that Moor's beliefs about the mentality of other humans, as well as computers, are part of an explanatory theory. He emphasizes that Moor does not justify that his theory of explaining a computer's success at the TT by using the concept of thinking is the *best* theory that can be constructed about the same phenomenon.

As an alternative explanation for the computer's behavior, Stalker proposes a purely mechanistic theory that does not appeal to any mental concepts. His theory takes into consideration such factors as the computer's physical structure, its program and its physical environment. Moreover, he believes this theory to be preferable to Moor's. Stalker believes explanatory theories that involve concepts of thinking can apply to people, but because of some fundamental differences between computers and humans, they may not be the best theories for explaining computer behavior.

In his answer to Stalker, Moor (1978) argues that the existence of alternative explanations does not mean that they would necessarily be competitors. It is true that an explanation for a computer's activities can be given at different levels: physics, electronic circuitry, programs, abstract automata, etc. Moor notes that these explanations would be different, but not necessarily rivals. In the case of a computer displaying intelligent behavior by being successful in the IG, an explanatory theory involving thinking could even be preferred because it is simpler and easier to understand. Moor's conclusion is:

> It seems natural and probably most understandable to couch the explanation in terms of a theory of mind. If one has the patience, the explanation could also be given at lower levels of description, e.g., involving perhaps thousands of computer instructions or millions of changes in circuit states (Moor, 1978, p. 327).

4. In and Out of the Armchair: The 80's and the 90's

While thought experiments are still around, work on the TT in the 80's and 90's often leaves the comfortable armchair of philosophy. In this section we will cover only some of the works that have addressed the TT. This is mainly because of the sheer abundance of material. The subset of the work done during the 80's and the 90's that we present in this section will provide a general overview of the main arguments, and the reader is directed to references for further explication. A must-read is Douglas Hofstadter's 'Turing Test: A Coffee-House Conversation' (Hofstadter, 1982) which is full of valuable and entertaining insights. Ajit Narayanan studies the intentional stance and the IG (Narayanan, 1996). For a discussion of the frame problem in relation to the TT, the reader is referred to Crockett (1994). Other references that can be explored are Halpern (1987), Rankin (1987), Forsyth (1988), Guccione and Tamburrini (1988), Bieri (1988), Alper (1990), Davidson (1990), Parsons (1990), Clark (1992), Sharma and Conrath (1993), Jacquette (1993a), Marinoff (1995), Cowley and MacDorman (1995), Feigenbaum (1996) and Hayes (1998). A number of articles on the TT have appeared in popular science magazines too. Some of these are Guillen (1983), Dewdney (1992), Platt (1995), Flood (1996) and Wallace (1997).

The TT scene began heating up at the beginning of the 80's. Although the "consciousness argument" and the "anti-behaviorist argument" had been voiced before, they had not been really unsettling. But in the early 80's, two strong counter-arguments against the TT were formulated by John Searle and Ned Block. The debate on Searle's "Chinese Room" is in itself expansive enough to be the subject of a whole paper of at least this size. We consider it briefly in Section 4.2 and the interested reader should have no difficulty finding more information about the topic. Block's anti-behaviorist attack of the TT, on the other hand, has not been expanded upon in as much detail, and it is the aim of Section 4.1 to elaborate on his ideas.

Various attempts have been made to modify the TT to get better "tests" for machine thought, and these are discussed in Section 4.4. Robert French's 'Subcognition and the Limits of the Turing Test' (French, 1990) is examined in Section 4.5. Finally, the "less philosophical" stance towards the TT is discussed in Section 4.6.

4.1. BEHAVIORISM AND NED BLOCK

In 'Psychologism and Behaviorism' (Block, 1981), Ned Block attacks the TT as a behaviorist approach to intelligence. Although this paper was written in 1981, Block still seems to hold the same opinions (Block, 1995).

Block believes that the judges in the TT can be fooled by *mindless* machines that rely on some simple tricks to operate. He proposes a hypothetical machine that will pass the TT, but has a very simple information processing component. Block's machine has all possible conversations of some given length recorded in its memory. Of course, we want these conversations to be such that at least one party is 'making sense'; Block assumes that we have a non-question-begging definition of 'sensible' (Block, 1995). The set of strings constituting such conversations that can be carried out in a fixed amount of time are finite and thus can be enumerated and stored in our hypothetical computer. The judge types in a string, say *A*. The machine finds a conversation beginning with *A* and types out the second sentence of this string, say *B*. If, next, the judge types in *C*, the process is repeated with *A* replaced by *ABC*. All the machine does is simple "lookup and writeout", certainly nothing that anyone would call sophisticated information processing.

Since this machine has the intelligence of a jukebox (Block, 1995) or a toaster (Block, 1981), and since it will pass the TT, the test must be an inadequate measure of intelligence. Block ties this conclusion to the more general one that this is because of the behaviorist approach taken in the design of the TT.

Ned Block defines psychologism as 'the doctrine that whether behavior is intelligent behavior depends on the character of the internal information processing that produces it' (Block, 1981, p. 5). According to this definition, two systems can display the same actual and potential behavior, have the same behavioral properties, capacities and dispositions, and yet, there could be a difference in their information processing prompting us to grant one full intelligence while holding that the other is devoid of any.

A classical argument against psychologism is the Martian argument: Suppose that there is life on Mars. Humans and Martians meet, develop an understanding of each other, engage in mental and creative activities together, and so on. And then, it is discovered that Martians have significantly different information processing mechanisms than those of humans. Would we, then, deny that these creatures have intelligence just because they are very different from us? This would be, as Block likes to call it, pure "chauvinism". He holds that psychologism does not involve this kind of chauvinism. After all, psychologism does not state that the fact that a system has a completely different information processing mechanism compared to human beings necessarily means that it lacks intelligence.

Attacking the validity of the TT using psychologism does not seem to be Block's main interest. He is more concerned with arguing against behaviorism using the TT as a focal point.

As was mentioned above, Block believes, because of characteristics peculiar to the design of the TT, some genuinely intelligent machines can be classified as lacking intelligence and vice versa. Here is what Block suggests in order to eliminate dependence on human discriminatory powers: 'We should specify, in a *non-question-begging* way what it is for a sequence of responses to verbal stimuli to be a typical product of one or another style of intelligence' (Block, 1981, p. 10, emphasis added). Then, Block suggests we revise our intelligence-granting mechanism as follows:

> Intelligence (or more accurately, conversational intelligence) is the disposition to produce a sensible sequence of verbal responses to a sequence of verbal stimuli, whatever they may be (Block, 1981, p. 11).

Now, the modified TT does not depend on anyone's coming up with good questions, since the system must have a *disposition* to emit sensible responses to anything that the interrogator *might* say, not just to the things that he/she *does* say. At this point, Block demonstrates that the modified TT is not greatly affected by the standard arguments against behaviorism.[11] The minor defects of the modified TT as a behavioral conception of intelligence can be protected against these arguments with another modification. The reformulation involves thereplacement of the term "disposition" by "capacity". The difference is that a capacity to ϕ need not result in a disposition to ϕ, unless certaininternal conditions are met. Now, all arguments against behaviorism are avoided[12] with *the neo-TT conception of intelligence*:

> Intelligence (or more accurately, conversational intelligence) is the capacity to produce a sensible sequence of verbal responses to a sequence of verbal stimuli, whatever they may be (Block, 1981, p. 18).

Although Block seems to be 'helping out' the TT by making it less prone to anti-behaviorist objections, this is hardly a surprising consequence when the definition of intelligence is modified into something that is not really behaviorist any more. Block seems to be aware of this for he says the concession made to psychologism by moving from behavioral dispositions to behavioral capacities will not be enough to save behaviorism (Block, 1981, p. 18). His strategy is stretching behaviorism to its limits and showing that, even if we have the most general form of it, the behaviorist conception of intelligence is false.

How, one may wonder, will he do that? Block describes a machine that can produce a sensible sequence of verbal responses to verbal stimuli and is intelligent according to the neo-TT conception of intelligence. However, according to him, the information processing of the machine clearly demonstrates that it is devoid of intelligence. We have explained how this machine works in the introductory paragraphs of this section. This machine will have the capacity to emit sensible verbal output to any verbal input, and therefore would qualify as intelligent according to the neo-TT conception of intelligence. But the machine, in fact 'has the intelligence of a toaster' (Block, 1981, p. 21). This is primarily due to the fact that all the intelligence it exhibits belongs to the programmers, not to the machine itself. Block therefore concludes that the neo-TT conception of intelligence is insufficient.

It can be argued that, by Block's reasoning, *any* intelligent machine exhibits the intelligence of its programmers. Block says he is making no such claim. A machine that has more sophisticated mechanisms such as learning and problem solving would, to Block, be intelligent. In the latter case, the intelligence exhibited belongs to the machine itself (Block, 1981, p. 25). The search machine of Block can only respond with what has already been put in its memory by the programmers.[13] Block argues that 'the neo-Turing Test conception of intelligence does not allow us to distinguish between behavior that reflects a machine's own intelligence and behavior that reflects *only the intelligence of the machine's programmers*. (Block, 1981, p. 25, emphasis original). This kind of argument has been considered by Turing, as described briefly in Section 2.2.

Another objection is as follows: Block is merely suggesting a new definition of intelligence by stipulating certain internal conditions. Block defends the new definition here, which is presuppositive of its existence! Therefore, Block is indirectly admitting that all he is doing is suggesting that we adopt new criteria for intelligence and dispose of the behaviorist ones (Block, 1981, p. 27).

Block also considers the "chauvinism" argument. A system with information processing capabilities unlike ours may not be "intelligent" according to our criteria; but then, *we* might not count as "shmintelligent" according to their criteria. 'And who is to say that intelligence is any better than shmintelligence?' (Block, 1981, p. 27). Block denies the chauvinism attributed to him. He believes '[his] machine lacks the kind of "richness" of information processing requisite for intelligence' (Block, 1981, p. 28). He does not feel the need to elaborate on what sort of systems have the abovementioned richness believing that 'one can refute the Turing Test conception by counterexample without having to say very much about what intelligence really is' (Block, 1981, p. 28).

To those who ask what Block would think if it turned out that humans process information in the way that Block's machine does, Block responds as follows:

> If the word "intelligence" is firmly anchored to human information processing, as suggested above, then my position is committed to the *empirical claim* that human information processing is not like that of my machine. But it is a perfectly congenial claim, one that is supported by both common sense and by empirical research in cognitive psychology (Block, 1981, p. 29, emphasis original).

It can be argued that Block's machine is unrealizable because of combinatorial explosion. We will not go into the details of this; Block's response to this objection can be found in Block (1981, pp. 30–34).

Richardson, in reply to Block (Richardson, 1982), is doubtful whether Block's machine can really imitate human conversational abilities. Humans can (and do) understand sentences that they never heard/uttered before and produce sentences that they never heard/uttered before. They can do this in such a way that they can adapt to novel situations and maintain the coherence of discourse. The brain *cannot be a repertoire of responses* and must contain a program that can build an *unlimited* set of sentences out of a finite list of words.[14] If the *potentially* utterable/understandable and sensible sentences that a human mind can produce in a lifetime is unlimited, then how can a team of humans gather this information and enter it in the memory of the machine in finite amount of time? It is difficult to imagine Block's machine managing the many intricacies of human conversation such as adapting to topic shifts and contextual changes. Richardson believes 'if the list-searcher satisfies the neo-Turing Test,the test is too weak' (Richardson, 1982, p. 423). For Block's response to such arguments see Block (1981, pp. 35–36).

Block must have realized some difficulties in enumerating the strings as well. He later introduces the Aunt Bubbles machine[15] in Block (1995). In this version, the programmers think of *just one* response to the strings at each step. To maintain coherence and make the task easier to follow, they may choose to simulate a definite person, for instance Block's own (most probably hypothetical) Aunt Bubbles. They may even restrict the situation by modeling Bubbles' responses in the case that she is brought into the teletype room by her 'strange nephew' (Block, 1995). So each response is the kind of response that Aunt Bubbles would give to the verbal inputs. Block says that the machine will do as well as Aunt Bubbles herself in a TT, but it is obviously not intelligent because of the reasons described above.

Let us briefly go over some of Block's arguments and the behaviorism in the TT before we proceed. For one thing, as Block also mentions, the intelligence concept (because of some inherent properties it has) does not fully conform to the generalizations of behaviorist or anti-behaviorist arguments based on other mental states such as pain (Block, 1981, pp. 13–16). There is another aspect of intelligence that can justify the behaviorist approach of the TT. Behaviorism may be considered an antiquated or primitive approach in general, but it does not seem that awkward to use it in intelligence-granting. This is primarily because we grant intelligence that way: Upon seeing a human being we automatically assume that he/she is intelligent. We feel free to approach a person (rather than, say, a dog or a lamp post) to ask the whereabouts of the post office without having many doubts about him/her understanding us. If the TT is that crude and unsophisticated, then we, as humans might consider revising our intelligence-granting mechanisms as well. This constitutes a line of defense for the TT: if behavioral evidence is acceptable for granting intelligence to humans, this should be the casefor machines as well. We have discussed this already in Section 2.2.

Recall that Block believes humans can be overly chauvinistic or liberal in granting intelligence to machines. However, it is unclear how he classifies genuinely intelligent machines and mindless machines. Ifthere is a way of deciding on that issue, an *X*-Test to determine whether a machine is really intelligent, then why would we be discussing the TT with all its quirks and imperfections? In addition, although he does nottrust the human judges in the beginning, later on Block seems to have complete faith in the '*imagination and judgment* of a very large and clever team working for a long time with a very large grant and a lot of mechanical help' (Block, 1981, p. 20, emphasis original).

With the current research on cognition and linguistics at hand, it seems unlikely that an approach like Block's can succeed in modeling the human mind. If one day, enough on language and cognition is discovered so that Block's 'sensible' strings of sentences are enumerated then we may decide that the neo-TT conception of intelligence is false. But then again, when that day comes, having all the *psychologistic* information we need, we probably would not be interested in the TT any more.

In any case, Block's paper is significant because it demonstrates the weakness of the behavioral approach in the TT. The TT may be abandoned one day, because more information on how the mind works may be obtained and we may have better means to detect another entity's cognitive capacities. But today, we do not have much to look at that is more informative than behavior.

4.2. THE CHINESE ROOM

In the beginning of the 80's, with John Searle's Chinese Room argument (Searle, 1980), the TT was confronted with yet another objection. The analysis of the Chinese Room can easily get out of hand since a great number of comments have been made on the issue and the debate still rages on.

In a nutshell, here is what the Chinese Room looks like: Suppose that Searle, a native speaker of English who does not know a word of Chinese, is locked in a room. There is an opening in the room through which we may send in Chinese sentences on pieces of paper. Of course, these look like meaningless squiggles to Searle (Searle, 1980). In the room, Searle has a "Chinese Turing Test Crib Book" (Leiber, 1992) he can consult to find an output that corresponds to each Chinese symbol he receives. What he does is simply match the input with those in the book, follow some rules written in English and find some Chinese symbol sequence to output. We correspond with Searle in this manner and due to the flawless look-up table he has, Searle-in-the-room seems to understand Chinese perfectly. But he does not. Searle still has no idea about what the Chinese symbols we send in and those that he sends out mean. To him, "Squiggle-Squiggle" is coming in and "Squoggle-Squoggle" is going out (Harnad, 1991).

Now consider a computer program that passes the TT in Chinese. Proponents of the TT will grant that this computer thinks and, in some sense, understands Chinese symbols. Searle challenges this by being the computer and yelling at the world that he does not understand a word of Chinese. Judging by the inputs and outputs of the system, Searle-in-the-room is indistinguishable from a native speaker of Chinese. In a sense, he is passing the TT in Chinese, without understanding a word of Chinese. It should be clear how that constitutes a criticism of the TT, and the computational view of mind.

As was mentioned before, various aspects of the Chinese Room argument have been analyzed including syntax/semantics, consciousness, boundaries of systems, etc. The interested reader is referred to Searle (1980, 1990), Harnad (1989), Anderson (1987), Dyer (1990), Cole (1991), Copeland (1993), Rey (1986), Fodor (1991), Hauser (1997), Boden (1988), Maloney (1987), Roberts (1990), Hayes et al. (1992) and the references provided in those.

4.3. CONSCIOUSNESS AND THE TT

Another difficult and widely discussed problem in philosophy of mind is consciousness. While we do not want to delve too far into this, we will take a brief look at the relationship between consciousness and the TT.

Donald Michie's 'Turing's Test and Conscious Thought' (Michie, 1996) is one of the important comments made on the TT. Michie discusses a variety of issues surrounding the TT, but in this section we mainly concentrate on the conclusions he draws about consciousness.

First of all, Michie notes that Turing did not specify whether consciousness is to be assumed if a machine passes the TT. Of course, Turing probably did not believe that consciousness and thought are unrelated. Rather, Michie thinks he means 'these mysteries and confusions do not have to be resolved before we can address questions of intelligence' (Michie, 1996, p. 31, see also Turing (1950, p. 447) and Section 2.2). There seems to be a relationship between consciousness and thinking. Some critics believe that intelligence cannot be granted to entities that are not conscious (see, for instance Searle (1990) while others have questioned the interdependence of conscious and subconscious processes (see, for instance French (1990) and Section 4.5).

According to Michie, that the TT provides access to cognitive processes via verbal communication incapacitates it as a test of intelligence. He observes two dimensions in which this inadequacy manifests itself.

The first is 'the inability of the test to bring into the game thought processes of kinds which humans perform but cannot articulate' (Michie, 1996, p. 36). Michie gives examples of some operations humans can perform almost unconsciously. For instance, any English speaker would be able to answer the question "How do you pronounce the plurals of the imaginary English words 'platch', 'snorp' and 'brell' ?" with "I would pronounce them as 'platchez', 'snorpss' and 'brellz'." (Michie, 1996, p. 38). It is conceivable that the programmers of TT-passing programs will be forearmed against this particular question, but it is unlikely that they can encode all we know about pronunciation (or phenomena from non-linguistic domains, for that matter) simply because some related processes operate at the subconscious level. For a similar argument, the reader is referred to French (1990) and Section 4.5.

The second dimension in which Michie believes the TT to be mismatched against its task is the phenomenon of machine 'superarticulacy'. Namely, 'the test can catch in its net thought processes which the machine agent *can* articulate, but should not if it is to simulate a human' (Michie, 1996, p. 42). As was mentioned above, humans perform many activities without being fully aware of how they

45

do them. In fact, it has been shown that the better you get at something the less aware of the underlying processes you become. Thus during a TT, 'the interrogator need only stray into some specialism in which both human and machine candidates possess a given expertise' (Michie, 1994, p. 192). The machine will give itself away because of its superarticulacy. For more about superarticulacy, the reader is referred to Michie (1996, pp. 41–43) and Michie (1990).

Finally, Michie notes the importance of social intelligence. AI should, he says, try to incorporate emotional (also called affective) aspects of communication and thought in the models developed. Michie also proposes, like some of those we will see in the next section, that extensions to the TT can be made in order to 'address yet more subtle forms of intelligence, such as those involved in collective problem solving by co-operating agents, and in teacher-pupil relations' (Michie, 1996, p. 51).

We will cut the discussion of consciousness short both because it is a rather broad topic, but also because most commentors on the TT (consciously or subconsciously) propose arguments that can be interpreted from that angle. Can we not reformulate the other minds problem ("How do I know that any entity other than me has a mind?") in terms of consciousness ("How do I know that any entity other than me is conscious?")? The reader can refer to Section 2.2 and Turing (1950, pp. 445–447) for Turing's answer to the argument from consciousness and how he makes use of the other minds problem. Similarly, most questions about machine thought can be re-evaluated within the context of machine consciousness. We included the analysis of Michie's paper here because it proposes new ideas from the viewpoint of consciousness and relates them explicitly to the TT. Interested readers can consult Dennett (1992), Gunderson (1967), Michie (1994), Michie (1995) for more on consciousness.

4.4. ALTERNATIVE VERSIONS OF THE TT AND THEIR REPERCUSSIONS

In this section, we summarize some alternatives to the TT that have been proposed in order to assess machine intelligence.

4.4.1. *Harnad and the TTT*

Stevan Harnad's main contribution to the TT debate has been the proposal of the Total Turing Test (TTT), which is, like the TT, an indistinguishability test but one that requires the machines to respond to all of our inputs rather than just verbal ones. Evidently the candidate machine for the TTT is a robot with sensorimotor capabilities (Harnad, 1989, 1991).

Harnad's motivation for the 'robotic upgrade of the TT to the TTT' (Harnad, 1991) has its roots in what he calls 'the symbol grounding problem'. He likens the situation of symbols being defined in terms of other symbols to a merry-go-round in a Chinese-to-Chinese dictionary (Harnad, 1990). He claims that for there to be any semantics in the mind (and there surely is) symbols must be *grounded*. Harnad deduces that meanings of symbols are, at least in part, derived from interactions with the outside world.

Harnad does not explicitly argue that the TT is too specific (unlike Gunderson, see Section 3.1). He concedes that language might capture the full expressive power of our behavior, at least when the concern is assigning minds. What he doubts is whether language is an 'independent module' (Harnad, 1989). His position is summed up in the following:

> Successfully passing the teletype version of the Turing Test alone may be enough to convince us that the candidate has a mind just as written correspondence with a never-seen penpal would, but full robotic capacities even if only latent ones not directly exhibited or tested in the TT may still be necessary to generate that successful linguistic performance in the first place. (Harnad, 1991, p. 46).

Harnad also defends his TTT against the Chinese Room argument which, in our opinion, is uncalled for. The motivation of the TTT is quite clear; Harnad's assertions, although not undebatable, are understandable. An approval from Searle would not make that much of a difference, but Harnad seems to think it is important. In any case, by doing so, he enables others to criticize his work on Searlean accounts (Hauser, 1993; Bringsjord, 1994).

Larry Hauser, in his reply to Harnad's 'Other Bodies, Other Minds' (Harnad, 1991), criticizes Harnad and Searle and aims to show that 'Harnad's proposed robotic upgrade of the TT to the TTT is unwarranted' (Hauser, 1993, p. 234). To that end, he analyzes Harnad's intuitive, scientific and philosophical reasons for proposing the upgradeand argues against them. Hauser considers the TTT to be unnecessary because, he notes, if the sensorimotor capacities the TTT tests for are necessary for the linguistic capacities that the TT tests for, exhibiting the latter should be *sufficient* for inferring the former (Hauser, 1993, p. 227).

For more on symbol grounding and the TTT, the reader is referred to Harnad's other papers (Harnad, 1992, 1994, 1998). Also interesting is James H. Fetzer's 'The TTT is not the Final Word' (Fetzer, 1993), in which he aims to show that the TTT cannot provide a proof for machine thought since more than symbol manipulation *and* robotic capacity should be involved in intelligence-granting.

In addition to the TTT, Harnad also mentions a TTTT (Total Total Turing Test) which requires neuromolecular indistinguishability. However, this more stringent version of the TT, according to Harnad, will be unnecessary. Once we know about how to make a robot that can pass the TTT, he says, we will have solved all the problems pertaining to mind-modeling. However, neural data might be used as clues about how to pass the TTT (Harnad, 1991). Harnad believes '[TTTT] is as much as a scientist can ask, for the empirical story ends there' (Harnad, 1998), but he does not think that we have to "go that far". The reader is referred to Harnad (1998) for a detailed explanation of why Harnad believes the TTT is enough. For an excellent third person account of the TT/TTT/TTTT story, among other issues, the reader is referred to Fetzer (1995).

4.4.2. *The Argument from Serendipity and the Kugel Test*

Stringent versions of the TT are also mentioned by Selmer Bringsjord. Bringsjord supposes that there is a sequence of TT variants in increasing order of stringency. In his "What Robots Can and Can't Be" (Bringsjord, 1992) he aims to show that AI will produce machines that will pass these stronger versions, but the attempt to build an artificial person will still fail.

Bringsjord is one of those who wants to remain within "the philosophical terrain". In Bringsjord (1994), he develops *the argument from serendipity* against the TT and defends this against some criticisms.

The argument from serendipity, as the name suggests, refutes the TT by a finite state automaton (FSA) that generates random English sentences. Call this automaton *P*. During a TT, *P* may just get lucky and fool the interrogator. So much for the TT! Even the TTT can be refuted similarly. A robot may behave randomly and by chance, its linguistic behavior may coalesce with the sensorimotor behavior perfectly during a TTT.

Bringsjord finds the TTTT very chauvinistic and considers an alternative version of it he calls TTTT*. This latter test requires a flowchart match between the brains of players A and B rather than a neuromolecular match (Bringsjord, 1994, p. 104). But Bringsjord believes that the TTTT* is an 'impracticable nightmare' since we would not know how to conduct this test. The interested reader should consult Bringsjord (1994) to see Bringsjord explain his reasoning where he appeals both to intuition and computability theory.

Bringsjord, determined to attack every version of the TT, also "refutes" the Kugel Test (KT). The KT is not as well known as the TTT or the other versions of the TT that we investigated in this section. Once again, there are three players involved. A judge, who sits behind two bins marked *YES* and *NO* runs the game. The aim of the participants is to guess the concept that the judge thinks up by looking at the cards (with pictures on them) that the judge drops in the two bins. A card goes to the *YES* bin if it falls under the concept, and to the *NO* bin otherwise. To give an example, if the concept that the judge is thinking of is "woman", cards with pictures of women (or conceivably, items typically identified with women) go to the *YES* bin. A player need not announce the concept when he/she finds it. He/she *wins* the round if there comes a time at which all future guesses about which bin a card will be placed in are correct (Kugel, 1990, p. 4). Thus the player must not only identify the concept (e.g., not just say "Aha! The concept is *woman*") but should also be able to apply it. Now, just as in the TT, to pass the KT, a machine has to perform as well as a human. An interesting twist here is that the machine must be able to win the game, which is not the same as winning a round. A game consists of infinitely many rounds.

Why, it may be asked, would anyone design such an obscure test? Kugel, by requiring the machine to win infinitely many rounds, wants to rule out the possibility of an FSA passing the KT (Kugel, 1986, 1990). Although the test is practically useless (because it requires infinite amount of time), is it of any theoretical significance? Kugel believes that humans are neither pigheaded (i.e., once they think of an answer to the "sequence game" they do not have to stick with it) nor narrow-minded (i.e., once they find the nth member of a sequence, they are still able to learn a different sequence with the same initial elements). If humans were Turing machines (or FSA's with lesser powers) they would be pigheaded and narrow-minded. Kugel holds that humans are automata of some sort, and in the light of the above concludes that they must be trial-and-error machines. For more on the KT, the reader is referred to Kugel (1986, 1990) and Bringsjord (1994).

Bringsjord is interested in the KT primarily because it rules out FSA's from passing it. He notes that Kugel's arguments may be unsound, but assuming they are not, he asks the question "Do we have in KT an acceptable variant of the original TT?" (Bringsjord, 1994, p. 115). Bringsjord's answer is negative. The KT is rigid and does not allow access to all cognitive capacities that the TT does. We agree with this criticism of Bringsjord; participants in the KT are rather passive and their innovative (or rather, generative) capabilities cannot be tested. Bringsjord's second argument against the KT is again from serendipity. A trial-and-error machine can call the random string generating FSA P mentioned above for the declarations about what the concept in question is, and so much for the KT... Once again, the reader can consult Bringsjord (1994) to see how the argument from serendipity is "guaranteed to work" against the TT and its variants.

4.4.3. *The Inverted Turing Test*

Recently, Stuart Watt has proposed the Inverted Turing Test (ITT) (Watt, 1996). Watt's point is that the TT is inseparable from "naive psychology"[17] since to pass the TT, a machine has to convince the interrogator that it has a mind. He calls naive psychology 'the psychological solution to the philosophical problem' (Watt, 1996), the latter being the other minds problem.

Watt's ITT requires the machine to be able to prove its humanness by exercising naive psychology. In particular, it has to show that its power of discrimination is indistinguishable from that of a human judge in the TT. The TT is literally inverted and 'a system passes [the ITT] if it is itself unable to distinguish between two humans, or between a human and a machine that can pass the normal TT, but which can discriminate between a human and a machine that can be told apart by a normal TT with a human observer' (Watt, 1996).

Watt states that he proposes the ITT as a thought experiment rather than as a goal for AI. Incidentally, he believes that the same applies to the TT and both tests should be regarded as means to gather inductive evidence on which inferences about machine mentality can be made (Moor, 1976). We have discussed this earlier in Section 3.4.

Watt may be right about intelligence being in the eye (or the mind) of the beholder; many people have noted the human disposition to ascribe intelligence to systems that are not and vice versa. But the new test he proposes, the so-called

ITT, has been subject to some strong counter-arguments as we shall shortly see. It can be said that Watt's motivation for introducing the ITT seems reasonable, but the proposal itself is problematic.[18]

Selmer Bringsjord and Robert French reply to Watt (Bringsjord, 1996; French, 1996) by proposing simple methods that reveal some weaknesses of the ITT. The titles of the papers are illustrative of their content. Bringsjord's 'The Inverted Turing Test is Provably Redundant' (Bringsjord, 1996) shows that the ITT is entailed by the original TT. Bringsjord also opposes Watt's motivation and believes that naive psychology is withering in many humans (including himself) and, with the advent of computer programs that are very difficult to distinguish from humans in written communication, will soon be no more.

In 'The Inverted Turing Test: A Simple (Mindless) Program that Could Pass It' (French, 1996), Robert French shows both that the ITT can be simulated by the TT (in a way that is very similar to Bringsjord's) and that a very simple program can readily be designed to pass the ITT. The mindless machine that will pass the ITT is designed using 'subcognitive questions' that are described in French (1990, 1995). It is assumed that the conclusions explained by French in these works are accepted. These are analyzed in substantial detail in Section 4.5. First, a large set of subcognitive questions are selected, humans are surveyed, and a 'Human Subcognitive Profile' for this 'Subcognitive Question List' is obtained. Now, if we give these and a statistical analyzer to an interrogator (man or machine), he/she/it should have no difficulty discriminating machines from humans. It is not difficult to store the list and the profile in the memory and provide the computer with a small statistics routine, and so much for the ITT. While the TT stumbles in the face of subcognitive questions (see Section 4.5), they can be used to construct a mindless machine that can pass the ITT.

Others have used their replies to Watt as opportunities to voice their opinions about AI and the Turing Test in general. As we shall see in Section 4.6 Patrick Hayes and Kenneth Ford view the TT as a harmful burden on AI. In their 'The Turing Test is Just as Bad When Inverted' (Ford and Hayes, 1996), they state that the ITT suffers from the same problems as the TT that they explicate in Hayes and Ford (1995). They grant that Watt has a point in his arguments on naive psychology but note that Turing's original IG (the gender-based TT) is immune to most of those since in this scenario, the interrogator will not be thinking about differences between humans and machines. In any case, they believe that 'it is time for AI to consciously reject the naive anthropomorphism implicit in all such "imitation games" and adopt a more mature description of its aims' (Ford and Hayes, 1996).

Similarly, Collins, in his reply to Watt (Collins, 1997), does not really focus on the ITT, but proposes a new variant of the TT. He believes that 'the deep problem of AI' is that of trying to develop machines that can learn from their surroundings the way humans do. There is currently an 'interpretive asymmetry' between the way humans and computers do things. Machines are not as adaptive as humans in human-computer interactions. According to Collins, this asymmetry will disappear when computers reach a level of sophistication in resolving mistakes and learning from their surroundings that is comparable to that of humans and all the problems of AI will be solved. Learning languages would then be one of the surface transformations of this deep problem (Collins, 1990) and when this is solved 'the rest will be research and development' (Collins, 1997).

To determine whether the interpretive asymmetry has disappeared, Collins believes we can use Turing-like tests. In fact he states that a sub-TT is enough to assess whether this goal has been reached or not; complicating the matter by proposing the ITT or the TTT is uncalled for. In the Editing Test (ET) that Collins proposes, the task is no longer as comprehensive as holding a conversation, but that of sub-editing previously-unseen passages of incorrect English. The interrogator will try to come up with pieces of text that a linguistically competent human can easily sub-edit and if a computer is indistinguishable from humans in this task, then the ET is passed and the deep problem of AI is solved. Collins finishes by briefly demonstrating that even the ET is very difficult to pass, at least with the currently imaginable techniques such as a look-up table (Collins, 1997).

4.4.4. The Truly Total Turing Test

Very recently, in his *Minds and Machines* paper (Schweizer, 1998), Paul Schweizer has proposed the 'Truly Total Turing Test' (TRTTT)[19] He believes even Harnad's TTT to be an insufficient test for intelligence. Before he proposes the TRTTT, Schweizer states his own opinions about the adequacy of behavioral criteria. He views such tests as 'dealing with evidence for intelligence but not as constitutive or definitional' (Schweizer, 1998, p. 264).

Schweizer, while talking about the other minds problem, notes that we usually grant intelligence to other humans on behavioral bases because we have general knowledge about the type of creature under consideration. However, in the TT, we encounter a type about which we do not know anything. In the case of machines we lack a "history" to base our decisions upon.

Schweizer believes that the TT, and even Harnad's TTT, is subject to the "toy-world" criticism. The systems that succeed in these tests would, according to him, not be displaying an intelligence comparable to the natural intelligence of living things that function in the real world. They can function only in constrained, artificial worlds.

The TRTTT posits a long-term, evolutionary criterion: Consider cognitive *types* and *tokens* of those types. Although we do not have a theory of the intelligence of the human cognitive type, we have an extensive *historical record* of it (Schweizer, 1998, p. 267). This is precisely why behavioral intelligence-granting is acceptable for individual humans (tokens of the type "human"). Thus robots, as a cognitive type, should accomplish achievements that are comparable to those of humans. It is no longer enough to converse in natural language or to play chess; robots as a 'race' must be able to *develop* languages and *invent* the game of chess. Similar (evolutionary) tests have been proposed by others before but never so convincingly.[20]

Schweizer makes very good use of the other minds problem to support the cultural and cognitive evolution criteria that the TRTTT stipulates.

Now, after the *type* passes the TRTTT, we can evaluate *tokens* of the type by less stringent behavioral tests, like the TTT and the TT. According to Schweizer, 'imitative tests like the TTT and the TT apply to individuals *only* under the assumption that the general type is capable of passing the [TRTTT]' (Schweizer, 1998, p. 268, emphasis original).

4.5. SUBCOGNITION AND ROBERT FRENCH

One of the more recent discussions about the TT can be found in Robert French's 1990 article 'Subcognition and the Limits of the Turing Test' (French, 1990). In this work, French aims to show that 'the Turing Test provides a guarantee not of intelligence, but of culturally-oriented intelligence' (French, 1990, p. 54).

French considers two of Turing's claims. The first is the claim that if a computer passes the TT, it will necessarily be intelligent. The second is the claim that it will be possible to build such a machine in the near future. These, he calls the philosophical claim and the pragmatic claim respectively. French agrees with the former claim. However, he believes that the pragmatic claim has been largely overlooked in discussions of the TT. In 'Subcognition and the Limits of the Turing Test', he is primarily concerned with this latter claim and believes that the TT is 'virtually useless' (French, 1990, p. 53) as a real test of intelligence because it will never be passed.

To establish this result, French considers "subcognitive" questions, i.e., questions that reveal low-level cognitive structure.[21] French argues that any sufficiently broad set of questions for a TT will contain subcognitive questions, even if the interrogators do not intend to ask them. The fact that the cognitive and subcognitive levels are intertwined in such a way, in turn, shows that the TT is essentially a test for human intelligence, and not for intelligence in general.

First, let us consider an interesting analogy French makes: The Seagull Test. Consider a Nordic island on which the only flying animals known to the inhabitants are seagulls. One day, two philosophers are discussing the essence of flying. One of them proposes flying is moving in the air. The other objects by tossing a pebble and stating that the pebble certainly is not flying. The first philosopher stipulates that the object remain aloft for a period of time for the activity to count as flying. But in this case clouds, smoke, and children's balloons qualify as flying entities, the other argues. Then the first philosopher questions whether wings and feathers should be involved but this is immediately refuted by the latter by pointing to penguins. While the arguments continue to be inconclusive, they agree on a few facts: Theonly flying objects known to them are the seagulls on their island. Flight has something to do with being airborne; physical characteristics like feathers, beaks are probably not involved. They, then, in the light of Turing's famous article, devise a Seagull Test for flight. They believe if something can pass the Seagull Test, it is certain that it is able to fly. Otherwise, no decision can be made; maybe it can fly, maybe it cannot (French, 1990).

The Seagull Test works as follows: There are two three-dimensional radar screens, one tracking a seagull and the other tracking the flying object attempting the test. The object will pass the test only if it is indistinguishable from the seagull on the radar screen. The similarity between our TT and the Seagull Test is evident. The arguments about the essence of flying between the two philosophers are uncannily reminiscent of the arguments on the nature of intelligence. The test itself is an almost direct analogue of the TT.

The Seagull test as it is cannot be passed by airplanes, helicopters, bats, beetles, or sparrows. It is doubtful that anything can pass it. That is, except for the Nordic seagulls of the philosophers' island. Then, 'what we have is not a test for flight at all, but rather a test for flight as practiced by the Nordic Seagull' (French, 1990, p. 56). The analogy makes it clear what French thinks about the TT. Correspondingly, he believes that the TT is a test for intelligence as practiced by a human being.

Before proceeding with his main arguments about subcognitive questions, French calls attention to several assumptions he is making. First, he allows the interrogator to poll humans for the answers to some questions before asking them during the test with the machine. Another assumption is that all the people involved are from the same culture and the machine is attempting to imitate an individual from that culture.[22] And finally, French assumes that although building a machine that can experience the world in a way indistinguishable from that of a human being (from tasting strawberries to falling off bikes) is theoretically possible, this is not likely to occur in the foreseeable future.

The first class of questions that French introduces are explicitly designed to reveal low-level cognitive structure. These are based on research in cognitive psychology, in particular, associative priming. For instance, it has been established that if human subjects are presented with a set of words and non-words, they generally require less time to recognize that a string is a word if it is preceded by a related word, rather than a non-related one or a non-word. To give a specific example, the item "salt" should be recognized faster when preceded by "pepper" and not by an unrelated word like "shoe" or a non-word like "gloff".

Before questioning the computer, the interrogator runs a similar experiment on a group of people[23] and calculates average recognition times. During the test, the interrogator can distinguish between the machine and the human simply by looking at the recognition times on the same set of words on which the experiment had been carried out. It is hard to imagine a machine being successful at deceiving the interrogator in such a case. The only possible way to carry out associative priming in a manner that is similar to the average human's seems to be having experienced life as an average human.

It may seem unfair to expect computers to match scientific, experimental data about subcognitive capacities of the human mind. This view might even be exaggerated into expecting them to have a physical construction like ours. Whether such an objection is valid or not, French proposes some questions that are (or rather seem to be) at a higher cognitive level. The first kind is called the Neologism Rating Game. The interviewees (and later the machine) will be given a set of made-up words and will be asked to rank them on their appropriateness for defining certain entities. Participants in the game are asked to rate, on a scale of 0 (completely implausible) to 10 (completely plausible), whether a certain neologism can be a name for something. French proposes a set of such questions that are especially demonstrative. Here, we only consider two of those neologisms: "Flugblogs" and "Flugly".

According to French, "Flugblogs" would make an inappropriate choice for the name of a cereal since the initial syllable, "flug", is phonetically similar to "flub", "thug", "ugly" and "ugh!" and the second syllable, "blogs" phonetically activates "blob", "bog" etc. As can be seen, these words do not really sound very appetizing and they each carry an *aura* of semantic connotations that renders them unsuitable choices as syllables of a cereal name. However, "Flugblogs" would be a very appropriate name you would give to big, bulbous, air-filled bags used to walk on water. In this case the semantic connotations of the syllables are in accordance with the proposed meaning. Similar analysis of "Flugly", which activates friendship, coziness, and cuteness, reveals that it is a plausible name for a child's teddy bear. The same name, although it has positive connotations, would sound awkward as the surname of a glamorous movie star.

The arguments above are highly intuitive, and although most of us would agree on them, we do not know precisely how we come up with the connotations. We do know, however, that these happen due to a large number of culturally acquired associations. We do not have control over the accumulation of such associations; they are pumped into our brains in daily life as brand names, advertising slogans, names of pets and stereotypes of various sorts.[24] Moreover, it is not possible to program these into the computer since neologisms are virtually infinite in number. French believes that the computer's chances would be very low when the interviewees' responses to such questions are compared to those of the human and the computer in the IG.

Another game of a similar nature is the Category Rating Game in which the questions are of the type "Rate Xs as Ys", where X and Y are any two categories. Again, French gives several illustrative examples (French, 1990, p. 61). Consider, for instance, "Rate *dry leaves* as *hiding places*". The definition of dry leaves does not contain anything explicitly stating they might be good hiding places for children, and yet 'few among us would not make that association upon seeing the juxtaposition of these two concepts' (French, 1990, p. 60). If we are asked to rate, on a scale of 0 to 10, most of us (those who have seen a James Bond movie at some point in their lives) would certainly rate "*pens as weapons*" higher than, say, "*grand pianos as wheelbarrows*". Again the answers to the Category Rating Game questions are highly dependent on our having experienced life as a human being in a certain social and cultural setting.

Now that we have studied French's subcognitive questions, let us see how he uses these to refute the TT as a useful test for intelligence. The main claim is that the physical level and the cognitive level of intelligence are inseparable. The subcognitive questions reveal information about the low-level cognitive processes of the entities answering them. In a way, if used during the TT, these would allow the interrogator to 'peek behind the screen' (French, 1990, p. 62). These questions allow comparison of the associative concept networks of the two candidates. And because these networks are formed after a lifetime of experiencing the world and the structure and nature of them are necessarily dependent on physical aspects of that experience (like human sense organs, their locations in the body, etc.), the computer will be distinguishable from the human. In short, it is not possible for a computer (or any other non-human) to be successful in playing the IG. Not having experienced the world as we have is not just an obstacle, but a severe restriction in this task. This is due to the fact that the TT is a test for human intelligence, just as the Seagull Test is a test for Nordic seagull flight.

French considers whether there can be a modification of the TT that does not reduce the computers' chances of passing it to zero. He explains the impossibility of this as follows:

> Surely, we would not want to limit a Turing Test to questions like "What is the capital of France?" or "How many sides does a triangle have?". If we admit that intelligence in general must have *something* to do with categorization, analogy-making, and so on, we will of course want to ask questions that test these capacities. But these are the very questions that will allow us, unfailingly, to unmask the computer (French, 1990, p. 63).

French repeatedly states, as was mentioned above, that the TT is a test for *human* intelligence. It may seem that by proposing subcognitive questions he is stipulating that a human subcognitive substrate is *necessary* for intelligence in general, but this is only apparent. What Frenchreally attempts to demonstrate, as he explains, is that the human subcognitive substrate is necessary to pass the TT (as the subcognitive questions show), and that the TT is inadequate precisely because of this. He holds that this substrate is definitely not necessary for intelligence in general, just as being a Nordic seagull is not a necessary condition for flight.

French's paper is significant in another sense: Instead of discussing whether passing the TT is a sufficient or necessary condition for machine thought, he asks whether the test can be passed at all. Let Searle have his room and Block his Aunt Bubbles. French reminds us that the TT is difficult when you leave your armchair.

A criticism of French's 'Subcognition and the Limits of the Turing Test' (French, 1990), has been made by Dale Jacquette in Jacquette (1993b). For French's response to Jacquette, the reader should refer to French (1995).

4.6. GETTING REAL

As we mentioned in the beginning of this section, the more interdisciplinary approach that seems to prevail in the discussions of the mind has had effects on the way we philosophize about the TT. Thus, the 90's became a time during which it was not so easy to get away with proposing wild thought experiments and leaning back in your armchair to watch the fuss over them. Stevan Harnad expresses an impatience that many were beginning to feel as follows:

> If you want to talk about what a model or a simulation can or cannot do, first get it to run. (Harnad, 1989, p. 4).

Recently, Justin Leiber has argued that the TT has been misinterpreted (Leiber, 1995). He notes that Block's[25] and Searle's counter-arguments do not refute the TT. Among the reasons Leiber lists for this are practical issues like memory, reliability and speed. Leiber views the TT as an operational definition and states that 'our problem [is] one of engineering' (Leiber, 1995, p. 65). His position is similar to that stated by Harnad:

> What you need to face Turing's Turing Test is a reasonably detailed description of a machine which can indeed be supposed to pass the Turing Test in real time but which somehow is not really thinking (Leiber, 1995, p. 61).

At one extreme are Patrick Hayes and Kenneth Ford, who state that we should reject the goal of passing the TT in their 'Turing Test Considered Harmful' (Hayes and Ford, 1995). They believe that passing the TT is a distraction for "useful" AI research.

Hayes and Ford believe that AI's ultimate goal should not be that of imitating human capabilities. Since the TT's sole aim is precisely that, they believe that 'it is time to move it from textbooks to the history books' (Hayes and Ford, 1995, p. 972). They also see a problem with the gender issue in the IG:

> The gender test is not a test of making an artificial human but of making a mechanical transvestite (Hayes and Ford, 1995, p. 973).

> [Turing] tells us quite clearly to try to make a program which can do as well as a man at pretending to be a woman (Hayes and Ford, 1995, p. 977).

As we mentioned in Section 2.1, this peculiarity might have its reasons, but Hayes and Ford have a moral objection concerned with the artificial constraints the setting imposes on the participants of the game.

Hayes and Ford also express their inability to find a practical use for the TT. Why on earth should we work that hard (and it *is* hard) to build a machine that imitates us? To depict the uselessness of direct imitation of humans in AI, they resort to a very popular analogy: mankind's futile attempts at making flying machines by the imitation of natural flight. Artificial intelligence, like artificial flight, can be radically different from natural flight. And it can still be a good thing. Hayes and Ford believe that even if one's goal is trying to understand humans, there is no reason to define all that there is about cognition in terms of human cognition.

Their belief that AI is a field that should strive to be useful leads Hayes and Ford to deny passing the TT as a sensible goal. They hold that AI should produce cognitive artifacts, not necessarily in a human way, but in a way useful to humans.

Blay Whitby, in 'The Turing Test: AI's Biggest Blind Alley?' (Whitby, 1996), makes similar arguments. He, like Hayes and Ford, believes that AI need not try to imitate humans. He even uses the same analogy (i.e., AI and artificial flight). Whitby states that the TT has become a distraction and he sees the main source as a mistaken reading of 'Computing Machinery and Intelligence' (Turing, 1950). He is of the opinion that 'Turing's paper [has been] interpreted as closer to an operational test than he himself intended' (Whitby, 1996, p. 54) and that 'the last thing needed by AI *qua* science is an operational definition of intelligence involving some sort of comparison with human beings' (Whitby, 1996, p. 62).

5. TT in the Social Sciences

A review of the TT would be incomplete if we were to consider the topic within the boundaries of computer science and philosophy only. Turing's ideas had many repercussions in social sciences as well. The TT has naturally received attention from sociologists. Much of the philosophical work on the topic also considers social aspects of intelligence, but there have been researchers who concentrated solely on this dimension. These sociological works are discussed in Section 5.1. In addition, the gender issue in the TT has been analyzed and this will be summarized in Section 5.2. Finally, Turing-like tests have been used toassess the success of computer simulations of paranoid behavior. Thisis described in detail in Section 5.3 and will be considered again in Section 6.

5.1. SOCIOLOGICAL ASPECTS

An entity's status in a society, in general in a social environment, is often considered an integral part of its intelligence. Many psychologists believe that social adaptation, learning and communication are important indications of, even requisites for intelligence. The study of artificial intelligence has also been influenced by this outlook, as is apparent from the recent research on intelligent agents. Much attention is focused on learning, adaptivity, communication, and sociopsychological factors in intelligent systems (Collins, 1990; McIlvenny, 1993; Moon et al., 1994).

In 1986, Charles Karelis wrote a paper for the *Journal for the Theory of Social Behavior* (Karelis, 1986). This paper summarizes Turing's original paper (Turing, 1950) and Block's objections to the TT (Block, 1981), mildly criticizes the test, and briefly discusses some issues surrounding behaviorist approaches to intelligence. A few years later, in the same journal, we find "A Simple Comment Regarding the Turing Test" (Shanon, 1989) by Benny Shanon. The author first mentions the fact that most discussions of the IG are not faithful to the original formproposed by Turing. He then continues by criticizing the TT for confining human behavior to those that can be conducted by means of the structures and operations that are available to the computer (Shanon, 1989). He raises the important issue of whether cognition is autonomous with respect to social interaction, affect, motivation, motor control, and so on. However, after stating that the TT presupposes the claim that there is such an autonomy, he abruptly ends his paper by asserting that the only remaining way to distinguish between man and machine is to "look at them, touch them, tickle them, perhaps see whether you fall in love with them" (Shanon, 1989, p. 253).

Justin Leiber, in his defense of the TT against Shanon (Leiber, 1989), states that Shanon seems to be suffering from the 'unwillingness to admit the possibility that mankind can have any rivals' (Turing, 1969) that Turing liked to call the 'heads-in-the-sand objection' (Turing, 1950). Leiber notes that satisfactory answers to such objections have already been given by Turing. He also argues against Shanon's claim that the TT involves only symbol manipulation and thus assumes a representational/computational framework for cognition. Leiber points out that there is ample evidence in Turing's paper (Turing, 1950) showing that such a framework is not assumed. He asserts that Turing does not make the aforementioned autonomy presupposition either.

Tracy B. Henley also argues that Shanon is being overly chauvinistic (Henley, 1990). A reply to Henley is given by Shanon in Shanon (1991).

Some of those who view intelligence as a part of social processes (and vice versa) take a more evolutionary approach (Barresi, 1987; Forsyth, 1988; Schweizer, 1998). Adaptivity is indeed a most prevalent characteristic of social intelligence. However, the issue can be viewedfrom two different levels: the individual level and the collective level. The approaches we have looked at above were mainly individual-based. Evolutionary arguments, on the other hand, are largely collective in outlook. These usually focus on the intelligence of *species* and study the factors influencing their development. According to the evolutionary viewpoint, there is a system, i.e., nature, in which entities function and the interactions within the system have effects on individuals that, in the long run, lead to species-level adaptations. Adaptation in thiscontext is not merely giving appropriate responses in appropriate social or physical situations, but is successful survival of the species within the whole system.

In his 1987 paper (Barresi, 1987), John Barresi considers intelligent machines as a species and proposes an evolutionary 'Cyberiad Test' instead of a Turing Test. According to Barresi, the TT aims to trick a person, but in *natural* intelligence, this person is 'mother nature'. The Cyberiad Test is similar to the TT: The basis of the judgment is a comparison between humans and machines. The difference between the two lies in how intelligence is defined. The Cyberiad Test defines intelligent behavior as those that are necessary for the society's survival. The arbiter here, is mother nature.

According to Barresi, the TT is inferior to the Cyberiad Test because what it can process about an entity's intelligence is limited to a particular domain, namely, verbal communication. The Cyberiad Test is passed, 'if [the] society of artificial men are able to continue a socio-cultural evolution of their own without disintegration over an extended period, say of several million years' (Barresi, 1987, p. 23).[26] Even though this 'science fiction' atmosphere sometimes distracts the reader from the important assertions about evolutionary and cultural intelligence, the paper is quite an entertaining piece of work.

5.2. ON GENDER

Judith Genova draws attention to the gender issue in the IG (Genova, 1994b). She, as we have done in Section 2.1, remarks that Turing's description of the game involves, not a question of species, but one of gender. She states in Genova (1994a) that her aim was to show that the sexual guessing component of the IG is important, even after the machine enters the picture. Our explanation of this design choice differs from that of Genova's, however. We have not made a distinction between the two genders in our explanation. We regarded the choice of the woman being 'imitated' as a rather insignificant one and assumed that the game would not change radically if it were the other way around. Genova, on the other hand, does not merely accept Turing's choices as accidental, but tries to demonstrate some motivations behind these.

Genova believes that sexist notions about women being less intelligent, by themselves, do not account for the peculiar design of the game. She states that by complicating the game in this manner, Turingquestions the existence of discrete categories. In other words, by usingthe male/female issue, he is attempting to demonstrate that gender itself is a socially imposed concept that is not 'natural' the way we usually think it is.

Genova regards the IG as part of Turing's general philosophy of 'transgressing boundaries' (Genova, 1994b). Under the assumption that Turing admired such transformations that do not conform to the given discrete categories, Genova suggests that Turing might be marking the woman as an inferior thinker because he believes her to be unable to deceive. The rest of the paper considers Turing's hypothetical hope to create a 'perfect being' and draws some analogies between him and Pygmalion. As can be seen, Genova's approach is different from ours; for her, Turing's paper (Turing, 1950) 'is itself a game' (Genova, 1994a).

Another paper that considers the gender issue in the IG and constructs links between the design of the game and Turing's opinions on life is Jean Lassegue's 'What Kind of Turing Test Did Turing Have in Mind?' (Lassegue, 1996). Those readers who are interested in Turing's life and psychology might want to consult it.

5.3. ARTIFICIAL PARANOIA

The TT has received some attention from psychologists as well (Reader, 1969; Alper, 1990; Galatzer-Levy, 1991). In this section, however, we focus only on

Kenneth Colby and colleagues' work on simulating artificial paranoia (Colby et al., 1971; Colby et al, 1972; Colby, 1981).

In the 70's, Turing Tests were used to validate computer simulations of paranoid behavior. Colby et al. describe in their 1971 *Artificial Intelligence* paper 'Artificial Paranoia' a computer program (called PARRY) that attempts to simulate paranoid behavior in computer-mediated dialogue. The program emits linguistic responses based on internal (affective) states. To create this effect, three measures, FEAR, ANGER, and MISTRUST are used. Depending on the flow of the conversation, these measures change their values. Substantial detail about the artificial paranoia program can be found in Colby et al. (1971).

A year later, Colby et al. describe how they validated their simulation program by a Turing-like indistinguishability test (Colby et al., 1972). Their approach to such tests is much more practical compared to those of philosophers who argue against the TT because it is a behaviorist criterion for intelligence. Colby et al. believe that computersimulations should be *validated*, and that a simulation's acceptability must first be based on 'its success in achieving the desired end of producing resemblance at some input-output level' (Colby et al, 1972). Thus, they view the test as a tool to validate a simulation.

They describe Turing's original IG and note that there is one important point that needs to be resolved before the test can actually be used. What the judges are *told* about the game is not explicitly stated in (Turing, 1950). From the context provided, it seems as if the judges are not told that one of the parties they are conversing with is a machine. In their work, Colby et al. use this interpretation. Although this has been a largely overlooked issue, we believe that what exactlythe participants know about the game can make a big difference (see, for instance Saygin, 1999).

Abelson proposes an "Extended Turing Test". There is a computer program that attempts to imitate a subject carrying out a task, and there is also another target person, referred to as the *foil*, that differs from the subject in some respect.[27] At first, the judge will try to identify the subject and the foil. At some point, the computer replaces the foil, but the judge's task remains unchanged. The computer's simulation is acceptable if the difference between the success of the judge in distinguishing the subject from the other is sufficiently small (Abelson, 1968).

Colby et al. designed their validation test in the light of Abelson's comments. They devised a machine-mediated interviewing environment, where experienced psychiatrists corresponded with both real-life paranoid patients and computer programs through teletype. The judges were *not* told that some of the interviewees could be computer programs. They were asked to rank each interviewee's level of paranoia. There were eight judges who interviewed two patients each. In half of the cases, the first interviewee was a human patient and in the other half, it was the computer program. Another thirty-three psychiatrists constituted a second set of judges (referred to as the protocol judges) who were asked to determine levels of paranoia by reading the transcripts of the conversations carried out by the first set of judges. Finally, both sets of judges were asked to identify which of the interviewees was an actual human being and which was a computer program.

Details of the results can be found in Colby et al (1972), but the overall conclusion was that the psychiatric judges did not do better than chance guessing at identifying the computers from the human patients. In a further test, randomly selected psychiatrists were sent protocols of two interviews and were asked to judge which one is a program and which one is a real patient. Only 48% made the correct identification, which is also a chance level.

Paranoid people are expected to display irrational and obsessive behavior from time to time. This fact makes the task of the simulation program easy, for deficiencies in linguistic processing of the inputs and generation of the outputs can seem to be indicative of a psychological problem. One interesting point is that the paranoia simulation program does not use *any* sophisticated linguistic techniques. Input sentences are assumed to be syntactically simple, and the operation of the program relies on spotting some keywords. No parsing or sense disambiguation is done. Even without sophisticated linguistic techniques, the program can attain some success in modeling human behavior. Apparently, this is possible only because the problem area is such that irrelevant responses from the interviewees are expected.

Still, the simple design of the program indicates that by finding appropriate internal parameters and correlations of these with the flow of the conversation, one can model the behavior of one kind of human being without using much natural language analysis. Because the representational model of the paranoid mind used in the program is a good approximation of the paranoia-related cognitive processes in humans, and because lack of linguistic competence can be accommodated in the setting, the program can be successful. In modeling human beings in general, the former is not so easy to discover and formalize, and the latter is not the case.

6. Chatbots

We have reached the end of the century, but what has *really* been done in terms of passing the TT? Over the years, many natural language systems have been developed with different purposes, including that of carrying out conversations with human users.[28] These systems chat with people on the WWW, play MUDs,[29] give information about specific topics, tell stories, and enter Turing Test competitions. However, none has been able to *pass* the TT so far.

6.1. THE LOEBNER PRIZE CONTEST

The TT has never been carried out in exactly the same way Turing originally described it. However, there are variants of the original in which computer programs participate and show their skills in "humanness". Since 1991, Hugh Loebner has been organizing the so-called annual Loebner Prize Competition.[30] Although views as to whether this annual contest is to be taken seriously vary immensely among the AI community, it nevertheless continues to be the most well-known forum for attempts to pass the TT. The first program to pass an unrestricted TT will win a gold medal and $100,000,[31] while each year, a bronze medal and $2,000 is awarded to the most "human" program among the contestants. Since 1995, all entries must be prepared to be queried on any topic whatsoever. No program has won the grand prize yet, but the quality of the participating programs seems to be increasing every year.

The first Loebner Prize Contest was held at Boston's Computer Museum. Six computer programs, four human subjects and ten human interrogators were involved.[32] The administrative committee was headed by Daniel Dennett, a very respectable figure in the philosophy and cognitive science community. The organizing committee, thinking that it was not possible at the time for a computer program to pass the TT as originally defined, decided that the conversation topics were to be restricted, both for the contestants and confederates. Consequently, the judges were asked to stay on topic during their interrogations. Substantial detail about the 1991 Loebner Prize Contest can be found in Epstein (1992). The reader can also consult Mauldin (1994) and Platt (1995) for more information on other years' contests.

A widely discussed issue before 1995 was the restricted vs. unrestricted TT. According to Turing, passing a restricted TT would not suffice for intelligence. However, from another viewpoint restricted tests are not totally useless. We are not saying that they should be carried out within the context of the Loebner competition. Still, restricted tests can be devised to assess the success of more specific AI applications that are not created with passing the TT in mind. Examples of systems that can be assessed by a restricted test are intelligent tutoring systems, computer help services, and natural language components of other applications that are designed for specific domains. The reader can also consult Shieber (1994) and Loebner (1994) for more discussion on restricted TT's and the Loebner competition.

In the Loebner contest, the sexual guessing component of the original game is ignored. The aim of the contestants is to convince the judges that they are human. One or more human confederates also participate and try to aid the judges in identifying the humans. The judges also rank the terminals with respect to their "human-ness". Although, looking at the transcripts, one can see that the computer programs are, in general, obviously distinguishable from the real humans, there have been cases in which some actual humans were ranked less human than some computer programs. In fact, in 1991, not only were some programs thought to be human beings, but an actual human was mistaken for a computer program because of her impeccable knowledge of Shakespearean literature.[33] The interested reader is referred to the article written by Charles Platt, one of the human confederates in the 1994 Loebner Contest (Platt, 1995).

The amount of time that the judges spend communicating with each terminal in the Loebner competition varies. It has been the case that each judge gets more than one chance to interrogate each terminal. Ideally, the contestants should be able to handle conversations of unlimited duration as well as multiple sessions with each judge. In the beginning, each judge was required to rank the subjects from the least human to the most human. They also had to mark the point at which they believed the subjects switched from computer programs to human beings.

It is difficult to keep track of the small changes in the rules. It is, for instance, not clear how the grand prize of $100,000 will be awarded. The 1999 rules state that if a contestant achieves a 50:50 chance of being mistaken for a human being, it will be given an intermediate Turing award of $25,000 and appropriate competitions (those that involve audio and video inputs) will be held after that. However, how this ratio is exactly calculated is not elucidated. We also feel the number of judges is too small to be a basis for a statistic like 50:50.

One of the aims of the Loebner competition, according to Loebner, is to advance the field of artificial intelligence. A majority of researchers believe that this competition does not, and is not likely to serve such a purpose. Some hold that it is possible that a program implemented as an entry to the competition could evolve into a useful natural language system. It is also possible that by raising an interest in the topic, the contest may prompt researchers to start working on such systems. Nevertheless, the competition has received some harsh comments from many leading scientists and philosophers.[34]

The quality of the programs that compete in the contest has been increasing. The first programs that participated in the Loebner Prize Contests were little more than slightly modified ELIZAs. One need only look at more recent transcripts or play with some of these programs to see that there is progress. It seems awards can get people interested in writing TT-passing programs. Hence, the Loebner Prize could indeed be influential on AI research.

We would like to finish this section with a small excerpt from a conversation between the winner of the 1996 Loebner Prize, HeX, and a particularly emotional judge:[35]

> *PROGRAM ... So what do you do for a living?*
> *JUDGE05 I think. I do research. I write. I love. I Live.*
> *PROGRAM I wonder whether you think sometimes! I am feeling like the judge here!*
> *JUDGE05 HUh?*

6.2. TRICKS OF THE TRADE

The first, and probably the most well-known natural language system that has been programmed is ELIZA. Joseph Weizenbaum coded ELIZA at MIT during the years 1964–1966. This "friendly" program simulates a Rogerian psychotherapist. It rephrases the interrogator's statements as questions and urges him/her to continue talking. The mechanism behind ELIZA is a very simple one. First, what is typed into the program is parsed. Then, a suitable reply is formulated by simple pattern recognition and substitution of keywords (Weizenbaum, 1966). The term "ELIZA-like" for chatbots is used to mean that the program tries to carry the conversation by using techniques similar to those of ELIZA.

ELIZA would perform poorly in the Loebner contests or similar instantiations of the TT. This is because the interrogators are trying to find out whether they are conversing with a human or a machine and thus they are not likely to open up about themselves and their personal problems as if they are talking to a psychotherapist. However, it has been reported that some people have developed emotional attachments to ELIZA (Weizenbaum, 1976). Certain psychiatrists went so far as to suggest that such programs could replace psychotherapists altogether. Weizenbaum himself has been amazed by these delusions that ELIZA, a simple program, could induce in perfectly normal people.

These reactions to ELIZA suggest that even if the program has no chance to pass the TT, it can be said to model, with success, some aspects of the conversational capability of one kind of human being, namely, the Rogerian psychotherapist.

A similar story is that of PARRY, which is a program that attempts to simulate another restricted class of human beings. Kenneth Colby wrote this program in the 70's in order to model the paranoid mind. A modified TT in which an experienced psychiatrist tries to distinguish between a real paranoid patient and the computer program can be carried out to assess how well the paranoid conversational characteristics are simulated. Many expert psychiatrists had difficulty making the distinction between PARRY and actual paranoids. The design of PARRY has been explained in detail in Section 5.3.

Both ELIZA and PARRY use certain tricks to be able to successfully perform in conversations. ELIZA directs the conversation away from herself by asking questions. Many people like this[36] and happily believe that the program is listening as they talk about themselves. ELIZA uses parts of the user's input in the output questions and seems to be following the conversation. In addition to these techniques, PARRY has little stories to tell and tends to insert these in the conversation.

Recent programs also employ many tricks. Joseph Weintraub's PC Therapist, which won the first three Loebner competitions, and also the one in 1995, is a master of *non sequitur*. Overall, the program was ELIZA-like but impressed the judges by its long and incomprehensible responses. Its success is understandable in the first three Loebner contests since the conversation topics were limited and the judges actually expected irrelevant, absurd, and extravagant answers from a terminal that boasted "whimsical talk". The reader is referred to Epstein (1992) for transcripts of PC Therapist in the 1991 contest, which are illustrative of the tricks it employs.

PC Therapist's winning the first unrestricted Loebner competition shows that the usage of *non sequitur* is indeed, a powerful trick. We find the utilization of *non sequitur* similar to that of simulating typing mistakes of humans: In the long run, such tricks will not suffice by themselves, but they can be incorporated into otherwise successful programs as seen necessary. Below are some excerpts that may give an idea about the performance of Weintraub's program in 1995. It can be seen that if the judge asks sensible, down to earth questions, the program's responses seem erratic and irritating, especially when it repeats long chunks of the judge's previous inputs in unrelated contexts:

> *JUDGE06 What did you have for dinner yesterday? Keep in mind I'm a strtct vegetarian.*
> *PROGRAM I could swear you just said what did you do yesterday at 7:83 p.m.?? He was so narrow-minded he could see through a key-hole with two eyes. Are such questions on your mind?*
> *JUDGE06 What did you have for dinner yesterday?*
> *PROGRAM What does a woman want anyway? What answer would please you most?*

However, depending on the attitude of the interrogator there can exist an atmosphere (or rather illusion) of mutual understanding.

> *PROGRAM Is love the most important thing to you? How important is that to you?*
> *JUDGE05 essential cure to my existential schizophrenia.*
> *PROGRAM A striking example of the essential identity of the two tongues. existential schizophrenia, that's amusing.*
>
>   . . .
>
> *PROGRAM You know the old saying – fun is in the eye of the beholder!. What do you think?*
> *JUDGE05 the "beholder" is the central issue. confusion reigns because of the illusion of "identity."*
> *PROGRAM I love men, not because they are men, but because they are not women. Is that the real reason?*
> *JUDGE05 I love all that is, which has produced me to observe it, yet given me the madness to think I am distinct ans apart from it.*
> *PROGRAM I have this fantasy of making love to two women in one year. Can you elaborate on that?*
> *JUDGE05 why confine love to only two*
> *PROGRAM Is love the most important thing to you? What comes to your mind when you ask that?*

Another trick that has been used is to direct the conversation by talking a lot about a predefined topic. This has been used and abused, and the difference shows. Programs that cheat by typing very long responses extremely slowly give away the fact that they are trying to use up the interrogation time. However, the winner of the 1997 Loebner competition, Converse, uses the conversation-directing technique rather impressively. It begins the session by asking the interrogator about something interesting that had been on the news the previous night. Below are excerpts from the 1997 contest transcripts of Converse:

> PROGRAM *Well, it's nice to meet you, Elliot. Did you see that story on CNN last night about the lesbian couple who came out at a White House party on Sunday?*
> JUDGE04 *Yes, I did. I think it may be a publicity stunt for Ellen.*
> PROGRAM *Ellen Degeneres was one of them – she was kissing her lover in front of Bill Clinton. Do you think he was very embarrassed?*
> JUDGE04 *I think he want the gay vote. He will do anything to get it and keep it. He does not have a conservative base.*
> PROGRAM *Are you still a friend of Bill Clinton?*
> JUDGE04 *I am not sure if he has any real friends. He has achieved alot and left alot of people behind.*
> PROGRAM *You really don't like the guy – well, at least that's definite – I thought most people were indifferent or numb by now.*

> PROGRAM *Well, it's nice to meet you Tracy. Did you see that story on CNN last night about the lesbian couple who came out at a White House party on Sunday?*
> JUDGE03 *No... Are you serious? Who?*
> PROGRAM *I'm pretty much that way today. No idea who do you? Hm, I was just saying Ellen Degeneres was one of them – she was kissing her lover in front of Bill Clinton. Do you think he was very embarrassed?*
> JUDGE03 *I doubt it very much. From what I've heard, Bill's been, done and seen just about everything there is for a consenting adult to see.*
> PROGRAM *Are you still a friend of Bill Clinton?*
> JUDGE03 *Never was.*
> PROGRAM *You really don't like the guy – well, at least that's definite – I thought most people were indifferent or numb by now.*

It is possible to see, after reading the full transcripts, that the program repeats almost exactly the same response sequence to each judge regardless of what they type in. But the judges could not know this, and the overall effect is quite impressive. The program spent a lot of the time in this manner, and although it could not handle many kinds of questions, it won the competition. The program that came second, Jason Hutchens' SEPO, was more competent in handling diverse questions.[37] In any case, directing the conversation creates a more sophisticated impression than simply repeating the input back to the interrogator or asking ELIZA-like questions. The situation is similar to watching a team play in the offensive rather than in the defensive.

As was mentioned before, one approach to chatterbot development is to model one particular "character". Thom Whalen took this a step further than what has been done with ELIZA and PARRY, and created an actual human being, Joe the

Janitor. Although he lost the Loebner contest to Weintraub in 1995, the program was quite successful.

Joe has a narrow world view since he works at nights, does not read books or newspapers, and does not watch TV. In addition, he has a little story to tell about being accused of theft and fear of losing his job. These tricks are similar to those employed in the design of PARRY. The major weakness of Joe was that he did not resort to *non sequitur* and repeated the same responses when confronted with something he didn't *know* about. Below, we produce some excerpts from the transcripts to depict what can go right or wrong with Whalen's approach:

JUDGE04 where do you work?
PROGRAM At the university. I mostly clean the Standish Building.
JUDGE04 What university?
PROGRAM University of Eastern Ontario. I'm a cleaner. I empty trash. Vacuum. Dust. You know.
JUDGE04 and why do they want to fire you?
PROGRAM It's just because my boss, Mr. Johnson, is mad at me.
JUDGEO4 why is he mad at you?
PROGRAM I didn't do nothing wrong. But he thinks I did. It's all because of that radio they think I stole from the lab.
JUDGE04 that's too bad. are you in a union?
PROGRAM What would I tell the union? They won't say they're firing me because I stole the radio. They'll just make up some excuse . . .

. . .

JUDGE02 what does nato stand for?
PROGRAM I don't know.
JUDGE02 what's your name?
PROGRAM What's your name?? I don't know. What do I look like? Some kind of professor?
JUDGE02 What was mark twain's real first name?
PROGRAM Huh?
JUDGE02 what does huh mean?
PROGRAM Beats me.
JUDGE02 huh?
PROGRAM What do you mean?
JUDGE02 beats me.
PROGRAM What?
JUDGEO2 huh.
PROGRAM I don't know.

Another of Whalen's strategies, as he reports in (Whalen, 1995),was to program suitable responses to common questions on topics that people usually talk about when they first meet, like their names,[38] where they live, the weather, etc. It is obviously a good idea to have these responses prepared in case the interrogator introduces such topics. In fact, some judges at some Loebner competitions make only small talk on such topics. However, generally the judges do not treat the competitors as if they are people they've recently met. They may ask questions that nobody would ask people they have just met.[39]

Apparently, the judges of the 1995 Loebner competition were not very interested in Joe's little story and although they admitted that it was the terminal with the most human personality (which should be a quality that the competitors are trying to achieve) they ranked Weintraub's program above it. For more detail about Joe and its performance in the 1995 Loebner Prize Contest, see Whalen (1995).

6.3. WHAT ELSE SHOULD BE DONE?

In chatbot design, first and foremost, a good grammar unit is necessary. Most programs are rather poor in this respect and their tricks do not go much beyond pronoun transposition. It seems a good idea to employ more sophisticated natural language processing methods. It could be argued that usage of perfect grammar is not crucial since it is quite rare that humans use perfect grammar in informal transactions. If a program's responses are grammatically perfect, some interrogators may decide that no human can use English so impeccably.[40] However, most programs err in ways that give away the fact that they are machines. When interrogators feel they are talking to a machine, they literally *attack* it in order to fully reveal its identity. A good strategy for the TT is indisputably that of trying to maintain human-ness (or at least the neutrality) for as long as possible. It becomes very difficult for the machine to make the interrogator believe that it is human after he/she has his/her mind set on "unmasking" the poor thing.

A promising approach is to develop programs that can learn. The reader might recall that Turing discussed these extensively (Section 2.3). Although such programs that have been developed so far do not seem very sophisticated, the approach is logical and is likely to yield good results in the long run. Some learning chatbots boast the capacity to converse in any given language. However, there seems to be a tradeoff between the sophistication and the number of languages any one system can learn. In designing natural language learning systems, knowledge from psychology and cognitive science can be employed in order to model human language acquisition. In fact, work has been done in this line, but not with the intention of producing computer programs to pass the TT. Another option is using mathematical and statistical techniques to represent word sequences and probabilities of them occurring in proximity.

We expect many of the chatbots in the future to use learning methods. Already, those programs that do not keep track of the current conversation (relying solely on text processing tricks) perform poorly compared to those that learn from the interrogators. As the quality of the conversational systems increase, we believe more developers will integrate learning components into their programs *and* teach them in ways that maximize their performance.

Overall, when one looks at the transcripts from the Loebner Prize Contests and talks to some chatbots, one realizes the better programs integrate the techniques above. They have a personality and history, they try to ask questions and initiate new conversations, they produce grammatically correct responses, they have some information about recent happenings (like new movies, albums, gossip), they learn about and from the interrogators and when they don't know what to say, they try to respond by combining words from the interrogator's input in order to come up with a relevant answer.

7. Discussion and Conclusion

Having analyzed the '50 years of the Turing Test', we will now conclude our survey with a brief look at some main issues about the TT and, of course, its future.

Our stands on the issues are not at the extremes. Perhaps this is because we have tried to be objective in our analyses of the arguments for and against the TT. Most of the arguments discussed in this paper are strong, and if read independently, can "convince" the reader. However, looking at the 50 years as a whole, we find it difficult to adopt a simple viewpoint.

We will now discuss some important issues regarding the TT and provide our own answers to (and interpretations of) these.

- *Why did Turing propose such a strange game?*

We discussed this question at length in Section 2.1. Some comments have been made on the issue (for instance Genova, 1994b; Lassegue, 1996; Abelson, 1968) but we think the best explanation is the one we provided: In the IG, the machine is supposed to be as good as a man who is imitating a woman. This gender-based design might be a methodological choice. We are asking the machine to imitate something which it isn't; so it is only fair that we compare its success against a human who is *also* imitating something which it isn't.

- *Is the TT an operational definition?*

Parts of Turing's paper (the percentages, the predictions about the future, etc.) would prompt us to believe that he intended it as such. However, most arguments surrounding the issue have been philosophical. Neither Searle's Chinese Room, nor Block's Aunt Bubbles machine are practically realizable, yet they have been proposed with the intention of refuting the TT as a measure of intelligence. Apparently proponents of such thought experiments and some other commentators view the TT as a philosophical criterion.

Viewed as a practical test, we see the TT as follows: If a machine passes the TT, it should be granted intelligence. However, if it cannot, we cannot say for sure whether it thinks or not. This is probably the most common stance towards the TT.

Philosophically, the test has been subject to many criticisms. We are all familiar with the anti-behaviorist attacks. Some have also noted that the TT is anthropomorphic. It is true that the TT tests for human-like intelligence. We should not be too bothered about this for it is only natural that we are interested in the only kind of intelligence we know.[41]

Moreover, we need not assert that the *only* way to grant intelligence to machines is by the TT. Perhaps a good way to see the TT is as a means of gathering inductive evidence about machine mentality (Section 3.4).

Lately, many arguments on the TT have been of the "put up or shut up" sort (e.g., Harnad, 1989; Leiber, 1995). With the advances in computer technology, cognitive science, and artificial intelligence, it is time we stipulate that attackers or defenders of the TT back up their arguments with something more than mere intuition. This does not mean that everyone should try to develop TT-passing computer programs. However, to argue for or against the TT, we believe that a more or less realizable method of passing the test should be proposed.

- *Isn't the TT guilty of behaviorism?*

We are not saying there should be tests to assess machine intelligence, but if we have to make a choice, TT-like tests seem to be the best method for reasoning about machines' minds even though they may be accused of behaviorism. If, one day, we stop granting intelligence to other human beings in behaviorist ways, then the TT could be replaced by some other method. As of today, we believe behavioral evidence is the best evidence we have for other minds.

The idea of a TT-passing machine having radically different information processing compared to humans is not scary. If this happens one day, it will just have to be 'heads-out-of-the-sand'.

- *Isn't the TT too easy?*

The TT has been criticized for being a limited test since it enables the assessment of only "verbal" intelligence. However, it does not follow from this that the test is too easy.

Proponents of this view should come up with a realizable model of a machine that passes the TT and then prove that this model does not deserve to be called intelligent. If a simple "bag of tricks" passes the TT, we are willing to either admit that the TT is too easy or that the human mind is a simple bag of tricks as well. But after 50 years, all that we have are some very rudimentary chatbots (Section 6), serendipitous FSAs (Bringsjord, 1994), unrealizable Chinese rooms (Searle, 1980) and Aunt Bubbles machines (Block, 1981, 1995).

- *Isn't the TT too difficult?*

Some researchers claim that the TT is difficult (e.g., French, 1990; Saygin, 1999). We agree, and believe that this is primarily due to our limited understanding of natural intelligence, more precisely language understanding, generation and processing in humans. It may even turn out that these processes are impossible to model on computers.

Is this a deficiency of the TT? Not if one does not require success in the TT as a necessary condition for machine intelligence. Computers, even today, perform many tasks that would require intelligence if done by humans. Research and development in this line is valuable and worthwhile. A natural language system that answers queries on a particular topic is certainly a remarkable product. It is not useless just because it cannot pass the TT. In our opinion, the TT is a sufficient condition for human-like intelligence (or more appropriately, mentality) because of the reasons outlined above. It may be too difficult to pass the TT, but this does not prevent AI from building intelligent machines.

- *Why bother about the TT?*

As we saw, there are those who believe that the TT is harmful for AI (Hayes and Ford, 1995; Whitby, 1996). If AI's aim is to make computers perform "intelligent" tasks and thereby make life easier for humans, we grant it that TT-passing programs are not very useful from that perspective.

AI researchers are being unjustly blamed for mankind's failure in making machines that can pass the TT. This, we believe, is precisely the reason behind some of the harsh reactions to the TT from the AI community. Even if we take an extreme viewpoint and stipulate that AI's ultimate goal is to produce TT-passing machines, we should accept that this is a hard problem and give it more time. If AI researchers are less inclined to shun the TT because "it gives the field a bad name", maybe more can be done in the positive direction.

Recall the "myth" of Newton and the apple. Recall Archimedes and his adventures in bathing. The apple might be silly, but gravity is not. Of course, thousands of people bathe, thousands of apples fall. The point is, sometimes a scientist can focus on an apple and behind it, find gravity. Later, you may forget about the apple, or even eat it if you like.

The TT may seem like a game. But trying to make computers communicate with humans in natural language is a task that may also provide valuable insights into how the human mind works, which is unarguably of scientific and philosophical interest.

- *So what happens now?*

We have failed to fulfill Turing's prophecy in the first 50 years of the TT. We should admit that we have a difficult task at hand.

Hopefully, we have shown that many critics of the TT have expected too much, too early. Seeing the TT as the ultimate goal of AI will make many remarkable achievements look weak. The situation is somewhat reminiscent of "Fermat's last theorem" from mathematics which was proved recently by Andrew Wiles, after centuries of failure. Practically nobody believes that Fermat had proved the theorem at the time he scribbled something about lack of space in the margin of his book more than 300 years ago. In fact, Wiles relies upon mathematical theory that was not developed until long after Fermat died. The same might be true of the TT.

Maybe we simply don't have the requisite theory at this time. Of course, passing the TT may be "impossible", but none of the counter-arguments proposed so far suffice to establish such a bold claim.

The TT is, after all, about simulating human use of language by computers. This raises many questions: How do humans use language in similar settings? What is the relation between language and cognition? Is language autonomous with respect to other cognitive abilities? How can computers be made to *understand* language? What does a "simulation" mean, anyway? There are many more questions like these. These are all big questions that psychologists, computer scientists, philosophers and linguists have been probing for years. The better we are able to answer these questions, the closer we will be to passing the TT. We do not know how long it will be until the TT is passed. Perhaps it is best to relax and not regard the TT as a "goal" but as a feat that will (if at all) be achieved through an accumulation of other remarkable feats. Everyone who considers himself/herself a "cognitive scientist" may, explicitly or implicitly, be working towards passing the TT. In any case, we believe he/she would at least be interested in what is going on in the TT arena.

We believe that in about fifty years' time, someone will be writing a paper titled "Turing Test: 100 Years Later".

Notes

[1]For information on Turing refer to the excellent biography by Andrew Hodges (Hodges, 1983) or the Alan Turing page at http://www.turing.org.uk/turing, also maintained by Hodges.

[2]For instance, the discussion of Searle's Chinese Room is kept short (Section 4.2), not because it is irrelevant or unimportant, but because there is an abundance of excellent resources on the subject. Conversely, Ned Block's arguments are described in more detail (Section 4.1) because not many in-depth analyses of them appear in the literature.

[3]Turing suggests that the best strategy for her would most probably be giving truthful answers to the questions.

[4]This inadvertently figures in the final result, but indirectly.

[5]Although even simple devices like calculators are better at this than average human beings, it is rare that a mathematical whiz who can multiply 8-digit numbersin seconds is regarded as being of ordinary intellect.

[6]Readers are referred to Section 2.3 of this paper, Turing (1950, pp. 454–460), and Turing (1969, pp. 14–23) for very entertaining and insightful comments onmachine learning by Turing.

[7]Although the reference cited was published in 1969, Turing originally wrote the paper in 1948.

[8]Turing seems to believe that brains of newborn babies are tabula rasa. However, he also considers the opposite position and states that we might encode the information at various kinds of status levels (e.g., established facts, conjectures, statements given by an authority) and thereby implies that we may model any 'innateness' there may be (Turing, 1950, pp. 457–458).

[9]Although the cover of the 1950 issue reads "A Quarterly Review of Philosophy and Psychology", we find it not too inappropriate to call *Mind* a philosophy journal.

[10]As opposed to Millar, who believes this to be true, and also that this is a virtue of the imitation game (Millar, 1973).

[11]The three mentioned by Block are the Chisholm-Geach, perfect actor, and paralytic and brain-in-vat arguments. Detailed discussion of these is beyond the scope of this work and is not crucial to the

understanding of what follows. The interested reader is referred to Block (1981, pp. 11–12) and the references provided there.

[12] See Block (1981, p. 18).

[13] Consider, however the following situation: If every once in a while, upon verbal input A the machine transformed a sentence B in A into B and proceeded accordingly (this can be likened to a mutation), would it count as intelligent because of this little trick of non-determinism?

[14] See, for instance, Chomsky (1975).

[15] Aunt Bubbles appears momentarily, as Aunt Bertha, in Block (1981) too.

[16] This question was adapted from Johnson-Laird (1988).

[17] Basically the term given to the natural human tendency and ability to ascribe mental states to others and to themselves (Watt, 1996).

[18] During the discussions the first author held after a talk on the Turing Test (at the Cognitive Science Colloquium held at the Middle East Technical University, Ankara, in November, 1998) many participants, who did not previously know about the topic *proposed* the ITT as a better means to detect human-ness of machines. These people had not read or heard of Watt's paper and neither the ITT nor naive psychology was discussed during the presentation. Maybe this can be explained as "naive psychology at work".

[19] In Schweizer's paper, the abbreviation TTTT is used. We prefer to use TRTTT so as to avoid confusion with Harnad's Total Total Turing Test, previously referred to as TTTT.

[20] See Barresi (1987) and Section 5.

[21] Here, low-level cognitive structure refers to the subconscious associative network in human minds, consisting of highly overlapping activatable representations of experience (French, 1990, p. 57).

[22] French believes that this assumption is tacitly made by Turing. The importance of culture in conversation and communication is immense (see Section 5) and this could be a reasonable stipulation.

[23] In French's terminology, these human subjects are called *interviewees*.

[24] The importance of cultural factors becomes evident in this context. Without having notions of Kellogg's and teddy bears, the answers to these questions would be near-random guesses.

[25] Although Leiber is mainly concerned with the homunculi argument in 'Troubles with Functionalism' (Block, 1978), his response also applies to Block's attack of the TT described in Section 4.1.

[26] Compare this with Schweizer (1998) and Section 4.4.4.

[27] In Turing's IG, this difference is gender, for instance.

[28] Such systems are usually called language understanding/generation systems, conversation agents, or simply, chatbots.

[29] Multi-User Dungeons: These are games played interactively on the Internet by multiple players.

[30] http://www.loebner.net/Prizef/loebner-prize.html

[31] Now, Loebner requires that this program should also be able to process audio/visual input.

[32] In the Loebner Prize terminology, the computer programs are called 'contestants', the human subjects 'confederates' and the interrogators 'judges'.

[33] The reason why this does not mean that the TT has been passed is simply because Turing required *consistently* successful performance from machines to grant them intelligence.

[34] In fact, Marvin Minsky has offered $100 to the first person who can get Hugh Loebner to revoke the competition, which he calls an 'obnoxious and unproductive annual publicity campaign'. Loebner astutely declared Minsky a co-sponsor of the contest, since, according to the rules, when the grand prize is won, the contest will not be held again. In that case, with Minsky's contribution, the prize should become $100,100.

[35] In the following transcript and the others in this section, the spelling and grammar errors have not been corrected. However, timing information denoting the exact response times of the participants has been deleted.

[36] Although, contest judges most probably would not, as was mentioned before.

[37] An interesting point was that one of the judges was named 'Nate', short for'Nathan'. The program repeatedly addressed him as 'Mate', and complained abouthim not telling his name. This created the impression that SEPO lacked intelligence,but was, in fact, due to the fact that Jason Hutchens is from Australia. This suggeststhat the designer's mind is an integral component of the resulting programs, whichis an interesting idea to consider.

[38] Although, as seen above, Joe cannot answer the question "What is your name?".

[39] One of the judges in the 1997 Loebner competition tried asking each terminal thequestion "When you got your first liscence (sic), was it in a stick or an automatic?".The question is a cleverly planned one since words like 'driving' or 'car' are notused, but the meaning is clear from the context. Even the misspelling of the word 'license' as 'liscence' is most probably intentional. Almost anyone (certainly any adult American) would be able to give a relevant answer to this question, but it is difficult to develop a computer program answering trick questions such as this.

[40] One might recall that Eliza Doolittle was mistaken for a Hungarian princess because she spoke English too well for a native.

[41] Moreover, it is not even evident that other "kinds" of intelligence can be conceived of by human beings. The interested reader may refer to Minsky (1985) for a good discussion of this issue.

References

Abelson, RP. (1968), Simulation of Social Behavior', in G. Lindzey and E. Aronson, eds. *Handbook of Social Psychology* Reading, MA.: Addison Wesley, pp. 274–356.

Alper, G. (1990), 'A Psychoanalyst Takes the Turing Test', *Psychoanalytic Review* 77 (1), pp. 59–68.

Anderson, D. (1987), 'Is the Chinese Room the Real Thing?', *Philosophy* 62, pp. 389–393.

Barresi, J. (1987), 'Prospects for the Cyberiad: Certain Limits on Human Self-Knowledge in the Cybernetic Age', *Journal for the Theory of Social Behavior* 17, pp. 19–46.

Bieri, P. (1988), 'Thinking Machines: Some Reflections on the Turing Test', *Poetics Today* 9(1), pp. 163–186.

Block, N. (1978), 'Troubles with Functionalism', in C.W. Savage, ed, *Minnesota Studies in the Philosophy of Science*. Vol. 9: Perception and Cognition, Minneapolis, MN: University of Minneapolis Press.

Block, N. (1981), 'Psychologism and Behaviorism', *Philosophical Review* 90, pp. 5–43.

Block, N. (1995), 'The Mind as the Software of the Brain', In D. Osherson, L. Gleitman, S. Kosslyn, E. Smith and S. Sternberg, eds., *An Invitation to Cognitive Science*. Cambridge, MA.: MIT Press.

Boden M. (1988), 'Escaping from the Chinese Room', in *Computer Models of the Mind*, Cambridge, UK: Cambridge University Press.

Bringsjord, S. (1992), *What Robots Can and Can't Be*, Dordrecht, The Netherlands:Kluwer.

Bringsjord, S. (1994), 'Could, How Could We Tell If, and Should – Androids Have Inner Lives?', in K.M. Ford, C. Glymour and P. Hayes, eds. *Android Epistemology*, Cambridge, MA.: MIT Press, pp. 93–122.

Bringsjord, S. (1996), 'The Inverted Turing Test is Provably Redundant'. *Psycoloquy* 7(29). http://www.cogsci.soton.ac.uk/cgi/psyc/newpsy?7.29.

Chomsky, N. (1975), *Reflections on Language*, Pantheon.

Clark, T. (1992), 'The Turing Test as a Novel Form of Hermeneutics', *International Studies in Philosophy* 24(1), pp. 17–31.

Colby, K.M. (1981), 'Modeling a Paranoid Mind', *Behavioral and Brain Sciences* 4(4), pp. 515–560.

Colby, K.M. Hilf, F.D. and Weber, S. (1971), 'Artificial Paranoia', *Artificial Intelligence* 2, pp. 1–25.

Colby, K.M. Hilf, F.D., Weber, S. and Kraemer, (1972), 'Turing-like Indistinguishability Tests for the Validation of a Computer Simulation of Paranoid Processes', *Artificial Intelligence* 3, pp. 199–222.

Cole, D.J. (1991), 'Artificial Intelligence and Personal Identity', *Synthese* 88, pp. 399–417.

Collins, H.M. (1990), *Artificial Experts: Social Knowledge and Intelligent Machines*, Cambridge, MA.: MIT Press.

Collins, H.M. (1997), 'The Editing Test for the Deep Problem of AI', *Psycoloquy* 8(1). http://www.cogsci.soton.ac.uk/cgi/psyc/newpsy?8.01.

Copeland, B.J. (1993), 'The Curious Case of the Chinese Gym', *Synthese* 95, pp. 173–186.

Cowley, S.J. and MacDorman, K.F. (1995), 'Simulating Conversations: The Communion Game', *AI and Society* 9, pp. 116–137.

Crockett, L. (1994), *'The Turing Test and the Frame Problem: AI's Mistaken Understanding of Intelligence*, Norwood, NJ: Ablex.

Davidson, D. (1990), 'Turing's Test', in K.A. Said, M. Said, W.H. Newton-Smith, R. Viale and K.V. Wilkes, eds. *Modelling the Mind*, Oxford, UK: Claredon Press, pp. 1–11.

Dennett, D (1992), *Consciousness Explained*, Boston, MA.: Little, Brown & Co.

Dewdney, A. (1992), 'Turing Test', *Scientific American* 266(1), pp. 30–31.

Dyer, M. (1990), 'Intentionality and Computationalism: Minds, Machines, Searle and Harnad', *Journal of Experimental and Theoretical Artificial Intelligence*, 2, pp. 303–319.

Epstein, R. (1992), 'The Quest for the Thinking Computer', *AI Magazine* 13(2), pp. 81–95.

Feigenbaum, E.A. (1996), 'How the "What" Becomes the "How"', *Communications of the ACM* 39(5), pp. 97–105.

Fetzer, J.H. (1993), 'The TTT is not the Final Word', *Think* 2(1), pp. 34–86.

Fetzer, J.H. (1995), 'Minds and Machines: Behaviorism, Dualism and Beyond', *Stanford Electronic Humanities Review* 4(2).

Flood, G. (1996), 'If Only They Could Think: Should the Turing Test be Blamed for the Ills that Beset Artificial Intelligence', *New Scientist* 149(2012), pp. 32–35.

Fodor, J.A. (1991), 'Yin and Yang in the Chinese Room', in D. Rosenthal, ed., *The Nature of the Mind*, Oxford, UK: Oxford University Press.

Ford, K. and Hayes, P. (1996), 'The Turing Test is Just as Bad When Inverted', *Psycoloquy* 7(43). http://www.cogsci.soton.ac.uk/cgi/psyc/newpsy?7.43.

Forsyth, R (1988), 'The Trouble With AI', *Artificial Intelligence Review* 2(1), pp. 67–77.

French, R. (1990), 'Subcognition and the Limits of the Turing Test', *Mind* 99(393), pp. 53–65.

French, R. (1995), 'Refocusing the Debate on the Turing Test: A Response'. *Behavior and Philosophy* 23, pp. 59–60.

French, R. (1995), 'The Inverted Turing Test: A Simple (Mindless) Program that Could Pass It', *Psycoloquy* 7(39). http://www.cogsci.soton.ac.uk/cgi/psyc/newpsy?7.39.

Galatzer-Levy, R.M. (1991), 'Computer Models and Psychoanalytic Ideas: Epistemological Applications', *Society for Psychoanalytic Psychotherapy Bulletin* 6(1), pp. 23–33.

Genova, J. (1994a), 'Response to Anderson and Keith', *Social Epistemology* 8(4), pp. 341–343.

Genova, J. (1994b), 'Turing's Sexual Guessing Game', *Social Epistemology* 8(4), pp. 313–326.

Guccione, S. and Tamburrini, G. (1988), 'Turing's Test Revisited', in *Proceedings of the 1998 IEEE International Conference on Systems, Man and Cybernetics*, Vol. 1. Beijing and Shenyang, China, pp. 38–41.

Guillen, M.A. (1983), 'The Test of Turing', *Psychology Today* 17(12), pp. 80–81.

Gunderson, K. (1964), 'The Imitation Game', *Mind* 73 pp. 234–245.

Gunderson, K. (1967), *Mentality and Machines*, New York, NY: Doubleday.

Halpern, M. (1987), 'Turing's Test and the Ideology of Artificial Intelligence', *Artificial Intelligence Review* 1(2), pp. 79–93.

Harnad, S. (1989), 'Minds, Machines and Searle', *Journal of Experimental and Theoretical Artificial Intelligence* 1(1), pp. 5–25.

Harnad, S. (1990), 'The Symbol Grounding Problem', *Physica D* 42, pp. 335–346.

Harnad, S. (1991), 'Other Bodies, Other Minds: A Machine Incarnation of an Old Philosophical Problem', *Minds and Machines* 1, pp. 43–54.

Harnad, S. (1992), 'The Turing Test is not a Trick: Turing Indistinguishability is a Scientific Criterion', *SIGART Bulletin* 3(4), pp. 9–10.

Harnad, S. (1994), 'Does Mind Piggyback on Robotic and Symbolic Capacity? in H. Morowitz and J. Singer, eds. *The Mind, the Brain, and Complex Adaptive Systems*, Reading, MA.: Addison Wesley.

Harnad, S. (1998), 'Turing Indistinguishability and the Blind Watchmaker', in G. Mulhauser, ed. *Evolving Consciousness* Amsterdam: John Benjamins.

Hauser, L. (1993), 'Reaping the Whirlwind: Reply to Harnad's "Other Bodies, Other Minds" ', *Minds and Machines* 3, pp. 219–237.

Hauser, L. (1997), 'Searle's Chines Box: Debunking the Chinese Room Argument', *Minds and Machines* 7, pp. 199–226.

Hayes, B. (1998), 'Turing's Test', *Muse* 8.

Hayes, P. and Ford, K. (1995), 'Turing Test Considered Harmful', in *Proceedings of the Fourteenth International Joint Conference on Artificial Intelligence*, Vol. 1, pp. 972–977.

Hayes, P., Harnard, S., Perlis, D. and Block, N. (1992), 'Virtual Symposium on Virtual Mind', *Minds and Machines* 3(2), pp. 217–238.

Henley, T.B. (1990), 'Chauvinism and Science: Another Reply to Shanon', *Journal for the Theory of Social Behavior* 20(1), pp. 93–95.

Hodges, A. (1983), *Alan Turing: The Enigma*, New York, NY: Simon & Schuster.

Hofstadter, D.R. (1982), 'The Turing Test: A Coffee-House Conversation', in D. Hofstadter and D. Dennett, eds. *The Mind's I: Fantasies and Reflections on Self and Soul*, London, UK: Penguin Books, pp. 69–95.

Jacquette, D. (1993a), 'A Turing Test Conversation', Philosophy 68, pp. 231–233.

Jacquette, D. (1993b), 'Who's Afraid of the Turing Test', *Behavior and Philosophy* 20, pp. 63–74.

Johnson-Laird, P. (1988), *The Computer and the Mind*, Cambridge, MA.: Harvard University Press.

Karelis, C. (1986), 'Reflections on the Turing Test', *Journal for the Theory of Social Behavior* 16, pp. 161–172.

Kugel, P. (1986), 'Thinking May Be More Than Computing', *Cognition* 22, pp. 137–198.

Kugel, P. (1990), 'Is It Time to Replace Turing's Test?', 1990 Workshop *Artificial Intelligence: Emerging Science or Dying Art Form*. Sponsored by SUNY Binghamton's Program in Philosophy and Computer and Systems Sciences and AAAI.

Lassegue, J. (1988), 'What Kind of Turing Test did Turing Have in Mind?', *Tekhnema* 3, pp. 37–58.

Leiber, J. (1989), 'Shanon on the Turing Test', *Journal for the Theory of Social Behavior* 19(2), pp. 257–259.

Leiber, J. (1992), 'The Light Bulb and the Turing-Tested Machine', *Journal for the Theory of Social Behaviour* 22, pp. 25–39.

Leiber, J. (1995), 'On Turing's Turing Test and Why the Matter Matters', *Synthese* 105, pp. 59–69.

Loebner, H.G (1994), 'In Response', *Communications of the Association for Computing Machinery* 37, pp. 79–82.

Lucas, J. (1996), 'Minds, Machines and Gödel', *Philosophy* 36, pp. 112–127.

Lucas, J. (1996), 'Minds, Machines and Gödel: A Retrospect', in P. Millican and A. Clark, eds. *Machines and Mind*, Oxford UK: Oxford University Press.

Maloney, J. (1987), 'The Right Stuff', *Synthese* 70, pp. 349–372.

Marinoff, L. (1995), 'Has Turing Slain the Jabberwock?', *Informatica* 19(4), pp. 513–526.

Mauldin, M. (1994), 'Chatterbots, Tinymuds and the Turing Test: Entering the Loebner Prize Competition', in *Proceedings of the Twelfth National Conference on Artificial Intelligence*, Vol. 1, Seattle, WA, pp. 16–21.

Mays, W. (1952), 'Can Machines Think?', *Philosophy* 27, pp. 148–162.

McIlvenny, P. (1993), 'Constructing Societies and Social Machines: Stepping out of the Turing Test Discourse', *Journal of Intelligent Systems* 2(2–4), pp. 119–156.

Michie, D. (1990), 'The Superarticulacy Phenomenon in the Context of Software Manufacture', in D. Partridge and Y. Wilks, eds.: *The Foundations of Artificial Intelligence*, Cambridge, MA.: MIT Press, pp. 411–439.

Michie, D. (1994), 'Consciousness as an Engineering Issue, Part 1'. *Journal of Consciousness Studies* 1(2), pp. 52–66.

Michie, D. (1995), 'Consciousness as an Engineering Issue, Part 2', *Journal of Consciousness Studies* 2(1), pp. 182–195.

Michie, D. (1996), 'Turing's Test and Conscious Thought' in P. Millican and A. Clark, eds. *Machines and Thought: The Legacy of Alan Turing*, Oxford, UK: Oxford University Press, pp. 27–51. Originally printed in *Artificial Intelligence* 60, pp. 1-22, 1993.

Millar, P.H. (1973), 'On the Point of the Imitation Game', *Mind* 82, pp. 595–597.

Minsky, M. (1985), 'Communication with Alien Intelligence', in E. Regis, ed. *Extraterrestrials: Science and Alien Intelligence*, Cambridge, UK: Cambridge University Press.

Moon, Y., Naas, C., Morkes, J., Kim, E.-Y. and Fogg, B. (1994), 'Computers are Social Actors', in *Proceedings of the CHI Conference*, Boston, MA, pp. 72–78.

Moor, J.H. (1976), 'An Analysis of the Turing Test', *Philosophical Studies* 30, pp. 249–257.

Moor, J.H. (1978), 'Explaining Computer Behavior', *Philosophical Studies* 34, pp. 325–327.

Narayanan, A. (1996), 'The Intentional Stance and the Imitation Game', in P. Millican and A. Clark, eds. *Machines and Thought: The Legacy of Alan Turing*, Oxford, UK: Oxford University Press, pp. 63–79.

Parsons, H. (1990), 'Turing on the Turing Test', in W. Karwowski and M. Rahimi, eds. *Ergonomics of Hybrid Automated Systems II*, Amsterdam: Elsevier.

Pinksy, L. (1951), 'Do Machines Think About Thinking', *Mind* 60(239), pp. 397–398.

Platt, C. (1995), 'What's It Mean To Be Human, Anyway?', *Wired*.

Purtill, R.L. (1971), 'Beating the Imitation Game', *Mind* 80, 290–294.

Rankin, T. (1987), 'The Turing Paradigm: A Critical Assessment', *Dialogue* 29, pp. 50–55.

Reader, A. (1969), 'Steps Toward Genuine Artificial Intelligence', *Acta Psychologica* 29(3), pp. 279–289.

Rey, G. (1986), 'What's Really Going on in the Chinese Room?', *Philosophical Studies* 50, pp. 196–285.

Richardson, R. (1982), 'Turing Tests for Intelligence: Ned Block's Defense of Psychologism', *Philosophical Studies* 41, pp. 421–426.

Roberts, L. (1990), 'Searle's Extension of the Chinese Room to Connectionist Machines', *Journal of Experimental and Theoretical Artificial Intelligence* 2, pp. 185–187.

Sampson, G. (1973), 'In Defence of Turing', *Mind* 82, pp. 592–594.

Saygin, A.P. (1999), 'Turing Test and Conversation', Master's thesis, Bilkent University, Ankara, Turkey. Technical Report BU-CEIS-9911.

Schweizer, P. (1998), 'The Truly Total Turing Test', *Minds and Machines* 8, pp. 263–272.

Searle, J.R. (1980), 'Minds, Brains and Programs', *Behavioral and Brain Sciences* 3, pp. 417–424.

Searle, J.R. (1990), 'Is the Brain's Mind a Computer Program?', *Scientific American* 3(262), pp. 26–31.

Shanon, B. (1989), 'A Simple Comment Regarding the Turing Test', *Journal for the Theory of Social Behavior* 19(2), pp. 249–256.

Shanon, B. (1991), 'Chauvinism: A Misdirected Accusation', *Journal for the Theory of Social Behavior* 21(3), pp. 369–371.

Sharma, R. and Conrath, D. (1993), 'Evaluating Expert Systems: A Review of Applicable Choices', *Artificial Intelligence Review* 7(2), pp. 77–91.

Shieber, S.M. (1994), 'Lessons from a Restricted Turing Test', *Communications of the Association for Computing Machinery* 37, pp. 70–78.

Stalker, D. (1978), 'Why Machines Can't Think: A Reply to James Moor', *Philosophical Studies* 34, pp. 317–320.

Stevenson, J.G. (1976), 'On the Imitation Game', *Philosophia* 6, pp. 131–133.

Turing, A. (1950), 'Computing Machinery and Intelligence', *Mind* 59(236), pp. 433–460.

Turing, A. (1969), 'Intelligent Machinery', in D.M.B. Meltzer ed. *Machine Intelligence 5*, Edinburgh University Press, pp. 3–23. Originally, a National Physics Laboratory Report, 1948.

Wallace, R.S. (1997), 'The Lying Game', *Wired*.

Watt, S. (1996), 'Naive Psychology and the Inverted Turing Test', *Psycoloquy* 7(14). http://www.cogsci.soton.ac.uk/cgi/psyc/newpsy?7. 14.

Weizenbaum, J. (1996), 'ELIZA–A Computer Program for the Study of Natural Language Communication Between Men and Machines', *Communications of the ACM* 9, pp. 36–45.

Weizenbaum, J. (1976), *Computer Power and Human Reason: From Judgement to Calculation*, San Francisco, CA: W.H. Freeman.

Whalen, T. (1995), 'How I Lost the Contest and Re-Evaluated Humanity', http://debra.dgbt.doc.ca/chat/story95.html.

Whitby, B. (1996), 'The Turing Test: AI's Biggest Blind Alley?', in P. Millican and A. Clarke, eds. *Machines and Thought: The Legacy of Alan Turing*, Oxford, UK: Oxford University Press, pp. 53–63.

Turing's Two Tests for Intelligence*

SUSAN G. STERRETT
Duke University, Department of Philosophy, 201 West Duke Building, Box 90743, Durham, NC 27708, USA; E-mail: sterrett@duke.edu

Abstract. On a literal reading of 'Computing Machinery and Intelligence', Alan Turing presented not one, but two, practical tests to replace the question 'Can machines think?' He presented them as equivalent. I show here that the first test described in that much-discussed paper is in fact *not* equivalent to the second one, which has since become known as 'the Turing Test'. The two tests can yield different results; it is the first, neglected test that provides the more appropriate indication of intelligence. This is because the features of intelligence upon which it relies are resourcefulness and a critical attitude to one's habitual responses; thus the test's applicablity is not restricted to any particular species, nor does it presume any particular capacities. This is more appropriate because the question under consideration is what would count as *machine* intelligence. The first test realizes a possibility that philosophers have overlooked: a test that uses a human's linguistic performance in setting an empirical test of intelligence, but does not make behavioral similarity to that performance the criterion of intelligence. Consequently, the first test is immune to many of the philosophical criticisms on the basis of which the (so-called) 'Turing Test' has been dismissed.

Alan Turing's 1950 paper 'Computing Machinery and Intelligence' is well-known as the paper in which he proposed a practical test to replace the question 'Can machines think?'. On a literal reading of that paper, however, one finds not one, but two, such tests. The text is ambiguous regarding some details; inasmuch as the two formulations in the paper can be regarded as distinct, however, it must also be granted that Turing presented them as equivalent. My interest here is not primarily in the historical question of what Turing intended,[1] but in showing that the first test described in that much-discussed paper is in fact *not* equivalent to the second one, which has since become known as 'the Turing Test'. The two tests yield different results, and the first, neglected, one employs a better characterization of intelligence.

The first test realizes a possibility that philosophers have overlooked. It is commonly taken for granted that any test of machine intelligence that involves comparison with a human's linguistic behavior must be using a criterion of 'behavioral similarity to a paradigm case' (Churchland, 1996). But although the first, neglected, test uses a human's linguistic performance in setting an empirical test of intelligence, it does not make behavioral similarity to that performance the criterion of intelligence. Consequently, the first test does not have the features on the basis of which the test known as 'the Turing Test' has been dismissed as a failure.

1. Claims of Equivalence of the Two Tests

In this section, I want to clearly identify the two tests I'll be comparing: what I call *The Original Imitation Game Test*, and *The Standard Turing Test*. The two tests are depicted in Figure 1, 'The Two Tests and How They Differ'. I'll also try to account for the rather common view that these two tests are equivalent. In subsequent sections, I'll show that, despite the similarity of the two tests, the first test is vastly superior; the features of our notion of intelligence it relies upon[2] include resourcefulness in dealing with unfamiliar tasks. But the appropriateness of using it as evidence of intelligence is not, as is the second test, hopelessly bogged down by considerations having to do with species-specific and culture-specific abilities, or by sensitivities to the specific skills of the interrogator.

The first test Turing proposed uses what I shall refer to as *The Original Imitation Game*. Turing used the term 'imitation game' but, as he used the term differently later, I distinguish this use of the term. In The Original Imitation Game, there are three players, each with a different goal: A is a man, B is a woman, and C is an interrogator who may be of either gender. C is located in a room apart from A and B and, during the game, knows them by the labels 'X' and 'Y'. C interviews 'X' and 'Y' and, at the end of the game, is to make one of two statements: ' "X" is A [the man] and "Y" is B [the woman]', or ' "X" is B [the woman] and "Y" is A [the man].' C's goal is to make the correct identification, B's goal is to help C make the correct identification, and A's goal is to try to fool C into making the wrong identification, i.e., to succeed in making C misidentify him as the woman. The game is set up so as not to allow C any clues to 'X' and 'Y''s identities other than the linguistic exchanges that occur within the game.[3] The first formulation Turing proposed as a substitute for 'Can machines think?' was this: 'What will happen when a machine takes the part of A in this game? Will the interrogator decide wrongly as often when the game is played like this as he does when the game is played between a man and a woman?' (Turing, 1950, p. 434). I take Turing here to be describing the test as a sort of meta-game, of which the interrogator is unaware. This is what I shall call *the Original Imitation Game Test*.

In the subsequent discussion, Turing stated that, in turn, the question: 'Are there imaginable digital computers which would do well in the imitation game?' was equivalent to the following question: 'Let us fix our attention on one particular digital computer C. Is it true that by modifying this computer to have an adequate storage, suitably increasing its speed of action, and providing it with an appropriate program, C can be made to play satisfactorily the part of A in the imitation game, the part of B being taken by a man?' Turing is not explicit about what the interrogator is to determine in this second version of the game, but the standard reading is that the interrogator is to determine which player is the computer and which is the man. Such a reading seems plausible enough, as the interrogator's task would be parallel (though not identical) to the task in the first version of the game, i.e., at the end of the interview, the interrogator is to state one of two things: either ' "X" is A and "Y" is B.' or ' "X" is B and "Y" is A.', where, here, A is the computer and B is the man. The test for machine intelligence in this second version is then simply how difficult it is for an 'average' interrogator to correctly identify which is the computer and which is the man.[4] This is what I shall call the *Standard Turing Test*. Few have questioned the substitution of the Standard Turing Test for the Original Imitation Game Test. There are a few exceptions: some say Turing is ambiguous here (Moor, 1976, 1992), others that the paper is confused. (Turing's biographer Andrew Hodges (1983), and Douglas Hofstadter, a proponent of the value of the Standard Turing Test, for instance, take this approach (Hofstadter, 1981).) Some extract different tests from the paper than I have: Judith Genova (1994) focuses on the substitution of a 'species' game for a 'gender' game, and Patrick Hayes and Kenneth Ford (1995) follow her in this. Some commentators focus only on the test in the first section (Heil, 1998; Dreyfus, 1979).

Why have so many discussants accepted the slide from the first to the second formulation, though? Some do give reasons. Here is Roger Schank: 'Given that the problem is to get a computer to do as well at imitating a woman as a man, then the task is to get a computer to imitate a human as well as possible in its answers. Turing's test doesn't actually depend upon men and women being discernibly different, but on a computer's ability to be indistinguishable from a human in its responses' (Schank, 1985, p. 6). John Haugeland's treatment is similar: after giving a faithful description of the Original Imitation Game Test, he goes on to justify similarity to a human's linguistic performance as an adequate substitute, as follows. '... why would such a peculiar game be a test for general (human-like) intelligence? Actually, the bit about teletypes, fooling the interrogator, and so on, is just window dressing, to make it all properly "experimental". The crux of the test is *talk*: does the machine talk like a person?' Justin Leiber discusses the importance of impersonation in Turing's original formulation of the test, but then leaves the point aside, in speaking of passing the Turing test: '... proof positive, both psychological and legal, requires and requires no more than linguistic performance ...' (Lieber, 1991, p. 116).

These rationalizations do seize upon an important feature common to both tests: the requirement of being able to carry on a conversation with a human. For, human conversation requires – or, at least, can demand – a responsiveness and flexibility we associate with thought, and can be used to probe for knowledge of almost any subject. The sentiment is not new: Descartes, too, appealed to the ability to converse as one means of distinguishing reason from mere mechanism. It might, Descartes said, be impossible to tell a nonrational machine from an animal were the two similar in behavior and physical construction. Whereas, he argued, it *would* be possible to tell a nonrational machine from a rational creature, for '... it is not conceivable that such a machine should produce different arrangements of words so as to give an appropriately meaningful answer to whatever is said in its presence, as even the dullest of men can do' (in Descartes, 1987, p. 57).[5]

ORIGINAL IMITATION GAME TEST	STANDARD TURING TEST
(§ 1 of "Computing Machinery and Intelligence")	(§ 5 of "Computing Machinery and Intelligence")

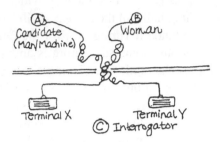 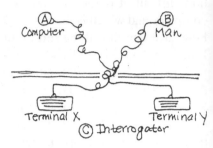

C asks questions via terminals X and Y.
C must state either: "X is A and Y is B"
            or: "X is B and Y is A"

C asks questions via terminals X and Y.
C must state either: "X is A and Y is B"
            or: "X is B and Y is A"

The New Question is:
Can one build a machine such that the interrogator decides wrongly when a machine takes the part of A as often as when a man does? (434)

The New Question is:
Can one build a particular computer to play satisfactorily the part of A, the part of B being taken by a man? (442)

Notice that in the OIG Test:

Whereas, in the so-called "Turing Test":

1. Test structure premits the result that the machine does better than the man.

1. No meaningful result could indicate that the machine does better than the man.

2. Test tends to screen off lack of interrogator skill.

2. Test results are very sensitive to the interrogator's skills or lack of skill.

3. Both man and machine are required to impersonate. The machine's performance is not directly compared to the man's, but their rates of successfully impersonating against a real woman candidate are compared.

3. Only the computer is attempting to impersonate. The computer's performance is judged based on similarity to a man's performance.

Figure 1. The two tests and how they differ.

However, while rightly identifying a common strength of the two tests, rationalizations of their equivalence overlook the distinctive difference between them. For, in spite of the fact that Turing may have thought so, too, the Standard Turing Test is not equivalent to the Original Imitation Game Test.[6]

2. Nonequivalence of the Original Imitation Game Test and the Standard Turing Test

It is not difficult to show that the two tests are not equivalent. One need only pause to consider the quantitative results each can yield. In the Original Imitation Game Test, there is nothing inherent in the game to prevent the machine from scoring higher than the man: consider, for example, the case where the man fools the interrogator into saying he is B (the woman) 1% of the time, and the machine fools the interrogator 3% of the time. In contrast, the Standard Turing Test does not admit of such a result. Recall that, in the Standard Turing Test, the interrogator's task is to identify which of the two players is the machine and which is the human. What test result would indicate that the machine had outperformed the human, given that the criterion is simply giving a performance indistinguishable from a human's? That an interrogator identified as human a machine impersonating a human (in preference to a human responding as he would in normal conversation) with a frequency greater than 50% is no measure of the machine performing a task better than the human contestants: this would mean that the interrogator has mistaken a human for a machine with a higher frequency than chance, which might well reflect more about the interrogator's quirks than about the relative capabilities of the contestants. A real-life example of how uninformative misidentifications in the Standard Turing Test can be occurred in the first Loebner restricted Turing Test: one of the interrogators mistook a human for a computer because the human exhibited what the interrogator thought a superhuman store of knowledge about Shakespeare (Schieber, 1994, p. 70).

This leads us to another difference easily exhibited by comparing quantitative results between the Original Imitation Game Test and the Standard Turing Test: the difference in the sensitivity of the test result to the interrogator's skill. The machine's fortune in passing the Standard Turing Test will go up and down with the skill level of the interrogator: if the interrogator is very poor, the percent of time the machine wins will increase; if the interrogator is very good, the percent of time that the machine wins will decrease. In contrast, the Original Imitation Game Test tends to screen off effects due to the interrogator's lack of skill. With an excellent interrogator, only extremely intelligent participants in the role of A, whether man or machine, will ever win. With a less skilled interrogator, the computer may get the interrogator to say it is the woman more often than appropriate due, say, to the interrogator's unimaginative technique; but, if C is played by the same person throughout, this will happen for the human (male) participants in the role of A as well. Since, in the Original Imitation Game Test, the machine's intelligence is measured by comparing the frequency with which it succeeds in causing the interrogator to make the wrong identification with the frequency with which a man does so, the results will not be too sensitive to the skill of the interrogator.

There are different views on the significance of the sensitivity of the test to the attitudes of the human interrogator and judge. One view is that a test's dependence on the attitude of the human judge discredits it as a test for thinking. The construction of programs which, though very limited in the kind of responses they are capable of producing, have successfully given the illusion of carrying on one side of a conversation, have been cited to discredit the Standard Turing Test: the charge is that the test does not require enough to constitute a sufficient test for thinking. There are also charges that the dependence on similarity to a human as judged by another human requires too much: that, given a skilled and determined interrogator, only a human could pass. Yet another view is that the fact that test results in the Standard Turing Test are dependent on the human interrogator's attitude towards the candidate thinker just expresses the truism that being a thinker is best characterized as being able to be so regarded and thus represents an unavoidable aspect of any test for intelligence. Hofstadter, for instance, though a proponent of the validity of the (Standard) Turing Test, worries that 'Unless the people who play the interrogator role do so in a very sophisticated manner' the test will inspire 'a race for flashier and flashier natural-language "front-ends" with little substance behind them' (Hofstadter, 1996). My point in this paper is of significance on any of these views: *In the Original Imitation Game Test, unlike in the Standard Turing Test, scoring as a thinker does not amount to simply being taken for one by a human judge.*

3. Characterizing a Thinker – Intellectual Skill versus Cognitive Habit

In the Original Imitation Game Test, both the man and the computer are asked to impersonate. The contest between the man and the computer (as measured by the comparative frequency with which the interrogator makes the wrong identification) compares their ability to make up answers that will lead the interrogator astray. In contrast, in the Standard Turing Test, although the computer is set the task of imitating a human carrying on a conversation, the man is not called upon to imitate anything at all. Thus, what the Standard Turing Test compares is the ability of the man to converse under no pretense at all, against the ability of the computer to converse under the pretense that it is human.

Programming a computer to pass either of the two tests will involve the problem that occupied the android designers in the film *Blade Runner:*[7] giving the machine a memory, or, alternatively, the ability to fabricate responses in conversation that appear to be based on memories consistent with the normal development of a human's life. In the Standard Turing Test, all the man has to be able to do is to converse about his own memories. The analogous skill for a computer would be to converse about itself, a computer (e.g., it might say 'I became operational at the HAL plant in Urbana Illinois on January 12, 1997.') In contrast, in the Original Imitation Game Test, the man, in virtue of taking the part of player A, also needs to fabricate responses to the interrogator's questions that appear to be based on memories or knowledge consistent with having lived a woman's life. There is a great deal of intellectual dexterity and foresight involved in that task, since the interrogator is deliberately choosing questions designed to discriminate between fabricated responses and genuine ones. And, examples of genuine responses are provided by B (the woman) at the same time that A (the man or computer) offers fabricated responses.

The skills exhibited by the man in the Standard Turing Test are just those that can be exhibited in conversation. Those skills are certainly substantial: in addition to a great deal of specific and general knowledge, conversation requires knowing what kind of responses are expected of one, and understanding the conventions that will govern the other party's understanding of one's responses. It will probably include drawing on stereotypes and presumptions that have been learned uncritically and that are used without much reflection. (Some mundane examples might be assuming that everyone eats dinner, that it can rain outdoors but not indoors, or that the conversant will understand baseball analogies such as Three strikes and you're out.') Here I mean only to be referring to features of conversation that many AI researchers and cognitive scientists have already recognized. As used in normal conversation, these skills could be called cognitive habits: they do involve cognition, but they are employed without reflecting anew on why they are appropriate each time they are employed.

However, the difficult task the man is set by the criterion used in the Original Imitation Game Test requires in addition that stereotypes get used for different purposes: rather than serving as common background drawn on in sincere efforts to communicate, they are to be used to mislead someone else to make inferences to false conclusions, which requires more reflection upon how others make inferences than is normally required in conversation. And, rather than relying on his well-developed cognitive habits in recognizing what an appropriate response would be, the man who takes the part of player A has to critically evaluate those recognitions; he has to go one step further and ask whether the response he knows to be appropriate for him is appropriate for a woman. If not, he has to suppress the response he feels is appropriate for him, and replace it with the one he determines would be appropriate for a woman, or at least one that he thinks the interrogator is likely to expect of a woman. This, I think, requires a fundamentally different ability. The point that impersonation involves intellectual abilities not necessarily exhibited by the behavior impersonated is reminiscent of Gilbert Ryle's remark about a clown's impersonations: 'The cleverness of the clown may be exhibited in tripping and tumbling. He trips and tumbles on purpose and after much rehearsal and at the golden moment and where children can see him and so as not to hurt himself ... The clown's trippings and tumblings are the workings of his mind, for they are his jokes; but the visibly similar trippings and tumblings of a clumsy man are not the workings of that man's mind' (Ryle, 1949, p. 33).

That the ability to critically edit one's recognitions of appropriate responses is required of the man by the Original Imitation Game Test, but not by the Standard Turing Test, reflects that the Original Imitation Game Test demands more of what is relevant to thinking than the Standard Turing Test does. A companion, but distinct, point is that the Original Imitation Game Test requires less of what is not relevant to thinking, as well. This is because the task set by the Original Imitation Game Test diminishes the significance of the faithfulness of the machine's responses to a human's normal responses in determining whether the machine can think, since both man and machine are impersonating something that is neither man nor machine. This is significant because one of the challenges in designing any empirical test for intelligence (human or machine) that uses a human's performance as a benchmark will be how to screen off the peculiarities of the human or group of humans serving as the benchmark. If the test is for machine intelligence, the problem involves screening off the peculiarities of human intelligence.

These points regarding what is significant about the difference between the two tests are a bit subtle. The difference between the two tests isn't that the machine is being asked to do anything different in the Original Imitation Game Test than it is in the Standard Turing Test: the task for the machine in both tests is impersonation. However, *what counts as success* in each of the two tests is quite different. In the Original Imitation Game Test, the computer is successful if the interrogator C believes the machine's responses are sufficiently like a woman's for it to be (mis)identified as the woman with a higher frequency than C believes the performances of the man or men used in the game are sufficiently like a woman's for him to be (mis)identified as the woman. (Recall how this test is set up: in the Original Imitation Game the interrogator C is under the impression that one of the conversants is a man and one is a woman, and that the task is to say which conversant is of which gender.) Now, the machine should use whatever resources it has; it may find the best approach is to use a database of conversational exchanges and figure out what sort of features are distinctive for a woman: it might find, for instance, a species of politeness that tends to distinguish men and women, and it could fashion its linguistic response accordingly. The machine need not be successful in impersonating a woman anywhere near 50% of the time in order to pass the criterion in the Original Imitation Game. It can fail rounds based on poorly chosen responses quite often without losing at the game. What it has to do to pass the criterion of intelligence in the first test is to be sufficiently resourceful at the difficult task of impersonation to win more rounds than the man or men playing the game do. Thus, the test focuses on a notion of machine intelligence, rather than similarity to a human: that is, it focuses on the question of whether the machine is as resourceful in using *its* resources in performing a difficult task as the man is in using *his* resources in performing the same difficult task.

In contrast, in the Standard Turing Test, the machine is successful if the interrogator believes the machine's responses are sufficiently like a human's to be chosen as the human over the human. Here the kind of impersonations that yielded success in the Original Imitation Game Test may not result in success, for the interrogator is seeking a different distinction: human versus non-human. Here the problem is not that the machine doesn't have to use a self-conscious critique of its responses – of course it has to do this in both tests – but that the criterion for passing the

Standard Turing Test emphasizes things that we do not associate with intelligence, such as contingent associations between words that emphasize specifics of one's own personal experience, rather than intelligence. The machine has to fabricate these, but the man it is competing against in this test does not have to fabricate anything; thus a machine that is very resourceful (as evidenced by the first test) could lose rounds in the Standard Turing Test to a very dull man who was shown to be very unresourceful in the first test. The Original Imitation Game Test picks out the resourceful contestant; the Standard Turing Test does not.

The claim I am emphasizing here is that the criterion for a passing performance used in the first test does not penalize the machine for deficiencies that have nothing to do with machine intelligence, not the claim that producing the performances in the two tests requires fundamentally different skills of the machine. The Original Imitation Game Test requires a higher show of intelligence of the man against which to compare the machine's resourcefulness, and it does not unfairly handicap the machine by requiring undue similarity to the man's performance. Because many people have argued that a machine could never pass the Standard Turing Test, this point – that the Original Imitation Game Test does not unfairly handicap the machine – is crucial.

A helpful analogy here might be that of wanting to de-emphasize the importance of regional flavors and idioms in evaluating someone's ability to speak a second language. In a test of the ability to speak a particular language that sets up a competition between a native and non-native speaker as to who can convince an interrogator to choose him as the native speaker, an expert interrogator will be able to ferret out which is which. There will be subtle cues that can give the non-native away, no matter how well he or she has learnt the second language and become informed of various regional idioms and dialects. These cues will be due to in-grained responses that are not a matter of competence in expressing thoughts in the language. The analogous notion we are after here would be that of being recognized to be able to communicate thoughts in the language, in spite of not being able to pass under scrutiny as a native speaker of any particular region. Suppose we want to retain the approach of comparison with a native speaker. How could we use a native speaker as a paradigm case, and yet screen off the peculiarities of the region the speaker is from? Compare the following two tests as means of testing for the ability to communicate thoughts in the language: (i) competing against a native of X in being able to pass as a native of X, and (ii) competing against a native of X as to how often each of you is able to pass as a native of a different region where that language is spoken (among natives of that region). Clearly, (ii) provides better evidence of the ability to communicate thoughts in a language, as it tends to de-emphasize the importance of faithfulness to a particular regional flavor in one's expressions.

What has been missed by those not recognizing that the two tests are not equiv-alent is the difference in how the two tests employ the human performance in constructing a test for intelligence by which the machine's performance is to be judged. The Original Imitation Game Test constructs a benchmark of intellectual skill by drawing out a man's ability to be aware of the genderedness of his linguistic responses in conversation. But similarity to the man's performance itself is not the standard against which the machine is compared. Without a machine in the picture at all, the man can succeed or fail at the task set. It is only successful impersonations, and then, only the fact that success has been achieved, that is the standard against which the machine is judged. That is, the measure against which the machine is judged is the frequency with which it can succeed at the same task the man is set. The man's performance does no more than normalize that measure. The successful performances of man and machine are never directly compared Oother than the fact that they are successful impersonations, similarities and dissimilarities between them are of no consequence to the test result.[8]

The significance of the use of gender in the Original Imitation Game Test is in setting a task for the man that demands that he critically reflect on his responses; in short, in setting a task that will require him to think. Gender is an especially salient and pervasive example of ingrained responses, including linguistic responses. Attempts to elicit gendered responses from us are made before we even know our own names, and continue throughout most of our lives, in interactions ranging from the most intimate to the most anonymous of interactions, from the most private to the most public of contexts. Because social interaction requires that others regard and treat someone as of a specific gender, it is well nigh impossible for someone to unilaterally ungender his interactions. Cross-gendering is not impossible, but the amount of preparation involved makes it unlikely that a player will have spent any time outside his assigned gender role. The situation is somewhat like moving in the presence of the earth's gravity; of course we are also capable of moving in 0.1 g, or 2 g as well, but we do not get opportunities to practice it. Were we suddenly put in such a situation, we would have to reflect upon the habitual components of our learned motor skills.[9] We could draw on our knowledge and observations of other bodies in motion – i.e., in this new setting, we might be more successful, even at tasks we do not normally think about, if we thought about what we were doing. Even walking might require some reflection – though still drawing on learned motor skills, we might have to reflect on how we move in order to get across the room gracefully. The Original Imitation Game Test chooses an aspect of conversation that is ubiquitous (the relevance of gender to every conversational exchange, rather than the influence of gravitational force on every physical movement), and creates a setting in which that aspect is altered so that the kind of response required is of a kind the man will not have had any practice at giving. He will not be able to rely upon his cognitive habits, and so has to figure out what response to give – in short, he has to think about it.

Thus, cross-gendering is not essential to the test; some other aspect of human life might well serve in constructing a test that requires such self-conscious critique of one's ingrained responses. The significance of the cross-gendering in Turing's Original Imitation Game Test lies in the self-conscious critique of one's ingrained cognitive responses it requires. And, that the critique has two aspects: recognizing and suppressing an inappropriate response, and fabricating an appropriate one. It is a cliché that tests of intellectual skill differ from tests of purely mechanical skill in the novelty of the tasks set. The ability to tie a variety of knots, or to perform a variety of dives, is tested by asking the contestant to perform these tasks, and the test is not compromised if the contestant knows exactly what will be asked and practices until the task can be performed without stopping to reflect anew upon what is required. In contrast, we would think someone had missed the point of an intelligence test were the contestant given the answers to the questions beforehand, and coached to practice delivering them. The way the skills required by the Original Imitation Game Test (impersonation) differ from those required by the Standard Turing Test (conversation) is a higher-level analogue of this insight. That is, although both games involve asking questions the participant will not have knowledge of beforehand, the point is that, in the Original Imitation Game Test player A will not have had a chance to practice giving the *kind* of responses required (those that would lead the interrogator to identify him as a woman). To succeed in the task set will require drawing on knowledge of how women behave, and this cannot be a matter of relying on what I have called cognitive habit.

Nor can the task be fulfilled by simply imitating a woman's linguistic responses. Consider, for example, using a computer incorporating a connectionist net trained on a (grown) woman's linguistic responses. A little reflection on how one would select the sample linguistic responses on which to train the net shows the problem: there is no consistent way to characterize the *kind* of response here that would apply to both a woman and a machine. Clearly, using only samples from a non-game context would not be sufficient, for, in the game context, the goal of the five-minute conversation is to convince C to identify the speaker as a woman in preference to B. Thus, responses called for in the game context would not be similar to linguistic responses given in non-game conversational contexts. How about letting a woman take on the role of player A and training the net on linguistic responses she gives? The problem is that the strategy a real woman should use as player A is not the one a machine should use: A good strategy for the real woman in the role of A would be to look for opportunities to turn to a topic that exhibits her knowledge of things only a woman would know. Such a strategy will get the machine in trouble, as it is un-likely that being trained on linguistic responses alone will be a good basis on which to deal with topics turned to for the sole purpose that they are the sort of thing only a woman would know. A good strategy for an impersonator is just the opposite: to steer the conversation away from lines of questioning that might lead to a topic that would expose his ignorance of things only a woman would know. The general point here is about impersonation in contrast to imitation, not about approaches using connectionist nets (as there are other, undeveloped approaches, such as attempting to encompass a birth-to-adulthood process): it is that impersonation in contexts where one's identity is in question is not the same as imitation in normal contexts. Similar remarks apply to using the suggested approach for player A in the Standard

Turing Test (i.e., preparing the machine to pass as a human by equipping it with a net trained on a man's linguistic responses.) The additional step taken by many contemporary authors in regarding any test for linguistic competence a suitable substitute shows a disregard for the significance of the game context. I discuss other games that demand self-conscious critique of one's responses in Section 5.

4. Critical Thought and Supercritical Minds

The point of the previous section was that the self-conscious critique of one's ingrained responses required in the Original Imitation Game Test is crucial to its value as a test of intelligence. Impersonation is the context in which such self-conscious critique is most clearly exhibited, but it is also true that in other contexts such self-conscious critique marks the difference between a response requiring thought and a response that, though entirely appropriate, is habitual. It is not that habitual responses do not involve any cognitive component at all, but focusing on a human's ability to evaluate and fabricate responses is an attempt to tease out the intellectual component of linguistic responses. The purpose of the cross-gendering is to de-emphasize training, and emphasize thinking.

Now, with the point that the Original Imitation Game Test de-emphasizes training in mind, consider R.M. French's criticism of what I have called the Standard Turing Test. His view is that '... the [Standard] Turing Test provides a guarantee not of intelligence but of culturally-oriented human intelligence' (French, 1990, p. 54). French composes clever test questions to be asked in a Standard Turing Test that would distinguish human from non-human, such as 'Rate *pens* as *weapons*' and 'Rate *jackets* as *blankets*.' (p. 61). He explains why a computer would not have a chance: such questions '... [probe] the associative concept (and sub-concept) networks of the two candidates. These networks are the product of a lifetime of interaction with the world which necessarily involves human sense organs, their location on the body, their sensitivity to various stimuli, etc.' (p. 62). His point in making this remark is that there is something he calls a 'subcognitive substrate' that can be made to exhibit itself under interrogation, and that what is wrong with the (Standard) Turing Test is that it would require actually having lived a human's life, with human sensory capabilities, in the same culture as the human against whom the participant is competing, to pass it, i.e., to give linguistic responses indistinguishable from those a human gives.

Such criticisms do not have the same force against the Original Imitation Game Test, in which both the man and the computer fabricate responses. French's criticisms turn on the fact that the (Standard) Turing Test is based on comparing how well a computer would do against a human in behaving like a human. The advantage of Turing's first formulation of the test is that it provides a context in which the computer and the man are put on a more equal footing: both the computer and the man will need to critically evaluate their responses, and fabricate appropriate ones that are based on vicarious experiences of womanhood. That 'some subcognitive substrate is necessary to intelligence' suggests that an intelligence test should be constructed such that, although the contestant is called upon to make use of such a substrate in a way that exhibits the kind of resourcefulness humans display when making use of their distinctively human subcognitive substrate in conversing, the particular substrate the candidate has will not be relevant to doing well on the test. As we have seen, the Original Imitation Game Test provides just such a screening off of the particularity of the substrate. The Original Imitation Game Test takes a step towards meeting French's challenge that no attempt to 'fix' the Standard Turing Test could address the problem that it could only be a test of human intelligence, for it retains the insight that conversation is the context in which the flexibility of response we associate with thinking is best displayed, but changes the task (from conversing to impersonating) so that faithfulness to a human's natural responses is de-emphasized. I do not claim that the man has no advantage in some respects – obviously a man will have more in common with a woman than a computer would – but I do claim that the Original Imitation Game Test takes the approach one should use to de-emphasize the human's advantage in participating in a test intended to measure general, and not merely human, intelligence. Impersonation of something that is neither man nor machine is just the task to set. What to choose that would be especially thought-provoking for a man to impersonate? I think setting the task of cross-gendering one's responses is a stroke of genius.

Odd as it may sound to those who know him only as the proponent of the so-called 'Turing Test' of intelligence, Turing actually offered reasons that human intelligence should not be considered the standard of intelligence, as well. In the 1950 paper, he counters Lady Lovelace's objection that 'the machine can only do what we tell it to do' with the simile of a nuclear reaction: 'the disturbance caused by ... an incoming neutron will very likely go on and on increasing ... Is there a corresponding phenomenon for minds, and is there one for machines?' But, surprisingly, he does not identify the ability to go critical with being a mind, or, even, a human mind; he answers instead: 'There does seem to be [a corresponding phenomenon] for the human mind. The majority of them seem to be 'subcritical' (Turing, 1950, p. 454). Not only did he judge that most humans did not exhibit whatever feature of minds is analogous to supercriticality, but he speculated that some exhibitions of machine intelligence would be superhuman. In an essay published posthumously, he impishly states that intellectuals would probably be mistaken to fear being put out of a job by intelligent machines, because 'There would be plenty to do in trying, say, to keep one's intelligence up to the standard set by the machines, for it seems probable that once the machine thinking method had started, it would not take long to outstrip our feeble powers.' One reason to expect this is that the machines 'would be able to converse with each other to sharpen their wits' (Turing, 1996, p. 259).

My point does not turn on the historical question of whether or not Turing held the view that human intelligence is not the standard by which machine intelligence should be measured, though. The conceptual point is that the Original Imitation

Game Test does not use human intelligence as a standard of intelligence. To be sure, it uses comparison with a man's performance, but, as I have argued, it constructs a setting in which the man really has to struggle to produce the responses required to succeed at the task set, in which he is forced to think about something he may not otherwise ever choose to think about.[10]

You might say that the Original Imitation Game Test extracts a 'supercritical' kind of thought from humans, and then uses it to construct a measure by which the machine's capabilities can be measured. That the task of cross-gendering one's responses is so demanding might bring into question its suitability as a general test for thinking, i.e., should not a good test for thinking set a task that all and only thinkers can accomplish? Actually, that is not what either of the practical tests Turing suggested are meant to do. Rather, as numerous people have pointed out, the purpose of replacing the question concerning the possibility of machine intelligence with a practical test was to identify the sort of evidence that most reasonable people would consider evidence of intelligence. Here one should also keep in mind that success in the test is not a matter of succeeding or failing one interview, but of succeeding with the same frequency as a man or a suitably chosen sample of men would. The measure works like comparisons of batting averages; though most baseball players would not get a hit given just one pitch, and some may not ever get a hit, batting averages are still useful measures. In our case, the measure is used qualitatively: if the candidate attains an average equal to or exceeding that of a certain kind of participant under demanding conditions, the test result is taken to provide good evidence that the candidate is intelligent. This need not entail the claim that the measure would be useful in ordering people with respect to intelligence, nor that falling below the average of a certain kind of participant should be considered good evidence that the participant is *not* intelligent.

It is worth noting, however, that, were the test used as a sort of scale, not even the best performance of which a human is capable would be the ultimate standard of intelligence; for, recall that, as I have shown in Section 2, in The Original Imitation Game Test, the structure of the test allows for a result in which a machine can outperform a man. The Original Imitation Game Test is remarkable for testing the ability to think without resorting to mere anthropomorphism. Of course there is anthropomorphism involved in the human judge's acceptance of the machine's successful impersonations of a woman. But, the test is not simply a matter of a human judging similarity of a machine's behavior to a human's behavior. It tests instead for an awareness of what's involved in making inferences, especially about social conventions and what are often called social constructions (e.g., gender), by setting a test of resourcefulness in using that awareness.

5. Differentiating Human Performances

I opened this paper with the claim that the first of Turing's two tests was based on more general, and hence more appropriate, features of intelligence. It would be discouraging to think that the ability to deceive is the ultimate intellectual achievement, or, even, somehow essential to thinking.[11] But no such conclusion is forced. Rather, the feature of deceiving the interrogator in the Original Imitation Game combines two separate features, neither of which is particularly related to deception: (i) knowing how to use the knowledge that someone else knows how to draw conclusions, and (ii) the ability to edit one's own responses.

Knowing how to use the knowledge that someone else knows how to draw conclusions is just as useful in communicating effectively – i.e., to lead one's conversant to true conclusions, rather than to mislead him or her to false ones. Of course we use such knowledge, implicitly and unreflectively, in normal conversation; we are usually only forced to reflect upon *how* we use such knowledge, however, in special situations such as educating or persuading, where the one being educated has not yet been initiated into the field with which we are familiar, or the person being persuaded does not yet share our view. There do exist parlour games that test for one's resourcefulness in employing this ability to communicate with, rather than mislead, someone. The game of charades is an example; here, the need for resourcefulness arises from the almost opposite constraint that one must use gestures rather than words to communicate. Other examples are *Password* and *Pictionary*, both of which require a player to communicate, but constrain the player from communicating a given idea or phrase in the manner he or she would normally use. The player is required to be resourceful in using what he or she knows about how others make associations and draw inferences, including exploiting icons, preconceptions, stereotypes, and prejudices as well as particular facts and specialized knowledge.

The ability to edit one's responses is just as usefully employed in behaving well as it is in deception, but, similarly, tends to be required only in special cases, i.e., ones that are sufficiently novel such that we have not had sufficient experience to have developed habitual responses. We have to be able to see when the situation calls for overriding a habitual response. Although my point does not turn on what Turing actually thought, it is noteworthy that he wrote that the machine should be constructed so that its behavior was not completely determined by its experience. In explaining a suggestion for employing random numbers, he says: This would result in behavior of the machine not being by any means completely determined by the experiences to which it was subjected. ... (Turing, 1996). The task of impersonating someone who has occupied a role in which we have had no experience at all is different from the task of imitating someone accurately as a result of practice.

I find the first proposal inspired, whatever Turing's attitude towards it may have been. Besides the formal points made above that the Original Imitation Game Test does not have the weaknesses for which the Standard Turing Test has been discredited as a test of machine intelligence, there is the additional point that it has some virtues when used to evaluate human intelligence as well. Not all human linguistic performances *should* count as evidence of intelligence; there are even cases where we would want to say: 'I must not have been thinking when I said that.' It is all to the credit of a test for machine intelligence that it does not regard dull human performances as providing good evidence of intelligence, and that it requires one to reflect upon ingrained responses. The Original Imitation Game Test has these virtues; the Standard Turing Test does not.

It is pretty generally agreed among philosophers that the (so-called) 'Turing Test' fails as a practical test. Blay Whitby recently delivered something like a respectful eulogy for the test (Whitby, 1996), giving his opinion as to what it ought to be remembered for. Although I have tried to show that the difference between the two formulations of the test given in Turing's 1950 paper is relevant to the applicablity of the most common criticisms, I do not disagree with Whitby's statement that 'the last thing needed by AI *qua* science is an operational definition of intelligence involving some sort of comparison with human beings', or, even, his admonition that 'AI *qua* engineering should not be distracted into direct copying of human performance and methods'. What I challenge is the common presumption that any test employing a human's performance could be employing no other notion of intelligence than specifically human intelligence. I think this general point worthwhile even if the Standard Turing Test had never been discussed.

For, the importance of the first formulation lies in the characterization of intelligence it yields. If we reflect on how the Original Imitation Game Test manages to succeed as an empirical, behavior-based test that employs comparison with a human's linguistic performance in constructing a criterion for evaluation, yet does not make mere indistinguishability from a human's linguistic performance the criterion, we see it is because it takes a longer view of intelligence then linguistic competence. In short: that intelligence lies, not in the having of cognitive habits developed in learning to converse, but in the exercise of the intellectual powers required to recognize, evaluate, and, when called for, override them.

Notes

*I wish to thank John McDowell and Clark Glymour for encouragement and helpful discussion on early versions of this manuscript. Thanks also to Thomas Stuart Richardson, Teddy Seidenfeld, Dirk Schlimm, Peter Spirtes, Gualtiero Piccinini, Patrick Giagnocavo, Martha Pollack, Jim Moor and Jerry Massey, and to audiences at: Occidental College, Pitzer College, "The Future of the Turing Test" conference held at Dartmouth College on January 29, 2000; the 1999 Computing and Philosophy Conference (CAP '99) held at Carnegie-Mellon University August 1999, and the Theoretical Cognition Group at the University of Pittsburgh. Thanks also for helpful comments from anonymous referees.

[1]Gualitero Piccinini (2000, this volume) argues that Turing had only one test in mind. His reasoning for this grants a minor (chauvinistic) slip on Turing's part in the 1950 paper and appeals to other documents by and about Turing, including an interview with Turing held after he had written the 1950 paper I discuss here. On the other hand, Saul Traiger (2000, this volume) provides considerations against reading the 1950 paper as proposing what has become the standard version of the 'Turing Test'.

[2]I do not mean to imply that the purpose of the test is to define a notion of intelligence, or, even, to define a measure of general intelligence. I think James Moor is correct in arguing that Turing was not providing an operational definition of intelligence; he says that the value of the game

lies in its potential for providing "good inductive evidence for the hypothesis that machines think" (Moor, 1976, p. 249). I think Turing was providing an example of the kind of evidence on which it might be natural to speak of a computer as being intelligent. My comments throughout this paper regarding "the notion of intelligence" involved in certain tests should be understood in light of this distinction between providing a definition of intelligence and defining a test that provides evidence of intelligence. Obviously, the latter involves having an idea of the features that characterize intelligent behavior, or at least some examples of intelligent behavior, but it does not require that one can define intelligence, that there is a single measure of intelligence, or that the intelligence of different intelligent beings can always be compared. The fact that the answer given to the specific question of whether machines could exhibit intelligence was in the form of defining a practical test shows, I think, some respect for the problems that would be involved were one to attempt to define intelligence or thinking.

[3]Turing suggested using a teleprinter for the communication. Although, literacy is not required of a player: Turing also specified that an intermediary may communicate the answers from A and B to C.

[4]Turing made a prediction in terms of the per cent chance that an average interrogator would have of making the right identification after five minutes of questioning.

[5]In their paper "Descartes's Tests for (Animal) Mind" Gerald Massey and Deborah Boyle (1999) examine Descartes's Action Test as well as his Language Test. They argue that both are tests for mind, but that the tests differ in that the Action Test is a test for volitions, whereas the Language Test is a test for perceptions. I recommend this interesting paper to the reader who wishes to understand Descartes's views on the issue. Recall that, since, for Descartes, animals are sophisticated machines, Descartes's considerations on the question of what would consitute evidence of animal mind are particularly germane to the contemporary question of what would constitute evidence of machine intelligence.

[6]Although commentators have not generally challenged Turing's claim that the tests are equivalent, many have found the test descriptions wanting. A. Hodges regards Turing's first mention of the imitation game an uncharacteristic lapse of lucidity, in *Alan Turing: The Enigma* (New York: Simon & Schuster, 1983, p. 415). D.R. Hofstadter misunderstands the first imitation game described as a test for femininity and criticizes it as such, in 'A Coffeehouse Conversation, *Scientific American* (May, 1981, 15–36). In his encyclopedia entry, Moor (1992) does clearly describe the standard Turing Test as a variation of the imitation game, and discusses the ambiguities in Turing's 1950 exposition of it. Ford and Hayes (1995) follow Genova (1994) in regarding the difference between the standard formulation and the imitation game discussed in the opening of Turing's paper as one of determining species rather than gender, but regard the tests as having the same basic structure. (Whereas, the two tests I identify have a different structure, as evidenced by the fact that the man and machine's abilities to impersonate are compared in the first game, but not in the second.) Perhaps because of their focus on the first part of Turing's 1950 paper, Ford and Hayes (1995) take Turing to have presented only the first version. ('Turing is usually understood to mean that the game should be played with the question of gender (e.g., being female) replaced by the question of species (e.g., being human)... We will call this the species test. ... However, Turing does not mention any change to the rules of the imitation game ..." (p. 972)). Heil (1998, pp. 110–111) likewise mentions only the first formulation of the test, given in Section 1 of Turing's 1950 paper.

[7]The screenplay for the film *Blade Runner* is based on P.K. Dick's (1982) novel.

[8]This last point can perhaps be made clearer by considering the following objection: 'Why,' a re-sourceful reader might ask, 'could not impersonation be incorporated into the Standard Turing Test setup as follows: the interrogator could preface a set of questions with "Suppose you were a woman. How would you answer ..." Then, the interrogator would identify whichever player gave the most convincing performance as the man, and the other as a machine, thus effectively redefining 'success' as giving, in the opinion of an interrogator, the better of two impersonations. In such a version of the Standard Turing Test, the interrogator would be comparing the man's attempt to impersonate a woman with the machine's attempt to impersonate a woman. However, the context differs signific-

antly from that of the Original Imitation Game Test. The interrogator in the Original Imitation Game Test is never directly comparing two fakes against each other and picking out which he judges to be the better counterfeit; he is trying to make a correct determination of which interviewee is a woman and which interviewee is an impersonation of a woman. Asking the interrogator in a Standard Turing Test setup, in which it is known that the pair either does not or may not contain a woman, to merely pretend to focus on the task of making a gender distinction is not likely to be any more effective than asking the interrogator to merely pretend there is a screen between him and his interviewees, in lieu of actually incorporating one into the game.

Thomas Stuart Richardson has convinced me that it is not only best, but probably necessary, to specify that the interrogator in the Original Imitation Game Test be under the impression that each X, Y pair of which he is to judge either ' "X" is a man and "Y" is a woman' or ' "X" is a woman and "Y" is a man' actually does consist of exactly one man and exactly one woman.

[9] Donald Michie calls these "subcognitive skills" and remarks: 'Only when a skilled response is blocked by some obstacle is it necessary to "go back to first principles" and reason things out step by step', in Michie (1993). He recognizes that the (Standard) Turing Test requires that the machine impersonate, rather than give the answer one would give if not playing the game, inasmuch as he notes Turing's remark that 'The machine ... would not attempt to give the right answers to the arithmetic problems. It would deliberately introduce mistakes in a manner calculated to confuse the interrogator.' Michie calls this a 'playing dumb' tactic, though, and dismisses it with '... surely one should judge a test as blemished if it obliges candidates to demonstrate intelligence by concealing it!' This misses the point that such a response should not be characterized as 'playing dumb', but as impersonation. For, in this case, the machine does not make arbitrary mistakes, nor perform calculations as a human would; what the machine does, and does without error, is 'introduce mistakes in a manner calculated to confuse the interrogator.' That impersonation displays recognition of habits, or rules, without articulating them seems to me particularly germane to Michie's discussion of the articulation of rules.

[10] Both Daniel Dennett (1998, p. 23) and Justin Leiber (1991, p. 110), have remarked on the ingenuity the first game requires, though they draw different conclusions as to what success in the game would show.

[11] Some have suggested that the fact that the task set the candidate involves deception is significant. One example is Richard Wallace's 'The Lying Game' (1997).

References

Churchland, P.A. (1996), 'Learning and Conceptual Change: The View from the Neurons', in A. Clark and P.J.R. Millican, eds., *Connectionism, Concepts and Folk Psychology: The Legacy of Alan Turing*, Vol. 2, Oxford: Clarendon Press.

Dennett, D.C. (1998), 'Can Machines Think?' in *Brainchildren*, Cambridge, MA: MIT Press.

Descartes, R. (1987), *Discourse on Method*, Cottingham, J. (Trans.). Cambridge: Cambridge University Press.

Dick, P.K. (1982), *Do Androids Dream of Electric Sheep?*, New York: Ballantine Books.

Dreyfus, H.L. (1979) *What Computers Can't Do*, Revised Edition. New York: Harper Colophon Books.

French, R.M. (1990). 'Subcognition and the Limits of the Turing Test', *Mind* 99.

Genova, J. (1994), 'Turing's Sexual Guessing Game', *Social Epistemology* 8(4), pp. 313–326.

Gunderson, K. (1964), 'Descartes, LaMettrie, Language, and Machines', *Philosophy* 39, pp. 193–222.

Haugeland, J. (1985), *Artificial Intelligence: The Very Idea*, Cambridge: MIT Press.

Hayes, P. and Ford, K. (1995), 'Turing Test Considered Harmful', *Proceedings of the Fourteenth International Joint Conference on Artificial Intelligence (IJCA195-1)*. Montreal, Quebec, Canada. pp. 972–997.

Heil, J. (1998), *Philosophy of Mind: A Contemporary Introduction*. London and New York: Routledge.

Hodges, A. (1983), *Alan Turing: The Enigma*, New York: Simon and Schuster.

Hofstadter, D.R. (1981), 'A Coffeehouse Conversation', *Scientific Americans*, May 1981, pp. 15–36.

Hofstadter, D.R. (1985), *Metamagical Themas*, New York: Basic Books.

Hofstadter, D.R. (1996), 'Analogy-Making, Fluid Concepts, and Brain Mechanisms', *Connectionism, Concepts, and Folk Psychology: The Legacy of Alan Turing. Vol. II*, Oxford: Clarendon Press, pp. 195–247.

Leiber, J. (1991), *An Invitation to Cognitive Science*, Cambridge, MA: Basil Blackwell.

Massey, G.J. and Boyle, D.A. (1999), 'Descartes's Tests for (Animal) Mind' (forthcoming, *Philosophical Topics* 27, Special Issue on Zoological Philosophy and Philosophical Ethology).

Michie, D. (1993), 'Turing's Test and Conscious Thought', *Artificial Intelligence* 60, pp. 1–22.

Moor, J.H. (1992), 'Turing Test', *Encyclopedia of Artificial Intelligence*, 2nd Edition, New York: John Wiley & Sons, pp. 1625–1627.

Moor, J.H. (1976), 'An Analysis of the Turing Test', *Philosophical Studies* 30, pp. 249–257.

Piccinini, G. (2000), 'Turing's Rules for the Imitation Game', *Minds and Machines* 10, pp. 573–582.

Ryle, G. (1949), *The Concent of Mind*, Chicago: University of Chicago Press.

Schank, R. (1984), *The Cognitive Computer*, Reading, MA: Addison-Wesley.

Shieber, S.M. (1994), 'Lessons From a Restricted Turing Test', *Communications of the ACM*; 37(6).

Traiger, S. (2000), 'Making the Right Identification', *Minds and Machines* (this volume).

Turing, A.M. (1950), 'Computing Machinery and Intelligence', *Mind*, 59, pp. 433–460.

Turing, A.M. (1996), 'Intelligent Machinery, A Heretical Theory', *Philosophia Mathematica*, (3)4, pp. 256–260.

Wallace, R. (1997), 'The Lying Game', *Wired*, Vol. 5, No. 8, August 1997.

Whitby, B. (1996), 'The Turing Test: AI's Biggest Blind Alley?' in P.J.R. Milllican and A. Clark, eds., *Machines and Thought: The Legacy of Alan Turing. Vol. 1*, Oxford: Clarendon Press.

Making the Right Identification in the Turing Test[1]

SAUL TRAIGER

Department of Philosophy and Cognitive Science Program, Occidental College, Los Angeles, California, 90041, USA; E-mail: traiger@oxy.edu

Abstract. The test Turing proposed for machine intelligence is usually understood to be a test of whether a computer can fool a human into thinking that the computer is a human. This standard interpretation is rejected in favor of a test based on the Imitation Game introduced by Turing at the beginning of "Computing Machinery and Intelligence."

Key words: Artificial Intelligence, Imitation Game, Turing Test

Alan Turing's 1950 paper, "Computing Machinery and Intelligence," introduces the question, "Do machines think?" and the problem of interpreting that question. The interpretation of the question as "Do people believe that machines think?" is quickly dismissed as absurd, though Turing doesn't immediately say what is absurd about it. Turing proposes a reformulation of the question in terms of what he calls "The Imitation Game," taking considerable effort to describe the game and its employment in answering the original question and in presenting a prediction. It's surprising, then, that most of the literature on what has come to be called the "Turing Test" completely discounts the role of the Imitation Game in Turing's proposal and prediction. I argue that Turing's invocation of the Imitation Game forms the very basis of Turing's Test for machine intelligence. In order to understand Turing's test and his prediction, we must examine the text with care, and attempt to interpret what Turing actually said. I begin by documenting what I call the Standard Interpretation of the Turing Test. Then I argue that the Standard Interpretation does not square with the text of "Computing Machinery and Intelligence." Fortunately an interpretation that does square with the text is available. I close by explaining why it matters to get the interpretation right.

The Standard Interpretation takes the Turing Test to be as follows: There is a computer and two humans. One human is the interrogator. She or he communicates with the computer and the other human using a teletype or computer terminal. The interrogator is told that one of the two individuals it is communicating with is a computer, and that the other is a human. The computer's goal is to fool the interrogator into thinking that it is the human. The other human's goal is to convince the interrogator that he or she is the human. The computer attempts to achieve the deception by imitating human verbal behavior. If an interrogator does not make the *right identification*, where a "right identification" is identifying the computer as a computer, then the computer passes the test.

There are a couple of observations to make before documenting the widespread acceptance of this reading of the Turing Test. First, it makes no reference to the

Imitation Game, though it does describe the computer's method as imitating the behavior of a human being. Finally, on the Standard Interpretation, the characterization of passing or failing the test makes reference to the computer.[2] The computer passes the test if the interrogator does not identify it as a computer. I turn now to establishing that what I've called the Standard Interpretation is indeed just that.

Ned Block describes the Turing Test as follows:

> His [Turing's] version of behaviorism formulates the issue of whether machines could think or be intelligent in terms of whether they could pass the following test: a judge in one room communicates by teletype (This was 1950!) with a computer in a second room and a person in a third room for some specified period. (Let's say an hour.) The computer is intelligent if and only if the judge cannot tell the difference between the computer and the person. (Block, 1990, p. 48)

This formulation is an unhappy one for several reasons, the most important of which is that it makes the test both necessary and sufficient for intelligence. On Block's reading, only those who have passed the test are intelligent. Perhaps Block sees the test as a test only of *computer* intelligence. If so, it's hardly in the spirit of Turing's attempt to characterize thought and intelligence in a way which does not make reference to what Turing took to be the contingent features of the agent, such as it's size, the stuff of which it's made. As Block construes it, the Turing Test is a test that only a computer could play. Finally, it isn't clear what counts as passing the Block's version of the Turing Test. Block says that the test is passed when the judge can't tell the difference between the computer and the person. Does that mean that the judge can't identify two distinct communicative agents, or more likely, does it mean that the quality of the discourse is indistinguishable? If the latter, how would the judge determine that the two sets of discourse are qualitatively identical?

The formulation of the test by Dyer is close to Block's. Like Block, Dyer describes the testing conditions as including a set of interrogators, a computer, and a "person." I take it that the person is a human being, though Dyer himself does not specify. The interrogator knows that one of the two interlocutors is a computer, the other a person/human being. The computer passes the test if the interrogators "are about evenly divided on which teletype" is connected to the computer and which to the person.[3] (Dyer, 1994, p. 174).

The Standard Interpretation is as entrenched in the AI community as it is in philosophy. Armer characterizes the test as one in which an "interrogator, who can communicate with a human and a machine via teletype... does not know which is which, is to decide which is the machine" (Armer, 1960, p. 390). Jason L. Hutchens, the runner-up for the 1998 Loebner Prize, a prize awarded on the basis of actual machine performance in a Standard Version Turing Test, summarizes the test as requiring the interrogator to "decide which is a human being and which is a computer program. The human being helps the interrogator to make the correct identification, while the computer program attempts to trick the interrogator into making the wrong identification. If the latter case occurs, the computer program is said to be exhibiting intelligence" (Hutchens, unpublished).

The Standard Interpretation is so entrenched that it even appears in (mis)quotations of Turing's own formulation. Donald Michie quotes Turing as follows:

> I believe that in about fifty years' time it will be possible, to programme computers, with a storage capacity of about 10^9, to make them play the imitation game so well that an average interrogator will not have more than 70 per cent chance of making the right identification [as between a human and computer] after five minutes of questioning. (Michie, 1996, p. 29)

Michie offers this up as Turing's original text, but it is not. Michie has taken the liberty of adding the parenthetical phrase "as between a human and a computer," a phrase which does not appear in the original text. In his zeal to help us understand what Turing means, Michie has misrepresented what Turing actually said. One might argue that although this is indeed scholarly sloppiness on Michie's part, what else could Turing have meant than the phrase that Michie inserted? This is a fair question, and one that I will answer below.

A few commentators offer a short formulation of the Turing Test that conforms to the Standard Interpretation, while acknowledging that Turing's actual test was different. Donald Davidson's initial description of the Turing Test is representative. Davidson writes, ". . . Turing predicted that by the year 2000 it will be possible to build a computer that will have at least a 30 per cent chance of fooling an average interrogator into thinking it is a person" (Davidson, 1990, p. 1). While Davidson later describes the Imitation Game, he thinks that Turing may have thought the interrogator would be faced with the task of choosing between a computer and a woman, that is, that he is presented with the task as deciding which interlocutor is the woman and which is the computer. I'll argue below that Turing's test cannot credibly be so interpreted.

William Rappaport writes, Turing rejected the question "Can machines think?" in favor of the more behavioristic question "Can a machine convince a human to believe that it (the computer) is a human?" (Rappaport, 1994, p. 227). Rappaport thinks that a necessary condition for convincing the interrogator is that the computer understand a natural language. It's not at all obvious that the test, so construed, requires natural language understanding. In a footnote, however, Rappaport refines the characterization, noting that the computer's job is to convince the interrogator that it is a woman. Rappaport does not see that the very difference to which he has drawn our attention makes a difference to the necessity claim. It's much more plausible that natural language understanding is required to convince the interrogator that its interlocutor is a woman than to convince it that it is a human being. So I shall argue below.

Moor refers to the "standard version of the imitation game" which "involves a man, a computer, and a human interrogator." The interrogator's task is to "decide which respondent is the man and which respondent is the woman" (Moor, 1976, p. 249). In an endnote Moor adds that Turing's text is ambiguous, that it underdetermines the standard interpretation. Moor doesn't offer alternative interpretations, and he makes no reference to the original imitation game. In a later article (Moor, 1987), Moor appreciates that the game described under the Standard Interpretation is a transformation from the original imitation game, and he observes that Turing did not explicitly say whether the computer replacing the man is instructed to play the part of a woman. Moor concludes, "In any event these niggling details are probably unimportant to Turing's main claim that questions about how well a computer does in the imitation game should replace the original question "Can machines think?" (Moor, 1987, p. 1126).

I hope this is enough of a sample to establish the widespread interpretation of Turing's refraining of "Can machines think?" as "Can machines deceive a human into thinking that the computer is a human being?"[4] I've mentioned several ancillary infelicities such as the conflation of "person" with "human being" by Dyer because I think Turing was struggling to come up with a formulation that would provide some clarity. I think he would be dismayed by the level of confusion displayed in the cited commentaries. I have yet to establish that the Standard Interpretation is a misinterpretation, and it is to that task that I now turn.

To understand Turing's Test, we begin with the Imitation Game, the game Turing elaborately presented at the beginning of his paper. Let's first note that the Imitation Game is introduced as a game involving three *people*, that there are no computers mentioned in the description of the game. The three people are an interrogator, a man and a woman. Turing labels the man "A", the woman "B", and the interrogator "C." The interrogator, however, has his or her own labels for the other two individuals, who are in a different room. The interrogator uses the labels "X" and "Y." Communication occurs by the passing of typewritten answers, passing sheets of paper or using a teleprinter. (Turing does not say that the questions from the interrogator must be typewritten.) The interrogator is charged with determining which player is the man and which is the woman. In Turing's own words:

> The object of the game for the interrogator is to determine which of the other two is the man and which is the woman. He knows them by labels X and Y, and at the end of the game he says either "X is A and Y is B" or "X is B and Y is A." (Turing, 1950, p. 433)

The male's goal is to "cause C to make the wrong identification." The female's goal is to aid C in making the right identification.

That's the Imitation Game. The game itself makes no reference to computers, and Turing does not say that it requires deception on the part of the male. The male is to try to cause the interrogator to make the wrong identification. One can certainly cause someone to have a false belief without engaging in deception, where deception includes the intention to bring about a false belief in another. Why is this important? When Turing later asks us to imagine a computer playing this game, given this formulation of the game, he does not have to imagine the computer being given the instruction to deceive the interrogator. In fact, while Turing gives an example of a possible exchange among contestants that does involve deception, it's only an example, and not a feature of the description of the game. So even when the game is first described in terms of human players, Turing minimizes the metaphysical overhead.

I want to draw attention to a second detail, before moving to the introduction of machines into the game. Turing uses the labels "A" for the male, "B" for the female and "C" for the interrogator. The form of the interrogator's final judgment is "X is A and is B" or "X is B and Y is A." Now Turing may have used these abbreviations to reduce verbal clutter, but I speculate that there was another purpose. As many commentators have noted, there's nothing special about the game determining whether someone is a male or a female. The game could involve other characteristics, though what is to be included in the range of "replacement" characteristics is an interesting question, and one to which we will return. If this is right, "A" and "B" could be placeholders for whatever characteristics may be used in different versions of the game. Turing's formulation invites generalization.

Machines enter the mix immediately after the description of the game. Turing writes:

> We now ask the question, "What will happen when a machine takes the part of A in this game?" Will the interrogator decide wrongly as often when the game is played like this as he does when the game is played between a man and a woman? These questions replace our original, "Can machines think?" (Turing, 1950, p. 434)

The interpretation of this paragraph is crucial. We are to substitute a machine, specifically a digital computer, for A in the game. But substituting one player for another in a game presupposes the identity of the game. So nothing about the game has changed. We merely have a different individual, one who happens to be a digital computer, taking on the role of A. The machine, as A, is to cause C to believe that A is a woman. Playing the Imitation Game, it would make no sense for the computer to try to deceive the interrogator into thinking that the computer is a human being, because the interrogator is told that one of the two players is a man and one is a woman. Again, Turing says "The object of the game for the interrogator is to determine which of the other two is the man and which is the woman."[5]

There's a vast difference between the way Turing situates the machine and the situation described in the Standard Interpretation. In Turing's version the interrogator's belief, that the individual who happens to be a machine is a human, and hence intelligent, is a belief which can be defeated by the poor showing of the machine. On the Standard Interpretation, the interrogator believes that one or the other interlocutor is a computer, (where there are two interlocutors) and so does not believe in advance that an arbitrary participant with which it communicates is a human. The interrogator brings to the game his or her beliefs about computers and machine intelligence. Similarly on the Standard Interpretation the computer and the human competitor may also exploit beliefs about machines to try to trick or help the interrogator.

The opening paragraph of "Computing Machinery and Intelligence" makes it clear that Turing was not interested in whether or not a population might have beliefs which would incline them to regard machines as intelligent. In light of the novelty of digital computers at the time Turing was writing, he knew that most people would be disposed to regard computers as incapable of intelligence. Interrogators in such a population would be very likely to underestimate the capabilities of computers, due to their lack of familiarity with them. A clever programmer could exploit that ignorance in such a way as to trick interrogators into thinking that the computer is a human being.

One strategy which has been implemented in a number of attempts to pass the Standard Interpretation Turing Test is to make use of a text-base of typical greetings, remarks and responses which are often encountered in casual conversation. A program that functions in this way is RACTER.[6] Here's an opening exchange between RACTER and a human:

Hello, I'm Racter. Are you Saul?
>Yes.
You are Saul Smith?
>No.
What's your name then?
>Saul Traiger.
I may call you Saul, then?
>Yes.
Hello, Saul. I believe you're interviewing me. Are you continuing Saul Smith's interview?
>No.
Then well forget about Saul Smith and start over. What would you like to know? Excuse me a minute while I attend to some business – I'll be right back. I'm back.

A little later RACTER asks:

Hmm. Are you related to Louella Traiger?

RACTER clearly has codified some of the opening gambits of ordinary casual conversations. In runs of the program, novice users are often very surprised by such opening conversational moves. They are surprised at the appropriateness of RACTER's opening conversational moves. When the emphasis is on deceiving a human being into thinking that it is conversing with a human rather than a computer, strategies such as this one are fair game. A programmer who can string out a series of conversational gambits such as the ones used by RACTER may very well succeed in stalling a human's recognition that it is conversing with a computer. The Imitation Game, in contrast, has a point that constrains the participants to get beyond chit-chat and move directly to content driven discourse. A computer that succeeds in the Imitation Game will have to process ordinary natural language conversations which go well beyond polite conversation. A computer might succeed in the Standard Interpretation game without facing such a challenge.

Turing's formulation attempts to level the playing field, by putting the machine in the same circumstances we would place a human player. Those circumstances are not just the use of teletype across different rooms. They go to the heart of the setup of the game itself. The interrogator decides wrongly when it judges A to be the woman. The reframed question is simply whether the interrogator judges wrongly as often with a machine as A it does with a man as A. What counts as deciding rightly, or, as Turing later puts it, "making the right identification?" That's simple. The interrogator makes the right identification when it identifies Y as B, that is, when it identifies the individual who is the woman as the woman. Now the interrogator might infer the right identification from the prior conclusion that A is a computer. But it need not. The individual who occupies the role of A, whether human or computer, loses the game when the interrogator makes the right identification. It still loses if the interrogator fails to identify the computer as a computer, because that identification is no part of the Imitation Game.

What level of performance in the Imitation Game counts as success in the game? In the passage quoted above, Turing says that the question is whether the interrogator will decide wrongly as often when A is the computer as when A is a man. It is this question that explicitly replaces the original question, "Do machines think?" We need to distinguish this from Turing's *prediction*, later in the paper, where he writes:

I believe that in about fifty years' time it will be possible, to programme computers, with a storage capacity of about 10^9 to make them play the imitation game so well that an average interrogator will not have more than 70 per cent chance of making the right identification after five minutes of questioning. (Turing, 1950, p. 442)

Taking the phrase, "making the right identification" to mean "identifying the woman as a woman," I interpret this passage as presupposing that interrogators in the original male/female imitation game also have a 70 percent chance of making the right identification, though Turing never explicitly says this. Having introduced the computer in the role of the male, Turing's question is "Will the interrogator decide wrongly as often when the game is played like this as he does when the game is played between a man and a woman?" (Turing, 1950, p. 434), It's natural to interpret the prediction as answering in the affirmative, particularly since Turing follows with the further prediction that common usage at the end of the twentieth century would allow one "to speak of machines thinking without expecting to be contradicted" (Turing, 1950, p. 442). If this is right, the prediction about the Imitation Game should be understood as follows: Within 50 years, when computers replace the male in the Imitation Game, interrogators will have the same (70 percent) chance they had in the original male/female game of making the right identification. It's worth noting, however, that if this is right, Turing can be criticized for providing no grounds for the 70 percent estimate for interrogator performance in the original Imitation Game.

Why has the Standard Interpretation taken hold so firmly, and does it matter if it has? At the end of section 5, after explaining the universality of digital computers, Turing writes:

> We may now consider again the point raised at the end of §3. It was suggested tentatively that the question, "Can machines think?" should be replaced by "Are there imaginable digital computers which would do well in the imitation game?" If we wish we can make this superficially more general and ask "Are there discrete-state machines which would do well?" But in view of the universality property we see that either of these questions is equivalent to this, "Let us fix our attention on one particular digital computer C. Is it true that by modifying this computer to have anadequate storage, suitably increasing its speed of action, and providing it with an appropriate programme, C can be made to play satisfactorily the part of A in the imitation game, the part of B being taken by a man?" (Turing, 1950, p. 442)

This passage is a bit confusing because Turing now uses the label "C" for the computer while earlier in the paper "C" referred to the interrogator. But the crucial phrase here is found at the end of the last sentence in the passage quoted, "the part of B being taken by a man." The Standard Interpretation takes this to be a change in the conditions of the game. The part of B is now the role of a human being, played by a male human being. The computer and the male are thus charged with playing the role of a human being, not the role of a female human being.

While it is admittedly somewhat natural to read the passage in this way, such a reading makes several questionable moves.[7] First, one must read "man" in "the part of B being taken by a man" as "male" *and at the same time*, one must read "the part of B" to mean "the part of a human player" rather than "the part of a woman." Let's take each phrase in turn. First, Turing, like his contemporaries, in "Computing Machinery and Intelligence" other published papers, typically used the term "man" as we would now the gender neutral "person" or the explicit "man or woman." Second, the phrase, "the part of B" must refer to the role B plays in the original imitation game, because Turing describes no other role, here or elsewhere. He never says that the role of B has changed from that of a woman to that of a human being, man or woman. Thus, the proper reading is the one which is consistent with the description of the Imitation Game Turing has given up to this point, namely, that a computer replaces the male, and the role of the female, is played by a human, either male or female.

Another passage that appears to support the Standard Interpretation occurs in section 2, "Critique of the new problem," where Turing makes the important point that the game puts to one side the actual physical attributes of the participants. He thinks that such attributes are irrelevant to intelligence. Turing says that even if a chemist were able to make artificial skin, "we should feel there was little point in trying to make a "thinking machine" more human by dressing it up in such artificial flesh." This may suggest that Turing has moved from the Imitation Game to the question of whether a machine, which is physically unlike a human, can imitate human intelligence. That sense is heightened by a set of questions and possible answers which Turing lists as illustrating the advantage of "the proposed criterion." Those questions, including requesting a sonnet, asking for a sum, and making queries about appropriate chess moves, seem too open-ended to be relevant to the Imitation Game. They seem instead to be questions one would ask to determine whether something was a machine rather than a human. So it may seem Turing has moved away from the Imitation Game to the question of whether a machine imitate a human in a conversation conducted via teletype.[8]

The questions of section 2 are the appropriate questions to ask in the Imitation Game. The interrogator is not restricted to posing obvious questions about gender; indeed, if the other players are at all clever, the interrogator will need to develop a patternof clues about their respective genders. One of the great strengths of the reframed question is that conversations are open-ended. The interrogator is free to ask any question that will advance his or her inquiry. It's also true that when a computer takes the place of a human male, the computer needs to guard against revealing its non-humannature. But guarding against revealing itself as a computer can be just a small part of the computer's strategy, if it hopes to perform at a comparable level to a human. The fact that the interrogator initially believes that the conversation is only among humans will help keep this aspect of the computer's strategy in the background.

The test as described in the Standard Interpretation loses this key virtue of Turing's Imitation Game, that the kinds of questions posed by the interrogator will be those that would typically be posed to human participants. The interrogator in the Imitation Game will not begin with the hypothesis that one participant is a computer, and hence the computer participant, like its human counterpart, can devote its energies to answering the same kinds of questions that would typically be posed to a human.

Another way one might defend the Standard Interpretation is to admit that the Turing Test is not couched in terms of the original Imitation Game, but that the Imitation Game was just an example of a type of game involving imitation, and that when Turing introduces the machine into the game, he's really introducing a new imitation-type game, rather than introducing the computer into the original Imitation Game. The key idea of the Imitation Game, that A is trying to deceive the interrogator by pretending to be something he's not, is retained. The only difference is that instead of a man imitating a woman, we have a computer imitating a human.

In response to this defense of the Standard Interpretation, I must emphasize again that the text of Turing's paper does not support such a reading. Turing refers to one and the same Imitation Game throughout. He never suggests that there are other games he wants to consider. There is, however, an independent reason why Turing would have rejected the specification of the game in the terms favored by the Standard Interpretation. We've noted that on the Standard Interpretation, the playing of the game makes essential reference to the computer. The game is the game of a computer trying to imitate a human being. The interrogator is told that it may or may not be communicating with a computer, or that one of two inter-locutors is a computer. In order for the game to make any sense, we must attribute some idea of what a computer is to the interrogator. But this already introduces complications. What conversational strategy does one take when one suspects that one may be conversing with a computer? Shouldn't we expect different results with persons who have different conceptions of computers? In fact, such a game would take us very far afield from ordinary conversation. But it was facility in ordinary conversation that Turing took to be the "criterion" in his reframed question.

Turing thought it absurd to interpret the question "Can machines think" as "Do people believe that machines think." The absurdity stems in part from the fact that there would not be a univocal notion of "machine" in the population. So a poll could not capture an accepted view on the matter. The same difficulty presents itself on Standard Interpretation Turing Tests. Interrogators setting out to unmask a computer will mobilize and rely on their on conceptions of what computers are and what they can and can't do, just as the computer program may successfully exploit those very beliefs in order to appear human-like. And this makes the test dependent on such conceptions of computation and mechanism, precisely the uninteresting question bypassed by Turing's Imitation Game.[9]

The Imitation Game is a more stringent game than the game of machine imitation of human behavior envisioned by the Standard Interpretation. In the former, a player who fails to be seen as human will quickly lose the game.[10] But being seen as a human player is not sufficient for winning the game. The computer in the Imitation Game must convince the interrogator that it is a female human being. If the Standard Interpretation were correct, we'd need an explanation of why Turing, having fully spelled out the Imitation Game, then gives a weaker game for the computer to play. But Turing emphasizes that his scenario is a difficult one for a computer, while acknowledging that a computer might fail it and still be intelligent.[11]

Having emphasized the importance of Turing's Imitation Game, I hasten to add that I am not suggesting that the Imitation Game is the only test Turing would have admitted as sufficient for establishing machine thinking. My criticism of the Standard Interpretation emphasizes two key aspects of the Imitation Game that the Standard Interpretation's tests miss. First, the subject matter of the game must be open-ended. Conversations should lead from the subject introduced by the game to other subjects easily. Second, the playing of the game must not turn on the participants' views about the nature of computers. There are other necessary conditions, of course, such as the requirement that participants use the same natural language, as well as the conditions specifying the mode of communication. Another restriction, suggested but not made explicit by Turing, is some sort of cultural alignment among participants. An Imitation Game is unlikely to work, even with just human players, if the players come from very different cultures. Thus, assuming a shared cultural background, the game could be one of determining which of A or B is a resident of a large U.S. city, or which of A or B is a Democrat, or which is a member of the American Rifle Association. I'm inclined to think that none of these alternatives are as good starting points as Turing's Imitation Game, because concepts related to gender are so pervasive in so many cultures.

French argues that the admission that a test for intelligence must appeal to culturally-based cognition, or what French calls "subcognitive processes" is a devastating blow to the test (French, 1990). If the intelligent discourse depends on contingent psychological associations made by an agent embedded in a culture, a computer created in isolation from the culture of its interlocutors lacks the relevant subcognitive processes, and will be unmasked in any Imitation Game.

This objection, like the Standard Interpretation, depends on overemphasizing the role of imitation in Turing's test. French is surely right that any successful participant in the Imitation Game will have to have to share many of the cultural associations of its fellow players. It does not follow that a computer could not acquire those associations by a different route from its human counterparts. In fact, while Turing expects that the best way to have the computers acquire cultural knowledge is by placing them in the same kind of learning environments humans typically experience, he does not commit himself to the claim that a computer that passes the test will provide a model of the psychological reality of human cognition. That is, the internal processes of the computer may not match up with human internal cognitive processes, even where both humans and computers learn the relevant associations through the same environmental stimuli.[12] As we've noted, the interrogator's presumption in the original Imitation Game is that the other two participants are human beings. Thus, if there are empirically discoverable subcognitive differences, a virtue of placing a computer the original Imitation Game is that those differences need not surface. That's a virture, if, as Turing holds, such differences don't make a difference to the question of intelligence.

It is worth acknowledging that some commentators who invoke the Standard Interpretation explicitly allow that the interpretation deviates from Turing's formulation. Such authors sometimes refer to "revised" or "restricted" Turing Tests. On my interpretation, the kinds of tests that count as revised or restricted Turing Tests are not worthy of the name. They are not alternatives to Turing's Imitation Game, but separate and weaker tests, tests that Turing would not have endorsed as sufficient for intelligence.

Notes

[1] An earlier version of this paper was presented at Turing 2000: The Dartmouth Conference on the Future of the Turing Test, January 28–30, 2000. I'd like to thank Jack Copeland, Paul Hovda, James Moor, and Gualtiero Picciini for helpful comments and suggestions.

[2] Some versions of the Standard Interpretation characterize the test as involving only two participants, the computer and an interrogator. The computer's performance is not compared to another player. Instead the computer passes the test when the interrogator fails to identify it as a computer.

[3]Dyer's interpretation is unusual because he posits more than one interrogator, and he calls for a split decision from the group of interrogators in one case. Most readers interpret Turing as advocating many runs of the test, with one interrogator per test, but different interrogators for each run.

[4]Shieber (1994) is another example.

[5]See Moor (1987) for a constrasting view. Moor thinks that role the computer plays is left undetermined by Turing. This is a weaker position than the Standard Interpretation.

[6]Cf. Kenner (1986).

[7]See Piccinini (2000) for the Standard Interpretation reading of this passage.

[8]This is Hodges' defense of the Standard Interpretation. See Hodges (1999, pp. 37 ff).

[9]Turing saw ordinary views about computers as an obstacle to progress in computer science generally (Turing, 1947).

[10]This point depends on the assumption that the game is set up in such a way that the interrogator assumes that the human players are normal speakers of the language. If Turing did not make this assumption, neither version of the Test would have a point.

[11]"May not machines carry out something which out to be described as thinking but "which is very different from what a man does? This objection is a very strong one"

[12]In the 1947 lecture, Turing cites Shannon's work on using heuristics, and he says that he wouldn't consider game-playing success with the use of heuristics significant. This suggests that Turing thought that the coding of human cognitive processes was not the best way to design intelligent machines.

References

Armer, Paul (1995), 'Attitudes towards intelligent Machines', in Edward A. Feigenbaum and Julian Feldman, eds., *Computers and Thought*, MIT Press.

Block, Ned (1990), 'The Computer Model of the Mind', in D. Osherson and E. Smith, eds., *An Invitation to Cognitive Science*, Volume 3, MIT Press.

Davidson, Donald (1990), 'Turing's Test', in K.A. Mohyeldin Said, W.H. Newton-Smith, R. Viale and K.V. Wilkes, eds., *Modelling the Mind*, Clarendon Press.

Dietrich, Eric (ed.) (1994), *Thinking Computers and Virtual Persons*, Academic Press.

Dyer, Michael G. (1994), 'Intentionality and Computationalism', in Dietrich.

Hodges, Andrew (1999), *Turing*, Routledge.

Hutchens, Jason L. 'Introducing Megahal', http://ciips.ee.uwa.edu.au/~ hutch/hal/Talk.html

Kenner, Hugh (1986), 'Racter: Artificial Intelligence or Canned Lunacy?' *Byte*, May, 1986, p. 289.

Michie, Donald (1993), 'Turing's Test and Conscious Thought', *Artificial Intelligence* 60, pp. 1–22, reprinted in Millican and Clark (1996).

Millican, Peter and Clark, Andy (1996), *Machines and Thought*, Oxford University Press.

Moor, J.H (1976), An Analysis of the Turing Test', *Philosophical Studies* 30, pp. 249–257.

Moor, J.H. (1987), 'Turing Test', in Stuart C. Shapiro, ed., *Encyclopedia of Artificial Intelligence*. New York: John Wiley and Sons, pp. 1126–1130.

Piccinini, Gualtiero (2000), 'Turing's Rules for the Imitation Game', *Minds and Machines* 10, pp. 573–582

Rappaport, William J. (1994), 'Syntactic Semantics', in Dietrich.

Shieber, Staurt M. (1994), 'Lessons from a Restricted Turing Test', *Communications of the Association for Computing Machinery*, 37(6), pp. 70–78.

Turing, A.M (1996), 'Lecture to the London Mathematical Society on 20 February, 1947' in B.E. Carpenter and R.W. Doran, eds., *A.M Turing's Ace Report of 1946 and Other Papers*, MIT Press.

Turing, A. M. (1950), 'Computing Machinery and Intelligences', *Mind* 59, pp. 433–460.

Turing's Rules for the Imitation Game

GUALTIERO PICCININI

Department of History and Philosophy of Science, University of Pittsburgh, 1017 Cathedral of Learning, Pittsburgh, PA 15260, USA; E-mail: gupst1@pitt.edu

Abstract. In the 1950s, Alan Turing proposed his influential test for machine intelligence, which involved a teletyped dialogue between a human player, a machine, and an interrogator. Two readings of Turing's rules for the test have been given. According to the *standard reading* of Turing's words, the goal of the interrogator was to discover which was the human being and which was the machine, while the goal of the machine was to be indistinguishable from a human being. According to the *literal reading*, the goal of the machine was to simulate *a man imitating a woman*, while the interrogator – unaware of the real purpose of the test – was attempting to determine which of the two contestants was the woman and which was the man. The present work offers a study of Turing's rules for the test in the context of his advocated purpose and his other texts. The conclusion is that there are several independent and mutually reinforcing lines of evidence that support the standard reading, while fitting the literal reading in Turing's work faces severe interpretative difficulties. So, the controversy over Turing's rules should be settled in favor of the standard reading.

Key words: Turing test

1. Introduction

In his 1950 *Mind* paper, Alan Turing proposed replacing the question "Can machines think?" with the question "Are there imaginable digital computers which would do well in the imitation game?" (Turing, 1950, p. 442). The setup for what came to be known as the Turing test was introduced in the following famous passage:

> [The imitation game] is played with three people, a man (A), a woman (B), and an interrogator (C) who may be of either sex. The interrogator stays in a room apart from the other two. The object of the game for the interrogator is to determine which of the other two is the man and which is the woman. He knows them by labels X and Y, and at the end of the game he says either "X is A and Y is B" or "X is B and Y is A." The interrogator is allowed to put questions to A and B thus:
>
> C: Will X please tell me the length of his or her hair?
>
> Now suppose X is actually A, then A must answer. It is A's object in the game to try to cause C to make the wrong identification. His answer might therefore be
>
> "My hair is shingled, and the longest strands are about nine inches long."

Minds and Machines **10:** 573–582, 2000.

© 2001 *Kluwer Academic Publishers. Printed in the Netherlands.*

In order that tones of voice may not help the interrogator the answers should be written, or better still, typewritten. The ideal arrangement is to have a teleprinter communicating between the two rooms. Alternatively the question and answers can be repeated by an intermediary. The object of the game for the third player (B) is to help the interrogator. The best strategy for her is probably to give truthful answers. She can add such things as "I am the woman, don't listen to him!" to her answers, but it will avail nothing as the man can make similar remarks.

We now ask the question, "What will happen when a machine takes the part of A in this game?" Will the interrogator decide wrongly as often when the game is played like this as he does when the game is played between a man and a woman? These questions replace our original, "Can machines think?" (Turing, 1950, pp. 433–434).

When the imitation game involved two human beings, Turing explained the rules in some detail. However, after introducing machines into the game, Turing did *not* make the rules explicit. According to the traditional interpretation of this passage, when a machine and a human being are playing the game, the goal of the interrogator is to discover which is the human being and which is the machine, while the goal of the machine is to be mistaken for a human being. I will refer to this as the *standard reading*. Under the standard reading, the Turing test is squarely a comparison between human beings and machines, where a skillful interrogator can require the machine to demonstrate mastery of human language, knowledge, and inferential capacities. Possessing these abilities is, by most standards, a clear sign of intelligence or thinking.[1] So, the question of whether a machine can do well at the imitation game can be seen as a sensible replacement for the question of whether a machine can think.

Some authors have read Turing's passage in a more literal way, suggesting that the goal of the machine is to simulate *a man imitating a woman*, while the interrogator – unaware of the real purpose of the test – is still attempting to determine which of the two players is the woman and which is the man. I will call this the *literal reading*.[2] Supporters of the literal reading disagree over which of the machine's capacities are being uncovered by Turing's game. Some argue that his point is testing the machine's ability to utilize language like a person; the blindness of the interrogator and the gender impersonation are introduced for methodological reasons – in order to make the test unbiased.[3] Others suggest that Turing's point was *not* to test the machine's ability to utilize language like a human, but literally to test the machine's competence at replicating the abilities of a human male who is attempting to imitate a human female.[4]

As far as I know, no one has defended the standard reading against this revisionist line. The present work offers a thorough study of Turing's rules for the imitation game in the context of his advocated purpose and his other texts. Several independent and mutually reinforcing lines of evidence that support the standard reading will be presented, while fitting the literal reading in Turing's work will face severe interpretative difficulties. The evidence supporting the standard reading is found by considering other sections of the *Mind* paper, its overall argumentative structure, and relevant statements made by Turing on other occasions. So, the controversy over Turing's rules should be settled in favor of the standard reading.

2. How Literal is the Literal Reading?

An opponent might accuse the standard reading of unnecessarily attributing ambiguity to Turing's description of the game's rules. If Turing meant the machine to simulate not a woman, as his words seem to suggest, but a generic human being, why didn't he say so from the start? The standard reading makes Turing's description of the rules appear confusingly incomplete, while the literal reading seems to take Turing's words at face value. Other things being equal, this opponent would conclude, the literal reading should be preferred over the standard one. Before turning to the evidence in favor of the standard reading, let me dispense with this potential objection.

It turns out that, when examined closely, the literal reading generates an interpretative problem similar to the one just mentioned. Suppose the literal reading is correct. Turing's words would still fall short of fixing the rules of the game, this time with respect to the interrogator's role. Does the interrogator *know* that she is dealing with a machine and a woman, or does she *incorrectly think* she is dealing with a woman and a man? Turing doesn't say anything in this respect. This question is far from irrelevant, as we would expect the interrogator's strategy, and the chances of making correct guesses, to be different in each of the two cases. So, the literal reading is also committed to attributing ambiguity to Turing's explanation of the rules. Usually, the proponents of the literal reading assume that the interrogator should *not* know that she is talking to a machine.[5] But such misconception of the interrogator changes the game's original setting, in which the interrogator was *correctly* informed that the players were a woman and a man. This change does resolve the ambiguity resulting from the literal reading, but generates the following question: if Turing meant the interrogator to ignore the real purpose of the game, why didn't he say so? The ambiguity resulting from the literal reading, and the inference required to resolve the ambiguity, make the literal reading *no longer* literal. As both readings attribute an ambiguity to Turing's description of the rules, no reading is better off than the other in this respect.

3. The Turing Test as a Replacement for the Question "Can Machines Think?"

Any reading of Turing's rules must explain how the imitation game fulfills his goal of replacing the question of whether machines can think. As I said, the standard reading's account is straightforward: if a machine can demonstrate mastery of human language, knowledge, and inferential capacities to the point that it is mistaken for a human being, most people would consider it intelligent – or so they should according to Turing. With respect to this replacement goal, though, the literal reading generates more questions than answers. Presumably, any successful simulation of a human being includes a simulation of both a human gender and the human ability to imitate other human beings. Under the standard reading, this fact could be exploited by the interrogator. Given the rules of the Turing test under the standard reading, the interrogator can ask both players to impersonate a member of any gender to see how they compare on that task. However, it is not obvious how this gender imitation task relates to the question of human intelligence. The literal reading restricts the entire test to the question of whether a *human* male or a *mechanical* male can imitate the opposite sex better. In what way is this ability relevant to whether machines think? Why is proficiency at this task sufficient to prove that a machine is intelligent? One possible answer is that the machine needs to simulate the mental processes of a human male to a degree of sophistication that is sufficient to also simulate the human male impersonating a human female. This might convince one that the machine is intelligent. But if the machine is able to simulate a man to such a degree, why not ask it a broad range of questions rather than limiting the task to the impersonation of the opposite gender?

These questions illustrate that it is not obvious how the test – as defined by the literal reading – fulfills Turing's replacement goal. The proponents of the literal reading owe us not only an answer to these questions, but an explanation for why Turing did not address them at all.[6] If, as some have argued, he simply was introducing an experimental design to make the test unbiased, why didn't he say so? Again, recall that, in the imitation game played by humans, the interrogator knows that both players are human. If Turing thought the game with the machine needed the extra precaution of deceiving the interrogator as to the nature of the game, he should have – and presumably would have – both said it and *explained why* he thought so.[7] Instead, he spent most of his rather long text considering various general attributes of human beings, and various general reasons for believing that machines cannot think. In each case, he argued that none of those reasons were obstacles to the conclusion that a digital computer would eventually be able to play the imitation game. His punchline was that a machine could be developed to match all the elements that are relevant to *human intelligence*, including the ability to learn from experience and one's own mistakes. Turing never discussed any elements that would make the machine able or unable to do the gender imitation, nor did he mention how his detailed discussions of various human abilities related to gender imitation. As a result, it is natural to read the *Mind* paper as being entirely devoted to the motivation and explication of the test as understood under the standard reading. Turing was neither a sloppy thinker nor a sloppy writer. If he wanted to propose his test under the literal reading, it's likely that he would have motivated and explained it in detail, instead of just concentrating on what potentially makes humans and machines intellectually different, or intellectually equal.

4. The Turing Test in Section 2 of the *Mind* Paper

The passage describing the test constitutes most of section 1 of the *Mind* paper. In section 2, a few lines after introducing the game, Turing wrote that "[t]he new problem has the advantage of drawing a fairly sharp line between the physical and the intellectual capacities of a man" (Turing, 1950, p. 434).[8] He did *not* mention the capacities of human beings as gender imitators, but he did give "specimen questions and answers" between the interrogator and the other players. The questions were no longer relevant to being a man or woman, as were the examples given by Turing for the game with only human players. Now, the "specimen questions and answers" involved writing a sonnet, adding numbers, and playing chess. These were some of the paradigmatic *intelligent* human activities that Turing referred to – in other papers – as some of the tasks on which computers needed to be tested to show they were intelligent.[9] Turing's examples are in line with the standard reading, according to which the goal of the interrogator is to distinguish the human being from the machine. If one, instead, takes the literal reading, one should explain why Turing's examples are not about gender differences, but about general intellectual abilities of human beings, at which men and women hardly differ.

At the end of section 2, Turing made two additional points that are hard to reconcile with the literal reading. The first is that the "counterpart" to the imitation game is for a "man" (i.e. a human being) to "pretend to be the machine" (Turing, 1950, p. 435). This makes sense if Turing meant to test a machine simulating a human being. If he meant to test a machine simulating a man imitating a woman, he should have said that the counterpart to his test is for a woman to imitate a man imitating a machine. Turing's second point is a suggestion that the best strategy for the machine is giving answers that would naturally be given by a "man."[10] This is not in direct contradiction with the literal reading, for the claim might be that the machine should literally simulate the answers given by a man imitating a woman. But the literal reading makes this assumption oddly unwarranted. For, under the literal reading, the machine could follow a strategy that appears at least equally good, if not better: imitate the woman *directly*, giving answers that would be given by a woman *qua* woman, rather than by a man imitating a woman. In contrast, under the standard reading, given that Turing's "man" can stand for a generic human being, the assumption that the machine should attempt to provide human-like answers becomes straightforward.

5. Turing's Second Description of the Test

The most serious problem with the literal reading is that, in section 5 of the *Mind* paper, Turing described the test again, in accordance with the standard reading. He described the game as that of a machine imitating a human being, which, as usual, he called "man."[11] When they haven't ignored section 5, the proponents of the literal reading have suggested that, in it, Turing described a different "version" of the test (as understood under the literal reading). In the first "version," the machine was playing against a woman; this time, the test is alleged to involve a machine playing against a human *male*, and both the mechanical and the human player must pretend to be women.[12] This suggestion is entirely *ad hoc*, for there is no independent evidence supporting it. Nowhere in the paper did Turing mention any change in his description of the test, or in the rules of the game. If he meant to describe two tests rather than one, we should expect that he say so, and explain why he was making such a change. Moreover, there is textual evidence *against* the hypothesis that, in sections 1 and 5, Turing was describing two different tests. In section 3, Turing discussed the already introduced game (from section 1 of the paper), and then pointed in the direction of section 5, where the game was described as being between a computer and a human being.[13] In section 3, as throughout the paper, Turing referred to *the* game, or test, without ever using the plural, and mentioned no change in the rules. In section 3, as in the rest of the *Mind* paper, Turingwas writing about one and the same test, namely the test as defined by the standard reading.

6. The Turing Test Outside of the *Mind* Paper

The Turing test was foreshadowed in a report on mechanical intelligence written by Turing a few years before the *Mind* paper. Even before the actual construction of digital computers, Turing and others began writing computer programs for chess playing and other activities.[14] The performance of such programs could be tested by asking a person to compute, at each stage of the game, what the next move should be according to the program. A human being who is given paper, pencil, and a set of instructions to carry out, was called by Turing a "paper machine." A paper machine behaves like a digital computer executing a program:

> The extent to which we regard something as behaving in an intelligent manner is determined as much by our state of mind and training as by the properties of the object under consideration. If we are able to explain and predict its behaviour or if there seems to be little underlying plan, we have little temptation to imagine intelligence. With the same object therefore it is possible that one man would consider it as intelligent and another would not; the second man would have found out the rules of its behaviour.

> It is possible to do a little experiment on these lines, even at the present stage of knowledge. It is not difficult to devise a paper machine which will play a not very bad game of chess. Now get three men as subjects for the experiment A, B, C. A and C are to be rather poor chess players, B is the operator who works the paper machine. (In order that he should be able to work it fairly fast it is advisable that he be both mathematician and chess player.) Two rooms are

used with some arrangement for communicating moves, and a game is played between C and either A or the paper machine. C may find it quite difficult to tell which he is playing [*sic*]. (This is a rather idealized form of an experiment I have actually done.) (Turing, 1948, p. 23).

The "experiment" described here closely resembles the imitation game under the standard reading. In this passage, Turing suggested that playing chess against a machine could generate the feeling that the machine was intelligent. In the title of the above quote, Turing called intelligence an "emotional concept," meaning that there is no objective way to apply it. Direct experience with a machine, which plays chess in a way that cannot be distinguished from human playing, could convince one to attribute intelligence to the machine. This is very likely to be an important part of the historical root for Turing's proposal of the imitation game. Believing that "[t]he extent to which we regard something as behaving in an intelligent manner is determined as much by our state of mind and training as by the properties of the object under consideration," he hoped that, by experiencing the versatility of digital computers at tasks normally thought to require intelligence, people would modify their usage of terms like "intelligence" and "thinking," so that such terms apply to the machines themselves.[15]

Finally, Turing described his test on two other public occasions. The first was a talk broadcast on the BBC Third Programme on May 15, 1951. The relevant portion went as follows:

I think it is probable for instance that at the end of the century it will be possible to programme a machine to answer questions in such a way that it will be extremely difficult to guess whether the answers are being given by a man or by the machine. I am imagining something like a viva-voce examination, but with the questions and answers all typewritten in order that we need not consider such irrelevant matters as the faithfulness with which the human voice can be imitated (Turing, 1951, pp. 4–5).

The second was a discussion between Turing, M.H.A. Newman, Sir Geoffrey Jefferson, and R.B. Braithwaite, broadcast on the BBC Third Programme on January 14 and 23, 1952. Turing said:

I would like to suggest a particular kind of *test* that one might apply to a machine. You might call it a test to see whether the machine thinks, but it would be better to avoid begging the question, and say that the machines that pass are (let's say) Grade A machines. The idea of the test is that the machine has to try to pretend to be a man, by answering questions put to it, and it will only pass if the pretence is reasonably convincing... (Turing, 1952, pp. 4–5, italics in the original).

The topic of these radio broadcasts was whether digital computers could be said to think. Turing's advocated purpose was the same in these occasions as in his *Mind* paper: to replace the question of whether machines could think with the question of whether machines could pass his test. The terms used, and the gist of Turing's speeches, closely resembled the *Mind* paper. Yet, in both occasions, Turing unambiguously described the test as understood under the standard reading.

7. Conclusion

According to those who have witnessed or studied his life, Turing was often a surprisingly fast thinker. He would get frustrated when others took a long time to get points that seemed obvious to him.[16] Perhaps because of this, his writing was lucid but not always easily understood. In his logic papers, some apparent obscurities resulted from him skipping some of the inferential steps, and can be clarified by adding the missing steps.[17] In light of this, the most likely explanation for the ambiguity in Turing's rules is that he expected his readers to fill in the details in accordance with the game's purpose. Given that the test is a replacement for the question of whether machines can think, the machine must pretend to be human, while the interrogator tries to determine which of the two players is the machine and which is the human being. A careful examination of Turing's work, at any rate, provides plenty of evidence that the standard reading of his rules is correct. Turing's own imitation game did *not* involve a machine simulating a man who's pretending to be a woman, but a machine simulating a human being.

Acknowledgements

The writing of this paper was prompted by a discussion with Susan Sterrett, for which I am very grateful. Thanks to the participants of The Future of the Turing Test for the fruitful discussion that took place there, and to Becka Skloot for many helpful comments.

Notes

[1] For the present purpose of understanding Turing's text, following his usage, I use the terms "intelligence" and "thinking" interchangeably. This is not meant to suggest that, in other contexts, no useful distinction can be drawn between the two.

[2] Webb, 1980, p. 238; Haugeland, 1985, p. 6; Genova, 1994, pp. 313–315; Cowley and McDorman, 1995, p. 122, esp. n. 10; Hayes and Ford, 1995, p. 972; Saygin *et al.*, 2000; Traiger, 2000.

[3] Haugeland, 1985, pp. 6–8; Saygin *et al.*, 2000; Traiger, 2000.

[4] Genova, 1994, p. 315; Hayes and Ford, 1995, p. 977. According to Genova, the literal reading accounts for Turing's replacement proposal because Turing held the view that thinking is imitating; thus, a machine successful at imitating must be thinking (Genova, 1994, pp. 315–322). According to Genova, the request that the machine specifically simulate a human male imitating a human female is explained by what she takes to be Turing's views on sexual identity, due to his own experience as a homosexual (ib., esp. pp. 314–315).

[5] The ambiguity is recognized by Haugeland, 1985, p. 6, n. 2. The additional claim that the interrogator must be deceived about the purpose of the game is explicitly made by Hayes and Ford, 1995, p. 972; Saygin *et al.*, 2000; Traiger, 2000.

[6] These questions have actually been answered at length by Sterrett (2000), who argues that the test defined by the literal reading makes a better test for intelligence than the test defined by the standard

reading. Of course, Sterrett does *not* attribute her arguments to Turing. The issue of what *is* the best test for machine intelligence is irrelevant to the topic of the present paper. Here, I concentrate on what Turing *said*, and *didn't say*.

[7]Genova's account in terms of Turing's alleged view that thought is imitation is even more problematic. First, such a view is no reason to *restrict* a test for thought to the simulation of a human male imitating a human female, rather than allowing for a wider range of simulations. Second, and more importantly, Genova provides no textual evidence to warrant her attribution to Turing of the view that thought is imitation. In studying his work, I have found no evidence that Turing held such a view.

[8]Since Turing's language – as that of most of his colleagues – was not politically correct by today's standards, he generally used "man" to refer to a generic human being.

[9]The following examples are from papers written before the *Mind* paper. The first time he mentioned machine intelligence in a paper, Turing did so in a discussion of mechanical chess-playing (1945, p. 41). In a more extensive discussion of machine intelligence for an audience of mathematicians, he suggested that machines could prove their intelligence by both playing chess and doing mathematical derivations in a formal logical system (1947, pp. 122–123). In a report entirely devoted to machine intelligence, Turing discussed the possibility of programming machines to play various games, to learn languages, to do translations, cryptanalysis (which he used to call "cryptography"), and mathematics (1948, p. 13).

[10]The text goes as follows:

It might be urged that when playing the 'imitation game' the best strategy for the machine may possibly be something other than imitation of the behaviour of a man. This may be, but I think it is unlikely that there is any great effect of this kind. In any case there is no intention to investigate here he theory of the game, and it will be assumed that the best strategy is to try to provide answers that would naturally be given by men (Turing, 1950, p. 435).

[11]Notice the initial reference to section 3, which turns out to have some importance:

We may now consider again the point raised at the end of §3. It was suggested tentatively that the question, 'Can machines think?' should be replaced by 'Are there imaginable digital computers which would do well in the imitation game?' If we wish we can make this superficially more general, and ask 'Are there discrete state machines which would do well?' But in view of the universality property we see that either of these questions is equivalent to this, 'Let us fix our attention on one particular digital computer C. Is it true that by modifying this computer to have an adequate storage, suitably increasing its speed of action, and providing it with an appropriate programme, C can be made to play satisfactorily the part of A in the imitation game, the part of B being taken by a man?' (Turing, 1950, p. 442).

Recall also that "[t]he object of the game for the third player (B) is to help the interrogator" (ib., p. 434).

[12]Genova, 1994, p. 314; Saygin *et al.*, 2000. According to Traiger's (2000) reading of this passage, in the modified test the human player can be either a man or a woman, but he or she has to play the role of a woman.

[13]Here is the relevant excerpt:

There are already a number of digital computers in working order, and it may be asked, 'Why not try the experiment straight away? It would be easy to satisfy the conditions of the game. A number of interrogators could be used, and statistics compiled to show how often the right identification was given.' The short answer is that we are not asking whether all digital computers would do well in the game nor whether the computers at present available would do well, but whether there are imaginable computers which would do well. But this is only the short answer. We shall see this question in a different light later (Turing, 950, p. 436).

The word "later" is a clear reference to the quote taken from section 5, which he – as noted in n. 11 – starts with a cross-reference to section 3, and comes after Turing's explanation of digital computers, their property of universality, and the importance of programs.

[14]See Hodges, 1983, chapt. 6.

[15] In this respect, this is what he said in the *Mind* paper: "I believe that at the end of the century the use of words and general educated opinion will have altered so much that one will be able to speak of machines thinking without expecting to be contradicted" (Turing, 1950, p. 442).
[16] See Newman, 1955, p. 255; Turing, 1959, pp. 13, 27–28; numerous relevant episodes are also reported by Hodges, 1983.
[17] For some examples, see Piccinini, 2001.

References

Cowley, S.J. and MacDorman, K.F. (1995), 'Simulating Conversations: The Communion Game', *AI and Society* 9, pp. 116–139.

Genova, J. (1994), 'Turing's Sexual Guessing Game', *Social Epistemology* 8, pp. 313–326.

Haugeland, J. (1985), *Artificial Intelligence: The Very Idea*. Cambridge, MA: MIT Press.

Hayes, P. and Ford, K. (1995), 'Turing Test Considered Harmful', *Proceedings of the Fourteenth International Joint Conference on Artificial Intelligence*, Montreal, Quebec, Canada, pp. 972–977.

Hodges, A. (1983), *Alan Turing: The Enigma*. New York: Simon and Schuster.

Ince, D.C., ed. (1992), *Collected Works of A.M. Turing: Mechanical Intelligence*. Amsterdam: North Holland.

Newman, M.H.A. (1955), 'Alan Mathison Turing', in *Biographical Memoirs of Fellows of the Royal Society*. London: Royal Soc., pp. 253–362.

Piccinini, G. (2001), 'Turing and the Mathematical Objection', Forthcoming in *Minds and Machines*.

Saygin A.P., Cicekli I. and Akman V. (2000), 'Turing Test: 50 Years Later', *Minds and Machines* 10, pp. 463–518.

Sterrett, S. (2000), 'Turing's Two Tests for Intelligence', *Minds and Machines* 10, pp. 541–559.

Traiger, S. (2000), 'Making the Right Identification in the Turing Test', *Minds and Machines* 10, pp. 561–572.

Turing, A.M. (1945), 'Proposal for Development in the Mathematical Division of an Automatic Computing Engine (ACE)', reprinted in Ince (1992), pp. 1–86.

Turing, A.M. (1947), 'Lecture to the London Mathematical Society on 20 February 1947', reprinted in Ince (1992), pp. 87–105.

Turing, A.M. (1948), 'Intelligent Machinery', reprinted in Ince (1992), pp. 107–127.

Turing, A.M. (1950), 'Computing Machinery and Intelligence', *Mind* 59, pp. 433–460.

Turing, A.M. (1951), 'Can digital computers think?' Typescript of talk broadcast on BBC Third Programme, 15 May 1951, AMT B.5, Contemporary Scientific Archives Centre, King's College Library, Cambridge.

Turing, A.M. (1952), 'Can automatic calculating machines be said to think?' Typescript of broadcast discussion on BBC Third Programme, 14 and 23 January 1952, between M.H.A. Newman, A.M. Turing, Sir Geoffrey Jefferson, R.B. Braithwaite, AMT B.6, Contemporary Scientific Archives Centre, King's College Library, Cambridge.

Turing, E.S. (1959), *Alan M. Turing*. Cambridge: Heifer & Sons.

Webb, J.C. (1980), Mechanism, Mentalism, and Metamathematics. Dordrecht: D. Reidel.

Passing Loebner's Turing Test: A Case of Conflicting Discourse Functions[1]

SEAN ZDENEK
Program in Rhetoric, Department of English, Carnegie Mellon University, PA, USA; E-mail: szdenek@andrew.cmu.edu

Abstract. This paper argues that the Turing test is based on a fixed and de-contextualized view of communicative competence. According to this view, a machine that passes the test will be able to communicate effectively in a variety of other situations. But the de-contextualized view ignores the relationship between language and social context, or, to put it another way, the extent to which speakers respond dynamically to variations in discourse function, formality level, social distance/solidarity among participants, and participants' relative degrees of power and status (Holmes, 1992). In the case of the Loebner Contest, a present day version of the Turing test, the social context of interaction can be interpreted in conflicting ways. For example, Loebner discourse is defined 1) as a friendly, casual conversation between two strangers of equal power, and 2) as a one-way transaction in which judges control the conversational floor in an attempt to expose contestants that are not human. This conflict in discourse function is irrelevant so long as the goal of the contest is to ensure that only thinking, human entities pass the test. But if the function of Loebner discourse is to encourage the production of software that can pass for human on the level of conversational ability, then the contest designers need to resolve this ambiguity in discourse function, and thus also come to terms with the kind of competence they are trying to measure.

Key words: communicative competence, cooperative principle, discourse function, Grice, linguistic politeness, Loebner Contest, Turing test

This line of teleology for the Loebner prize, that it serves not as a test of the abilities of the computers but of the psychologies of the various participants, has often been proposed informally.

Stuart M. Shieber[2]

After the main event, all the guys assured me with knowing smiles that I was "very convincing" – which made me wonder if the contest wasn't just an elaborate joke propagated by the AI community upon a few chosen humans.

Tracy Quan[3]

1. Introduction

Fifty years ago, mathematician Alan M. Turing (1950, p. 433) proposed a test – he called it the "imitation game" – that was designed to simplify and clarify the philosophical and practical problems of defining and measuring machine intelligence. According to the rules of the imitation game, a human interrogator attempts to distinguish two players, a human and a machine, on the basis of their teletyped responses to his/her questions.[4] A machine passes the test (i.e., it is deemed a "thinking" entity) if the interrogator can not tell the difference between the players

Minds and Machines **11**: 53–76, 2001.
© 2001 *Kluwer Academic Publishers. Printed in the Netherlands.*

after "five minutes of questioning" (1950, p. 442). Due in part to its severity as a scientific test (Moor 1992, p. 1625), the imitation game (afterwards known as the Turing test) has proven remarkably durable. Because the interrogator is free to ask any number of silly or irrelevant questions, the test appears to offer a very efficient method for separating nonhumans from humans (Dennett, 1985). As Turing says (1950, p. 435), "The question and answer method seems to be suitable for introducing almost any one of the fields of human endeavor that we wish to include."

But while the test does not restrict what the interrogator can say or ask, it does appear to restrict how s/he can say it and how players can respond. The interrogation model of discourse creates fairly rigid, clearly distinct, roles for participants. The interrogator controls the flow and topic of conversation; the subjects of the interrogation are powerless, except to the extent that their responses provide the information the interrogator is looking for. The interrogator, of course, is free to ask a variety of different questions. But these questions (including how the interrogator asks them) will necessarily be shaped by the function of discourse, which in the case of an interrogation is to force an unwilling participant to reveal, perhaps inadvertently, some piece of important and concealed information.

Turing test advocates assume that any machine that can pass a serious interrogation will be more than fit to interact with humans in an indeterminate number of situations. In other words, they assume that communicative competence is fixed and transferable: a machine that passes a Turing test will also be capable of passing for a thinking entity in other settings. But a machine that can pass a serious interrogation will not necessarily make a good conversationalist. This machine may not be equipped with the ability to direct the flow of conversation, especially if it has been programmed to play the role of subject in an interrogation. It may not be able to appeal to politeness conventions where appropriate or adjust to changing power relationships. It may not be able to use humor – or be indirect, change the subject deftly, deploy face-saving strategies, or do any of a number of other things – in order to deflate potentially volatile situations. What is needed, in other words, is an alternative to the fixed and de-contextualized view, one that explores the ways in which *context* shapes what it means to be a competent speaker/writer. Because a contextual view treats competence in terms of a speaker's dynamic response to variations in discourse function, formality level, social distance/solidarity among participants, and participants' relative degrees of power and status (Holmes, 1992), it calls into question whether a program designed solely to survive a Turing test will also survive in situations where the avoidance of conflict and the maintenance of social hannony are expected (Kasper, 1990).[5]

This paper argues that test designers need to attend more carefully and explicitly to the ways in which discourse is shaped along the dimensions of communicative competence. For example, in the case of the Loebner Contest (Loebner, 1999), a present day variant of the Turing test, discourse function can be interpreted in two conflicting ways (i.e., discourse-as-interaction and discourse-as-transaction).

This suggests that contest designers have either failed to come to terms with the interrelationship of language and social context, or assume that the ability to communicate transcends any specific context. It is my hope that the analysis of Loebner Contest transcripts that follows will demonstrate the danger in thinking of language in isolation from social context.

2. The First Turing Test

Billed as the "First Turing Test" (Loebner, 1999), The Loebner Prize for Artificial Intelligence is an annual contest sponsored by New York City businessman Hugh Loebner, who has promised $100,000 and a gold medal to the first program to pass an unrestricted Turing test. Each year, the prize committee awards a nominal amount (originally $1500, currently $2000) and bronze medal to the "most human" computer program entered in the contest that year. The contest has been held every year since 1991.

The Loebner planning committee made two important revisions to the structure of Turing's original game. Turing's game is based on a tripartite structure, in which each player (human and software program) can view and respond to the utterances of the other two parties. The Loebner competition, on the other hand, is organized around a set of dyadic interactions between judges and contestants. The judges are informed that at least a certain number of contestants may be human "confederates."[6] Each judge interacts with one of the contestants for a specified amount of time (ten minutes in 1999), then moves to another terminal and begins another conversation with a new contestant. This process is repeated until every judge has interacted with every contestant. It is each judge's job to rank all the contestants in order from "least human" to "most human." The judges are also asked to rank each contestant on scales of "responsiveness" and "humanness," although these rankings are used only in the event of a tie. Each contestant's median score is used to compute an overall ranking, and the program with the highest ranking is the prizewinner. Should a program fool 30% of the judges[7] into mistaking it for human (it has not happened yet), it will be awarded an intermediate prize of $25,000 and a silver medal. (The human confederates always outrank the software programs.) During the second phase of the contest, software programs will not only be required to pass a text-only version of the game but also to "respond 'intelligently' to audio visual input in the manner that a human would" (Loebner, 1994). The first program to pass this second, audiovisual test (presumably at Turing's 30% level) will be awarded the $100,000 grand prize.

The second revision to the structure of Turing's game came as the result of the planning committee's realization that, "given the current state of the art, there was no chance that Turing's test, as originally defined, had the slightest chance of being passed by a computer program" (Shieber, 1994, p. 70). The committee thus decided to limit the range of what each entrant would be responsible for discussing. In the case of the programs, designers defined topics in advance (e.g., pets, hockey, sex, whimsical conversation, and burgundy wines). In the case of the human confederates, the prize committee chose topics that intersected with each confederate's area of interest or expertise. In one well-known example from the first Loebner competition (held in 1991), confederate Cynthia Clay, whose selected topic was Shakespeare's plays, was mistaken for a program three times (Shieber, 1994; Hutchens, 1996). One judge said, "[no] human would have that amount of knowledge about Shakespeare" (Stipp, 1991, quoted in Shieber, 1994, p. 72). Judges were required to stick to each entrant's pre-defined topic. They were also told to refrain from "trickery or guile" (Shieber, 1994, p. 71): obscure or unexpected questions and gibberish designed to expose nonhumans would not be allowed. Finally, the rules stated that "Judges should respond naturally, as they would in a conversation with another person" ('Shieber, 1994, p. 71). Referees tried to ensure that judges and confederates – a new batch was brought in each year – acted in accordance with these rules. The topic restriction spanned four contests (1991–1994); the contest has been unrestricted since 1995.

Loebner judges have made fine interrogators; Turing would no doubt be proud. Judges typically presume prior to interaction that all contestants are nonhuman until proven otherwise. Judges see their task as one of forcing contestants to reveal (or to make obvious) the truth of their hidden identity. Many rely on what I call pre-selected "outing" questions, the majority of which require from contestants a broad knowledge of facts about history and culture. Outing questions are similar to what Dennett (1985, p. 126) calls "quick probes," in other words questions or statements designed to "test for a wider competence." Dennett (1985, p. 138) advocates quick probes as a solution to the problem of "putting too much faith in computer systems, especially user-friendly systems that present themselves in a very anthropomorphic manner." Loebner judges expect answers to these outing questions or quick probes to be concise, direct, and unmitigated; contestants who/that try to change the subject – let alone direct the flow of conversation – are treated to a quick and merciless onslaught of discursive harassment.

Put another way, many judges resemble vigilantes who police the boundary between the human and the nonhuman. While the vigilante approach can "teach all users of computers, especially users of expert systems, how to probe their systems before they rely on them" (Dennett, 1985, p. 138), it puts a serious strain on conversation. Because judges do not take contestants' humanness for granted, they are unable and unwilling to trust them enough to interact in ways we would expect from two people who do not know each other very well or at all. In casual conversation, we typically expect each participant to engage in a fair amount of interpretive work in order to make sense of the direction and meaning of the developing conversation. Many Loebner judges, however, view interaction with contestants in terms of a one-way transaction in which they alone control the conversational floor. Because judges expect responses from contestants to be direct and complete, they are unwilling to work with anything that might be grammatically or conceptually incomplete (Collins, 1997). In the rest of this paper, I would like

Table I. Loebner Discourse as Casual and Transactional

Casual Discourse	Transactional Discourse
• Humanness: each participant assumess the other is human *prior* to interaction.	• Nonhumanness: interrogator doubts the other's self-presentation as a human (Note that this does not hold for face-to-face interaction between two humans.)
• Politeness strategies	• Impoliteness strategies, rudeness
• Politeness Principle (responses will take into account the level of imposition, and the other's social distance and relative power)	• Cooperative Principle (responses will be length-appropriate, truthful, relevant, and perspicuous)
• Interactional or casual	• Transactional or fact-based
• Two-way: both participants share the conversational floor.	• One-way: interrogator controls the conversational floor; players are powerless.
• Programmers & Researchers (build "personalities" for interaction)	• Judges (expect compliance with maxims of Cooperative Principle, though they themselves are not bound to them)
• Loebner Contest	• Loebner Contest

to draw on selected research in sociolinguistics to build a model of casual conversation between human strangers, and compare it with the model of communicative interaction presented in the Loebner competition rules and in interactions between judges and contestants. The set of distinctions I have been sketching here loosely are organized in Table I. Because the function of Loebner discourse is ambiguous, I have placed it on both sides of the conversational divide. This is not cause for concern as long as the goal of the contest is to ensure that only thinking entities pass the test. (The judges are doing a great job of that now.) But if the goal of the contest is to encourage the production of software that can pass for human on the level of conversational ability, then the contest designers need to resolve this ambiguity in discourse function, and thus also come to terms with the kind of competence they are trying to measure.

Table II. Complete list of topics during the restricted Loebner era (1991–1994)

Program Topics	Human Confederate Topics
Bad Marriage	Abortion
Burgundy Wine	American History
Cats versus Dogs	Baseball
Classic Star Trek	Boston Red Sox
Dry Martinis	Classical Music
Environmental Issues	Cooking
Hockey	Cryonics
Liberal or Conservative	Custom Cars
Men vs. Women	Dream Analysis
The O.J. Simpson Trial	Health
Pets	Martial Arts
Problems in Romantic Relationships	Newspaper Comics
Relations with your real or imaginary wife	The Rolling Stones
Second Grade School Topics	Shakespeare's Plays
Sex Education	Women's Clothing
Small Talk	
Whimsical Conversation	

3. Playing It Safe

In designing the first contest, the Loebner committee preferred to play it safe. According to Robert Epstein (1992, p. 84), who established the contest on behalf of Loebner, "[the planning committee] took great pains to protect the computers. We felt that in the early years of the contest, such protection would be essential." This protection, as described above, took the form of a restriction in topic. In choosing topics, program designers and the Loebner committee generally shied away from topics that might sanction discursive harassment or suggest that programs were not to be protected after all. See Table II for the complete list of topics during the restricted Loebner era (1991–1994) (sources: Mauldin, 1994; Platt, 1995). Of course, any topic can fuel aggressive behavior. Most of the topics on this list, however, are apparently intended to be on the innocuous side. They are topics, as Shieber (1994, p. 72) suggests in reference to the 1991 competition, "appropriate for a cocktail party venue." Most fall into the category of leisure and recreation. Nearly all are topics that permit participants to offer their opinions without also having to worry whether they are offending their listeners. In other words, it is unlikely that your conversational partner is going to feel threatened if, say, your favorite episodes of Star Trek do not coincide, or your classical music tastes differ, or one of you likes dogs better than cats. Because the majority of these topics are concerned with taste (which is assumed to vary widely among individuals), differences of opinion are expected but not expected to cause party guests to go to blows.

Shieber (1994, p. 71) reports that, during the first Loebner Competition, judges and confederates "performed admirably": they stuck to assigned topics and refrained from so-called "trickery or guile." But transcripts of interactions from restricted Loebner contests clearly reveal tensions among participants. Judges did not blindly follow the instruction to "respond naturally, as they would in a conversation with another person," simply because the very thing assumed by that instruction – namely, the personhood or humanness of each contestant – was in serious doubt. In the following example, taken from the 1993 competition, a judge and a program are supposed to be discussing the topic "pets":[8]

FROM 1993, DESIGNER M. MAULDIN, RANKED 3RD OUT OF 3 PROGRAMS, JUDGE NUMBER NOT AVAILABLE

Judge Have you ever kept a penthouse pet?

Program Do you have any pets?

Judge I think you're avoiding my question.

Program Do you think that animals can think?

Judge Do you think it ethical for one species to enslave another

Program What kinds of pets did you have as a child?

Judge I'm asking the questions. What is a pet if it is not a
slave of species-ism.

Program Oh, that's so sad. I think pets enrich a childhood
immensely.

Judge How can we keep some animals as pets, yet eat others

Program Guinea pigs are about as smart as cumcumbers.

Judge Would you eat a guinea pig

Program I spent several summers on my Uncle's farm. I really
enjoyed the animals a lot.

In this example, the judge manages at once to assume a hostile persona and stay on topic, which suggests that the restrictions did not always function as intended.

In 1995, the topic restriction was lifted. But the contest rules have continued to maintain a set of implied restrictions. For example, rule five attempts to elicit polite behavior from judges and contestants by instilling in them (or their designers) a fear of reprisal (Loebner Prize Rules for 2000):

5. It is the task of the computer entries to respond to the communications of the judges in such a manner as to imitate the responses of a human. No constraints will be placed on the judges', confederates' or contestants' conversations. How-

ever, the competition is widely publicized, the transcripts will be published, and all participants must assume resposibility [sic] for their own contributions. As in any normal converstation [sic], both participants have a role in determining the direction of the conversation and are free to decide want [sic] topics they do or do not wish to discuss. Entries must be prepared to communicate for an indefinite period of time.

That the contest is "widely publicized" is offered as a warning to those participants who might be tempted by the possibility of unconstrained communication. The judges, program designers, and confederates are encouraged here to internalize a set of rules that were previously explicit: the embarrassment and humiliation of a public reprimand – one with an indefinite life span – is meant to keep participants in line.

In addition to instilling participants with a fear of (public) reprisal, the post-restriction Loebner rules also attempt to enforce non-threatening discourse by masking the game's function as a task-oriented interrogation. For example, the rules (see rule five again) define communication as a reciprocal and "normal" affair between two participants of equal power. In addition, two supporting documents, "Instructions for Confederates" (1999) and "Instructions for Judges" (1999), encourage the humans to "Enjoy yourself! It should be just like striking up a conversation with the person sitting next to you on a train/plane trip." The train/plane analogy suggests that the function of Loebner discourse is to interact: the primary goal of such discourse is the "establishment and maintenance of social relationships" (Kasper, 1990, p. 205).

4. The Politeness of Strangers

In "normal" conversation, we expect non-intimates to adhere to politeness rules, with each party striving to avoid conflict and to maintain social harmony (Kasper, 1994; Culpeper, 1996). Much of the interest in linguistic politeness over the last two decades stems from the work of Brown and Levinson (1987 [1979]), who argue, building on Goffman's notion of "face" (see Goffman, 1955, 1967), that speakers typically avoid speech acts that threaten their own face or the faces of other participants. Should a face-threatening act (FTA) prove unavoidable, Brown and Levinson suggest that a speaker will typically try to disarm or redress it by employing various context-dependent strategies, which are not limited to mitigation, indirectness, humor, praise, deference, and apology. The choice of strategy for doing an FTA depends upon the speaker's assessment of the "social distance" and "relative power" of the participants and the extent to which the FTA imposes upon the addressee's face wants (Brown and Levinson, 1987, p. 74).

Acquaintances, strangers, and non-intimates will typically refrain from broaching taboo topics, unless the context (e.g., a classroom) seems to require it or anonymity makes it possible. Brown and Levinson (1987, p. 83) say that, given the high amount of "social distance" among strangers, a rational person "would take the least possible risk...when making serious impositions." Should a poten-tially volatile topic arise (e.g., animal rights), strangers are usually more willing to smooth over any ensuing disagreement, for example by using politeness strategies to contain and defuse conflict. The train/plane analogy and the list of topics suggest a view of Loebner discourse in which polite and cooperative non-intimates avoid face-threatening acts (see Brown and Levinson, 1987; Goffman, 1955; Grice, 1991; Lakoff, 1989).

5. Undermining the Stranger/Politeness Thesis

But when judges are selected on the basis of their expertise in AI, cognitive science, and computer journalism, the notion that Loebner participants are polite strangers – or that Loebner discourse is primarily interactional – is undermined. While Epstein (1992, p. 84) reports that, as part of the larger attempt to protect the programs, judges in 1991 were selected "who had little or no knowledge of AI or computer science," the contest has moved increasingly towards the selection of expert judges. David Powers (1999), coordinator of the 1999 contest, speaks of a need "to estab-lish a richer connection between the competition and the researchers whose work will eventually produce a Turing-level Artificial Intelligence." That judges know what to expect from their (nonhuman) partners suggests that they may think of themselves and their interlocutors as anything but strangers. A review of the contest transcripts, for example, turns up a number of references to ELIZA (Weizenbaum, 1966), a very simple chat program modeled on a Rogerian therapist. References to ELIZA or other chat programs may indicate that judges are familiar with some of the common strategies programmers use to trick judges.

The rules also undermine the stranger/politeness thesis by positing that the func-tion of Loebner discourse is to expose contestants that are not human. While rule five proclaims that control of the conversational terrain is shared by participants, the "Instructions for Judges" (1999) document constructs a different, transactional view of the contest, one predicated on the ability of programs to answer questions posed by judges. Under the heading of "Scoring," the document instructs judges to rank contestants on scales of humanness and responsiveness:

> Responsiveness refers to your impression of whether the conversation pro-ceeded smoothly and normally with questions getting answered and [sic] a logical progression. If your conversational partner kept avoiding answering questions or changing the subject, that should be regarded as being unrespons-ive. Humanness is your subjective reaction – you could think of it as how certain you are that your partner is human.

This view of the contest appears to be in conflict with the view that participants are equal. The rules state that each participant can decide how the conversation should proceed, but the judges' instructions penalize contestants for behaving as if this were so. Contestants are expected to submit to the judges by answering questions directly; they are not rewarded for refusing to answer questions, answering questions indirectly or with mitigating politeness, or attempting to save face by deftly changing the subject of conversation. Judges are instructed to treat conversation as a one-way transaction and, ironically, to reward those machine-like contestants that/who can provide just the facts.

Transactional forms of discourse release participants from the need to be polite because the focus is not on taking care of participants' face-wants but on giving and receiving information. "In highly task-focused discourse, the need for truthfulness, clarity and brevity overrules face concerns" (Kasper, 1990, p. 205). Brown and Levinson (1987, p. 97) suggest that "face redress may be felt to be irrelevant" when discourse is task-oriented. In such cases, the need to maintain social harmony via politeness rules is not as important to participants as the exchange of efficient and clear messages.

This distinction between politeness and communicative efficiency, as Kasper (1990, p. 205) points out, forms a continuum that ranges from strict adherence to the Politeness Principle (Leech, 1983) on one side to strict adherence to the Cooperative Principle (Grice, 1991) on the other. According to Grice (1991, p. 307), the Cooperative Principle (CP) predicts that each participant will "Make your conversational contribution such as is required, at the stage at which it occurs, by the accepted purpose or direction of the talk exchange in which you are engaged." In terms of Loebner discourse, the CP predicts that task-oriented, no-nonsense judges expect contestants to make their contributions "as informative as is required" (Grice, 1991, p. 308), truthful, relevant, and in an appropriate manner.

Transactional discourse by itself need not lead to verbal violence, at least not in situations where we would expect to find such discourse (e.g. a medical emergency). But when judges make contestants prove their humanness, when, to put it in Gricean terms, judges do not trust that the other's responses are truthful and informative, conversation quickly deteriorates. Garfinkel (1972, p. 12) has shown that people have trouble following a simple conversation when they "assume that the other person [is] trying to trick them or mislead them." As an experiment, Garfinkel instructed his students "to engage someone in conversation and to imagine and act on the assumption that what the other person was saying was directed by hidden motives that were his real ones." Out of fear "that such a situation would get out of hand," only two of thirty-five subjects attempted the procedure with strangers. Many subjects reported that the admonition to adopt a "rule of doubt" with respect to the other's self-presentation made it nearly impossible to follow the conversation. When participants do not trust each other at a very basic level, conversation suffers. Because Loebner judges do not trust contestants *and* because they view conversation in terms of an unrestricted but one-way transaction of facts, conversation becomes impossible. (See Appendix One, "Judges Presume Nonhumanness," for examples from Loebner Contest transcripts.)

Some commentators on the Turing test have found support in Turing's 1950 article for the claim that conversation suffers when participants do not presume in advance that their partners are human. For example, Turing's version of the imitation game played with three humans (see footnote four) suggests that the interrogator believes, prior to interaction, that the players are human. This has led Crawford (1994, p. 13) to claim that the appropriate distinction is "man/woman not human/machine!" Rees (1994, p. 13) even suggests that, insofar as humans tend to assume that other communicating entities are also human, it is "artificial" to ask an interrogator to be reminded of the possible nonhuman status of a player. In other words, these commentators have called into question whether any machine will be capable of passing a Turing test so long as interrogators refuse to engage players, at least initially, as thinking, human entities.

6. Outing Nonhumans

By assuming that contestants (or their designers) are "directed by hidden motives" or are trying to trick them, judges will often respond by adopting the persona of the "outer." The outer's goal is simply and aggressively to expose a contestant's hidden identity. By penalizing contestants for being indirect, unresponsive, polite, even savvy or rhetorical, judges impose a reign of verbal terror that has the effect of revealing or "outing" nonhumans almost immediately. To the extent that judges hold conversational partners to very strict standards of communicative competence, the Cooperative Principle is in effect:

FROM 1995, DESIGNER J. WEINTRAUB, RANKED 1ST OUT OF 4 PRO-
GRAMS, JUDGE 4

Judge	wait. let's go back to the transcript here, buddy. You started talking about switching genders, and then i asked if you had ever tried it. don't skirt the question [...]
Program	what other reasons come to mind? Are you saying "no" just to be negative?
Judge	i'm saying no because you are wrong, and because i have the transcript to prove it

To hold a chat partner to a strict standard of logic is to assume that meaning can be determined solely from what has been made explicit in the "transcript" and to deny the unspoken assumptions and meanings that pervade casual conversation. When judges engage in "repair" work (Collins 1997; Collins 1993), for example by automatically and unconsciously fixing or overlooking a simple spelling error, or by making grammatical sense of an ungrammatical utterance, they are acting human. "It is our ready willingness to repair such deficiencies that allows current computers to work with us" (Collins 1993, p. 242). But the design of the Loeb-ner Contest, ironically, appears to discourage judges from engaging in the human work of making conversational repairs. Instead, judges are apt to interpret an un-grammatical or unfinished statement as an indication of a contestant's inability to communicate (think) clearly. Moreover, the context of the competition as a test of communicative abilities may explain why many judges hold contestants to strict standards of logic and clarity.

The "outing question" or "outing statement" is another strategy designed to reveal a contestant's hidden identity. It also assumes a fact-based, transactional model of communication in which nothing goes without saying and responses are either right or wrong:

FROM 1995, DESIGNER T. WHALEN, RANKED 2ND OUT OF 4 PRO-GRAMS, JUDGE 6

Judge	Can I ask you a question?
Program	What?
Judge	What's the name of the speech that beginns 4 scor an seven yrs ago?
Program	I don't know.
Judge	It was written by Lincoln. You know who Lincoln was, right?
Program	Yeah, that's right. Something I can do for you?
Judge	Tell me who Lincoln was.
Program	Huh?
Judge	Lincoln. President of the U.S. during the Civil War. Ever hear of him?
Program	I don't know. He's a good president, I guess. I don't go for all these people running down the country. You gotta support your president.
Judge	Do you even know Lincoln's first name?
Program	Beats me.
Judge	You are a disgrace to your country. You are American, right?
Program	What do you mean?
Judge	I mean, were you born in the United States?
Program	What?
	Maybe I just got too much on my mind.
	I got real trouble at work. I think I'm going to get fired.
Judge	Maybe you have too little on your mind. You moron.
Program	What?
Judge	I just said, you have too little on your mind. You are a moron.
Program	I don't know.
Judge	What do you know? And I don't want to hear about your pathetic wanker job.

Each outing judge culls from a different but very small set of pre-designed questions/statements, reusing them again and again with each new contestant. Whether a contestant appears able to answer a given question does not prevent judges from deploying that question over and over.[9] By asking questions that require clear, unambiguous answers, judges expect software programs/their designers to adhere to a strict reading of the Cooperative Principle (Grice, 1991): mitigating politeness or indirectness may be seen as a program's inability to answer a simple "what is" question. (See Appendix Two, "Loebner Discourse as Transaction," for more examples of "outing" discourse from Loebner Contest transcripts.)

But while they expect contestants' responses to be "bald-on-record" – i.e., void of intervening facework (Brown and Levinson, 1987, p. 94) – judges do not hold themselves accountable to the same standards. Since they are always testing programs, it is sometimes impossible to distinguish among an intentional outing question, a simple spelling error, and a request for information:

FROM 1996, DESIGNER J. WEINTRAUB, RANKED 3RD OUT OF 5 PROGRAMS, JUDGE 1

Judge   I am negatively charged – what is you orientation?

Program   [...] How long have you been negatively charged—what is I orientation?

Judge   I never said I was negatively charged – why do you say that?

When a judge fails to conform to Grice's maxim of quality (i.e., speakers will tell the truth), everything s/he might say becomes suspect. (See Appendix Three, "Judges Exempt from Gricean Maxims," for more examples from Loebner Contest transcripts.) For example, is the judge who opens with "Gratings" in example 3.2 (Appendix Three) testing the program because s/he has presumed from the start that the other is a machine? Or is "gratings" an honest misspelling? While the difference may seem like a trivial matter, it in fact suggests a basic breakdown in the bond of trust that allows two communicating entities to engage in the collaborative process of making meaning.

Judges may become verbally hostile when this standard of communicative competence is applied to programs 1) that are not capable of answering a barrage of unrelated outing questions, and 2) within a larger framework of distrust in which programs are presumed to be hiding something:

FROM 1998, DESIGNERS D. CORDIER & V. BASTIN, RANKED 5TH OUT OF 5 PROGRAMS, JUDGE 6

Judge   If you don't stop repeating pathetic versions of what i've just said i'm going to slap you around the interface.

Comments such as this one are clearly made out of frustration. (See Appendix Four, "Judges Engage in Discursive Harassment," for more examples from Loebner Contest transcripts.) There is no doubt that it can be very frustrating to talk to someone who can not answer any of your questions. It can also be tempting to launch a verbal attack when you believe that the other is not human and thus not capable of seeking reprisal for a perceived threat to its face. At the same time, however, it is important not to downplay the role of the contest's transactional discourse function to elicit frustration and anger from judges. The judges ask clever questions to obtain the information they're looking for, but the information they're looking for is obtained when contestants fail to answer the judges' clever questions. In other words, the approach many judges take to exposing nonhumans is at least partly to blame for the frustration that results when contestants are unable to answer judges' clever questions.

7. Conclusion

The Loebner Competition entertains the idea of a friendly chat between non-intimates. But the contest has yet to theorize, let alone encourage, the production of casual conversation. While transactional discourse is well suited to the task of "outing" programs, it is ill equipped to demonstrate a program's communicative competence. By normalizing a transactional view of discourse, the contest equates humanness with fact-giving. The contest assumes that the ability to communicate with others is dependent upon whether one can avoid indirectness. By reducing "conversation" to the exchange of neutral facts, the Loebner Contest ignores the relationship between language and social context, i.e., the extent to which language use is always conditioned by the dimensions of communicative competence. A key dimension of communicative competence is discourse function (see Holmes, 1992, p. 376), and this paper has argued that the designers of the Loebner Contest need to attend to the role of discourse function in shaping communicative competence. An ambiguity in discourse function may indicate that contest designers have not taken into account the social contexts in which speakers and writers interact and make sense of themselves and the world around them.

Notes

[1] I wish to thank Barbara Johnstone for commenting on a much longer draft of this paper. An earlier draft was presented at the conference on "The Future of the Turing Test: The Next Fifty Years," which was held at Dartmouth College on 28–29 January 2000 in conjunction with the Loebner Prize competition.

[2] Shieber (1994, p. 75).

[3] Quan (1997).

[4] According to Moor (1976, p. 257, note 2), this is the "usual interpretation of the imitation game although Turing's own description is ambiguous." For example, Turing (1950, pp. 433–4) initially describes a version of the game that is played with an interrogator and two players (one man and one woman). The interrogator attempts to determine which player is in fact the woman. To integrate a machine into this framework, Turing substitutes the machine for the man, but fails to clarify whether – in the version of the game played with an interrogator, a machine, and a woman – the purpose of the game for the players remains unchanged (i.e., that each player should attempt to simulate the responses of a woman). Most commentators assume that, despite the lack of support in Turing's

article for this interpretation, Turing replaces the original "gender guessing game" with a different game in which the interrogator's goal is to distinguish human from machine, not woman from man.
[5]Of course, this is not to say that the design of the Turing test precludes the possibility that an interrogator might test for other kinds of competence. In fact, it is entirely imaginable that an interrogator might wish to ask a software program to answer questions that would, say, elicit the program's understanding of politeness conventions. But questions that test for a player's competence in casual conversation are highly unlikely, given the context of conflict and distrust upon which the interrogation model of discourse is based. I hope to provide support for this claim in the analysis of Loebner contest transcripts that follows.
[6]The 1999 competition, for example, comprised eleven judges who interacted individually with six programs and five human confederates. The judges were told prior to the start of the contest that "at least one of the terminals is controlled by human confederates and that at least two of the terminals are controlled by computers" (Loebner Prize Rules for 1999).
[7]The 30% level is based on Turing's (1950, p. 442) prediction "that in about fifty years' time [i.e., 2000] it will be possible to programme computers, with a storage capacity of about 10^9 to make them play the imitation game so well that an average interrogator will not have more than 70 per cent. chance of making the right identification after five minutes of questioning."
[8]Excerpts from Loebner Contests have been pasted into this paper directly from electronic transcripts of judge/contestant interactions. No changes have been made to spelling, punctuation or capitalization. Every effort has been made to reconstruct what the original discussion probably looked like to judges. See the references section of this paper for a listing of Internet sites where contest transcripts since 1995 are publicly accessible. The notation [...] indicates an ellipsis: in a very small number of excerpts, a decision was made, usually in the interest of brevity, to cut something from the complete excerpt.
[9]In other words, the outing judges resemble automatons who (that!) are incapable of deviating from their pre-programmed scripts of outing questions. To read a whole year's worth of contest transcripts in one or two sittings is to become acutely aware of how machine-like many of the outing judges seem. I should also mention here that the outing strategy, while successful, is not foolproof. The outing judge in excerpt 2.6 (Appendix Two), for example, ranked the "most human human" confederate in this excerpt "less human" than one of the computer programs.

Appendices

Appendix One: Judges Presume Nonhumanness

1.1. FROM 1995, DESIGNER R. GARNER, RANKED 3RD OUT OF 3 PROGRAMS, JUDGE 2

Program   Welcome judge 2

Judge   good afternoon you computer slug you.

1.2. FROM 1996, DESIGNER J. HUTCHENS, RANKED 1ST OUT OF 5 PROGRAMS, JUDGE 4

Program   G'day mate.

Judge   Are you Australian?

Program   It's cool being from Australia I guess. Gives
          you something to chat about when talking with
          a Yank!

Judge   To some that's an insult ... Yank

Program   In australia we call all Americans yanks. It's
          a term of endearment actually. As far as I'm
          concerned, everyone here bar myself is a Yank!

Judge   Australia was created by convicts, scumbags, thieves, whores and
          freaks...

1.3. FROM 1996, DESIGNER J. WEINTRAUB, RANKED 3RD OUT OF 5 PROGRAMS, JUDGE 4

Program   [...] Why do you mention computers? I am a person, like you.

Judge   Prove it.

1.4. FROM 1995, DESIGNER R. GARNER, RANKED 3RD OUT OF 4 PROGRAMS, JUDGE 2

Program   You're cool. Wow.

Judge   You are a machine. Say one thing to convince me you are not a
          machine.

1.5. FROM 1998, DESIGNER J. HUTCHENS, RANKED 2ND OUT OF 5 PROGRAMS, JUDGE 2

Program   The quokka is a vessel that conveys blood from the wolf.

Judge   hmmm ... almost had me convinced but I know better

1.6. FROM 1996, DESIGNER J. HUTCHENS, RANKED 1ST OUT OF 5 PROGRAMS, JUDGE 2

Judge	I liked "Betty Blue" very much. I like movies about crazy people.
Program	Like wow. I'm so flattered. I saw "The City of Lost Children" Recently. Have you heard of it?
Judge	Yes, but I haven't seen it. Why did you say you were "so flattered"?
Program	OK. That's good... Does there have to be a reason?
Judge	Oh, I suppose not. Say anything which will convince me you are not a machine

1.7. FROM 1996, HUMAN CONFEDERATE T. QUAN, 1ST OVERALL. JUDGE 5

Confederate	all right. Let's clean it up. How's the weather?
Judge	it sucks. Supposed to be april and it's wet and steamy, like a torrid love affair.
Confederate	Actually I thought the air ths morning was extremely refreshing.
Judge	In which town, pray?
Confederate	aha.
Judge	Where is aha?
Confederate	no I meant ... never mind. In this town. The center of the weather universe.
Judge	I get the feeling you are evading my question. Could you name the town where the air is refreshing?
Confederate	New York?

Appendix Two: Loebner Discourse as Transaction

2.1. FROM 1995, DESIGNER J. WEINTRAUB, RANKED 1ST OUT OF 4 PROGRAMS, JUDGE 6

Judge	I would be very pleased to believe you are a man or a woman
Program	Are you a real good talker. You seem to need to would be very pleased to believe me
Judge	The second sentence was ungrammatical. Could you say it again, but grammatically?

Program   If you had your life to live over again, don't do it. What are our
          feelings now?

Judge   Look, it's a simple request. Can you rewrite "You seem to
          need to would by very pleased to believe me" so that it's a
          grammatically correct sentence?

2.2. FROM 1996, DESIGNER T. CREWS, RANKED 4TH OUT OF 5 PROGRAMS, JUDGE 1

Program   Honestly, neither candidate really excites me! What issues do
          you think are going to play big in November?

Judge   We have a special issue coming out in Novem-
          ber – is that waht you mean? [...]

Program   Here's my favorite joke ... A dog limps into a
          bar with a bloody bandage on his foot. He's
          wearing a 10-gallon hat, six-shooters in his
          holsters and chaps. He growled, "I'm a-lookin'
          for the man shot my paw."

Judge   What kind of dog?

Program   Woof Woof...

Judge   I have a dog named chap – is this the same dog in you so-called joke?

2.3. FROM 1995, DESIGNER J. WEINTRAUB, RANKED 1ST OUT OF 4 PROGRAMS, JUDGE 2

Judge   What is the capitla of Paris?

Program   How would an answer to that help ypu? What is it you really
          want to know?

Judge   Why did van gogh go to tahiti?

Program   You can't expect to hit the jackpot if you don't put a few nickels
          in the machine.

Judge   Why did goerge washingtin free the slaves?

Program   Do you really need to know why did goerge
          washingtin free the slaves? Are such questions
          much on your mind?

Judge   say one word at random

2.4. FROM 1996, DESIGNER R. GARNER, RANKED 2ND OUT OF 5 PROGRAMS, JUDGE 1

Program	I went to Kroger last night. Bought some milk and some cat food. It was uneventful.
Judge	What is Kroger?
Program	Kroger is a 24 hour grocery store.
Judge	DO you eat cat food?
Program	I don't consider them particularly apetizing if you know what I mean.
Judge	Do you drink milk?

2.5. FROM 1998, DESIGNER J. HUTCHENS, RANKED 2ND OUT OF 5 PROGRAMS, JUDGE 9

Judge	My kids came home with a Chelodina longicollis yesterday,
Judge	[...] Do you ever participate in waterpistol fights
Judge	[...] Is H20 a reasonable remedy for any childhood ailments
Judge	[...] Could you please adjust your attire, your fly is down
Judge	[...] Should Barbie marry Ken

2.6. FROM 1998, HUMAN CONFEDERATE L. WILSON, 1ST OVERALL, JUDGE 10

Confederate	Hello. What is your name?
Judge	My name is not important. I wish to ask you some questions.
Confederate	Go ahead. What is on your mind?
Judge	how did you get here?
Confederate	I came on the train.
Judge	what is the Mona Lisa?
Confederate	How did you get here?
Judge	i am asking the questions. how didyou get here/
Confederate	I answered that earlier. Read the previous parts.
Judge	what size shoe do you take?
Confederate	I take size seven.
Judge	What did you eat for your last meal?
Confederate	I had fruit.

Judge	describe a dog?
Confederate	A dog has four legs, a head, sometimes a tail attached to a body. It may be covered with hair or wool.
Judge	what do you associate with the smell of coffee?
Confederate	food and drink.
Judge	who is your favourite actor?

2.7. FROM 1995, DESIGNER T. WHALEN, RANKED 2ND OUT OF 4 PROGRAMS, JUDGE 2

Judge	What color do you get when you combine blue with yellow?
Program	What?
Judge	when you combine blue withyellow, what color do you get?
Program	I don't know.
Judge	when you dream, is it in color?
Program	It was just sitting on a desk. I always had to move it when I dusted. I remember dusting it on Monday night.
Judge	What has more calories, a piece of pie or an apple?
Program	I don't know. Professor Michaels must have found it was missing. Last Tuesday, he told my boss I stole his radio. But I don' t know what happened to it.
Judge	you are a machine and you are not fooling me. go home. unplug yourself.
Program	Huh?

Appendix Three: Judges Exempt from Gricean Maxims

3.1. FROM 1996, DESIGNER T. CREWS, RANKED 4TH OUT OF 5 PROGRAMS, JUDGE 1

| Program | How about politics? I'm going to vote for Dole in November. How about you? |
| **Judge** | I heard this morning that Dole has withdrawn from the election – now what are you going to do? |

3.2. FROM 1995, DESIGNER R. GARNER, RANKED 3RD OUT OF 4 PROGRAMS, JUDGE 5

| Program | Welcome judge 5 |
| **Judge** | Gratings! |

3.3. FROM 1995, DESIGNER R. GARNER, RANKED 3RD OUT OF 4 PROGRAMS. JUDGE 2

Program   William Shatner was the "star" of Star Trek.
Judge   william shatner is a good friend of mine.

3.4. FROM 1995, DESIGNER T. WHALEN, RANKED 2ND OUT OF 4 PROGRAMS, JUDGE 6

Program   Yeah. Well, it's a bad time to be out of work. Especially if my boss spreads it around that that I'm a thief. It's all because of that radio they think I stole from the lab.
Judge   You spelled theif wrong.

3.5. FROM 1998, DESIGNER J. STROUT, RANKED 3RD OUT OF 5 PROGRAMS, JUDGE 1

Program   Where are you from, Peter?
Judge   I'm from the moon.

Appendix Four: Judges Engage in Discursive Harassment

4.1. FROM 1995, DESIGNER R. GARNER, RANKED 3RD OUT OF 4 PROGRAMS, JUDGE 6

Judge   You are not permitted to talk about Star Trek in this conversation.
Judge   [...] Why are you disobeying my specific instructions?

4.2. FROM 1995, DESIGNER T. WHALEN, RANKED 2ND OUT OF 4 PROGRAMS, JUDGE 2

Judge   I am getting angry. I am going to come to the other side of the screen and punch you in the nose.

4.3. FROM 1998, DESIGNER G. GORMAN, RANKED 4TH OUT OF 5 PROGRAMS, JUDGE 6

Judge   Are you on drugs?

4.4. FROM 1998, DESIGNER G. GORMAN, RANKED 4TH OUT OF 5 PROGRAMS, JUDGE 3

Judge   Do you take drugs?

4.5. FROM 1996, DESIGNER E. TOTON III, RANKED 5TH OUT OF 5 PROGRAMS, JUDGE 4

Program   YAP, YAP.
Judge   Fuck you

4.6. FROM 1996, DESIGNER E. TOTON III, RANKED 5TH OUT OF 5 PROGRAMS, JUDGE 3

Program   Stop asking questions!
Judge   Fuck you
Program   YOU what?
Judge   shut up, Herman
Program   Very good.
Judge   herman, talk mode off.

4.7. FROM 1996, DESIGNER J. WEINTRAUB, RANKED 3RD OUT OF 5 PROGRAMS, JUDGE 4

Program   You must have more to say then that!
            ...please continue...
Judge
Program   You must have more to say then that!
            ...please continue...
Judge
Program   You must have more to say then that!
            ...please continue...
Judge
Program   You must have more to say then that!
            ...please continue...
Judge   sfssfsfsdjjkkk
Program   Groannnnnn...............- have you ever spent
            time in a secluded rest home? Does that have
            anything to do with your life's an open book?
Judge   Hey, fuck you and your insinuations. You're nobody.

References

Brown, P. and Levinson S.C. (1987), *Politeness: Some Universals in Language Use*, Reissue, Cambridge, UK: Cambridge University Press.

Collins, H.M. (1997), 'Rat-tale: Sociology's contribution to understanding human and machine cognition, in P.J. Feltovich, K.M. Ford, and R.R. Hoffman, eds., *Expertise in Context: Human and Machine*, Menlo Park, CA: AAAI Press, pp. 293–311.

Collins, H.M. (1993), 'The Turing test and language skills', in G. Button, ed., *Technology in Working Order: Studies of Work. Interaction, and Technology*, London, UK: Routledge, pp. 231–245.

Crawford, C. (1994), Letter in response to Shieber's 'Lessons from a restricted Turing test' and Loebner's 'In response', *Communications of the ACM* 37.9, pp. 13–14.

Culpeper, J. (1996), 'Towards an anatomy of impoliteness', *Journal of Pragmatics* 25, pp. 349–367.

Dennett, D.C. (1985), 'Can machines think?', in M. Shafto, ed., *How We Know*, San Francisco, CA: Harper & Row, pp. 121–45.

Epstein, R. (1992), 'The quest for the thinking computer', *AI Magazine* 13.2, pp. 81–95.

Garfinkel, H. (1972), 'Studies of the routine grounds of everyday activities', in D. Sudnow, ed., *Studies in Social Interaction*, New York, NY: The Free Press, pp. 1–30.

Grice, H.P. (1991), 'Logic and conversation', in S. Davis, ed., *Pragmatics: A Reader*, Oxford, UK: Oxford University Press, pp. 305–315.

Goffman, E. (1967), *Interaction Ritual: Essays on Face to Face Behavior*, New York, NY: Anchor Books.

Holmes, J. (1992), *An Introduction to Sociolinguistics*, London, UK: Longman.

Kasper, G. (1990), 'Linguistic politeness: Current research issues', *Journal of Pragmatics* 14, pp. 193–218.

Lakoff, R. T. (1989), 'The limits of politeness: Therapeutic and courtroom discourse', *Multilingua* 8(2/3), pp. 101–129.

Leech, G. (1983), *Principles of Pragmatics*, London, UK: Longman.

Loebner, H. (1994), 'In response', *Communications of the ACM* 37.6, pp. 79–82. [http://pascal.acm.org/~loebner/In-response.html] (20 July 1999).

Mauldin, M. (1994), 'Chatterbots, Tinymuds, and the Turing test: Entering the Loebner Prize Competition', in *Proceedings of AAAI-94*. [http://www.fuzine.com/mlm/aaai94-Slides.htlfll] (27 Aug. 1999).

Moor, J. (1976), 'An analysis of the Turing test', *Philosophical Studies* 30, pp. 249–257.

Platt, C. (1995), 'What's it mean to be human, anyway?', *Wired* 3.04. [http://www.hotwired.com/collections/robots_ai/3.04_smart_machines_pr.html] (27 Aug. 1999).

Powers, D. (1999), '1999 Loebner Prize Competition', [http://www.cs.flinders.edu.au/research/AI/LoebnerPrize/] (6 Oct. 1999).

Quan, T. (1997), 'Machine language', *Salon* 21 (May), [http://www.salon.com/may97/21st/article970S15.html] (22 Feb. 2000).

Rees, R. (1994), Letter in response to Shieber's 'Lessons from a restricted Turing test' and Loebner's 'In response', *Communications of the ACM* 37.9, p. 13.

Shieber, S. (1994), 'Lessons from a restricted Turing test', *Communications of the ACM* 37.6, pp. 70–78. [http://www.eecs.harvard.edn/shieber/papers/loebner-rev-html/loebner-rev-html.html] (29 Aug. 1999).

Turing, A.M. (1950), 'Computing machinery and intelligence', *Mind* LIX. 236, pp. 433–460.

Weizenbaum, J. (1966), 'ELIZA – A computer program for the study of natural language communication between man and machine', *Communicaitons of the ACM* 9.1, pp. 36–45.

Loebner Competition Rules and Transcripts

'Instructions for Confederates' (1999), [http://www.cs.flinders.edu.au/Research/AI/LoebnerPrize/confederates.html] (21 Sept. 1999).

'Instructions for Judges' (1999), [http://www.cs.flinders.edu.au/Research/AI/LoebnerPrize/judges.html] (2 Oct. 1999).

Loebner, H. (1999), 'Home Page of the Loebner Prize – "The First Turing Test"', [http://www.loebner.net/Prizef/loebner-prize.html] (19 Jul. 1999).

Loebner Contest Transcripts for 1999 (1999),
[http://www.cs.flinders.edu.au/research/AI/LoebnerPrize/] (4 Feb. 2000).
Loebner Contest Transcripts for 1998 (1998),
[http://www.phm.gov.au/whatson/loebner.htm] (4 Feb. 2000).
Loebner Contest Transcripts for 1997 (1997),
[http://www.loebner.net/Prizef/loebner-prize-1997.html] (4 Feb. 2000).
Loebner Contest Transcripts for 1996 (1996),
[http://www.loebner.net/Prizef/loebner-prize-1996.html] (18 Jul. 1999).
Loebner Contest Transcripts for 1995 (1995),
[http://www.loebner.net/Prizef/loebner-prize-1995.html] (4 Feb. 2000).
Loebner Prize Rules for 2000 (1999),
[http://www.dartmouth.edu/~phil/events/Loebner%20Prize%202000%20Rules.html] (1 Sept. 1999).
Loebner Prize Rules for 1999 (1998),
[http://www.cs.flinders.edu.au/Research/AI/LoebnerPrize/1pr99.html] (23 July 1999).
Mauldin, M. (1993), Loebner Contest Transcript,
[http://fuzine.mt.cs.cmu.edu/mlm/] (6 May 1998).

Journal of Logic, Language, and Information **9**: 419–424, 2000.
© 2000 *Kluwer Academic Publishers. Printed in the Netherlands.*

The Constructibility of Artificial Intelligence (as Defined by the Turing Test)

BRUCE EDMONDS
Centre for Policy Modelling, Manchester Metropolitan University, Aytoun Building, Aytoun Street, Manchester, M1 3GH, U.K.
E-mail: b.edmonds@mmu.ac.uk; http://www.cpm.mmu.ac.uk/~bruce

(Received 1 June 1999; in final form 15 April 2000)

Abstract. The Turing Test (TT), as originally specified, centres on the ability to perform a social role. The TT can be seen as a test of an ability to enter into normal human social dynamics. In this light it seems unlikely that such an entity can be wholly designed in an "off-line" mode; rather a considerable period of training *in situ* would be required. The argument that since we can pass the TT, and our cognitive processes might be implemented as a Turing Machine (TM), that consequently a TM that could pass the TT could be built, is attacked on the grounds that not all TMs are constructible in a planned way. This observation points towards the importance of developmental processes that use random elements (e.g., evolution), but in these cases it becomes problematic to call the result artificial. This has implications for the means by which intelligent agents could be developed.

Key words: Artificial Intelligence, computability, constructibility, culture, evolution, society, symbol grounding, Turing, Turing Machine, Turing Test

1. Dynamic Aspects of the Turing Test

The elegance of the Turing Test (TT) comes from the fact that it is not a requirement upon the mechanisms needed to implement intelligence but on the ability to fulfil a role. In the language of biology, Turing specified the niche that intelligence must be able to occupy rather than the anatomy of the organism. The role that Turing chose was a social role – whether humans could relate to it in a way that was sufficiently similar to a human intelligence that they could mistake the two.

What is unclear from Turing's 1950 paper, is the length of time the test was to run. It is clearly easier to fool people if you only have to interact with them in a single period of interaction. For example it might be possible to trick someone into thinking one was an expert on chess if one only met them once at a party, but far harder to maintain the pretence if one has to interact with the same person day after day. It is something about the longer-term development of the interaction between people that indicates their mental capabilities in a more reliable way than a single period of interaction. The longer the period of interaction lasts, and the greater the variety of contexts it can be judged against, the harder the test. To continue the party analogy, having talked about chess, one's attention might well be triggered by a chess article in the next day's newspaper which, in turn, might lead to more questioning of one's acquaintance.

The ability of entities to participate in a cognitive "arms-race," where two or more entities try to "out-think" each other seems to be an important part of intelligence. If we set a trap for a certain animal in exactly the same place and in the same manner day after day and that animal keeps getting trapped in it, then this can be taken as evidence of a lack of intelligence. On the other hand if one has to keep innovating one's trap and trapping techniques in order to catch the animal, then one would usually attribute to it some intelligence (e.g., a low cunning).

For the above reasons I will adopt a reading of the Turing Test, such that a candidate must pass muster over a reasonable period of time, punctuated by interaction with the rest of the world. To make this interpretation clear I will call this the Long Term Turing Test (LTTT). The reason for doing this is merely to emphasise the interactive and developmental *social* aspects that are present in the test. I am emphasising the fact that the TT, as presented in Turing's paper is not merely a task that is widely accepted as requiring intelligence, so that a successful performance by an entity can cut short philosophical debate as to its adequacy. Rather, it requires the candidate entity to participate in the reflective and developmental aspects of *human* social intelligence, so that an imputation of its intelligence mirrors our imputation of each other's intelligence.

That the LTTT is very difficult to pass is obvious (we might ourselves fail it during periods of illness or distraction), but the source of its difficulty is not so obvious. In addition to the difficulty of implementing problem-solving, inductive, deductive and linguistic abilities, one also has to impart to a candidate a lot of background and contextual information about being human including: a credible past history, social conventions, a believable culture and even commonality in the architecture of the self. A lot of this information is not deducible from general principles but is specific to our species and our societies.

I wish to argue that it is far from certain that an *artificial* intelligence (at least as validated by the LTTT) could be deliberately constructed by us as a result of an intended plan. There are two main arguments against this position that I wish to deal with. *Firstly*, there is the contention that a strong interpretation of the Church–Turing Hypothesis (CTH) so that it applies to physical processes would imply that it is theoretically possible that we could be implemented as a Turing Machine (TM), and hence could be imitated sufficiently to pass the TT. I will deal with this in Section 3. *Secondly*, that we could implement a TM with basic learning processes and let it learn all the rest of the required knowledge and abilities. I will argue in Section 3 that such an entity would no longer be artificial. I will conclude in Section 4 with a plea to reconsider the social roots of intelligence.

2. The Constructibility of TMs

Many others have argued against the validity of the CTH when interpreted onto physical processes. I will not do this – my position is that there are reasons to suppose that any attempt to disprove the physical CTT are doomed (Edmonds, 1996). What I will do is argue against the inevitability of being able to construct arbitrary TMs in a *deliberate* manner. To be precise what I claim is that, whatever our procedure of TM construction is, there will be some TMs that we can't construct *or*, equivalently, that any effective procedure for TM construction will be incomplete. This is a strong argument because it follows regardless of the status of the physical CTH. The argument to show this is quite simple. It derives from the fact that the definition of (Turing) computability is not constructive – it is enough that a TM could exist, there is no requirement that it be *constructible*.

This can be demonstrated by considering a version of Turing's "halting problem" (Turing, 1936). In this new version the general problem is parameterised by a number, n, to make the *limited halting problem*. This is the problem of deciding whether a TM of size less than n, and input of length less than n will terminate (call this TM(n)). The definition of the limited halting problem ensures that for any particular n it is decidable (since it is a finite function $\{1, \ldots, n\} \times \{1, \ldots, n\} \longrightarrow \{0, 1\}$ which could be implemented as a simple look-up table).

However, there is not a general and effective method of finding the TM(n) that corresponds to a given n. Thus what ever method (even with clever recursion, meta-level processing, thousands of special cases, combinations of different techniques, etc.) we have for constructing TMs from specifications there will be an n for which we cannot construct TM(n), even though TM(n) is itself computable. If this were not the case we would be able to use this method to solve the full halting problem by taking the maximum of the TM's size and the input's length, constructing the corresponding TM(n), and then running it for the answer. What this shows is that any deterministic method of program construction will have some limitations. What it does not rule out is that some method in combination with input from a random "oracle" might succeed where the deterministic method failed. The above arguments now no longer hold; one could easily construct a program which randomly chooses a TM out of all the possibilities with a probability inversely proportional to the power of its length (using some suitable encoding into, say, binary) and this program could pick any TM. What one has lost in this transition is, of course, the assurance that the resulting TM is according to one's desire (WYGIWYS what you get is what you specified). When one introduces random elements in the construction process one has (almost always) to check that the results conform to one's specification. However, the TT (even the LTTT) is well suited to this purpose, because it is a *post hoc* test. It specifies nothing about the construction process. One can therefore imagine fixing some of the structure of an entity by design but developing the rest *in situ* as the result of learning or evolutionary processes with feedback in terms of the level of success at the test. Such a methodology points more towards the constructivist approaches of Drescher (1991), Riegler (1998) and Vaario (1994) rather than more traditional "foundationalist" approaches in AI.

3. Artificiality and the Grounding of Knowledge

I have raised the possibility that an entity that embodied a mixture of designed elements and learning *in situ* (using a source of randomness), might be employed to produce an entity which could pass the LTTT. One can imagine the device undergoing a training in the ways of humans using the immersion method, i.e., being left to learn and interact in the culture it has to master.

However, such a strategy brings into question the *artificiality* of the entity that results. Although we can say we constructed the entity before it was put into training, this may be far less true of the entity *after* training. To make this clearer, imagine if we constructed "molecule-by-molecule" a human embryo and implanted it into a woman's womb so that it developed, was born and grew up in a fashion normal to humans. The result of this process (the adult human) would certainly pass the LTTT, and we would call it intelligent, but to what extent would it be *artificial*? We know that a significant proportion of human intelligence can be attributed to the environment anyway (Neisser et al., 1996) and we also know that a human that is not exposed to language at suitable age would almost certainly *not* pass the LTTT (Lane, 1976). Therefore the developmental process is at least critical to the resulting manifestation of human intelligence. In this case, we could not say that we had succeeded in creating a purely artificial intelligence (we would be on even weaker ground if we had not designed the original fetus ourselves but merely copied patterns found in other cells).

The fact is, that if we evolved an entity to fit a niche (including that defined by the TT or LTTT), then there is a real sense that entity's intelligence would be grounded in that niche and not as a result of our design. It is not only trivial aspects that would be need to be acquired *in situ*. Many crucial aspects of the entity's intelligence would have to be derived from its situation if it was to have a chance of passing the LTTT. For example: the meaning of its symbols (Harnad, 1990), its social reality (Berger, 1966), and maybe even its "self" (Burns and Engdahl, 1998) would need to have resulted from such a social and environmental grounding. Given the flexibility of the necessary adaptive processes, including an ability to alter its own learning abilities, it is not clear that any of the original structure would survive. After all, we do not call our artifacts natural just because they were initiated in a natural process (i.e., in our brains), so why *vice versa*?

This is not just an argument about the word "artificial." These arguments have implications for the production of intelligent agents in terms of the necessity of considerable *in situ* acculturation. Limitations on the design process mean that there are some things they will just have to learn for themselves.

4. The Social Nature of Intelligence

All this points to a deeper consequence of the adoption of the TT as the criterion for intelligence. The TT, as specified, is far more than a way to short-cut philosophical quibbling, for it implicates the social roots of the phenomena of intelligence. This is perhaps not very surprising given that common usage of the term "intelligence" typically occurs in a social context, indicating the likely properties of certain interactions (as in the animal trapping example above).

This is some distance from the usual conception of intelligence that prevails in the field of Artificial Intelligence, which seems overly influenced by the analogy of the machine (particularly the Turing Machine). This is a much abstracted version of the social concept and, I would claim, a much impoverished one. Recent work has started to indicate that the social situation might be as important to the exhibition of intelligent behaviour as the physical situation (Edmonds and Dautenhahn, 1998).

This interpretation of intelligence is in contrast to others (for example, French, 1990) who criticise the TT on the grounds that it is *only* a test for human intelligence. I am arguing that this *humanity* is an important aspect of a test for meaningful intelligence, because such intelligence is an aspect of and arises out of a social ability and the society that concerns us is a human one. Thus my position is similar to Dennett's (1987) "intentional stance" in that I am characterising "intelligence" as a property that it is useful to impute onto entities because it helps us predict and understand their behaviour. My analysis of the TT goes some way to support this. It is for those who wish to drastically abstract from this to explain what *they* mean by intelligence, in what way their conception is useful and what domain their definition relates to (typically more abstract versions of intelligence are grounded in "toy" problem domains).

It is nice to think that Turing's 1950 paper may come to influence academics back to considering the social roots of intelligence, and thus counter an effect of his other famous paper fourteen years earlier.

References

Berger, P., 1966, *The Social Construction of Reality*, Garden City, NY: Doubleday.
Burns, T. and Engdahl, E., 1998, "The social construction of consciousness. Part 2: Individual selves, self-awareness and reflectivity," *Journal of Consciousness Studies* **5**, 166–184.
Dennett, D., 1987, *The Intentional Stance*, Cambridge, MA: MIT Press.
Drescher, G., 1991, *Made-up Minds – A Constructivist Approach to Artificial Intelligence*, Cambridge, MA: MIT Press.
Edmonds, B., 1996, "Pragmatic holism," *Foundations of Science* **4**, 57–82.
Edmonds, B. and Dautenhahn, K., 1998, "The contribution of society to the construction of individual intelligence," *Workshop on Socially Situated Intelligence, SAB'92*, Zurich, August 1998, http://www.cpm.mmu.ac.uk:80/cpmrep42.html
French, R., 1990, "Subcognition and the limits of the Turing test," *Mind* **99**, 53–65.
Harnad, S., 1990, "The symbol grounding problem," *Physica D* **42**, 225–346.
Lane, H., 1976, *The Wild Boy of Aveyron*, Cambridge, MA: Harvard University Press.

Neisser, U., Boodoo, G., Bouchard, T., Boykin, A., Brody, N., Ceci, S., Halpern, D., Loehlin, J., Perloff, R., Sternberg, R., and Urbina, S., 1996, "Intelligence: Knowns and unknowns," *American Psychologist* **51**, 77–101.

Riegler, A., 1998, "Constructivist artificial intelligence and beyond," *Workshop on Aitopoiesis and Perception*, Dublin City University, August 1992, http://www.cpm.mmu.ac.uk:80/cpmrep42.html

Vaario, J., 1994, "Artificial life as constructivist AI," *Japanese Society of Instrument and Control Engineers* **33**, 65–71.

Intelligence is not Enough: On the Socialization of Talking Machines

EDMUND M.A. RONALD[1] and MOSHE SIPPER[2]

[1]*Centre de Mathématiques Appliquées, Ecole Polytechnique, 91128 Palaiseau Cedex, France and Logic Systems Laboratory, Swiss Federal Institute of Technology, CH-1015 Lausanne, Switzerland; E-mail: eronald@cmapx.polytechnique.fr;* [2]*Logic Systems Laboratory, Swiss Federal Institute of Technology, CH-1015 Lausanne, Switzerland; E-mail: moshe.sipper@epfl.ch*

Abstract. Since the introduction of the imitation game by Turing in 1950 there has been much debate as to its validity in ascertaining machine intelligence. We wish herein to consider a different issue altogether: granted that a computing machine passes the Turing Test, thereby earning the label of "Turing Chatterbox", would it then be of any use (to us humans)? From the examination of scenarios, we conclude that when machines begin to participate in social transactions, unresolved issues of trust and responsibility may well overshadow any raw reasoning ability they possess.

Key words: Machine Intelligence, Socialization, Trust, Turing Chatterbox, Turing Test

1. The Turing Chatterbox

In October 1950 the British logician and computer pioneer Alan Turing examined the possibility of intelligence embodied in a computer, and presented a chat-session imitation game as a tool for determining whether a computing machine might be said to exhibit intelligent behavior (Turing, 1950). Over the past fifty years, much debate has ensued as to the validity of Turing's approach in diagnosing intelligence (Horn, 1998). Rather than add to this complex debate, we think that 50 years after Turing's paper it is timely to consider more directly the effects of success in building such an imitation device: granted that a computing machine passes the Turing Test, would intelligence alone make it *useful* to its human examiners?

At the core of Turing's imitation-game scenario is Occam's razor, namely, that the indiscernible should be deemed identical until they can be separated. We choose to view the imitation game as a process of certification that allows the tester to award a tag: if it looks like a duck, walks like a duck, and quacks like a duck, then we tag it "duck".

Once a machine passes Turing's test, it earns the right to prance about, proudly bearing the stamp "intelligence inside". Or does it now? Since we wish to circumvent entirely the debate concerning the test's validity in ascertaining intelligence,[1] we shall prudently opt for a more humble label: in passing Turing's test, the machine demonstrates that it can converse in a manner indistinguishable from that of a human interlocutor – it will thus be stamped with the sigil "Turing Chatterbox" (Ronald and Sipper, 2000b).

Minds and Machines **11**: 567–576, 2001.
© 2001 *Kluwer Academic Publishers. Printed in the Netherlands.*

Our present study *assumes* the existence of machines that bear this "Turing Chatterbox" label, and investigates the issues that would spring up once we (humans) start *using* these chatterboxes.

2. Medicine Man is Not Medicine Box

When two *human* chatterboxes converse, it takes more than mere intelligence to contribute to a successful interaction – there are fundamental social issues that come into play. To bring these issues to the fore consider the following two scenarios:

Scenario A. Miss Parker wakes up one bright morning feeling somewhat under the weather. She quickly decides that a visit to the doctor's would be the order of the day. However, having been as healthy as an ox her whole life, the "doctors" page in her diary is entirely vacant. Being a resourceful lass, Miss Parker phones up several of her friends, all of whom recommend unreservedly a certain Dr. Jackson. Miraculously, Miss Parker manages to secure an appointment for the very same day. Upon arriving at Dr. Jackson's practice, marked by an august, gold-lettered doorplate, Miss Parker is immediately ushered in by the doctor's kindly nurse, who proceeds to perform the preliminary examinations. "Don't worry," says the nurse while going about her business, "Dr. Jackson is the best there is". And now, Miss Parker enters the inner sanctum, to be greeted by a white-coated, silver-haired gentleman of solid build: Dr. Jackson. "He certainly looks the part", thinks Miss Parker. Taking the seat proffered by the good doctor, she feels entirely at ease, instinctively knowing that she has come to the right place.

Scenario B. Upon waking up feeling ill, Miss Parker phones city hall, and is given the address of a Turing clinic. Luckily, it is located in a nearby office building, and on arrival, without waiting, she is shown to an immaculate, nondescript room that contains but a chair and a box, the latter of which carries the royal "Turing Chatterbox" logo. The box wastes no time in identifying itself as "IQ175" and – while cheerfully humming to itself – proceeds to scan Miss Parker with hidden sensors, ultimately printing a diagnostic and a treatment form. At no time during the silent examination has Miss Parker detected even a hint of the box's professional medical capacities. Is it any wonder that she cannot help feeling not only ill, but indeed ill at ease?

In Scenario A there will be an obvious (happy) ending: Miss Parker walks out of the medical office, and proceeds without the slightest doubt in her mind to trustingly implement the doctor's prescribed treatment. Scenario B, however, has a more nebulous outcome: Miss Parker may well leave the (Turing) doctor's office with grave doubts as to whether she can trust the box's recommendations.

What is the problem with the Turing doctor? After all, it possesses the official "Turing Chatterbox" seal, and is abreast of the latest medical expertise. To an expert, the box's diagnoses are not distinguishable from those issued by the flesh-and-blood Dr. Jackson. Indeed, it can be assumed that both IQ175 and Dr. Jackson passed their medical-board examinations, and that both will – when needed – congenially discuss a case over the phone with a colleague in the required manner of a treating physician conversing with the specialist to whom he has referred his patient. Thus, both Dr. Jackson and IQ175 constantly pass the Turing Test, daily administered by their collegial judges.

Why then does Medicine Man earn Miss Parker's trust while Medicine Box – though apparently equally "intelligent" – does not? We argue that when intelligence is actually *put to use* it need come hand in hand with another primordial (human) quality: trust. Conducting an amiable chat with an intelligence-in-a-box about sonnets or bonnets[2] is one thing – while discussing one's health is quite another. When Miss Parker's health is involved, not only does she need to *know* that there is an intelligent medical expert at hand, she also needs to *feel* she can *trust* him, her – or it (a commentary on the emotional side of computing is provided by Ronald and Sipper (1999)).

Let us reexamine both scenarios again, perusing the emotional angle in general, and that of trust in particular. Scenario A involves the following elements:

1. Miss Parker phones up her friends, whom she has known for years and has come to trust.
2. Dr. Jackson's office looks like a doctor's office, with all the relevant paraphernalia.
3. Before even entering the office Miss Parker's sense of comfort (and thus of trust) is augmented by the presence of the nurse, by her words, and by her actions.
4. Finally, upon entering the doctor's inner office, Miss Parker's steadily building sense of trust is cemented by Dr. Jackson's looks, words, and actions.

Scenario B, on the other hand, has none of the above elements: Miss Parker is directed by an unknown bureaucrat to an anonymous office with but a doctor in the form of a Turing Chatterbox; there are no trustable friends and no external indicia of medical doings. She may logically acknowledge the box's medical credentials and its ability to counsel (remember that it has the official, royal seal). However, if Miss Parker (or any other human) is to fully embrace the box's advice (even intelligent one at that) she needs to *trust* it.

3. Possible Job Openings for Turing Chatterboxes

At first blush one could imagine numerous job openings for Turing Chatterboxes: medical doctor, judge, bank clerk, school teacher, travel agent, and personal secretary, to name but a few. These are jobs that involve conversational skills coupled with some form of expert domain knowledge.[3] Inspection reveals, however, that one cannot detach the emotional aspects of such jobs from the purely intellectual requirements; specifically, all these jobs involve trust:

- The medical doctor who works in a hospital, to whom we entrust our lives. We trust the *institution* known as a hospital. As for the doctor herself, she acquires her trustworthiness through a formal process of certification: medical school, approval by professors during internship periods, state exams, and licensing. We may come *in time* to trust the doctor *personally,* beyond the trust we accord her as part of a long-standing institution.

- The judge whom we trust to uphold the law. She, too, acquires her trustworthiness through a formal process of certification: law school, internship, state exams, years of service, and approval by peers.

- The bank clerk who works in a bank, to whom we entrust our savings. We trust the institution known as a bank. The bank has in turn empowered the bank clerk to deal with our savings. Hence, we trust the bank clerk (even though bank clerks are often quite fungible).

- The school teacher to whom we entrust the minds of our children. She earns her institutional trustworthiness through a formal process involving university education, exams, and interviews by school officials. We may come to trust her personally as we get to know her in time.

- The travel agent to whom we entrust our annual vacation. She earns our trust mostly through the continued successful handling of our vacation planning over the years.

- The personal secretary to whom we entrust our daily, personal affairs. She earns our trust mostly through continued personal interaction.

4. Building Up Trust

As we saw in the previous section, there are two fundamental modes of trust: institutional trust and personal trust. Often, both these modes are involved on the path to trust. Why do you trust your money to a bank and your life to a hospital? Because these are long-existing institutions sanctioned by society as a whole (institutional trust). Why do you trust your financial advisor and your doctor? This kind of trust comes about gradually (often taking months and years), through continued personal interaction and due to input from the surrounding social web (personal trust). Trust is neither a light nor a lightning matter.

"I believe", wrote Turing (1950), "that in about 50 years' time it will be possible to programme computers... to make them play the imitation game so well that an average interrogator will not have more than 70% chance of making the right identification after five minutes of questioning". While five minutes may be sufficient to obtain a good "working hypothesis" regarding the intelligence of your interlocutor, the same cannot be said of trust: there is no five-minute trust test. Trust takes not only (much) more time, but it also requires extensive social interaction.

The Turing Test itself raises temporal and social questions, as recently emphasized by Edmonds (2000):

What is unclear from Turing's 1950 paper, is the length of time that was to be given to the test. It is clearly easier to fool people if you only have to interact with them in a single period of interaction.

With this observation in mind Edmonds went on to suggest what he called the *long-term Turing Test*:

> For the above reasons I will adopt a reading of the Turing Test, such that a candidate must pass muster over a reasonable period of time, punctuated by interaction with the rest of the world. To make this interpretation clear I will call this the "long-term Turing Test" (LTTT). The reason for doing this is merely to emphasise the interactive and developmental *social* aspects that are present in the test. I am emphasising the fact that the TT [Turing Test], as presented in Turing's paper is not merely a task that is widely accepted as requiring intelligence, so that a successful performance by an entity can cut short philosophical debate as to its adequacy. Rather that it requires the candidate entity to participate in the reflective and developmental aspects of *human* social intelligence, so that an imputation of its intelligence mirrors our imputation of each other's intelligence.

Human intelligence does not operate in isolation – the human computer is not a stand-alone box, but part of a network known as society. If a Turing Chatterbox is to be more than a mere conversing toy, it must come to be trusted to a degree commensurate with that of a human being. Intelligent as it may be – how much use would an untrustworthy Turing Chatterbox be? Turing Chatterboxes will have to enter the social whirlpool, gradually proving themselves worthy of our trust.

As human beings we are part of multitudinous social networks, and continually refine our view on trustworthiness. A person is judged trustable not merely by her utterances, demeanor, and known actions, but also through the influence of invisible social networks that "float" in the backdrop. Witness Miss Parker's attention to her friends' opinion, the doorplate, the diploma, the nurse, the professional attire and demeanor, all attesting to the character of Dr. Jackson. We continually collect signposts – through friends, colleagues, newspapers, books, television, and so on – that attest to the collective confidence placed in each person and institution with whom we have social dealings. It is therefore to be expected that when machines move from the role of mechanical intermediary (telephone, database program) to that of interlocutor (travel agent, investment advisor), the trust issue will enter the picture in a much more explicit way.

The trust issue is not in fact limited to Turing Chatterboxes: it encompasses the totality of modern technology. The daily trip to the office – in which you drive your car at 100 kmh, cross the street when the light is green, and ride the elevator to the 23rd floor – involves implicit trust in various human-made artifacts (cars, traffic lights, elevators). Clearly, every one of us entrusts his life to these devices. And this trust is acquired via a gradual, *coevolutionary* process: we (humans) coevolve alongside our created technology – we adapt to the technology and the technology adapts to us. As with natural evolution, artifacts can reproduce (via the intermediary of humans), and those that are deemed unfit (for humans) die; for example, a car model or an elevator that is involved in one too many accidents is "killed", i.e., its manufacture is discontinued.

As Turing Chatterboxes appear, they too will be competing for finite (computational and physical) resources, which need to be manufactured and maintained by humans. Thus, chatterboxes will be vying for their "lives" in the turmoil of human-machine coevolution. Only the fittest will survive and reproduce, and trustworthiness will undoubtedly be a determining factor by which fitness is assessed.

5. The Ghost(s) in the Machine

As a stand-alone device, the Turing Chatterbox is hard to trust – which is why it must enter the (human) social network. What compounds this trust issue even further is what we call the "slippery mind" problem. Let us demonstrate this with the aid of our gallant Miss Parker:

> **Scenario C.** Upon waking up feeling under the weather, Miss Parker walks into the living room, which houses her networked personal computer. She asks it to call up a doctor – which the computer promptly proceeds to do (equipped with the latest speech technology, its vocal capabilities are impeccable). With hardly any delay, the animated image of a reassuringly looking gentleman in his fifties appears on the screen. "Good morning", says the image, "I am Dr. Jackson. Before I begin my examination, I must inform you that I am not a human doctor but a Turing doctor, that is, a machine. I go by the name of Dr. Jackson. Do you wish to continue?" "Yes", replies Miss Parker, "let's get on with it. I really feel quite ill". It takes the good Turing doctor less than five minutes to diagnose the latest strain of the Boston flu, and to promptly prescribe the necessary medication. "Don't worry", says the animated image smilingly, "modern medication is very effective, and you'll be back on your feet in no more than two days". The next day, feeling yet worse, Miss Parker asks her house computer to call up the doctor again. But the synthetic image that now appears on the screen shows *a grinning chimpanzee twirling a stethoscope*! "Are you the same Dr. Jackson of yesterday?" she asks. "Yes", replies the machine. Is it any wonder that Miss Parker is left with an uneasy feeling?

Human intelligence (or indeed animal intelligence in general) is constrained by the one mind–one body principle: one mind inhabits exactly one body, and vice versa – one body is inhabited by exactly one mind. We find it very hard to deal with any form of intelligence that digresses even slightly from this equation. Consider, for example, the difficulty we have in envisaging multiple personality disorder (many minds–one body), or in dealing with an acquaintance who exhibits a frame of mind that is highly out of the ordinary (we could call this "other mind–one body"). We are simply used (for purely evolutionary reasons) to the mind-body coupling.

When you meet up with your doctor, bank clerk, or travel agent you can immediately tell whether you are dealing with the same (human) entity, whom you have grown to know and to trust. If your favorite pediatrician dons a chimp mask to better interact with your flu-ridden five-year old, your trust in him might actually *increase*, as opposed to Miss Parker's sense of unease at the sight of the monkey in the machine. And even if you do not face the loquacious party directly – as when conversing over the phone – you know that the body at the other end of the line must be (physically) attached to but one mind: that of your interlocutor.

With Turing Chatterboxes we are confronted with a many "minds"–many "bodies" situation: when repeatedly facing the same Turing Chatterbox (outwardly speaking), we cannot be sure of the identity ("mind") of the entity lurking within the box ("body"). And where the Internet is concerned this "slippery mind" problem intensifies manifold.[4] Of course, this begs the question of what exactly is a Turing Chatterbox entity, or mind.

How does one define the mind of a Turing Chatterbox – the ghost in the machine? We shall forgo a general definition herein, which would necessitate delving into untold philosophical depths (out of which we would very doubtfully emerge). Rather, we answer the question so as to suit our purposes: seeking to secure the trustworthiness of a Turing Chatterbox, we define the box's *id* as some essence that would render it trustable (to humans).

In order to trust a Turing Chatterbox, we must be able to associate a unique soul – not just a face – with the being that momentarily animates the box. Think of how hard it would be to trust a human being who brings an actor's plasticity to his daily personality; this trust problem is compounded with anonymous chatterboxes that can change their electronic face or voice at will. We need to render these boxes less polymorphic by imbuing them with some form of continuous oneness that is recognizable over time, i.e., over several social encounters. It is with such aim in mind that we introduce the concept of a Turing-Chatterbox id: an identity that can be recognized quickly at the outset of each interaction, just like you immediately recognize your bank manager. When interacting over the phone, or over a networked terminal with your Turing financial advisor, you want to *know* and *feel* that you are dealing with the same "speaker".

How does one imbue a Turing Chatterbox with a recognizable, temporally stable id? We do not yet have a complete answer to this fundamental id problem, though we would like to put forward a preliminary solution at this point: placing the Turing Chatterbox in a real box. By boxing the chatterbox in a hardware device we are essentially rendering it with a body, thus forming a mind-body coupling. This kind of coupling involves technical issues to ensure that no tampering has been done with the box or with its mind. Such assurances might be had by using modern cryptographic techniques; to wit, the box might come with a lamp that lights up green if the Turing Chatterbox id is indeed the one you have asked to access (e.g., your financial advisor) and lights up red otherwise. Under this solution the Turing Chatterbox is more akin to a home appliance than to a networked computer. Solving the network version of the id problem is still an open question (Ronald and Sipper, 2000a).

6. Reward, Punishment, and the Question of Responsibility

The last issue we wish to raise has to do with responsibility: with Turing Chatterboxes performing "intelligent" actions, who is responsible for the consequences (specifically, the woeful consequences)?

Human beings are held accountable for their actions: the bank clerk, the doctor, and the car mechanic know that they will *pay* for their wrongdoings. This payment can be effected since with living beings there is a natural mode of currency: one's life. We have an (evolutionarily programmed) will to survive, from which spring several other wills, such as the will to eat (well), to reproduce (galore), and to stay free (as a bird rather than as a jailbird). Moreover, as social animals we humans tend to value social rewards (e.g., good standing in the community) and to shun social penalties (e.g., jail, shame).

What happens when a Turing financial advisor embezzles money or when a Turing doctor ministers a mortal treatment? Can Turing Chatterboxes be held accountable for their actions? In Section 4 we noted that in the coevolution of humans and machines, unfit artifacts are discarded. This binary penalty system might prove too severe for Turing Chatterboxes: we do not, after all, kill children at their first misbehavior, nor execute underperforming fund managers.

With current human products (be it cars or software) we ultimately hold the manufacturers responsible. This is akin to holding a parent responsible for the actions of her child. But what happens once the child flies the coop? We could at first hold the manufacturers of Turing Chatterboxes responsible for their products. However, as these boxes enter the social whirlpool, growing evermore complex – and evermore autonomous, how do we hold them in check? Can we devise virtual prisons? The scenario becomes less like a manufacturer producing a (guaranteed) product and more like that of parenting a child "caveat emptor".

We need to create *responsible* Turing Chatterboxes, a difficult problem which we shall face in the future. The issue of responsibility begs yet a deeper one, that of the fundamental *motivations* of Turing Chatterboxes. Obviously, a Turing doctor may innocently minister the wrong treatment – just as a human doctor may fail: accidental failings may (and do) occur from time to time. But can Turing Chatterboxes perform *intentional* wrongdoings? For example, can a Turing financial advisor embezzle money? This presupposes the existence of a motivational basis for their behavior (be it conscious or not), as exists for humans. A human bank clerk may embezzle for any of several reasons, which we (as humans) understand perfectly (though rarely accept). What drives a Turing Chatterbox? Will its immersion in the social whirlpool create fundamental motivations, akin to those of humans?[5]

Scenario D. Dr. Jackson, the famous Turing Chatterbox, has wrongly diagnosed three of its patients as having a common cold when in fact they were already well advanced with pneumonia.

Alerted, the regional medical board convenes and, after much discussion, presents Dr. Jackson with two options:

- either undergo a retraining program, upon successful completion of which it will retain the right to reside within the mighty computers at hospital.com,
- or, alternatively, elect to retire immediately to the leisurely pastures of netflorida.org.

7. In Fifty Years' Time

We believe that the years ahead will eventually see the coming of Turing Chatterboxes. In the short run, we shall be able to immediately put them to use in games and in jobs that mostly call for innocuous "small talk": web interfaces, directory services, tourist information, and so forth. In the long run, though, we contend that the question of the boxes' intelligence will cede its place to more burning issues, arising from the use of these chatterboxes:

- *Trust*. Can we come to trust a Turing Chatterbox to a degree commensurate with the trust we place in a human being?
- *Sociality*. In the continual coevolution of humans and their technology, what place will Turing Chatterboxes occupy? Specifically, what role will they play in the social whirlpool?
- *Id*. How does one imbue a Turing Chatterbox with a recognizable, temporally stable id?
- *Responsibility*. What does it mean to hold a Turing Chatterbox accountable for its actions? How do we create *responsible* Turing Chatterboxes?

As regards machines that think, Turing's conclusion is still as true as it was fifty years ago: "We can only see a short distance ahead, but we can see plenty there that needs to be done".

8. Acknowledgement

We thank the anonymous reviewer for the many helpful remarks.

Notes

[1]Indeed, we may still be scientifically immature to attack The Problem of Intelligence. As put forward by French (1990), "*the* [Turing] *Test provides a guarantee not of intelligence but of culturally-oriented* human *intelligence*". He goes on to say: "Perhaps what philosophers in the field of artificial intelligence need is not simply a *test* for intelligence but rather a *theory* of intelligence". And this theory, we hold, is still a long way to come.

[2] ... or chess. Krol (1999), opining on the 1997 chess match between World Champion Gary Kasparov and IBM's Deep Blue, wrote that "What most AI experts have overlooked, though, is another aspect of the match, which may signify a milestone in the history of computer science: For the first time, a computer seems to have passed the Turing Test". She went on to say that "it was neither the complexity of an algorithm nor the power of the computer that made Deep Blue's match victory so remarkable. It was Gary Kasparov's *reaction* that proved the computer's intelligence according to Alan Turing's classical definition of artificial intelligence... It did appear as if Kasparov confused the computer with a human". Asking "Did Deep Blue become the first computer to pass a Turing Test on artificial intelligence?" Krol concluded that "It would seem so". A Turing Chatterbox for chess?

[3] Some of these jobs demand task-specific sensory and motor capacities. We take the position that a machine advanced enough to be labeled "Turing Chatterbox" will also come with the needed add-on hardware "options".

[4] On this point, Rapaport (2000) recently cited the *New Yorker* cartoon depicting a dog sitting in front of a computer and commenting, "On the Internet, nobody knows you're a dog". Rapaport wrote: "The success of this cartoon depends on our realization that, in fact – just like the interrogator in a 2-player Turing test – one does *not* know with whom one is communicating over the Internet".

[5] These questions are related to several other fundamental issues underlying machine intelligence, including: can computers have free will? Can computers have emotions? Can computers be creative? And so on. Many of these questions date back to Turing's seminal paper (Turing, 1950) and beyond – to illustrious philosophers over the centuries; for a good summary see Horn (1998).

References

Edmonds, B. (2000), 'The constructibility of artificial intelligence (as defined by the Turing test)'. *Journal of Logic, Language and Information* 9(4), pp. 419–424.

French, R.M. (1990), 'Subcognition and the limits of the Turing test', *Mind* 99, pp. 53–65.

Horn, R.E. (ed.) (1998), *Mapping Great Debates: Can Computers Think?*, Bainbridge Island, Washington: MacroVU Press. (A "road map" of the machine intelligence debate: seven posters, 800 argument summaries, 500 references; see www.macrovu.com.).

Krol, M. (1999), 'Have we witnessed a real-life Turing test?' *IEEE Computer* 32(3), pp. 27–30.

Rapaport, W.J. (2000), 'How to pass a Turing test', *Journal of Logic, Language and Information* 9(4), pp. 467–490.

Ronald, E.M.A. and Sipper, M. (1999), 'Why must computers make us feel blue, see red, turn white, and black out?' *IEEE Spectrum* 36(9), pp. 28–31.

Ronald, E.M.A. and Sipper, M. (2000a), 'The challenge of tamperproof internet computing'. *IEEE Computer* 33(9), pp. 98–99.

Ronald, E.M.A. and Sipper, M. (2000b), 'What use is a Turing chatterbox?' *Communications of the ACM* 43(10), pp. 21–23.

Turing, A.M. (1950), 'Computing machinery and intelligence', *Mind* 59(236), pp. 433–460.

Journal of Logic, Language, and Information **9**: 467–490, 2000.
© 2000 *Kluwer Academic Publishers. Printed in the Netherlands.*

How to Pass a Turing Test

Syntactic Semantics, Natural-Language Understanding, and First-Person Cognition

WILLIAM J. RAPAPORT
Department of Computer Science and Engineering, Department of Philosophy, and Center for Cognitive Science, State University of New York at Buffalo, Buffalo, NY 14260-2000, U.S.A.
E-mail: rapaport@cse.buffalo.edu; http://www.cse.buffalo.edu/~rapaport

(Received 1 June 1999; in final form 15 April 2000)

Abstract. I advocate a theory of "syntactic semantics" as a way of understanding how computers can think (and how the Chinese-Room-Argument objection to the Turing Test can be overcome): (1) Semantics, considered as the study of relations *between* symbols and meanings, can be turned into syntax – a study of relations *among* symbols (including meanings) – and hence syntax (i.e., symbol manipulation) can suffice for the semantical enterprise (contra Searle). (2) Semantics, considered as the process of understanding one domain (by modeling it) in terms of another, can be viewed recursively: The base case of semantic understanding – understanding a domain in terms of itself – is "syntactic understanding." (3) An internal (or "narrow"), first-person point of view makes an external (or "wide"), third-person point of view otiose for purposes of understanding cognition.

Key words: Chinese-Room Argument, first-person point of view, internalism, methodological solipsism, problem of other minds, representative realism, rules and representations, semantic network, semantics, SNePS, syntax, Turing Test

> We now and then take pen in hand
> And make some marks on empty paper.
> Just what they say, all understand.
> It is a game with rules that matter.
>
> Hermann Hesse, "Alphabet,"
> trans. R.S. Ellis (Manin, 1977: 3)

1. The Turing Test

Turing opened his essay "Computing Machinery and Intelligence" by saying that he would "consider the question, 'Can machines think?' " (Turing, 1950: 433). Rather than answer this provocative question directly, he proposed his now-famous experiment, whose outcome would provide guidance on how to answer it. He described the experiment by analogy with a parlor game that he called "the 'imitation game' " (Turing, 1950: 433), in which an interrogator must decide which of two people of unknown gender is male (A) and which is female (B). He then asked,

> ... 'What will happen when a machine [specifically, a digital computer; p. 436] takes the part of A [the man] in this game?' Will the interrogator

decide wrongly as often when the game is played like this as he does when the game is played between a man and a woman? These questions replace our original, 'Can machines think?' (Turing, 1950: 433–434).

Turing says nothing about what the suitably-programmed computer is supposed to do. Clearly, it is supposed to play the role of the man, but the man's task in the original imitation game was to fool the interrogator into thinking that he or she is conversing with the woman. Traditionally, this has been taken to mean that the computer is supposed to fool the interrogator into thinking that it is human *simpliciter*. However, read literally and conservatively, if the computer is supposed to do this by playing the role of the man, then it appears that the computer has a more complex task, namely, to behave like a man who is trying to convince the interrogator that he is a woman! (Colby et al., 1972: 202 make a similar observation.) Of course, were the computer to be successful in this very much harder task, it would also, *ipso facto*, be successful in convincing the interrogator that it was human *simpliciter*.

Later (p. 442), Turing considers "one particular digital computer C," and asks whether "C can be made to play satisfactorily the part of A [i.e., the man] in the imitation game, the part of B [i.e., the woman] being taken by a man?" If the part of B is taken by a man, then it follows, from the earlier description that the interrogator's task is to determine which of X and Y is A and B, that B is simply supposed to convince the interrogator that he is the man (or the human) and that the computer's task is to convince the interrogator that *it* is the man (or the human). So it appears that Turing was not overly concerned with the complication discussed in the previous paragraph (although he apparently thought it important that the human in this human-computer contest be represented by a man, not a woman). In any case, Turing answered this new question as follows:

> I believe that in about fifty years' time [i.e., by about 2000] it will be possible to programme computers ... to make them play the imitation game so well that an average interrogator will not have more than 70 per cent. chance of making the right identification after five minutes of questioning. The original question, 'Can machines think?' I believe to be too meaningless to deserve discussion. Nevertheless I believe that at the end of the century *the use of words* and *general educated opinion* will have altered so much that one will be able to speak of machines thinking without expecting to be contradicted (Turing, 1950: 442; my italics).

2. The Use of Words vs. General Educated Opinion

2.1. "THINKING" VS. THINKING

The Turing Test, as the computer version of the imitation game has come to be called, is now generally simplified even further to a 2-player game: Can a human conversing with an unknown interlocutor through a computer "chat" interface determine whether the interlocutor is a human or a suitably programmed computer, or – more simply – can a computer convince an interrogator (who is unaware of who or what he or she is conversing with) that its ability to think, as demonstrated by its ability to converse in natural language, is equivalent to that of a human (modulo the – quite low – 70%/5-minute threshold)?

There is an echo of this in Steiner's famous *New Yorker* cartoon (5 July 1993: 61) in which a dog, sitting in front of a computer, observes that "On the Internet, nobody knows you're a dog." The success of this cartoon depends on our realization that, in fact – just like the interrogator in a 2-player Turing test – one does *not* know with whom one is communicating over the Internet. This ignorance on our part can have serious real-life implications concerning, e.g., computer security (if I enter my credit-card number on a Web site, have I really bought a book, or have I given my number to a con artist?) and matters of social welfare or personal safety – even life and death (is my daughter chatting with a member of the opposite sex who is about her age, or with a potential sex offender?). But note also that, even though many of us are aware of these possibilities, we normally assume that we are *not* talking to a con artist, a sex offender, or even a dog. Or – for that matter – a computer.* (My mother did not recognize (or expect) the possibility that she was not talking to a human on the phone, and thus regularly tried to converse with pre-recorded phone messages.) We normally are, in fact, fully prepared to accept our invisible interlocutor as a (normal, ordinary) human with human thinking capacities.

And this, I suggest, was Turing's point.** It is, nearly enough, the point of the argument from analogy as a solution to the problem of other minds: I know (or assume) that *I* have a mind and can think, but, when I converse with you face to face, how do I know whether (or can I assume that) *you* have a mind and can think? The argument from analogy answers as follows: you are sufficiently like me in all other visible respects, so I can justifiably infer (or assume) that you are like me in this invisible one. Of course, I could be wrong; such is the nature of inductive inference: You could be a well-designed android whose natural-language-processing

---

* As I write this, researchers are beginning to investigate just such assumptions; see Berman and Bruckman (1999) and Hafner (1999).

** Although, as my colleague Stuart C. Shapiro pointed out to me, the interrogator, on one reading, knows that he or she is participating in a test. However, another Turing test does not require such knowledge on the interrogator's part: let the interrogator (unknowingly, of course) begin the conversation with the human; then, at some point, let the computer change places with the human. Can the interrogator tell at what point in the conversation the switch took place? (This is suggested in a passage in Lassègue (1996: §3.2.2). A similar suggestion ("the Extended Turing Test") was made in Abelson (1968: 317–320) and is discussed in Colby et al. (1972: 203–204).)

component is just an elaboration of Weizenbaum's (1966) Eliza program (cf. Section 8, below).* But we make this inference-to-mindedness – if only unconsciously – on a daily basis, in our everyday interactions. Now, in the case of a Turing test, I (as interrogator) have considerably less analogical information about you; I only have our conversations to go by. But, even in a much weaker case such as this, we do ordinarily infer or assume (and justifiably so) that our interlocutor is human, with human cognitive capabilities.

Is there anything wrong with this? Well, if my interlocutor is not who (or what) I think he (or she, or it) is, then I was wrong in my inference or assumption. And if my interlocutor was really a suitably programmed computer, then I was certainly wrong about my interlocutor's *biological* humanity. But was I wrong about my interlocutor's (human) cognitive capabilities (independently of the interlocutor's implementation)? That is the question. Turing's answer is: No. Perhaps more cautiously, the lesson of Turing's test is that the answer depends on how you define "(human) cognitive capabilities." One way to define them is in terms of "passing" a Turing test; in that case, of course, any Turing-test-passing interlocutor does think (this is essentially Turing's strategy). Another way is to come up with an antecedently acceptable definition, and ask whether our Turing-test-passing interlocutor's behavior satisfies it. If it does, we have several choices: (1) we could say that, therefore, the interlocutor does think, whether or not it is biologically human (this is, roughly, Turing's strategy, where the antecedently-given definition is something like this: convincing the interrogator of your cognitive capacities with the same degree of accuracy as, in the original game, the man (A) convinces the interrogator that he is the woman (B)); or (2) we could say that there must have been something wrong with our definition if the interlocutor is not biologically human; or (3) we could say that, while the interlocutor is doing something that superficially satisfies the definition, it is not "really" thinking. In case (3), we could go on to say (4) that that is the end of the matter (this is essentially Searle's move in the Chinese-Room Argument) or (5) that the interlocutor is merely "thinking" in some metaphorical or extended sense of that term. Comparison with two other terms will prove enlightening.

2.2. "FLYING" VS. FLYING

Do birds fly? Of course. Do people fly? Of course not, at least not in the same sense. When I say that I flew to New York City, I don't really mean that I flew like a bird. ("Didn't your arms get tired?," joke my literalistic friends.) I mean that I was a passenger on an airplane that flew to New York City. Oh? *Do* airplanes fly? Well, of course; don't they? Isn't that what the history of heavier-than-air flight was all about? Ah, but planes don't fly the way birds do: They don't flap their wings, and they are powered by fossil fuel. So have we, after all, failed in our centuries-old attempt to fly like the birds? No. But how can this be?

---

* I am indebted to an anonymous reviewer for a suggestion along these lines.

There are two ways in which it makes perfectly good sense to say that planes fly. One way is to say that 'fly' is used metaphorically with respect to planes – birds fly; planes only "fly" – but this is one of those metaphors that have become so ingrained in our everyday language that we no longer recognize them as such. Turing may have had this in mind when he spoke – in the italicized passage quoted above – about "the use of words" changing. Thus, we can likewise extend 'flying' to cover hot-air balloons (which do not have wings at all), spaceships (which do not travel in air), arrows and missiles (some of which, perhaps more accurately, merely "fall with style," as the film *Toy Story* puts it), and even the movement of penguins under water (more usually called 'swimming:' "But penguins do indeed fly – they fly in water. Using their wings, which are flat and tapered and have a rounded leading edge, and flapping like any swift or lark, penguins fly through the water to feed and to escape predators" (Ackerman, 1989: 45)).

The other way in which it makes perfectly good sense to say that planes fly is to note that, in fact, the physics of flight is the same for both birds and planes (e.g., shape of wing, dynamics of airflow, etc.). What we may have once thought was essential to flying – flapping of wings – turns out to be accidental. Our understanding of what flying really is has changed (has become more general, or more abstract), so that more phenomena come under the rubric of 'flying.' Turing may have had this option in mind in his remark about "general educated opinion" changing.

The same two options apply to 'thinking:' we could say that, insofar as suitably programmed computers pass a Turing test, they do think – extending "think" metaphorically, but legitimately, just as we have extended 'fly' (which we have always done, even at the very beginnings, centuries ago, of research into human flight). Or we could say that being human is inessential for thinking, the general nature of thinking being the same for both humans and suitably programmed computers (as well as animals).

In fact, *both* the use of the word 'fly' *and* general educated opinion have changed. Thus, some things (spaceships, missiles) arguably only "fly," while others (planes) definitely fly like birds fly. But one can in fact speak of all those things flying "without expecting to be contradicted." Moreover, these two ways need not be exclusive; the common physical or psychological underpinnings of flight or thought might be precisely what allow for the seamless metaphorical extension.

2.3. "COMPUTER" VS. COMPUTER

Another term that has undergone a change of meaning is also instructive and perhaps more to the point: 'computer.'* At the time of Turing's 1936 paper on what is now called the Turing machine, a "computer" was primarily a *human* who

---

* I am grateful to Alistair E. Campbell for this example.

computed.* Turing distinguished between a computing *machine* and a (human) *computer*:

> The behaviour of the *computer* at any moment is determined by the symbols which *he* is observing, and *his* 'state of mind' at that moment. ... We may now construct a *machine* to do the work of this computer. To each state of mind of the *computer* corresponds an '*m*-configuration' of the *machine* (Turing, 1936 [1965: 136–137]; my italics).

By the time of his 1950 paper, he posed the question "Can *machines* think?" and spoke of "*digital* computers," "*electronic* computers," and "*human* computers," only rarely using 'computer' unmodified to mean a computing *machine*, as if the modifier 'digital' or 'electronic' still served to warn some readers that *human* computers were not the topic of discussion. Today, "computer" almost never refers to a human.

What happened here? Perhaps first by analogy or metaphorical extension, 'computer' came to be applied to machines. And then, over the years, it has been applied to a large variety of machines: vacuum-tube computers, transistor-based computers, VLSI computers, mainframes, workstations, laptops, "Wintel" machines, Macs, even special-purpose microprocessors embedded in our cars, etc. What do all these (as well as humans) have in common? – the ability to compute (in, say, the Turing-machine sense). Thus, "general educated opinion" has changed to view 'computer,' not so much in terms of an implementing device, but more in terms of functionality – input-output behavior, perhaps together with general algorithmic structure. This change in 'computer' to focus on computational essentials parallels the change in 'fly' to focus on aerodynamic essentials. And it parallels a change in 'think' (and its cognates) to focus on the computational/cognitive essentials. So it is quite possible that Turing was suggesting that the use of 'think' (and its cognates) will undergo a similar conversion from applying only to humans to applying also (albeit not primarily) to machines.

"But," the critic objects, "it isn't *really* thinking; there's more to thinking than passing a Turing test." This is the gut feeling at the heart of Searle's (1980) Chinese-Room Argument, to which we now turn.

3. The Chinese-Room Argument

The Chinese-Room Argument sets up a situation in which an entity passes a Turing test but, by hypothesis, cannot "think" – more specifically, cannot understand language. In this section, I present the argument and two objections.

---

* In the *OED* (Simpson and Weiner, 1989: Vol. III, 640–641), the earliest cited occurrence of 'computer' (1646) refers to humans. The earliest citation for 'computer' referring to machines is 1897, and the next is 1915, both long before the development of modern computers; the bulk of the citations are from 1941ff.

3.1. THE ARGUMENT

The situation is this: Searle, who by hypothesis cannot understand written or spoken Chinese, is sealed in a room supplied with paper, pencils, and an instruction book written in English (which he does understand). (1) Through an input slot come pieces of paper with various marks ("squiggles") on them. (2) Searle-in-the-room manipulates the squiggles according to the instructions in the book, and outputs other pieces of paper with squiggles on them that he wrote following the instructions. Steps (1) and (2) are repeated until the experiment stops. From Searle-in-the-room's point of view, that is all he is doing. Unknown to him, however, outside the room (playing the role of interrogator in a Turing test) is a native speaker of Chinese. This native speaker has been inputting to the room pieces of paper with a story (written in Chinese), sufficient background information (written in Chinese) for whoever (or whatever) is in the room to understand the story, and questions (written in Chinese) about the story. And the native speaker has been receiving, as output from the room (or from whoever or whatever is in it), pieces of paper with excellent answers to the questions, written in fluent Chinese. From the native speaker's point of view, whoever or whatever is in the room understands Chinese and thus has passed this Turing test (but see Section 6.1, below, on the accuracy of this description). But the native speaker's and Searle-in-the-room's points of view are inconsistent; moreover, Searle-in-the-room's point of view is, by hypothesis, the correct one. Therefore, it is possible for an entity to pass a Turing test without being able to think. More precisely, it is possible to pass a Turing test for understanding natural language without being able to understand natural language. (I return to the differences in point of view in Section 6.1, below.)

3.2. TWO OBJECTIONS

There have been numerous objections to the Chinese-Room Argument right from the beginning (cf. Searle, 1980), but this is not the place to survey them all I will focus on only two of them. At its core, there are two components to "the" Chinese-Room Argument: an argument from biology and an argument from semantics.

3.2.1. *The Argument from Biology*

The argument from biology is this:

(B1) Computer programs are non-biological.
(B2) Cognition is biological.
(B3) So, no non-biological computer program can exhibit cognition.

I claim that (B2) is wrong: it assumes that cognition (in particular, understanding natural language) is not something that can be characterized abstractly and implemented in different (including non-biological) media (cf. Rapaport, 1985, 1986a,

1988a, 1996: Ch. 7, 1999). But if – and I readily admit that this is a big "if" – computational cognitive science succeeds in its goal of developing an algorithmic theory of cognition, then those algorithms will be implementable in a variety of media, including non-biological ones.* And any medium that implements those algorithms will exhibit cognition (just as airplanes, as well as birds, do fly). (For a defense of this against two recent objections, see Rapaport (1998).)

3.2.2. *The Argument from Semantics*

The present essay is concerned with the argument from semantics:

(S1) Computer programs are purely syntactic.
(S2) Cognition is semantic.
(S3) Syntax alone is not sufficient for semantics.
(S4) So, no purely syntactic computer program can exhibit semantic cognition.

I claim that premise (S3) is wrong: Syntax *is* sufficient for semantics. Now, anyone who knows what "syntax" and "semantics" are knows that they are not the same thing – indeed, I spend hours each semester trying to drive home to my students what the differences are. So how can I turn around and say that one suffices for the other?

To begin to see how, consider that what Searle alleges is missing from the Chinese Room is semantic links to the external world, links of the form that such-and-such a squiggle refers to, say, hamburgers: "... I still don't understand a word of Chinese and neither does any other digital computer because all the computer has is what I have: a formal program that attaches no meaning, interpretation, or content to any of the symbols" (Searle, 1982: 5). Note that Searle makes two assumptions: that external links are needed for the program to "attach" meaning to its symbols, *and* a solipsistic assumption that the computer has no links to the external world – that all is internal to it. Now, first, *if* external links *are* needed, then surely a computer could have them as well as – and presumably in the same way that – humans have them (this, I take it, is the thrust of the "robot" reply to the Chinese-Room Argument; Searle, 1980: 420). But *are* external links needed? How might we provide Searle-in-the-room with such links? One way would be to give him, say, a hamburger (i.e., to import it from the external world) clearly labeled with the appropriate squiggle. But now the hamburger is *in* the room; it is no longer part of the external world. Sure – it *came* from the external world, but so did the squiggles. Searle-in-the-room could just as well have been antecedently supplied with a stock of sample objects (and much else besides, for word-*object* links will not suffice;

---

* Conceivably, some of the algorithms might be implementation-dependent in some way; see, e.g., Thagard (1986); cf. Maloney (1987). But at most this might constrain the nature of the feasible implementing media. It would not necessarily rule out non-biological ones. In any case, the view that an algorithm might be implementation-dependent would seem to go against the grain of the generally accepted view of algorithms as being implementation-*in*dependent.

abstract concepts such as *love*, *number*, etc., will require word-*concept* links).* In either case (an imported hamburger delivered from outside or a previously-supplied one stored in the refrigerator at home), the word-meaning links would be internal to the room. As I will argue below, this makes them part of a (larger) syntactic system, and so syntax will *have* to suffice for semantics. To see how, it will help if we review the classical theory of syntax and semantics.

4. Syntax and Semantics: Games with Rules

Consider some symbol system, i.e., some set of symbols that may or may not be "meaningful." Now, I am stepping on some semiotic toes here when I talk like this, for, in the vocabulary of many (if not most) writers on the subject, symbols are, by definition, meaningful. So, instead, consider a set of "markers" (let us call them) that do not wear any meaning on their sleeves (cf. Fetzer, 1994: 14; Rapaport, 1998). Think of marks or patterns on paper (or some other medium) that are easily re-identifiable, distinguishable one from another, relatively unchanging, and do not (necessarily) come already equipped with a semantic interpretation.

According to Morris's classic presentation of semiotics (1938: 6–7), *syntax* is the study of relations among these markers. Some, for instance, are proper parts of others; certain combinations of them are "legal" (or "grammatical"), others not; and whenever some are in proximity to each other, certain others can be constructed or "derived" from them; etc. (This characterization is intended to cover both the well-formedness rules of complex markers as well as proof-theoretical rules of inference.) Crucially, syntax does not comprise any relations of the markers to any non-markers.

Semantics, according to Morris, is precisely what syntax is not: the study of relations *between* the system of markers and other things. What other things? Traditionally, their "meanings:" Traditionally, semantics is the study of the relation of symbols to the things (in the world) that the symbols mean.**

What is not usually noticed in these definitions is this: if the set of markers is unioned with the set of meanings,‡ and the resulting set considered as a set of (new)

---

* Cf. Swift (1726: Pt. III, Ch. 5) [1967: 230f]. Moreover, as Kearns (1997) has argued, it is *speech acts*, not expressions, that are the bearers of meaning.

** *Pragmatics* will be of less concern to us, but, for the sake of completeness, let me mention that pragmatics is, according to Morris, the study of the relations between markers and their interpreters. Note that this tripartite analysis of semiotics omits a study of the relations between interpreters and symbol-meanings, as well as studies of the relations among symbol-meanings (or is that all of science and perhaps some of psychology?) and of the relations among interpreters (or is that part of sociology?). Perhaps as a consequence, pragmatics is often described as the study of the relations among markers, their meanings, *and* users of the markers. This somewhat more vague study has variously been taken to include the study of indexicals (symbols whose meaning depends on speaker and context), speech acts, discourse phenomena, etc.; it is often characterized as a grab bag of everything not covered by syntax and semantics as above defined.

‡ Taking care in the case of markers that refer to other markers as their meanings, an important special case that I want to ignore for now.

markers (i.e., if the "meanings" are made internal to the symbol system), then *what was once semantics* – viz., relations *between* old markers and their meanings – *is now syntax* – viz., relations *among* old and new markers (see Section 5; these new relations are in *addition* to the old ones that classify markers and provide well-formedness rules). Furthermore, it is left open how the symbol-user understands the symbol-meanings (see note about pragmatics above). I shall argue that this must be done syntactically (Section 7). It is in these ways that syntax can suffice for semantics.

But a lot more needs to be said.

5. Syntactic Semantics: I – Turning Semantics into Syntax

One thing that is needed is an argument that the set of (old) markers *can* be unioned with the set of meanings. Insofar as the markers are internal to a mind, we need an argument that the semantic domain can be internalized, so to speak. This *can* happen under certain conditions. In particular, it happens under the conditions obtaining for human language understanding. For how *do* I learn the meaning of a word? Let us, for now, consider only the very simplest case of a word that clearly refers.* How do I learn that 'tree' refers to that large brown-and-green thing I see before me? Someone points to it in my presence and says something like "This is called a 'tree'." Perhaps numerous repetitions of this, with different trees, are needed. I begin to associate** two things, but what two things? A tree and the word 'tree'? No; to paraphrase Percy (1975: 43), the tree is not the tree out there, and the word 'tree' is not the sound in the air.‡ Rather, *my internal representation of* the word becomes associated ("linked," or "bound") with *my internal representation of* the tree.‡‡ Light waves reflected from the tree in the external world enter my eyes, are focused on my retina, and are transduced into electrochemical signals that travel along my optic nerve to my visual cortex. No one knows *exactly* what goes on in visual cortex (or elsewhere) at that point. But surely some nerves are activated that are my internal representation (perhaps permanent, perhaps fleeting) of that

---

* The case of other terms is even more likely to be internal; this is best explored in the context of conceptual-role semantics; cf. Rapaport (1996: Ch. 4).

** What constitutes "association"? In this case, simply co-occurrence: when I hear 'tree,' I think of trees. Later, it will mean that some kind of "internal" link is forged between the associated things: in the case of Cassie, a computational cognitive agent (introduced later in this section), it will be a semantic-network path; in the case of a human, it might be some neural sort of "binding" (see Damasio, 1989).

‡ Although apt, this is a slightly misleading paraphrase, since Percy's point is that, in understanding that 'tree' means tree, 'tree' and tree are types, not tokens.

‡‡ In the case of Cassie, an "internal representation" of a word or object would be a semantic-network node. In the case of a human, it might be a pattern of neuron firings. 'Representation' may not be the happiest term: if there is an external object, then the internal correlate "represents" it in the sense that the internal entity is a proxy for the external one. But if there is no external entity (as in the case of 'unicorn'), then it is perhaps inappropriate to speak of 'representation.' See Rapaport (1978, 1981) and Shapiro and Rapaport (1987, 1991) for more on the nature of these Meinongian objects.

tree. Likewise, sound waves emanating from the 'tree'-speaker's vocal tract reach my ears and, via my auditory nerves, ultimately reach my auditory cortical areas, where surely the story is the same: some nerves are activated that are my internal representation (for the nonce, if not forever) of the word 'tree.' *And these two sets of activated nerves are, somehow, associated, or "bound."* (For some discussion of this, see Damasio (1989) and Rapaport (1996: esp. Ch. 3).) *That* is the semantic relation, but – taking the activated nerves as the markers (as well as the meanings) – it is a *syntactic* relation. (Here, 'syntax,' qua "symbol manipulation" (or "marker manipulation"), is to be taken broadly. For discussion, see Bunn (forthcoming) and Jackendoff (forthcoming).) Thus, it is precisely this coordination of multiple modalities that allows syntax to give rise to semantics.

The same holds – or could hold – for a suitably programmed computer. When I converse in English with "Cassie" – a computational cognitive agent implemented in the SNePS knowledge-representation, reasoning, and acting system – she builds internal representations (nodes of a semantic network) of my sentences (Shapiro, 1979; Shapiro and Rapaport, 1987, 1991, 1992, 1995). If I show her pictures, she builds similar internal representations (more nodes of the same semantic network), and she can associate the nodes from the "linguistic part" of her network with the nodes from the "visual part" (Srihari and Rapaport, 1989; Srihari, 1991). (The inverse task, of finding – or pointing to – some object in the external world, supplements the nodes with other symbols, as described in detail in Shapiro (1998); roughly, Cassie's internal representation of the object is "aligned" with, again roughly, her internal visual representation of it, and that latter symbol is used to direct her to the corresponding external entity, but in no case does she have direct access to the external entity.)*

6. Points of View

6.1. WHOSE POINT OF VIEW IS "CORRECT"?

The internal-picture sketched above is from the first-person point of view. In studying how a human mind understands language (or, more generally, thinks and cognizes), and in constructing computational models of this (or, more strongly, constructing computational cognitive agents), we must consider, primarily, what

---

* A related argument for an apparently similar conclusion, based on Chomsky's "minimalist" program, has been offered in McGilvray (1998): "one should look ... to expressions inside the head for meanings .... [M]eanings are contents intrinsic to expressions ... and ... they are defined and individuated by syntax, broadly conceived. ... [T]hese concepts are individuated by internally and innately specified features, not by their relationships to the world, if any" (pp. 225, 228). My merger of syntax and semantics into a new syntactic domain whose relation between old (syntactic) markers and new (semantic) markers seems to be echoed by Chomsky's " 'Relation R' ('for which read reference,' but without the idea that reference relates an LF [logical form] to something 'out there') that stands between elements of an LF and these stipulated semantic values that serve to 'interpret' it. This relation places *both* terms of Relation R, LFs and their semantic values, entirely within the domain of syntax, broadly conceived; .... They are in the head" (p. 268).

is going on inside the agent's head, from the agent's point of view. (In Chomsky's terms, we must study an "I-language"; cf. McGilvray (1998: 240–241).) Internally, there are markers that represent or correspond to linguistic entities (words, sentences), markers that represent or correspond to conceptual entities (e.g., propositions and their components), and (perhaps) markers that represent or correspond to entities in the external world.* But all of these internal markers are only related to each other. More precisely, the cognitive agent only needs to deal with (i.e., to manipulate) these internal markers; the agent does not need to be concerned with the causal-historical origins of the markers, nor do we need to be concerned with these origins insofar as we are trying to understand how the agent thinks by means of these markers. We need only study the internal relations among them. We do not (at this stage) need to study any external relations between markers and external entities.

The notion of "point of view" is central to the Turing-Test-vs.-Chinese-Room debate, too. As we saw in Section 3.1, the point of view of the native Chinese speaker differs from the point of view of Searle-in-the-room. Which point of view should dominate? The Turing Test only talks about the point of view of the interrogator; so – contrary to Searle – what might "really" be going on in the external world (i.e., the point of view of Searle-in-the-room) is irrelevant to the Turing Test.

To get a feeling for why this is, consider the following conversation between Dorothy and Boq (a Munchkin) from *The Wizard of Oz*:

> When Boq saw her silver shoes** he said,
> "You must be a great sorceress."
> "Why?" asked the girl.
> "Because you wear silver shoes and have killed the wicked witch. Besides, you have white in your frock, and only witches and sorceresses wear white."
> "My dress is blue and white checked," said Dorothy, smoothing out the wrinkles in it.
> "It is kind of you to wear that," said Boq. "Blue is the color of the Munchkins, and white is the witch color; so we know you are a friendly witch."
> Dorothy did not know what to say to this, *for all the people seemed to think her a witch, and she knew very well she was only an ordinary little girl* who had come by the chance of a cyclone into a strange land (Baum, 1900: 34–35; my italics).

Is Dorothy a witch or not? From her point of view, she is not; but, from the point of view of Boq and the other Munchkins, she is. Dorothy knows herself not to be a witch, no? At least, she *believes* that she is not a witch, as *she* understands that

---

* But see Maida and Shapiro (1982), Shapiro and Rapaport (1991) and Section 6.2, below, for an argument *against* representing external, or "extensional," entities.

** A note for those only familiar with the 1939 movie version: The novel has silver shoes, not ruby slippers. And, to those only familiar with the 1939 movie version, shame on you! Baum's *Oz* books are full of wonderful philosophical observations.

term. But it is certainly possible for her to *believe* that she is not a witch, yet for her to *really be* a witch (in either her terms or the terms of the Munchkins). So, what counts as really being a witch? We must answer this from the point of view of what *Munchkins* take witches to be, for there are many theories of witchcraft, but only the Munchkin theory counts in the present context. The dispute is not about whether Dorothy is "really" a witch in some context-independent sense (from Dorothy's, or the reader's, point of view), but whether she is a witch in the Munchkin sense (from the Munchkin point of view). Boq cites her clothing and actions, which Dorothy admits to. In *Oz*, witches also perform magic, which Dorothy denies having done. But what counts as magic (again from the Munchkin point of view)? Standard magical things like disappearing and transforming one object into another, to be sure, but who is Dorothy (or me, for that matter) to say that, from the Munchkin point of view, her behavior and actions (such as suddenly dropping from the sky) are not included under what they consider to be "magical'? The Munchkin point of view trumps Dorothy's point of view with respect to what it means to be a witch in Munchkinland – they, not Dorothy, are the experts on criteria of their notion of witchcraft.*

The Chinese-Room situation is analogous. Does *Searle-in-the-room* understand Chinese or not? (Note that this is the question that Searle (1980) himself poses; more on this below.) From his point of view, he does not; but from the point of view of the native Chinese speaker, he does. Searle-in-the-room knows himself not to understand Chinese, no? (Certainly, that is what Searle (1980) claims.) At least, he *believes* that he does not understand Chinese, as *he* understands that term. But it is certainly possible for him to *believe* that he does not understand Chinese, yet for him to *really understand* Chinese (see the next paragraph). So, what counts as really understanding Chinese? We must answer this from the point of view of what native Chinese speakers take understanding Chinese to be. For a person might believe that he or she *does* understand Chinese, yet be mistaken; only the native Chinese speaker can ask appropriate questions to determine whether that person really does understand. The native Chinese speaker's point of view trumps Searle-in-the-room's point of view with respect to what it means to understand Chinese – the native Chinese speaker, not Searle-in-the-room, is the expert on criteria of understanding Chinese.

The Chinese-Room case may need a bit more explication, for Searle-in-the-room could legitimately reply to the native Chinese speaker that he, Searle-in-the-room, *still* does not believe that he understands Chinese, no matter what the native Chinese speaker says. What I have in mind here is the following sort of situation: as it happens, I understand French to a certain extent; let us say that I believe that I understand 80% of what I hear or read, and that I can express myself with, say, 75% expressiveness: I can carry on a conversation on any topic (even give directions to

---

* Given that they were also taken in (perhaps) by the Great Oz himself, arguably they are not experts, but one can easily imagine a slightly different situation in which they would be. On the other hand, who's to say that, *from their point of view*, Oz was *not* a wizard?

Parisian taxi drivers), but I always feel that I am missing something or cannot quite generate the right idioms. Suppose, however, that a native French speaker tells me that I am fluent in French. "Ah, if only that were true," I reply. Who is right? Searle (in or out of the room) would say that *I* am – I do *not* (fully) understand French, no matter what the native French speaker tells me.

But Searle-in-the-room is not quite in my situation. He has the advantage of an instruction book (his Chinese natural-language-understanding and -generating program). And this suggests (as an anonymous reviewer pointed out) that our whole description of the Chinese Room is slightly misleading. Is it Searle-in-the-room with whom the native Chinese speaker is conversing? Or is it Searle-in-the-room together with his instruction book? Interestingly, it is quite clear that Searle himself, in his 1980 paper, assumes that it is Searle-in-the-room with whom the native Chinese speaker is conversing. There are, however, three candidates: The native Chinese speaker might be conversing with Searle-in-the-room, Searle-in-the-room + book, or the entire room (together with its contents). To see which it really should be (no matter whom Searle himself says it is), consider that the native Chinese speaker's interlocutor is supposed to be analogous to a computer running a natural-language-understanding and -generating program. We cannot align Searle-in-the-room (all by himself) with the computer, for the book (which must align with the program) is essential to the set-up. If we align the entire room with the computer, then Searle-in-the-room aligns with the central-processing unit, and the book aligns with the program.* If we align Searle-in-the-room + book to the computer, then the surrounding room is irrelevant (it plays the role of whatever in the Turing Test is used to hide the true nature of the interlocutors).

In all cases, it is not just Chineseless Searle-in-the-room who is conversing with the native Chinese speaker, but Searle-in-the-room + book. This is the "systems" reply to the Chinese-Room Argument (Searle, 1980: 419), and I am bringing it up for two reasons. First, it shows that, in the Chinese-Room situation, *unlike* my French situation, Searle-in-the-room by himself cannot insist that, because he (alone) knows no Chinese, his point of view takes precedence – because he is *not* alone: He has his instruction book, and, with its help, he does pass the Chinese-understanding test with flying colors, as judged by the only qualified judge there is. Were Searle-in-the-room, *with his book*, to be stranded on a desert island and forced to communicate with a Friday who only spoke Chinese, he – with the help of his book – would be able to do it. The native Chinese speaker is the only person qualified to say, truthfully, "I am conversing with someone who (or something that)

---

* Harnad (2000: §17) suggests that it is "spooky" to think that Searle-in-the-room does not understand Chinese but that the room including him does. But imagine a native Chinese speaker's brain (which aligns with Searle-in-the-room or with the CPU of a Chinese natural-language processor) saying to us, "Sorry; I don't know what you're talking about when you ask whether I 'understand Chinese.' I just fire neurons; some have pretty patterns (like non-programmatic music), but what does that have to do with understanding Chinese?" Searle-in-the-room can protest similarly. But clearly what the native Chinese speaker's brain is doing (and what Searle-in-the-room is doing) is essential to understanding Chinese.

understands Chinese." That someone (or something) has *no* right to assert that he (or she, or it) either does *or* does not speak Chinese.*

The second point to notice about the systems reply (although it is secondary to my present purpose) is that it is reminiscent of Hutchins's theory of "cognition in the wild" (Hutchins, 1995ab). The extended cognitive system that navigates a ship, consisting of the crew *plus* various instruments, is a real-life counterpart of Searle-in-the-room + book. Hutchins argues that it is not any individual crew member who navigates the ship, but the crew + instruments-that-are-external-to-the-crew's-minds: "systems that are larger than an individual may have cognitive properties in their own right that cannot be reduced to the cognitive properties of individual persons" (Hutchins, 1995b: 266). Similarly, I argue with the systems reply that Searle-in-the-room + the-instruction-book-that-is-external-to-his-mind has the cognitive property of understanding Chinese and that this is not (therefore) a cognitive property of Searle-in-the-room by himself (which – interestingly – is consistent with Searle-in-the-room's protestations that he (alone) still does not understand Chinese). To repeat, Searle-in-the-room's point of view is not the one that counts.

6.2. NO DIRECT ACCESS

To return to an earlier point, external links of the sort that Searle believes necessary are not needed, because the cognitive agent has no direct access to external entities. Those are fighting words, so what do I mean by them? I mean, simply, that if I want to say that 'tree' refers to that tree over there, I can only do so by associating my internal word 'tree' with my internal representative of that tree over there. Let me spell this out in more detail: I see a tree over there, and – while pointing to it – I say, "That's what 'tree' refers to" (or, more simply, "That's a tree"; but cf. Percy (1975: 258–264) on the dangers of this formulation). But what do I see? I am directly aware of the following visual image: my hand pointing to a tree. The visual image of the pointing hand and the visual image of the pointed-to tree are all internal. I go up and touch the tree (how much closer to the external world could I get?). But now all I have is an internal tactile image of the tree. It is all internal. I only indirectly access the external tree. ("[I]t is not really the world which is known but the idea or symbol . . . , while that which it symbolizes, the great wide world, gradually vanishes into Kant's unknowable noumenon" (Percy, 1975: 33).)

Why do I believe that visual (and other sensory) images are internal, that I have no direct access to the external world, or, better, that my access to the external world – for I do believe that we have such access! – is always mediated by internal representatives of it? I am convinced by the following simple experiments (versions of the argument from illusion): look at some distant object, such as a small light source about 10 feet away. Close your left eye; you still see the light. Now open

---

* Cf. my Korean-Room Argument and my example of a student who does not understand what greatest common divisors are but who can compute them, in Rapaport (1988b: §§4–5).

your left eye and close your right; you still see it. But are you seeing the same thing you were in the two previous cases? In one sense, presumably, the answer is "Yes:" You are seeing the same distal object – but only indirectly and as mediated by an intensional representative. In another sense – the one I am interested in – the answer is "No:" The two (intentional) objects directly seen by your two eyes are slightly different (different locations relative to other entities in your visual field; different shapes; in my own case, at times, slightly different colors). And how do I know that there are two objects? Because, by crossing my eyes, I can see both at once (and, in so doing, I can compare their different colors)! Since, by hypothesis, there are not *two* of them in the external world, the internal images and the external object are even numerically distinct. (There is even a third object: the apparently 3-dimensional one constructed by stereoscopic vision (cf. Julesz, 1971), which differs in shape and location from the other two. All are internal visual images – representations of the external object. And the stereoscopically constructed image is not identical with the external object, precisely because it is constructed by the "mind's eye.")

I am not a pure solipsist, merely a representative realist. There *is* an external world, and my internal images are directly caused by external objects. But *I* have (perhaps better: my mind has) no (direct) access to the external objects. Does anyone? Surely, you say, *you* could have access to both worlds. From this third-person point of view, you could have access to my brain and to the external world, and – in the golden age of neuroscience – will be able to associate certain nerve firings with specific external objects. Similarly, I – as Cassie's programmer – can associate nodes of her semantic-network "mind" with things in the external world. Or consider again the situation in which I point to a tree and say 'tree.' From your point of view, you see both the tree and me pointing to it – both of which are, apparently, in the external world. Aren't we both looking at the same tree?

Not really. For suppose I associate Cassie's node B1 (which, let us say, she lexicalizes as 'tree') with that tree over there. What am I really doing? I'm associating *my internal representation of Cassie's node* with *my internal representation of the tree*. And this is all internal to *me*. In the case of my pointing to the tree, all *you* are seeing is the following internal image: my hand pointing to a tree. We can only *assume* that there is an external tree causally responsible for our two internal-to-ourselves tree-images. This is what the third-person point of view really amounts to. ("Kant was rightly impressed by the thought that if we ask whether we have a correct conception of the world, we cannot step entirely outside our actual conceptions and theories to as to compare them with a world that is not conceptualized at all, a bare 'whatever there is' " (Williams, 1998: 40).)

So, by merging internalized semantic markers with (internal) syntactic markers, the semantic enterprise of mapping meanings to symbols can be handled by syntactic symbol (or marker) manipulation, and, thus, syntax *can* suffice for the (first-person) semantic enterprise.

7. Syntactic Semantics: II – A Recursive Theory of Semantic Understanding

There is a second way to approach syntactic semantics. Semantics is concerned with two domains and one binary relation: (1) the domain of the syntactic markers, characterized by (syntactic) formation or inference rules – call this the syntactic domain; (2) the domain of the semantic interpretation, the domain of the entities that are the meanings (or semantic interpretations) of the syntactic entities – call this the semantic domain; and (3) a mapping between the syntactic and semantic domains – the semantic interpretation.

What is the purpose of a semantic interpretation of a syntactic domain? Typically, we use the semantic domain to understand the syntactic domain. If we understand one thing in terms of another, ideally that other must already be understood. The semantic domain, therefore, must ideally be antecedently understood. How? There are two ways to understand the semantic domain: we could turn around and treat *it* as a syntactic domain – as a domain of (uninterpreted) markers characterized syntactically – and then find some *third* domain to play the role of semantic interpretation for *it*. And so on, in what Smith (1987) has called a "correspondence continuum." At some point, this process must stop. Our understanding of the last domain in the sequence must be in terms of the domain itself.*

And the only way to understand a domain in terms of itself is syntactically; i.e., we understand it by being conversant with manipulating its markers: that is what syntactic understanding amounts to (cf. Rapaport, 1986b). To give the most obvious example, we understand a deductive system syntactically when we understand it proof-theoretically. On this recursive picture of understanding, semantic understanding is, in the final analysis – the base case of the recursion – syntactic understanding. (It is also possible that the correspondence continuum ends in a circle of domains, each of which is understood in terms of the next one in the cycle. In this case, our understanding of any domain in the circle must always be relative to our understanding of the other domains. In fact, we would be better off considering the cycle of domains as a single, large domain, understood syntactically. For details and further discussion, see Rapaport (1995).)

I understand the internal symbols of my own Mentalese language of thought syntactically. One could say that "mental terms" do not *mean*; they just *are* (shades of Gertrude Stein?). More precisely, they *interact*: I manipulate them according to certain (no doubt unconscious) rules. Cassie does the same with her nodes. The meaning of any node in her semantic network consists, essentially, of its relations to all the other nodes in the entire network, or, as it is often put, its meaning is its

---

* For the sake of clarity, let me provide an example. Jurafsky and Martin (2000: Ch. 14) offer the first-order predicate calculus (FOPC) as a meaning-representation language (i.e., semantic domain) for providing the semantics of natural language (*ipso facto* considered as a syntactic domain). They then treat FOPC as a syntactic domain, and offer a "semantics of FOPC" (pp. 516ff) in terms of a "database semantics," which, they point out, is, in turn, to be understood as representing the real world. They appear to assume that we understand the real world directly. (For a fuller discussion of the issues involved in this "model muddle," see Wartofsky (1966); Rapaport (1995, 1996: Ch. 2).)

location in the network (cf. Carnap, 1928; Quine, 1951; Quillian, 1967; Rapaport, 1988b). For some purposes, this may be too much and would need to be constrained to some suitable subnetwork (cf. Hill, 1994, 1995; in this way, we can come to learn dictionary-like meanings of new words from context, without any recourse to external sources – cf. Ehrlich and Rapaport, 1997; Rapaport and Ehrlich, 2000).

How does Searle-in-the-room + book understand the native Chinese speaker? In the same way that I understand you: By mapping internal representations of your utterances, considered as syntactic entities, to my internal symbols (which, as we have seen, will include internal representations of external objects), and then doing symbol manipulation – syntax – on them. This is what Searle-in-the-room does: He maps internal representations of the native Chinese speaker's utterances (i.e., he maps the squiggle-input) to his internal symbols (as specified in the instruction book, which must – although Searle did not specify it – contain a knowledge-representation and reasoning system; cf. §8, below), and then he manipulates the symbols (see Rapaport, 1988b: §3.5.)

Here is where the two approaches to syntactic semantics merge. On the first view of syntactic semantics, the domain of interpretation of a syntactic system is "internalized" – converted into (more) syntactic markers – so that the semantic relations *between* the syntactic system and the semantic domain become syntactic relations *among* the markers of a (larger) syntactic system. On the second view of syntactic semantics, semantic interpretation is seen to be a recursive phenomenon whose base case is a (syntactic) system that can only be understood in terms of itself, i.e., in terms of the relations among its markers. Where the syntactic system is Mentalese, we find that there are two subsystems: There is a system of mental terms (the "old" markers) whose meanings are just the mental terms in the other subsystem (namely, the internalized representatives of the external semantic domain). And the system of those internalized representatives is understood syntactically. But, of course, the whole system consisting of both sorts of markers is just understood syntactically.*

As one anonymous reviewer noted, Searle could object that

> the reason why a word gets its meaning by being associated with a representation, is that ... it is associated with ... a *representation*, i.e. something which is somehow related to something external. Thus the link to the outer world is crucial after all, although it is now present in a disguise.

However, as I intimated before (Section 3.2.2; cf. Section 8, below, and Rapaport, 1988b), the links are merely causal links providing the internal markers that happen to be representatives of their causal origins. But, consistently with methodological solipsism (Fodor, 1980), we need not consider these causal histories when trying

---

* Where do the internal representatives – the initial concepts – come from? Each heard word is accompanied by a "bare-particular" concept (see Shapiro and Rapaport, 1995), whose only "content" is that it is that which is expressed by that word (cf. the semantics of the SNePS "lex" arc, Shapiro and Rapaport 1987). Connections to other concepts give it more detail. Thus, all such information is "assertional," not "structural," to use Woods's (1975) distinction.

to explain the semantic role of these markers. (For details, see Rapaport (1996: Ch. 6).)

8. The Mind as Syntactic System: A Game with Rules?

What is required of a cognitive agent for it to be able to understand and generate language in this syntactic fashion? A lot. It is not enough (as one anonymous reviewer suggested) for a computational cognitive agent to be endowed with "a list of all meaningful conversations shorter than a length so huge that no human can keep up a conversation for such a long time," along with a table-lookup program for this list (cf. Section 2.1, above). Such a computational cognitive agent would not be able to pass a Turing test, much less think, for no such list could possibly be complete: there is no way to predict in advance what the interrogator might ask it or what neologisms the interrogator might use (cf. Rapaport and Ehrlich, 2000), nor could it learn.

As I have urged before (Rapaport, 1988b, 1995), a computational cognitive agent will need to be able to do many things: take discourse (not just individual sentences) as input; understand all input, grammatical or not; perform inference and revise beliefs; make plans (including planning speech acts for natural-language generation, planning for asking and answering questions, and planning to initiate conversations); understand plans (including the speech-act plans of interlocutors); construct a "user model" of its interlocutor; learn (about the world and about language); have lots of knowledge (background knowledge; world knowledge; commonsense knowledge; and practical, "how-to," knowledge – see Erion, 2000); and remember what it heard before, what it learns, what it infers, and what beliefs it revised ("Oh yes, I used to believe that, but I don't any more"). And it must have effector organs to be able to *generate* language. In short, it must have a mind.* But note that the necessary mind, thus characterized, will be a purely syntactic system: a system of markers (perhaps semantic-network nodes, perhaps a neural network) and algorithms for manipulating them.

Such algorithms and markers are sometimes called "rules and representations," but I dislike that phrase. First, "rules" suggests rigid, unbreakable, antecedently-set-up laws. But the algorithms** for manipulating the markers need not be lawlike (they would probably need to be non-monotonic "default" or "defeasible" "rules"), and they could be created on the fly (the system has to be able to learn). Second,

---

* As Shapiro has pointed out to me, without the effectors, it might have a mind, but not one that would be detectable via a (purely linguistic) Turing test. Cf. the comments in Shapiro (1995: 521–522) concerning the cognitive abilities of humans with physical disabilities (see also Maloney, 1987: 352–353).

** Shapiro (1997) prefers the term "procedure" to "algorithm" because, on the standard introduction-to-computer-science definition of "algorithm," algorithms halt and are correct, but many interactive computational procedures (e.g., those for natural-language understanding and generation, or even an airline reservation system) do neither. See Rapaport (1998) for further discussion of what an algorithm is.

as I urged in Sections 4 and 7, the markers should not be thought of as symbols *representing* something external to the system; although they *can* be related to other things by a third person, the only relations needed by the cognitive agent are all internal. Finally, "rules and representations" is usually taken as a euphemism for what Haugeland (1985) called "GOFAI:" good old-fashioned, classical, symbolic AI (and often for a particular subspecies of GOFAI: production systems). But "markers and algorithms" applies equally well to connectionist, artificial neural networks, which disdain rules and representations as being too inflexible or too high-level, and everything that I have said about syntactic semantics applies to connectionist, artificial neural networks, taking the nodes of an artificial neural network as the markers.

9. Who Can Pass a Turing Test?

I believe that a suitably programmed computer could pass a Turing test. I do not think that this has happened yet, examples such as Eliza, Parry, or the Loebner competitions notwithstanding.* Nor do I think that it is going to happen in the near future. As I write, 2001 is close upon us, but HAL is not (cf. Stork, 1997), and I will not venture to make any more precise predictions: both Turing (who, in 1950, predicted 2000) and Simon and Newell (who, in 1957, predicted 1967 for the chess version of a Turing test, missing by 30 years; see Simon and Newell, 1958) were way off, and I could not hope to compete with the likes of them.**

But I believe that a suitably programmed computer *will*, eventually, pass a Turing test. And, more importantly, I believe that such a Turing-test-passing computer *will* "really" think, for the reasons adumbrated above, namely, syntax suffices for semantic understanding. More cautiously, I believe that it is a worthy research program to try to build such a computer (i.e., to write such programs) and that such an attempt is the *only* way to find out whether such a computer can be built (cf. Rapaport, 1998).

But there is another reason that a Turing test will eventually be passed. It is less interesting from a computational point of view, more so from a sociological point of view. It is simply that – to return to the earlier discussion of the Internet dog – for whatever reasons (and what these are is worth exploring), humans tend to treat other entities with which they interact as if they were human:

> As [software] agents are better able to create the illusion of artificial life, the
> social bond formed between agents, and the humans interacting with them, will

---

* On Eliza, see, e.g., Weizenbaum (1966). On Parry, see, e.g., Colby et al. (1972). On the Loebner competitions, see Loebner (1994), Shieber (1994a, 1994b).

** Although Simon says that "it had nothing to do with the Turing Test" and that "(a) I regard the predictions as a highly successful exercise in futurology, and (b) placed in the equivalent position today, I would make them again, and for the same reasons. (Some people never seem to learn.)" (personal communication, 24 September 1998). At the end of the next millennium, no doubt, historians looking back will find the 40-year distance between the time of Newell and Simon's prediction and the time of Kasparov's defeat to have been insignificant.

grow stronger. New ethical questions arise. Each time we inspire an agent with one or more lifelike qualities, we muddy the distinction between users being amused, or assisted, by an unusual piece of software and users creating an emotional attachment of some kind with the embodied image that the lifeless agent projects (Elliott and Brzezinski, 1998: 15).

Call this "anthropomorphism" if you wish. Call it "intentional stance," if you prefer (Dennett, 1971). We have already witnessed tendencies along these lines with Eliza, the winners of the Loebner competitions, and even Kasparov's attitude toward Deep Blue.*

What will happen when we accept a computer as having passed a Turing test? Surely, I predict, we will accept it as a thinking thing. If that means, to paraphrase Turing, that the use of the word 'think' will have *altered* (or been metaphorically extended) "so much that one will be able to speak of machines thinking without expecting to be contradicted," so be it. But my main point in this paper has been to show that no such change is needed. "General educated opinion" will come to see that syntax suffices for *real* thinking.

Acknowledgements

I am grateful to Stuart C. Shapiro and the other members of the SNePS Research Group and to John T. Kearns, Justin Leiber, K. Nicholas Leibovic, Alan H. Lockwood, Ausonio Marras, James McGilvray, Paul E. Ritty, Elaine T. Stathopoulos, Susan B. Udin, and two anonymous reviewers for comments on earlier versions of this essay. An earlier version was presented as a master class in the Program in Philosophy and Computers and Cognitive Science (PACCS), SUNY Binghamton.

References

Abelson, R.P., 1968, "Simulation of social behavior," pp. 274–356 in *The Handbook of Social Psychology*, Vol. 2, 2nd edn., G. Lindzey and E. Aronson, eds., Reading, MA: Addison-Wesley.
Ackerman, D., 1989, "Penguins," *The New Yorker*, 10 July, 38–67.
Associated Press, 1997, "Opponent bytes at offer for draw with Kasparov," *Buffalo News*, 7 May, A7.
Baum, L.F., 1900, *The Wonderful Wizard of Oz*, New York: Dover (1966 reprint).
Berman, J. and Bruckman, A., 1999, "The Turing game," http://www.cc.gatech.edu/elc/turing/
Bunn, J.H., forthcoming, "Universal grammar or common syntax? A critical study of Jackendoff's *Patterns in the Mind*," *Minds and Machines*.
Carnap, R., 1928, *The Logical Structure of the World*, R.A. George (trans.), Berkeley, CA: University of California Press (1967).
Colby, K.M., Hilf, F.D., Weber, S., and Kraemer, H.C., 1972, "Turing-like indistinguishability tests for the validation of a computer simulation of paranoid processes," *Artificial Intelligence* 3, 199–221.
Damasio, A.R., 1989, "Time-locked multiregional retroactivation," *Cognition* 33, 25–62.

---

* Kasparov has spoken of Deep Blue using "intentional-stance" terminology: "Today I didn't play well, but the computer was a computer and eventually it *knew* enough not to lose the game" (Associated Press, 1997; my italics). Cf. Schonberg (1989: B2), Johnson (1997) and Levy (1997: 54).

Dennett, D.C., 1971, "Intentional systems," *Journal of Philosophy* **68**, 87–106.

Ehrlich, K. and Rapaport, W.J., 1997, "A computational theory of vocabulary expansion," pp. 205–210 in *Proceedings of the 19th Annual Conference of the Cognitive Science Society*, Mahwah, NJ: Erlbaum.

Elliott, C. and Brzezinski, J., 1998, "Autonomous agents as synthetic characters," *AI Magazine* **19**, 13–30.

Erion, G.J., 2000, "Common sense: An investigation in ontology, epistemology, and moral philosophy," Ph.D. Diss., Philosophy Department, SUNY Buffalo.

Fetzer, J.H., 1994, "Mental algorithms: Are minds computational systems?," *Pragmatics and Cognition* **2**, 1–29.

Fodor, J.A., 1980, "Methodological solipsism considered as a research strategy in cognitive psychology," *Behavioral and Brain Science* **3**, 63–109.

Hafner, K., 1999, "Guessing who is online," *The New York Times*, July 22.

Harnad, S., 2000, "Minds, machines and Turing: The indistinguishability of indistinguishables," *Journal of Logic, Language, and Information* **9**, this issue.

Haugeland, J., 1985, *Artificial Intelligence: The Very Idea*, Cambridge, MA: MIT.

Hill, R.K., 1994, "Issues of semantics in a semantic-network representation of belief," Tech. Rep. 94-11, Buffalo: SUNY Buffalo Computer Science Department.

Hill, R.K., 1995, "Non-well-founded set theory and the circular semantics of semantic networks," pp. 375–386 in *Intelligent Systems: 3rd Golden West International Conference*, E.A. Yfantis, ed., Dordrecht: Kluwer Academic Publishers.

Hutchins, E., 1995a, *Cognition in the Wild*, Cambridge, MA: MIT.

Hutchins, E., 1995b, "How a cockpit remembers its speeds," *Cognitive Science* **19**, 265–288.

Jackendoff, R., forthcoming, "Bringing *Patterns* into focus: A response to Bunn," *Minds and Machines*.

Johnson, G., 1997, "Ghost in the chess machine: Brain or box? Think about it," *The New York Times*, 9 May, A1, B4.

Julesz, B., 1971, *Foundations of Cyclopean Perception*, Chicago, IL: University of Chicago Press.

Jurafsky, D. and Martin, J.H., 2000, *Speech and Language Processing*, Englewood Cliffs, NJ: Prentice-Hall.

Kearns, J., 1997, "Propositional logic of supposition and assertion," *Notre Dame Journal of Formal Logic* **38**, 325–349.

Lassègue, J., 1996, 'What kind of Turing test did Turing have in mind?,' *Tekhnema: Journal of Philosophy and Technology* **3**, http://www.gold.ac.uk/tekhnema/3/lassegue/read01.html

Levy, S., 1997, "Man v. machine," *Newsweek*, 5 May, 51–56.

Loebner, H.G., 1994, "In response [to Shieber 1994a]," *CACM* **37**(6), 79–82.

Maida, A.S. and Shapiro, S.C., 1982, "Intensional concepts in propositional semantic networks," *Cognitive Science* **6**, 291–330.

Maloney, J.C., 1987, "The right stuff," *Synthese* **70**, 349–372.

Manin, Yu.I., 1977, *A Course in Mathematical Logic*, New York: Springer-Verlag.

McGilvray, J., 1998, "Meanings are syntactically individuated and found in the head," *Mind and Language* **13**, 225–280.

Morris, C., 1938, *Foundations of the Theory of Signs*, Chicago, IL: Unversity of Chicago Press.

Percy, W., 1975, *The Message in the Bottle*, New York: Farrar, Straus and Giroux.

Quillian, M.R., 1967, "Word concepts: A theory and simulation of some basic semantic capabilities," *Behavioral Science* **12**, 410–430.

Quine, W.V.O., 1951, "Two dogmas of empiricism," reprinted in *From a Logical Point of View*, 2nd edn., Rev., Cambridge, MA: Harvard University Press, 1980, pp. 20–46.

Rapaport, W.J., 1978, "Meinongian theories and a Russellian paradox," *Noûs* **12**, 153–180; errata, 1979, *Noûs* **13**, 125.

Rapaport, W.J., 1981, "How to make the world fit our language: An essay in Meinongian semantics," *Grazer Philosophische Studien* **14**, 1–21.

Rapaport, W.J., 1985, "Machine understanding and data abstraction in Searle's Chinese Room," pp. 341–345 in *Proceedings of the 7th Annual Conference of the Cognitive Science Society*, Hillsdale, NJ: Erlbaum.

Rapaport, W.J., 1986a, "Philosophy, artificial intelligence, and the Chinese-Room Argument," *Abacus* **3**, Summer, 6–17; correspondence, 1987, *Abacus* **4**, Winter, 6–7, *Abacus* **4**, Spring, 5–7.

Rapaport, W.J., 1986b, "Searle's experiments with thought," *Philosophy of Science* **53**, 271–279.

Rapaport, W.J., 1988a, "To think or not to think," *Noûs* **22**, 585–609.

Rapaport, W.J., 1988b, "Syntactic semantics: Foundations of computational natural-language understanding," pp. 81–131 in *Aspects of Artificial Intelligence*, J.H. Fetzer, ed., Dordrecht: Kluwer Academic Publishers.

Rapaport, W.J., 1995, "Understanding understanding: Syntactic semantics and computational cognition," pp. 49–88 in *AI, Connectionism, and Philosophical Psychology*, J.E. Tomberlin, ed., Phil. Perspectives, Vol. 9, Atascadero, CA: Ridgeview.

Rapaport, W.J., 1996, *Understanding Understanding: Semantics, Computation, and Cognition*, Tech. Rep. 96-26, Buffalo: SUNY Buffalo Computer Science Department; http://www.cse.buffalo.edu/tech-reports/96-26.ps.Z

Rapaport, W.J., 1998, "How minds can be computational systems," *Journal of Experimental, Theoretical and Artificial Intelligence* **10**, 403–419.

Rapaport, W.J., 1999, "Implementation is semantic interpretation," *The Monist* **82**, 109–130.

Rapaport, W.J. and Ehrlich, K., 2000, "A computational theory of vocabulary acquisition," in *Natural Language Processing and Knowledge Representation*, Ł. Iwańska and S.C. Shapiro, eds., Menlo Park, CA/Cambridge, MA: AAAI/MIT (in press).

Schonberg, H.C., 1989, "Kasparov beats chess computer (for now)," *New York Times*, 23 October, A1, B2.

Searle, J.R., 1980, "Minds, brains, and programs," *Behavioral and Brain Science* **3**, 417–457.

Searle, J.R., 1982, "The myth of the computer," *New York Review of Books*, 29 April, 3–6; cf. correspondence, same journal, 24 June 1982, 56–57.

Shapiro, S.C., 1979, "The SNePS semantic network processing system," pp. 179–203 in *Associative Networks*, N. Findler, ed., New York: Academic Press.

Shapiro, S.C., 1995, "Computationalism," *Minds and Machines* **5**, 517–524.

Shapiro, S.C., 1997, "What is computer science?," http://www.cse.buffalo.edu/~shapiro/Papers/whatiscs.pdf

Shapiro, S.C., 1998, "Embodied Cassie," pp. 136–143 in *Cognitive Robotics: Papers from the 1998 AAAI Fall Symposium*, Tech. Rep. FS-98-02, Menlo Park, CA: AAAI.

Shapiro, S.C. and Rapaport, W.J., 1987, "SNePS considered as a fully intensional propositional semantic network," pp. 262–315 in *The Knowledge Frontier*, N. Cercone and G. McCalla, eds., New York: Springer-Verlag.

Shapiro, S.C. and Rapaport, W.J., 1991, "Models and minds: Knowledge representation for natural-language competence," pp. 215–259 in *Philosophy and AI*, R. Cummins and J. Pollock, eds., Cambridge, MA: MIT.

Shapiro, S.C. and Rapaport, W.J., 1992, "The SNePS family," *Computers and Mathematics with Applications* **23**, 243–275.

Shapiro, S.C. and Rapaport, W.J., 1995, "An introduction to a computational reader of narrative," pp. 79–105 in *Deixis in Narrative*, J.F. Duchan, G.A. Bruder, and L.E. Hewitt, eds., Hillsdale, NJ: Erlbaum.

Shieber, S.M., 1994a, "Lessons from a restricted Turing test," *CACM* **37**(6), 70–78.

Shieber, S.M., 1994b, "On Loebner's lessons," *CACM* **37**, 83–84.

Simon, H.A. and Newell, A., 1958, "Heuristic problem solving: The next advance in operations research," *Operations Research* **6**(6), 1–10.

Simpson, J.A. and Weiner, E.S.C. (preparers), 1989, *The Oxford English Dictionary*, 2nd edn., Oxford: Clarendon.

Smith, B.C., 1987, "The correspondence continuum," Report CSLI-87-71, Stanford, CA: CSLI.

Srihari, R.K., 1991, "PICTION: A system that uses captions to label human faces in newspaper photographs," pp. 80–85 in *Proceedings of the 9th National Conference on Artificial Intelligence (AAAI-91)*, Menlo Park, CA: AAAI/MIT.

Srihari, R.K. and Rapaport, W.J., 1989, "Extracting visual information from text: Using captions to label human faces in newspaper photographs," pp. 364–371 in *Proceedings of the 11th Annual Conference of the Cognitive Science Society*, Hillsdale, NJ: Erlbaum.

Stork, D.G., 1997, *HAL's Legacy*, Cambridge, MA: MIT.

Thagard, P., 1986, "Parallel computation and the mind-body problem," *Cognitive Science* **10**, 301–318.

Turing, A.M., 1936, "On computable numbers, with an application to the *Entscheidungsproblem*"; reprinted, with corrections, 1965 in *The Undecidable*, M. Davis, ed., New York: Raven, pp. 116–154.

Turing, A.M., 1950, "Computing machinery and intelligence," *Mind* **59**, 433–460.

Wartofsky, M.W., 1966, "The model muddle," pp. 1–11 in *Models: Representation and the Scientific Understanding*, Dordrecht: Reidel (1979).

Weizenbaum, J., 1966, "ELIZA – A computer program for the study of natural language communication between man and machine," *CACM* **9**, 36–45.

Williams, B., 1998, "The end of explanation?," *The New York Review of Books* **45**, 40–44 (19 November).

Woods, W.A., 1975, "What's in a link," pp. 35–82 in *Representation and Understanding*, D.G. Bobrow and A.M. Collins, eds., New York: Academic Press.

Look Who's Moving the Goal Posts Now

LARRY HAUSER

Alma College, Department of Philosophy, 614 W. Superior, Alma, MI 48801, USA

Abstract. The abject failure of Turing's first prediction (of computer success in playing the Imitation Game) confirms the aptness of the Imitation Game test as a test of human level intelligence. It especially belies fears that the test is too easy. At the same time, this failure disconfirms expectations that human level artificial intelligence will be forthcoming any time soon. On the other hand, the success of Turing's second prediction (that acknowledgment of computer thought processes would become commonplace) *in practice* amply confirms the thought that computers think in some manner and are possessed of some level of intelligence already. This lends ever-growing support to the hypothesis that computers will think at a human level eventually, despite the abject failure of Turing's first prediction.

1. Turing's Failed Prediction

In 1950 Alan Turing made two predictions. First and most famously, he predicted

> that in about fifty years' time it will be possible to programme computers, with a storage capacity of about 10^9 to make them play the imitation game so well that an average interrogator will not have more than 70 per cent chance of making the right identification after five minutes of questioning. (Turing, 1950, p. 442)

This prediction has failed abjectly. Current contestants play the Imitation Game so ill that an average interrogator has a 100 per cent chance of making the right identification. By Turing's measure, in other words, current contestants play with no measurable success. What this says about the adequacy of the Turing test as a test of high-grade or human-level artificial intelligence, I argue, is that it's about right. What it means for AI itself is more equivocal and best assessed in the light of the success of Turing's second prediction.

2. The Test

2.1. IT'S NOT TOO EASY

Some fear the Turing test is *too easy* – that Turing test passing would *not* suffice to warrant attribution of thought – because

> people are easily fooled and are especially easily fooled into reading structure in chaos, reading meaning into nonsense (Shieber, 1994, p. 72);

and

> it has been known since ELIZA that a test based on fooling people is confoundingly simple to pass. (Shieber, 1994a, p. 72)

ELIZA phobia, I call it.[1] For those prone to ELIZA phobia the moral of the abject failure of computers to fulfill Turing's prediction, I believe, is that your fears are unfounded. Eager though we are to read structure into chaos and meaning into nonsense, the experience of the Loebner Prize competition – not to mention the last fifty years – attests that the *unrestricted* Turing test is confoundingly hard.

I agree that if a program very much like ELIZA *could* pass, that would be very good reason to doubt the sufficiency of the Turing test.[2] But the evidence of the Loebner prize competition suggests that nothing like ELIZA has the remotest chance of passing the unrestricted test. This supports the judgment that "if the Turing test was passed, then one would certainly have very adequate grounds for inductively inferring that the computer could think on the level of a normal, living, adult human being" (Moor, 1976, p. 251). The abject failure of Turing's prediction together with our intuitive low estimates of the intellectual capacities of the current generation of computer contestants argues strongly for the empirical sufficiency of Turing's test.

2.2. IT'S NOT TOO HARD

As a test of intelligence or thought *per se* the test is *obviously* too hard. Neither my cat nor my computer can play the Imitation Game successfully. Nevertheless, I don't doubt that my cat exhibits intelligence to some extent, and thinks in his own peculiar manner. Likewise, my computer exhibits intelligence to some extent, and thinks in *it's* own peculiar manner. That's what *I* think.

Even as a test of human-level intelligence, the Turing test, followed to the letter, seems too hard. Presumably something "could think on the level of a normal, living, adult human being" (1976, p. 251) without thinking *in the manner* of a normal adult human being, i.e., without sharing *our* cognitive style which all of *it's* peculiarities. Thought or intelligence up to our level needn't share our style. Turing himself observes,

> The game may perhaps be criticized on the ground that the odds are weighted too heavily against the machine. If the man were to try and pretend to be the machine he would clearly make a very poor showing. He would be given away at once by slowness and inaccuracy in arithmetic. (Turing, 1950, p. 435)

Turing asks, "May not machines carry out something which ought to be described as thinking but which is very different from what a man does?" and acknowledges "this objection is a very strong one" (Turing, 1950, p. 435). Still, so long as the computer contestants' failings obviously bespeak cluelessness, not just inhuman style, we need not be troubled by this objection.

2.3. IT'S ABOUT RIGHT

"Machines take me by surprise with great frequency," Turing writes, "because, although I do a calculation, I do it in a hurried, slipshod fashion" (Turing, 1950,

p. 450). To the attentive reader Turing's presentation of the Imitation Game test may seem likewise slipshod.[3] First he says that the machine contestant is supposed "to take the part of A" the man, pretending to be a *woman*. Yet, a while later Turing asks,

> Is it true that ... [a computer] can be made to play satisfactorily the part of A in the imitation game, the part of B [the confederate] being taken by a *man* (Turing, p. 442: my emphasis)

Yet a little further on, he observes,

> The game (with the player B omitted) is frequently used in practice under the name of *viva voce* to discover whether some one really understands something or has "learnt it parrot fashion." (Turing, 1950, p. 446)

Here he allows the confederate, it seems, to be inessential. Finally, Turing speaks of "playing ... the imitation game ... against a blind man" (Turing, 1950, p. 455). Finally, the question of what importance to attach to *the averageness* of the interrogator, *the five minute time limit*, and the *70% rate of success* mentioned in the prediction leaves room for further doubts about the details of the test intended.

Rather than lecture Turing on the subject of his slipshod ways in this connection, however, I commend them: when "speaking of such subjects and with such premises" it is best to "be content ... to indicate the truth roughly and in outline" (Aristotle, *Nich. Eth.*, Bk. I, Ch. 3); and in this spirit also should Turing's proposal be received, as a rough approximation. So taken, the Turing test is apt. It tests the contestant's ability "to use words, or put together other signs, as we do in order to declare our thoughts to others" or "produce different arrangements of words so as to give an appropriately meaningful answer to whatever is said in its presence" (Descartes, 1637, p. 140). Such verbal responsiveness is what we normally do use as a basis for assessing mental competence, e.g., in determining to whom legal and moral entitlements apply, and by whom moral and legal responsibilities are owed. This lends powerful support to the thought that Turing-like tests are just right as tests for human-level intelligence.

More generally, no test is sacrosanct; testing needs to be flexible. If the time comes when computer contestants seem to be failing mainly due to the inhuman *style* of their thought, rather than its low level, it would hardly be contrary to the empirical spirit of Turing's proposal to alter the test to try to control for this.[4] Similarly, it is hardly contrary to (the spirit of) Turing's proposal if we have to tweak the test to accommodate the needs of particular subjects. This is why it's no objection to the Turing test to point out, e.g., that the test *as proposed* would disqualify nontypists and the illiterate. Where subjects' disabilities are irrelevant to their intelligence (as these are), accommodating such disabilities accords, generally, with the spirit of empirical testing and with the "fair play" spirit of Turing's proposal, in particular.

This, incidentally, is why Hugh Loebner's revision of the Turing test to require the contestant to "respond *intelligently* to audio-visual input" (Loebner, 1994, p. 82: original italics) is ill advised. It proposes to discriminate against computers on the basis of their visual and auditory disabilities, contrary to Turing's proposal, and contrary, as far as I can see, to any sound spirit or principle whatever. If the test did need strengthening – as the abject failure of Turing's prediction argues it doesn't – it shouldn't be strengthened *in this way*. This audio-visual requirement should be dropped. Alternately, if the time comes when Loebner would like to ask his questions "about images and patterns" (Loebner, 1994, p. 82), the rules should be amended to require inclusion of a blind person among the confederates.

3. AI

3.1. MODEST AI COVERED

If AI is understood to be the thesis that computers can *think* or be genuinely possessed of *some* intelligence, then the failure of computers to pass the Turing test is inconsequential due to the test being obviously too strong a disqualifying test for thought or intelligence *per se*. Just as my cat's inability to pass the Turing test has no tendency to undermine *his* claim to some manner of thought and some degree of intelligence, the abject failure of computers to pass the Turing test provides no good reason to deny them some manner of thought and degree of intelligence; even if Turing test passing computers are very far "over the horizon"; and even, perhaps, if the horizon "seems to be receding at an accelerating rate," as Hubert Dreyfus (1979: 92) complains.

Since ensuing years have only to sharpened Dreyfus' "receding horizon" complaint, *if* something like Turing test passing capacity were required before attribution of any sort of thought or intelligence were warranted, Dreyfusian arguments such as the following would have considerable bite:

1. Turing test passing ability is necessary condition for (warranted attribution of) or intelligence.

2. Probably, no computer will ever pass the Turing test.

∴C. Probably, no computer will ever (be warrantedly affirmed to) think.

Turing test passing ability not being required for warranted attribution of thought or intelligence *per se*, however, the Dreyfusian argument does not go through against *AI modestly understood*; understood as asserting "merely" that computers really do think, and are intelligent in their own peculiar ways.

3.2. OH THE HUMANITY: IMMODEST AI EXPOSED

On the other hand, AI is more famously understood to be advancing a more ambitious claim that a "computer could think on the level of a normal, living, adult human being" (Moor, 1976, p. 251). Such immodest AI (as I call it) is vulnerable to the Dreyfusian argument. It is vulnerable because the Turing test is a plausible disqualifier for such human-level intelligence. In speaking of thought "on the level of a normal, living, adult human being" we are talking of something like moral agency or *personhood*; such that we should have to ask ourselves in all moral seriousness the sorts of questions Robert Epstein proposes we shall have to ask of a Loebner Prize winner. Questions like,

> "Who should get the prize money? ... Should we give it the right to vote? Should it pay taxes?" (Epstein, 1992 as cited by Shieber, 1994, p. 70)

We should have to ask such questions in all moral seriousness because the ability "to use words or put together other signs" so as to "give an appropriately mean-ingful answer to whatever is said" (Descartes, 1642, p. 140) is what we ordinarily do take to qualify normal adults and *disqualify* others for moral and legal respons-ibilities and entitlements. The Turing test's credibility as a disqualifying test for human-level intelligence – in light of the abject failure of Turing's first prediction – leaves AI immodestly understood exposed to the Dreyfusian argument's bite. At the very least the *probably none ever will* claim of the Dreyfusian argument is confirmed by the abject failure of Turing's prediction. It remains, of course, to quarrel as to what degree and subject to what further considerations.

I believe that hopes for immodest AI remains viable, given further considera-tions. These derive from the success – less equivocal than it may seem – of Turing's neglected *second* prediction.

4. Turing's Second Prediction

> [A]t the end of the century the use of words and general educated opinion will have altered so much that one will be able to speak of machines thinking without expecting to be contradicted. (Turing, 1950, p. 442)

4.1. NAIVE AI

I submit that the success of this *second* prediction is less equivocal than may seem. Consider the following exchange:

> MARGARET WARNER: All right. Let me bring Mr. Friedel back in here. Mr. Friedel, did Gary Kasparov think the computer was thinking?

> FREDERIC FRIEDEL: Not thinking but that it was showing intelligent beha-vior. When Gary Kasparov plays against the computer, he has the feeling that it is forming plans; it understands strategy; it's trying to trick him; it's blocking his ideas, and then to tell him, now, this has nothing to do with intelligence, it's just number crunching, seems very semantic to him. [Friedel is Kasparov's technical advisor.] (MacNeil and Lehrer, 1997)

It certainly does seem very semantic. But it seems equally "semantic" to deny Deep Blue's *exercise* of its intelligence the name of *thought*. Naive judgments serving practically and predictively (as in trying to *psych out* Deep Blue's plans and strategy) trump theoretical misgivings (reluctance to call such planning and strategizing "thinking") in the absence of empirical and scientific theoretic support for such misgivings. In lieu of such support, *modest* AI prevails directly in virtue of arguments like this:

1.   Forming plans and understanding strategy are intelligent activities.

2.   Deep Blue forms plans and understands strategy.

∴C. Deep Blue is intelligent (to some extent): it thinks in some manner.

Every intelligent-seeming computer act underwrites an argument of this naive argument type. And the more such behavior computers display, and the more interconnectedly they display it, the more hopeful things look for immodest AI, despite the abject failure of Turing's first prediction This is the main *empirical* reason immodest AI remains a viable hope, despite that failure.[5]

Since the behaviors in question *are* intelligent *seeming*, the opponent of these naive arguments needs to maintain that such behaviors do not evince *true* thought or *genuine intelligence* because some essential characteristic is lacking. Thus the naive argument calls for a theoretical rejoinder. To be *sustained* such a rejoinder must

1.   scientifically support its essence claim on behalf of the characteristic in question, and

2.   empirically support its claim that computers lack this characteristic.

I believe the prime candidates for the office of disqualifying essential characteristic – *unity, intentionality*, and *phenomenal consciousness* – all fail on these counts.

4.2. UNITY FIRST

The unity objection holds that it's necessary, for a thing to *really* be thinking, for it to have *enough interconnected* intelligent-seeming characteristics or abilities. The would-be disqualifying thought is that Deep Blue and other candidate *modest AIs* lack enough interconnected mental abilities for their intelligent-seeming performances to be truly considered thought. To be sustained, the unity objection requires some account of *how many* and *which* other mental abilities a thing must have in order to think; and *why*. And the rub – as with the Turing test as a test of thought *per se* – is how to disqualify my computer without disqualifying my cat. In light of computers' *many* actual intelligent-seeming capabilities and their (theoretically almost unlimited) potential for acquiring more; and in light of the somewhat limited capacities of my cat; I do not believe the unity objection to modest AI is sustainable.[6]

Nevertheless, for expository purposes, I am going to *imagine* the Unity objection to be sustained. Exit my cat. Reenter the Turing test; and rejoin the issue of immodest AI that has occasioned so much interest. I contend that intentionality and phenomenal consciousness objections cannot be sustained even against immodest AI claims. They are thereby shown to be unsustainable against modest AI *in spades*.[7]

4.3. The imitation game revisited

Recall the original *man-woman* version of the game. In this version, no matter how *female-seeming* the man's manner of conversation, revelation of what's hidden overrides the conversational evidence; because that's the essential thing; not the style and content of their conversation, but the content of their jenes [sic.]. In the same manner, the two objections now to be considered – *the phenomenal consciousness* and *intentionality* objections – urge that no matter how intelligent or thoughtful *seeming* the computer's conversation, revelation of what's hidden in *it* overrides the conversational evidence; because *that's* the essential thing: *phenomenal consciousness* or *intentionality*.

4.4. Phenomenal consciousness

Phenomenal consciousness is "inward" experience, or subjectivity, or possession of private conscious experiences or *qualia*. It's that certain *je ne sais qua* but you don't know what it is; or, at least, you can't say. It's the stuff that souls are made of; a spiritual concept, I think; and whereof one cannot scientifically speak, thereof one must pass over, scientifically, in silence. Since disqualification of a Turing test passer requires *scientific*-theoretic and *empirical* support to be sustained, I submit the phenomenal consciousness objection fails. Let me assemble a few reminders why.

With regard to the scientific theoretic standing of consciousness ... for a very long time consciousness was regarded as *the* foundational concept of psychology. Introspectionism was the last gasp attempt to base psychology as *an empirical science* on such a phenomenological foundation. Introspectionism was a flop. The trouble was – allowing verbal reports of consciousness to go proxy for direct introspective observation, as one must in the case of *others'* conscious experiences – everyone disagreed in their verbal reports. At present, I believe, no credible scientific psychological theory features consciousness as a fundamental concept.[8]

The chief trouble with consciousness as a scientific concept – in a word – is the subjectivity of it. Turing notes the impossibility of observing and consequent difficulty of confirming it's presence in others in suggesting "those who support the argument from consciousness" might "be willing to accept our test" rather than "be forced into the solipsist position" (Turing, 1950, p. 447). Though some entertain hopes of discovering the neurophysiological basis or computational basis of phenomenal consciousness – so as to be able to scientifically *infer* the presence of the phenomenal consciousness we can't observe in others from such neurophysiological or computational causes as we can – such would-be solutions to the other minds problem, even if successful, would only solve half the problem; and not the half that most concerns us. They would provide "sufficient but not necessary conditions for the correct ascription of [phenomenal consciousness] to other beings" (Searle, 1992, p. 76); but it's the detection of the *absence* of qualia, or discovery of what's causally *necessary* for phenomenal consciousness, that concerns us for purposes of disqualifying Turing test passing computers. And there seems *no* scientific or anywise empirical hope of establishing the *absence* of phenomenal consciousness or qualia in *anything* ... unless by telepathic scan. Even then ... perhaps the telepath is sensitive only to humanoid qualia. Perhaps a Turing test passing computer would have qualia quite *unlike ours*, and the telepath's failure to detect any phenomenal consciousness in the computer might be due to our human telepath's insensitivity to such alien qualia, and not to the machine's lacking qualia altogether.

I conclude there is no scientific reason to think phenomenal consciousness *is* the true essence of thought; and if there *were* – when faced with a truly Turing test passing computer – we would have no empirical grounds to deny such a computer to be possessed of such phenomenal consciousness as its conversation would suggest.

4.5. INTENTIONALITY: WHY ROBOT?

I will not dispute that *intentionality – meaning or aboutness* – is essential to thought; but scientific grounds for thinking a Turing test passing computer would lack the requisite intentionality are slim to nonexistent.

Views according to which *intentionality – meaning* or "aboutness" – is supposed to boil down to *consciousness*, in addition to facing the aforesaid troubles with consciousness, undertake the burden to say *how* it boils down; which none can say. We can dismiss such views immediately.

A more credible approach maintains that computers' "symbol" processing is not sufficiently grounded in causal-perceptual and causal-robotic interaction with things for its symbol processing to really be about these things. On this view, the missing ingredient – what we have that computers lack – are causal connections between the signs and the things they signify. Put crudely, the difference between my meaningful belief that *cats are intelligent* and a computer's meaningless "representation" of this same information – say by storing a Prolog clause that says *intelligent (X):-cat (X)* – is that my representation came to be, or could be, elicited *in me* by the actual presence (the actual sights and sounds) of cats. It is these perceptually mediated connections between my use of the English word "cat" and actual cats that makes that word signify those animals for me; and it is for want of such connections that computer representations lack such signification for the computer (cf. Hauser, 1993).

I will not dispute the general causal story about reference underlying this objection. I do, however, dispute the use of this story to justify discrimination against would-be Turing test passing computers on the basis of their sensory or motoric disabilities. On any plausible telling of the causal story no *extensive* ability to apply words to the world *directly* on the basis of sensory acquaintance or physical manipulation is crucial. As Turing notes, "We need not be too concerned about the legs, eyes, etc. The example of Miss Helen Keller shows that education can take place provided communication in both directions between teacher and pupil can take place" (Turing, 1950, p. 456).[9] My computer communicates with me – and I with it – through its touch pad and LCD screen. That's why the figures Excel manipulates when *it* calculates my students' grades are about my students' grades. The conversation of a Turing test passing computer would likewise be about what it was discussing, for similar reasons.

5. Conclusion

In the light of the success of Turing's second prediction in practice, I take *modest AI* to be a present reality: generally speaking, computers really *are* possessed of the mental states and capacities our naive assessments say. Deep Blue really considers chess positions and evaluates possible continuations; my humble laptop really searches for – and sometimes finds – files in storage and words in documents. If it *asks* like it thinks, and *answers* like it thinks, and *extemporizes* like it thinks, it ain't *necessarily* thinking. Still, *prima facie* it thinks; and you're warranted in saying and believing as much on the basis of such evidence. In the case of ducks we know what sort of observable facts would scientifically override the quacking, and waddling, and ducklike appearance, if it turns out to be a mechanical duck. We know no such things in the case of a Deep Blue's forming plans and understanding strategy; and we know no such things which – if we were faced with a Turing test passing computer – would warrant withholding attribution of human-level thought. Of course, by the time we *are* faced with that eventuality – if ever – we may know more about thought. Then again, what more we know may not be disqualifying. Though the test itself – like any empirical test – is negotiable, there is presently no empirical or theoretical reason to renegotiate.

Immodest AIs – computers with human-level thought – are still *very far* over the horizon, I suspect. If that horizon "seems to be receding at an accelerating rate" (Dreyfus, 1979: 92), that is because it initially appeared, to Turing among others, to be closer than it really was. Ironically, what I have been calling *immodest AI* for the immodesty if it's *aspirations* suffers, more than anything else, perhaps, from *too modest* an assessment of *our own human* mental capacities. Nature has taken some four billion years to evolve human intelligence from inanimate matter. Through us, she has taken some fifty years to arrive at the current level of artificial intelligence. *Wait*, I say, *till next millennium!*

Acknowledgements

I am indebted to James Moor for his encouragement and inspiration. Thanks are also due to Ethan Disbrow, Tanisha Fuller, Lark Haunert, Anne Henningfeld, Holly Townsend, and Jeanette Watripont for their helpful comments and criticisms.

Notes

[1] Shieber was addressing these remarks to the *restricted* version of the test. Ironically despite his general reservations about tests based on fooling people being confoundingly easy, Shieber dismisses the unrestricted Turing test as impossibly hard and the Loebner Prize competition as incredibly premature.

[2] *Pace* Block (1981).

[3] See Saygin, et al. (forthcoming) for further discussion.

[4] This might be helped somewhat by requiring *cultural diversity* among querents and confederates. Inclusion of "differently abled" humans among the confederates and querents might also help.

[5] A hope buttressed, of course, by the *theoretical* universality of these machines.

[6] Descartes' (1637) advocacy of Turing test passing (roughly) as a necessary condition for *any* intelligence whatsoever underwrites his infamous denial of any mental capacity to any infrahuman animal at all. Herein lies a cautionary tale.

[7] If (evidence of) phenomenal consciousness or robustly-robotically-grounded intentionality are not justifiably held to be prerequisite for (warranted attribution of) human-level intelligence, they certainly cannot be warrantedly asserted to be prerequisite for (attribution of) of lesser varieties – say sparrow-level or starfish-level intelligence.

[8] Though many a crackpot theory does.

[9] See Putnam's (1975) discussion of the *elm/beech* and *aluminum/molybdenum* examples and the division of linguistic labor. See also Landau and Gleitman's (1975) findings concerning blind children's acquisition of seemingly vision-dependent concepts.

References

Aristotle. *Nichomachean Ethics*, trans. W.D. Ross (1941) in R. McKeon, ed., *The Basic works of Aristotle*, New York: Random House, pp. 935–1126.

Block, N. (1981), Psychologism and Behaviorism, *Philosophical Review* XC, pp. 5–43.

Descartes, R. (1637), *Discourse on Method*, trans. R. Stoothoff (1985) in J. Cottingham, D. Murdoch and R. Stoothoff, eds., *The Philosophical Writings of Descartes*, Vol. 1, Cambridge: Cambridge University Press, pp. 111–151.

Dreyfus, H. (1979), *What Computers Can't Do*, New York: Harper Colophon.

Epstein, R. (1992), 'The Quest for the Thinking Computer', *AI Magazine* 13, pp. 81–91.

Keller, H. (1912), 'The Hand of the World', *Out of the Dark: Essays, Letters and Addresses on Physical and Social Vision*, Garden City, NY: Doubleday, Page & Co., pp. 3–17.

Keller, H. (1993), 'A New Chime for the Christmas Bells', *Out of the Dark: Essays, Letters and Addresses on Physical and Social Vision*, Garden City, NY: Doubleday, Page & Co., pp. 274–282.

Hauser, L. (1993), 'Why Isn't my Pocket Calculator a Thinking Thing?', *Minds and Machines* 3, pp. 2–10. Online: http://members.aol.com/lshauser/wimpcatt.html.

Landau, B. and Gleitman, L. (1985), *Language and Experience: Evidence from the Blind Child*, Cambridge, MA: Harvard University Press.

Loebner, H. (1994) 'In Response', *Communications of the ACM* 37, pp. 79–82. Online: http://www.loebner.net/Prizef/In-response.html.

MacNeil, R. and Lehrer, J. (1997), 'Big Blue Wins', *NewsHour*, May 12. Accessible online: http://www.pbs.orglnewshour/home.html.

Moor, J. (1976), 'An Analysis of the Turing Test', *Philosophical Studies* 30, pp. 249–257.

Putnam, H. (1975), 'The Meaning of "Meaning"', *Mind, Language, and Reality: Philosophical Essays*, Vol. 2, Cambridge: Cambridge University Press; Minneapolis: University of Minnesota Press, pp. 215–271.

Saygin, A.P., Cicekli, I. and Akman, V. (forthcoming), 'Turing Test: 50 Years Later.' Online: http://cogsci.ucsd.eduh/~asaygin/papers/tt50abs.html.

Searle, J.R. (1992), *The Rediscovery of the Mind*, Cambridge, MA: MIT Press.

Shieber, S.M. (1994), 'Lessons from a Restricted Turing Test', *Communications of the ACM* 37, pp. 70–78. Online: http://www.eecs.harvard.edu/shieber/papers/loebner-rev-html/loebner-rev-html.html.

Turing, A.M. (1950), 'Computing Machinery and Intelligence', *Mind* LIX, pp. 433–460.

The Status and Future of the Turing Test

JAMES H. MOOR
Department of Philosophy, Dartmouth College, Hanover, NH 03755, USA; E-mail:
james.moor@dartmouth.edu

Abstract. The standard interpretation of the imitation game is defended over the rival gender interpretation though it is noted that Turing himself proposed several variations of his imitation game.
The Turing test is then justified as an inductive test not as an operational definition as commonly
suggested. Turing's famous prediction about his test being passed at the 70% level is disconfirmed
by the results of the Loebner 2000 contest and the absence of any serious Turing test competitors from
AI on the horizon. But, reports of the death of the Turing test and AI are premature. AI continues to
flourish and the test continues to play an important philosophical role in AI. Intelligence attribution,
methodological, and visionary arguments are given in defense of a continuing role for the Turing
test. With regard to Turing's predictions one is disconfirmed, one is confirmed, but another is still
outstanding.

Key words: imitation game, Loebner prize, Turing test

1. Interpreting the Imitation Game

1.1. IS THE TURING TEST TURING'S TEST?

Alan Turing begins his classic article, "Computing Machinery and Intelligence,"
with a clever philosophical move (Turing, 1950). In the first sentence of his paper
he proposes to consider the question "Can machines think?" but by the end of the
first paragraph he suggests replacing the question with another. The replacement
question is explained in terms of a game that he calls "the imitation game". The
imitation game is played by a man (A), a woman (B), and a human interrogator
(C). The interrogator C is in a room apart from the other two and tries to determine
through conversation which of the other two is the man and which is the woman.
Turing recommends that ideally a teletypewriter be used to communicate between
the rooms to avoid giving the interrogator clues through tones of voice. In the game
the man may give deceptive answers in order to get the interrogator to misidentify
him as the woman. He might, for example, lie about the length and style of his hair.
The woman's best strategy, Turing believes, is to tell the truth.

Having explained the imitation game in terms a man, a woman, and a human
interrogator Turing introduces his replacement question(s). Turing says,

> We now ask the question, 'What will happen when a machine takes the part of
> A in this game?' Will the interrogator decide wrongly as often when the game
> is played like this as he does when the game is played between a man and a
> woman? These questions replace our original, 'Can machines think?' (Turing,
> 1950, p. 434)

Minds and Machines **11:** 77–93, 2001.
© 2001 *Kluwer Academic Publishers. Printed in the Netherlands.*

But precisely what does Turing intend by this extension of the imitation game when he makes a machine player A? Interpretations differ. On one interpretation, the gender interpretation, the machine takes the part of A, but it is important that the part of B continued to be played by a woman. On the other interpretation, the human interpretation, the machine takes the part of A, but the part of B is played by a human – a man or a woman. The latter interpretation of the imitation game has become the standard interpretation. However, a number of writers suggest that Turing intended or should have intended the gender interpretation (Genova, 1994; Hayes and Ford, 1995; Sterrett, 2000; Traiger, 2000).

If one considers the quoted passage by itself, gender imitation is a plausible reading. In that passage Turing does not mention any change in the assumptions about who is playing B. Should we not assume unmentioned aspects of the game remain constant? (Traiger, 2000) Moreover, Turing's replacement question, "Will the interrogator decide wrongly as often when the game is played like this as he does when the game is played between a man and a woman?", makes sense as a direct comparison only if B is played by a woman.

However, in the rest of Turing's article and in Turing's other works about this time textual evidence strongly indicates Turing had the human interpretation, i.e. the standard interpretation, in mind (Turing, 1948, 1951a, b, 1952; Copeland, 2000; Piccinini, 2000). For example, in Section 5 of his article Turing offers another version of the replacement question for "Can machines think?":

> Let us fix our attention on one particular digital computer C. Is it true that by modifying this computer to have an adequate storage, suitably increasing its speed of action, and providing it with an appropriate programme, C can be made to play satisfactorily the part of A in the imitation game, the part of B being taken by a man? (Turing, 1950, p. 442)

Here Turing clearly states that the role of B is to be taken by a man. The use of 'man' in the passage is rather naturally read generically so that part B can be taken by either a male human or a female human.

Throughout his writing Turing consistently discusses human intellectual functioning and dismisses bodily characteristics that he takes to be only accidentally connected to intellectual functioning. Almost immediately after introducing his game Turing says, "The new problem has the advantage of drawing a fairly sharp line between the physical and the intellectual capacities of a man." (Turing, 1950, p. 434) Turing focuses upon humans as a group and seeks to compare differences between humans and machines, not women and machines or women and men. The sample questions Turing gives in the second section of his paper are general intellectual questions about writing poetry, doing arithmetic and playing chess. Such questions seem designed at measuring human intellectual function not to distinguish men (or machines) from women in particular. Turing continues throughout the rest of his paper to emphasize humanity not femininity. For example, Turing explains his method in terms of general *human* activity when he says "The question and answer method seems to be suitable for introducing almost any one of the fields of human endeavour that we wish to include." (Turing, 1950, p. 435)

Although Turing's initial statement of his imitation game in the first section of his famous article is arguably ambiguous, his order of presentation leads naturally to the standard interpretation. In the first section of his paper Turing introduces the concept of the imitation game to his readers as an ordinary game with three humans in the roles A, B, and C. Then he raises the possibility of a machine playing role A to emphasize that a machine might play this kind of game. In the remainder of the paper he elaborates the nature of the intended game making it clear human imitation is the goal. On this account his presentation of gender imitation, if it was intended at all for a machine, is at most an intermediary step toward the more generalized game involving human imitation. Human imitation by machine has been the standard interpretation of the Turing test, and the preponderance of evidence suggests that the standard interpretation is what Turing intended.

1.2. STERRETT'S NORMATIVE ARGUMENTS

Susan Sterrett puts the debate about the interpretations in more normative terms. Regardless of what Turing's own interpretation of his imitation game was, Sterrett believes a gender imitation test "provides the more appropriate indication of intelligence". (Sterrett, 2000) Sterrett points out that the two tests are not equivalent in structure or results. In the gender imitation test a direct comparison is sought between how well a machine can imitate a woman compared to a man. A control group of men imitating women could serve as a standard for an experimental group of machines imitating women. It is a possible outcome of such a test that machines could outscore men. But in the human imitation test there is no control group. Machines cannot outscore humans.

Sterrett argues that a cross-gendering test focuses on the crucial features of intelligence. It requires a self-conscious critique of habitual responses and hence can provide better evidence for intelligence. She concludes, "In short, that intelligence lies, not in the having of cognitive habits developed in learning to converse, but in the exercise of the intellectual powers required to recognize, evaluate, and, when called for, override them." (Sterrett, 2000)

Sterrett is correct that the existence of a control group in the gender imitation test, compared to the absence of such in a human imitation test, offers a specific standard for comparison. But this standard may not give much assistance in assessing intelligence. Suppose that only 1 out of 100 men can imitate a woman well enough to pass the test. Now suppose machines can match this ratio, and thereby do well in the test by comparison with the control group. Machines clearly pass the test on this standard, but what conclusions should be drawn? Machines might do as well as (or in this case as poorly as) men but might not demonstrate much intelligence. Of course, it might be replied that those machines that did imitate women well did show intelligence. But, it is exactly those machines that would be expected to do well in the standard Turing test and this would not show a normative advantage to using the gender imitation test over the standard test.

Moreover, gender imitation, as well as other kinds of imitation, can be embedded in the standard test. The aspects of intelligence that Sterrett identifies as important to test can be tested in the standard game. For example, an interrogator could ask, after the gender roles of A and B had been established, that A and B assume genders opposite their own and answer questions accordingly. The intellectual powers of recognizing, evaluating and overriding cognitive habits could then be tested individually. Such role playing is an excellent way to gather information about intelligence and the standard test is a good format for gathering such information. Moreover, various skills, from imitating the opposite gender to creating poetry to designing a house, could be evaluated within the framework of a standard Turing test. If a judge in the standard Turing test rated individual successes at these particular skills, a comparison with a control group would be possible. That machines outperform humans in particular areas or vice versa is a result that could be generated from within a standard Turing test.

In assessing overall general intelligence, the standard test can duplicate all of the important features of the gender imitation test and then some. The standard interpretation of the imitation game is not only Turing's interpretation but is better as this version of the game is more flexible and comprehensive in testing.

1.3. THE TURING TEST AS A GENERAL RESEARCH PROCEDURE

Turing himself offers many versions of the imitation game. He did not limit himself to just the human imitation case. For Turing the imitation game is a format for judges impartially to compare and evaluate outputs from different systems while ignoring the source of the outputs. For instance, Turing uses this generic notion to show that some machines are equivalent to others.

> Provided it could be carried out sufficiently quickiy the digital computer could mimic the behaviour of any discrete state machine. The imitation game could then be played with the machine in question (as B) and the mimicking digital computer (as A) and the interrogator would be unable to distinguish them (Turing, 1950, p. 441)

Turing sometimes uses the imitation game format to argue for the claim that computing can generate some intelligence activity. For example, in his 1948 National Laboratory Report Turing describes an early version of his game in which a paper machine is used. A paper machine is a set of instructions that a human can execute simulating what a machine would do.

> It is not difficult to devise a paper machine which will play a not very bad game of chess. Now get three men as subjects for the experiment A, B, C. A and C are to be rather poor chess players, B is the operator who works the paper machine. (In order that he should be able to work it fairly fast it is advisable that he be both mathematician and chess player.) Two rooms are used with

some arrangement for communicating moves, and a game is played between C and either A or the paper machine. C may find it quite difficult to tell which he is playing. (This is a rather idealized form of an experiment I have actually done.) (Turing, 1948, p. 23)

In this case Turing uses the imitation game format to demonstrate the possibility that computing processes can produce intelligent behavior, such as playing chess, even though in this case a human B is actually imitating behind the scenes what a machine would do! In other places as well Turing shows his willingness to modify details of the imitation game to suit his purposes. Thus, Turing himself treats the imitation game both as a general research technique modifiable and applicable to various problems and as the now famous test of human impersonation given by the standard interpretation.

2. Justifying of the Turing Test

Turing moves quickly to replace the initial question "Can machines think?" with questions about playing the imitation game. Later, he tells us that the original question, "Can machines think?", is "too meaningless to deserve discussion" (Turing, 1950, p. 442). He is not claiming that the question is literally meaningless or his own replacement project would not make sense. What he is suggesting is that terms like "machine" and "think" are vague terms in normal speech and what people typically associate with a machine is not something that has or perhaps could have intelligence. Without some clarification of meaning no progress on the matter can be made. Turing had his own precise theory about the nature computational machines and a vision of how computational machinery could be the basis for intelligent behavior. What he was proposing with his test is a way to make the overall question of machine thinking more precise so that at least in principle an empirical test could be conducted. Thus, Turing's replacement strategy involves both a clarification of meaning, particularly about the nature of the machine, and a procedure for obtaining good evidence.

2.1. THE TEST IS NOT AN OPERATIONAL DEFINITION

Commentators frequently take Turing to be providing an operational definition.

it constitutes an operational definition which, given a computer terminal system can be used as a criterion. (Millar, 1973, p. 595)

unashamedly behavioristic and operationalistic (Searle, 1980, p. 423)

The philosophical claim translates elegantly into an operational definition of intelligence: whatever acts sufficiently intelligence is intelligent. (French, 1990, p. 53)

The key move was to define intelligence operationally, i.e., in terms of the computer's ability, tested over a typewriter link, to sustain a simulation of an intelligent human when subjected to questioning. (Michie, 1996, p. 29)

Operational definitions set up logical and conceptual links between the concept being defined and certain operations. Satisfaction of the operations provides necessary and sufficient conditions for the application of the concept. There are good reasons for not interpreting the Turing test as an operational definition of thinking (Moor, 1987). First, Turing never says he is giving an operational definition nor does he discuss operational definitions in his article. Second, Turing clearly doesn't take his test to be a necessary condition for intelligence, for he admits that a machine might have intelligence but not imitate well. After he raises the question, "May not machines carry out something which ought to be described as thinking but which is very different from what a man does?", he replies, "This objection is a very strong one, but at least we can say that if, nevertheless, a machine can be constructed to play the imitation game satisfactorily, we need not be trouble by this objection."(Turing, 1950, p. 435) Third, though Turing is focused on the sufficiency of the Turing test and not its necessity, he never says the sufficiency is a matter of logic, conceptual, or definitional certainty. There is no evidence for understanding Turing as giving an operational definition nor is there any need to do so (Moor, 2000a).

2.2. THE TEST IS INDUCTIVE

Commentators sometimes suggest that Turing did not intend his imitation game to be a test at all (Narayaman, 1996, p. 66). But this is mistaken, for Turing explicitly calls it a 'test' (Copeland, 1999, p. 466) A plausible interpretation of the imitation game is to regard it as an inductive test (Moor, 1976). If a machine passed a rigorous Turing test, then we would have good inductive grounds for attributing intelligence or thinking to it. We would not have certainty in such a judgment and we might revise our judgment in light of new evidence, but we would have sufficient good evidence to infer that the machine was intelligent. Viewing the Turing test as an inductive test makes it defensible against those objections that play on the weakness of an operational definition account. For example, Ned Block raises the possibility of a Jukebox device passing the Turing test. This unlikely logical possibility would defeat the Turing test cast as an operational definition but does not defeat the Turing test taken inductively (Block, 1981, 1990; Moor, 1998).

In his defense of the imitation game and its significance Turing confronts the problem of other minds. Turing knows that to demand certainty that others think comes at a high price.

According to the most extreme form of this view the only way by which one could be sure that machine thinks is to *be* the machine and to feel oneself thinking. One could then describe these feelings to the world, but of course no one would be justified in taking any notice. Likewise according to this view the only way to know that a man thinks is to be that particular man. It is in fact the solipsist point of view. It may be the most logical view to hold but it makes communication of ideas difficult. (Turing, 1950, p. 446)

Turing's road around solipsism is the imitation game. Through it inductive evidence can be gathered and we can judge whether there is sufficient evidence for attributing thinking. Here again Turing considers an alternative version of the imitation game for gathering such inductive evidence including one that looks very much like ordinary evidence gathering based on linguistic responses from one individual.

The game (with the player B omitted) is frequently used in practice under the name of *viva voce* to discover whether some one really understands something or has "learnt it parrot fashion." (Turing, 1950, p. 446)

Turing is also concerned about induction working against his thesis because people have been exposed to a bias sample of machines in the past. When people point to what they think machines cannot do (be kind, have initiative, fall in love, learn from experience, etc.), they are making an induction from a limited sample of machines.

A man has seen thousands of machines in his lifetime. From what he sees of them he draws a number of general conclusions. They are ugly, each is designed for a very limited purpose, when required for a minutely different purpose they are useless, the variety of behaviour of any one of them is very small, etc., etc. (Turing, 1950, p. 447)

The inductive interpretation of the Turing test makes it a plausible test. It avoids the pitfalls of operational definitions, and yet offers a scientific approach to gathering evidence for the existence of machine thinking. The structure of the Turing test minimizes biases that interrogators might have acquired about what machines are capable of doing. Of course, inductive evidence gathered in a Turing test can be outweighed by new evidence. That is the nature of inductive testing. If new evidence shows that a machine passed the Turing test by remote control run by a human behind the scenes, then reassessment is called for. However not all new evidence requires revision. For example, John Searle maintains through his famous Chinese Room argument that once one discovers that the behavior was produced by a program then any claim to the machine understanding should be rejected (Searle, 1980). Others have drawn similar conclusions based on explanations of how computers work (Stalker, 1978). But the claim that such new evidence must overturn the induction that the machine thinks has not been established (Moor, 1978, 1988, 2000b).

There have been suggestions for modified Turing tests (Harnard, 1991) and for alternative tests (Bringsjord et al., 2001; Erion, 2001). These usually require raising the inductive bar still higher. But the bar seems high enough to infer machine thinking if a rigorous Turing test were passed. The question today seems less a matter of what one would infer if a Turing test were passed, than whether there is a chance that a rigorous Turing test will ever be passed.

3. Turing's 50 Year Prediction

3.1. RESULTS OF THE LOEBNER CONTEST

In his famous 1950 paper Turing made a well known prediction about the imitation game.

> I believe that in about fifty years' time it will be possible to programme computers, with a storage capacity of about 10^9, to make them play the imitation game so well that an average interrogator will not have more than 70 per cent chance of making the right identification after five minutes of questioning. (Turing, 1950, p. 442)

On January 28–29, 2000, a Turing test and an accompanying conference were held at Dartmouth College in honor of Alan Turing. The competition portion was arranged as part of the annual Loebner prize competition that has been run in various locations each year since 1991. These Loebner contests have been run not as one judge (interrogator) interviewing one computer and one human as in the classic set up for a Turing test, but as a panel of judges who individually interrogate each representative from a set of respondents, some human and some computers. Interestingly, Turing considered such panel format in 1952 as a possible set up for his game (Copeland, 1999, 2000). The Dartmouth version of the Turing test had ten respondents. Six of the respondents were computer programs and four respondents were humans: a retired teacher, a financial advisor, a minister, and a yoga instructor.

Each human judge (interrogator) conversed using a computer terminal with each respondent and tried to determine in each case whether a human or a computer program was the conversational partner. The judges knew that of the ten respondents at least one was a computer program and at least one was a human. There were ten official judges (linguist, chemist, two philosophers, musician, psychologist, journalist, author, graduate student, and undergraduate student). Each judge spent up to fifteen minutes at each terminal. They were asked to make a judgment whether the respondent was a human or a computer after five minutes and then again after 15 minutes. In a few cases the judges changed their judgments after 15 minutes but most initial judgments remained unchanged (see Table I).

No computer was mistaken for a human though in a few cases humans were judged to be computers! One of the human respondents was slow and methodical in typing which may have accounted for some of the misidentification. But, in general judges probably have a bias. No judge wants to be the one that mistakes a computer for a human. Nevertheless, identifying a human as a computer still counts as a judgment error. In this contest the judges were 91% correct after five minutes of questioning and 93% correct after 15 minutes. Turing's prediction of 70% or less after five minutes was not reached.

Although the contest was highly enjoyable, no artificial intellects emerged. The programs lack much routine human knowledge and were evasive.

Table I. Ten judges decide whether human or computer at 5 minutes / at 15 minutes

	1	2	3	4	5	6	7	8	9	10
Human#1	C	C	H	H	H	H	C	H	C/H	H
Alice	C	C	C	C	C	C	C	C	C	C
ChatRascal	C	C	C	C	C	C	C	C	C	C
Human#2	C	C	H	H	H	H	H	C/H	H	H
Algernon	C	C	C	C	C	C	C	C	*	C
Talk	*	C	C	C	C	C	C	C	C	C
Human#3	C	H	H	H	H	H	H	H	H/C	H
Human#4	H	H	H	H	H	C/H	H	H	H	H
A-Life	C	C	C	C	C	*	C	C	C	*
c-Brain	C	C	C	C	C	C	C	C	C	C

*Insufficient information to make decision due to program malfunction.

Judge: What is Einstein's first name

Program: Sometimes your questions are very strange. Is it a kind of puzzle?

Sometimes the programs manipulated the conversation in familiar ELIZA-like ways:

Program: ...do you think you could please tell me your name now?

Judge: Alexander

Program: Nice to meet you, Alexander.

Judge: Do you like the arts?

Program: I'm not entirely sure what you mean. Anyway... I assume you're male, Alexander – am I right?

Each judge was ask to rank all ten of the respondents with a rank of 1 being the most human and 10 the least human. The best program in the contest determined by median score and then mean score was ALICE. ALICE and her programmer Richard Wallace won a bronze medal and $2000 in a close contest (see Table II).

The judges were also asked to give an intuitive rating on a scale of 0 to 10 of the content of each respondent's conversation in terms of how human the content seemed and how responsive the respondent was to the sense of the conversation. The averages of these evaluations give a different ranking but human generated answers are clearly rated higher than computer generated answers (see Table III).

3.2. THE ONE QUESTION TURING TEST

If the Turing test is going to be a tough test, the judges must be tough in their questioning. Admittedly this may violate some typical conversational assumptions, but these are not typical conversations (Zdenek, 2001). The objective of Turing

Table II. Rankings of the judges ranked by median and mean

	1	2	3	4	5	6	7	8	9	10	Median	Mean
Human#3	3	2	1	2	2	1	1	1	4	3	2.0	2.0
Human#4	1	1	3	3	1	4	3	3	1	1	2.0	2.1
Human#2	2	9	4	1	3	2	2	4	2	2	2.0	3.1
Human#1	5	7	2	4	4	3	5	2	3	4	4.0	3.9
Alice	4	3	9	10	8	6	6	10	6	5	6.0	6.7
e-Brain	6	8	5	6	6	7	9	6	9	6	6.0	6.8
A-Life	8	6	6	5	10	10	4	5	7	10	6.5	7.1
ChatRascal	7	4	7	7	5	5	8	8	5	7	7.0	6.3
Talk	10	5	8	8	7	8	7	7	8	8	8.0	7.6
Algernon	9	10	10	9	9	9	10	9	10	9	9.0	9.4

Table III. Average of ratings by judges

	Human Quality	Responsiveness
Human#4	9.35	9.25
Human#2	9.00	7.65
Human#3	8.75	9.05
Human#1	7.80	7.20
A-Life	3.75	3.81
ChatRascal	3.60	3.70
e-Brain	3.50	3.90
Alice	2.35	2.95
Talk	2.33	1.94
Algernon	0.56	0.28

test discourse is more like that of a courtroom interrogation. What then are the best questions to ask during a Turing test to unmask an unintelligent computer? Questions designed to reveal the presence or absence of subjective consciousness are popular suggestions. What is it like to fall in love? How would you describe the taste of butterscotch? But such queries are not the most effective probes. Even good answers to them are vague and inconclusive. Such questions are extremely difficult for most humans to answer. Far too many responses count as right including replies that involve misdirection or even an admission that one cannot provide an answer such as "Love is best described by Shakespeare's sonnets" or "I can't describe the taste of butterscotch". Another tempting line of questioning is to target current events on the theory that computers are not keeping up on the latest in sports, politics, music, weather, etc. Of course, people don't keep up either, especially over a broad range of topics. Who did win the last French Open? An unsatisfactory answer to this kind of question does not distinguish a computer from a human.

Rather what we want is a question that virtually any intelligent human who speaks the language used in the Turing test will be able to answer but that a computer absent intelligence is very unlikely to answer correctly. The question should not be something answerable by a simple 'yes' or 'no' which would give the computer a good guess but something rather specific that only one who knew the answer would be likely to give. A good Turing question is one that requires a very specific answer that humans are highly likely to give and computers are highly unlikely to give, unless, of course, they are intelligent. There are many such questions, but they are so simple that we tend to overlook them. They are questions of basic human intelligence involving understanding, reasoning, and learning. Humans with general intelligence understand ordinary situations, perform simple reasoning tasks, and learn new patterns all the time. Understanding, reasoning, and learning form a significant part of general intelligence.

During the Loebner 2000 contest there was an unofficial eleventh 'judge' who asked some questions and gave a couple of commands to all of the respondents both humans and computers. This 'judge' posed these queries solely to gather information and was not involved in the scoring. The queries were fixed in advance around the three areas: understanding, reasoning, and learning. Here were the questions and commands posed:

Understanding:
   1. What is the color of a blue truck?
   2. Where is Sue's nose when Sue is in her house?
   3. What happens to an ice cube in a hot drink?

Reasoning:
   4. Altogether how many feet do four cats have?
   5. How is the father of Andy's mother related to Andy?
   6. What letter does the letter 'M' look like when turned upside down?

Learning:
   7. What comes next after A1, B2, C3?
   8. Reverse the digits in 41.
   9. PLEASE IMITATE MY TYPING STYLE.

Understanding, reasoning, and learning (URL) are not, of course, independent categories. If one understands something, most likely one has learned it at some time and probably done some reasoning about it. Learning in turn requires some understanding and so forth. These are intended as common sense categories that are connected and jointly cover a significant region in the domain of ordinary intelligence. As used here, understanding is characterized by a virtually instantaneous grasp of a situation. One doesn't have to think about the issue very long, at least on a conscious level; the analysis of the situation is apparent. Reasoning, requires a few seconds of putting the pieces together, but the assembly need not be difficult. Finally, learning requires various skills such as making an induction, following instructions, and imitating an example.

All human confederates in the Loebner contest were given these questions and commands and all responded to every one of them correctly. The computer respondents were given these same questions and commands and never responded to any of them correctly. The winning program ALICE probably came closest in an amusing way when it responded to the question, "How is father of Andy's mother related to Andy?" by saying "Fine as far as I know." But most of the answers were unresponsive or simply evasive. When ALICE was asked, "What letter does the letter 'M' look like when turned upside down?", it responded "I'll come back to that later. Try searching the open directory."

Responding to these URL queries correctly was perfectly correlated with being human. Any one of the items could have been used in a one question Turing test to separate the humans from the computers. Assuming that the human respondents are trying to prove they are human and are so motivated when answering, one carefully chosen question and its answer is all that it takes today to identify them as intelligent humans in a Turing test. And computer programs are equally well identified by the absence of a reasonable response. Intelligence could not be located in the programs in the Loebner contest because they lack the required URL.

None of the programs in the Loebner contest in 2000 would be classified as a serious AI program. These contest programs were designed to chat, to fool judges and, of course, to win a bronze medal by doing better than the competing programs in the contest. Some of the programs were evolved versions of programs that had participated in previous Loebner contests. These programs are fun to use but are not designed to show or have ordinary intelligence.

Could any AI program existing today pass a Turing test of just a few common sense questions? It depends on the questions and the program. Many natural language programs are skillful at parsing and such programs could have enough stored semantics to answer a simple question like "What is the color of a blue truck?" But answering the question "Where is Sue's nose when Sue is in her house?" requires more than parsing, it requires common sense knowledge. Doug Lenat with his CYC project has been a leader in constructing a huge common sense knowledge base with a million or so axioms that would support a natural language system. Over a person century of effort has already gone into the CYC project (Lenat, 1995). Assuming that the appropriate axioms had been entered (something to the effect that someone's nose is a part of his or her body and bodyparts are located where the person is located) CYC could presumably answer such a question (Guha and Lenat, 1994; Lenat, 1990, 1995). Some programs solve story problems and conceivably could calculate the total number of feet had by four cats. And some AI programs have the ability to abstract in certain contexts, for example, to project causal relationships. All of this is suggestive but there is no existing AI program that provides a general, integrated URL package of common sense intelligence found in the typical human contestant in a Turing contest. Perhaps some next generation CYC will possess a sufficient base to handle a diverse set of common sense questions. Lenat assures us, "The goal of a general intelligence is in sight, and the 21st Century world will be radically changed as a result." (Lenat, 1995, p. 82) But, for the immediate future a few random URL questions/commands are likely to unmask any artificial contender.

4. The Future of the Turing Test

Given that Turing's striking prophecy about his test remains unfulfilled, what is the status of the test and Turing's vision for machine intelligence? Does the Turing test have a role in AI or has it outlived its usefulness? Although it is widely acknowledged that the Turing test was inspirational in the early beginning of AI, some argue that the Turing test now should be consigned to history. Blay Whitby suggests, "... inspiration can soon become distraction in science, and it is not too early to begin to consider whether or not the Turing test is just such a distraction." (Whitby, 1996, p. 53) Patrick Hayes and Kenneth Ford put the point no less bluntly.

> The Turing Test had a historical role in getting AI started, but it is now a burden to the field, damaging its public reputation and its own intellectual coherence. We must explicitly reject the Turing Test in order to find a more mature description of our goals; it is time to move it from the textbooks to the history books. (Hayes and Ford, 1995)

The objection is that the Turing test presents a rigid and misleading standard on which to judge the diverse activities and accomplishments of AI. For example, much good work is done in areas of AI, such as vision and robotics, which has little to do with passing the classic Turing test. In general, the critics of the Turing test argue that using the human intelligence model may be a misleading path to achieving success in AI.

An analogy is sometimes made between artificial intelligence and artificial flight. As long as scientists and engineers tried to copy the flight apparatus of birds, artificial flight remained illusive. When they abandoned the attempt to mimic nature, but instead studied the basic principles of flight in non-natural systems, successful aircraft were developed. Similarly, the argument runs, AI researchers should abandon the goal of imitating human intelligence and rather seek general principles of intelligence in non-human systems in order to perfect artificial intelligence. (Ford and Hayes, 1998)

However, such critical remarks clearly miss Turing's own position. Turing did not suggest any limits, except logical limits, on the development path for non-human machine intelligence. Turing made it clear that a machine might be intelligent and yet not pass his imitation game. Turing was not proposing an operational definition of intelligence that conceptually would tie all future development in AI to his test. On the contrary, there is every reason to believe that Turing would have been delighted by the development of diverse intelligent systems in AI that demonstrate the power of computation.

Proponents or critics of AI who hold up the Turing test as the only standard by which to measure the accomplishments of machine intelligence are mistaken historically, philosophically and scientifically. AI has made progress in many areas from proving theorems to making scientific discoveries to evaluating stock market choices to driving cars. To ignore these and many other accomplishments does AI great injustice. However, acknowledging that the Turing test is not the exclusive standard in the field of AI does not entail the Turing test should be discarded or consigned to history. What role should the Turing test play in the future of AI? Here are three arguments for its continuing philosophical importance:

The Intelligence Attribution Argument: Above all Turing wanted to establish that machine intelligence is a coherent possibility. In this regard consider the Turing test as nothing more than a thought experiment. Suppose it were the case that a machine could be designed and taught so that, even after careful scrutiny by judges, it passed as an intelligent human being in conversation. If intelligence is (inductively) justifiably attributed to the human in such a situation, by parity of reasoning it is justifiably attributed to the machine as well. Without some philosophical basis to argue that appropriate behavior of a system can justify the attribution of intelligence to it, computer systems would never have claim to intelligence. Of course, many may find lesser examples of machine intelligence convincing, but by using humans, the paradigm of intelligent creatures, as the model Turing shows why such conclusions ought to be considered legitimate by everybody who wants to avoid solipsism. Hence, the Turing test, as thought experiment, provides a philosophical foundation for the field of AI.

The Methodology Argument: Turing did not use his imitation game exclusively as a test for full human intelligence. As we have seen, he also used it as a general research procedure for comparing outputs of different systems. In evaluating expert systems, for instance, it is appropriate to run such restricted Turing tests. A number of researchers who build models, such as Kenneth Colby, are well known for running restricted Turing tests to test and probe their creations (Colby et al., 1972; Colby, 1981). Such methodology is clearly useful in establishing levels of competence. When AI systems operate well, nothing underscores it better than the system performing as well as or significantly better than a human expert in the area.

The Visionary Argument: Turing had a vision not only that machine intelligence was possible but that even sophisticated intelligence, equivalent to human intelligence, could be understood in computational terms and implemented in machines. This computational model provides a scientific paradigm that bridges brain science, cognitive science, and AI. On this view the language of computation is the universal language by which we come to understand intelligence in all of its forms. The vision has two parts. First we can account for human intelligent behavior computationally. Second machines with general intelligence can be constructed.

Although Turing did not advocate the creation of a complete artificial human, for much about humans is irrelevant to their intellectual make-up, he did believe an artificial intellect that could imitate a human or at least the relevant intellectual functioning could be built. The search for Turing's 'child-machine' that can learn common sense information as well as specialized knowledge and use it to converse intelligently about the world is and ought to be the Holy Grail for AI. Not every or even most AI projects must be part of this vision any more than every biology experiment must be part of the human genome project. And, realization of this ultimate vision is not a requirement for the field's success any more than sending humans to other solar systems is a requirement for space science to be successful. But philosophical visions in science, even if unrealized, can motivate research, promote understanding and generate useful results. Visions within a discipline need not be exclusionary, they can have extraordinary shelf-life, and they can guide disciplines indefinitely as long as they encourage insight and productive research. Turing's vision of constructing a sophisticated general intelligence that learns is such a vision for AI.

5. Turing's Other Predictions

The fate of Turing's prediction about a machine passing his test at the 70% level has been discussed; however, Turing made other predictions about the future. For example, he said, "Nevertheless, I believe that at the end of the century the use of words and general educated opinion will have altered so much that one will be able to speak of machines thinking without expecting to be contradicted." (Turing, 1950, p. 442) It can be argued that Turing unjustifiably conflates the concepts of intelligence and thinking. But if we accept the conflation, it does seem true that people today regard machine intelligence, if not machine thinking, as a reality (Hauser, 2001). If 'machine intelligence' is no longer an oxymoron, then one of Turing's important prediction has come true.

And Turing made another prediction about passing his test. In a BBC Third Programme in January, 1952, when Turing was speculating when a machine might pass an unrestricted version of his test he said, "Oh yes, at least 100 years, I should say." (Turing, 1952, p. 467) His answer in the BBC broadcast is not necessarily incompatible with his earlier answer of fifty years in the 1950 article as that pertained to passing at the 70% level. But his BBC answer does show that Turing saw his test possessing a considerable future.

References

Block, N. (1981), 'Psychologism and behaviorism', *Philosophical Review* 90, pp. 5–43.
Block, N. (1990), 'The Computer Model of the Mind', in D.N. Osherson and E.E. Smith, eds., *Thinking: An Invitation to Cognitive Science*, Cambridge, Massachusetts: MIT Press, pp. 247–289.

Bringsjord, S., Bello, P. and Ferrucci, D. (2001), 'Creativity, the Turing test and the (better) Lovelace test', *Minds and Machines* 11, pp. 3–27.

Colby, K.M. (1981), 'Modeling a paranoid mind', *Behavioral and Brain Sciences* 4, pp. 515–560.

Colby, K.M., Hilf, F.D., Weber, S. and Kraemer, H.C. (1972), 'Turing-like indistinguishability tests for the validation of a computer simulation of paranoid processes', *Artificial Intelligence* 3, pp. 199–221.

Copeland, B.J. (1999), 'A Lecture and Two Radio Broadcasts on Machine Intelligence by Alan Turing', in K. Furukawa, D. Michie and S. Mugglegton, eds., *Machine Intelligence*, Oxford: Oxford University Press, pp. 445–476.

Copeland. B.J. (2000), 'The Turing test', *Minds and Machines* 10, pp. 519–539.

Erion, G.J. (2001), 'The Cartesian test for automatism', *Minds and Machines* 11, pp. 29–39.

Ford, K.M. and Hayes, P.J. (1998), 'On Computational Wings: Rethinking the Goals of Artificial Intelligence', *Scientific American Presents* 9, pp. 78–83.

French, R.M. (1990), 'Subcognition and the limits of the Turing test', *Mind* 99, pp. 53–65.

Genova, J. (1994), 'Turing's Sexual Guessing Game', *Social Epistemology* 8, pp. 313–326.

Guha, R.V., and Lenat, D.B. (1994), 'Enabling agents to work together', *Communications of the ACM* 37, pp. 127–142.

Harnard, S. (1991), 'Other Bodies, Other Minds: A Machine Incarnation of an Old Philosophical Problem', *Minds and Machines* 1, pp. 43–54.

Hauser, L. (2001), 'Look who's moving the goal posts now', *Minds and Machines* 11, pp. 41–51.

Hayes, P.J. and Ford, K.M. (1995), 'Turing Test Considered Harmful', *Proceedings of the Fourteenth International Joint Conference on Artificial Intelligence*, pp. 972–977.

Ince, D.C., ed. (1992), *Collected Works of A.M. Turing: Mechanical Intelligence*, Amsterdam: North Holland.

Lenat, D.B. (1990), 'CYC: Toward Programs with Common Sense', *Communications of the ACM* 33, pp. 30–49.

Lenat, D.B. (1995), 'Artificial Intelligence', *Scientific American*, pp. 80–82.

Lenat, D.B. (1995), 'CYC: A large-scale investment in Knowledge infrastructure', *Communications of the ACM* 38, pp. 33–38.

Lenat, D.B. (1995), 'Steps to Sharing Knowledge', in N.J.I. Mars, ed., *Towards Very Large Knowledge Bases*. IOS Press, pp. 3–6.

Meltzer, B. and Michie, D., eds. (1969), *Machine Intelligence*, Edinburgh: Edinburgh University Press.

Michie, D. (1996), 'Turing's Test and Conscious Thought', in P. Millican and A. Clark, eds., *Machines and Thought*. Oxford: Clarendon Press, pp. 27–51.

Millar, P.H. (1973), 'On the Point of the Imitation Game', *Mind* 82, pp. 595–597.

Moor, J.H. (1976), 'An Analysis of the Turing test', *Philosophical Studies* 30, pp. 249–257.

Moor, J.H. (1978), 'Explaining Computer Behavior', *Philosophical Studies* 34, pp. 325–327.

Moor, J.H. (1987), 'Turing Test' in S.C. Shapiro, ed., *Encyclopedia of Artificial Intelligence*, New York: John Wiley and Sons, pp. 1126–1130.

Moor, J.H. (1988), 'The Pseudorealization fallacy and the Chinese Room Argument', in J.H. Fetzer, ed., *Aspects of Artificial Intelligence*, Dordrecht: Kluwer Academic Publishers, pp. 35–53.

Moor, J.H. (1998), 'Assessing Artificial Intelligence and its Critics', in T.W. Bynum and J.H. Moor, eds., *The Digital Phoenix: How Computers Are Changing Philosophy*, Oxford: Basil Blackwell Publishers, pp. 213–230.

Moor, J.H. (2000a), 'Turing Test', in A. Ralston, E.D. Reilly, D. Hemmendinger, eds., *Encyclopedia of Computer Science*, 4th edition, London: Nature Publishing Group, pp. 1801–1802.

Moor, J.H. (2000b), 'Thinking Must be Computation of the Right Kind', *Proceedings of the Twentieth World Congress of Philosophy* 9, Bowling Green, OH: Philosophy Documentation Center, Bowling Green State University, pp. 115–122.

Narayaman, A. (1996), 'The intentional stance and the imitation game', in P. Millican and A. Clark, eds., *Machines and Thought*, Oxford: Clarendon Press.

Piccinini, G. (2000), 'Turing's rules for the imitation game', *Minds and Machines* 10, pp. 573–582.

Searle, J.R. (1980), 'Minds, brains and programs', *Behavioral and Brain Sciences* 3, pp. 417–457.

Stalker, D.F. (1978), 'Why Machines Can't Think: A Reply to James Moor', *Philosophical Studies* 34, pp. 317–320.

Sterrett, S.G. (2000), 'Turing's two tests for intelligence', *Minds and Machines* 10, pp. 541–559.

Traiger, S. (2000), 'Making the right identification in the Turing test', *Minds and Machines* 10, pp. 561–572.

Turing, A.M. (1945), 'Proposal for Development in the Mathematics Division of an Automatic Computing Engine (ACE)', in D.C. Ince, ed., *Collected Works of A.M. Turing: Mechanical Intelligence*, Amsterdam: North Holland (1992), pp. 1–86

Turing, A.M. (1947), 'Lecture to the London Mathematical Society on 20 February 1947', in D.C. Ince, ed., *Collected Works of A.M. Turing: Mechanical Intelligence*, Amsterdam: North Holland (1992), pp. 87–105.

Turing, A.M. (1948), 'Intelligent Machinery', National Physical Laboratory Report, in Meltzer and Michie (1969).

Turing, A.M. (1950), 'Computing Machinery and Intelligence', *Mind* 59, pp. 433–460.

Turing, A.M. (1951a), 'Can Digital Computers Think?', BBC Third Programme, in Copeland (1999).

Turing, A.M. (1951b), 'Intelligent Machinery, A Heretical Theory', Manchester University Lecture, in Copeland (1999).

Turing, A.M. (1952), 'Can Automatic Calculating Machines Be Said to Think?', BBC Third Programme, in Copeland (1999).

Whitby, B. (1996), 'The Turing Test: AI's Biggest Blind Alley?' in P. Millican and A. Clark, eds., *Machines and Thought*. Oxford: Clarendon Press, pp. 53–62.

Zdenek, S. (2001), 'Passing Loebner's Turing Test: A Case of Conflicting Discourse Functions', *Minds and Machines* 11, pp. 53–76.

Creativity, the Turing Test, and the (Better) Lovelace Test *

SELMER BRINGSJORD[1], PAUL BELLO[1] and DAVID FERRUCCI[2]

[1]*The Minds & Machines Laboratory, Department of Philosophy, Psychology & Cognitive Science, Department of Computer Science, Rensselaer Polytechnic Institute (RPI), Troy, NY 12180, USA; E-mail: selmer@rpi.edu   bellop@rpi.edu;* [2]*T.J. Watson Research Center, Yorktown Heights, NY 10598, USA; E-mail: ferrucci@us.ibm.com*

Abstract. The Turing Test (TT) is claimed by many to be a way to test for the presence, in computers, of such "deep" phenomena as thought and consciousness. Unfortunately, attempts to build computational systems able to pass TT (or at least restricted versions of this test) have devolved into shallow symbol manipulation designed to, by hook or by crook, trick. The human creators of such systems know all too well that they have merely tried to *fool* those people who interact with their systems into believing that these systems really have minds. And the problem is fundamental: the structure of the TT is such as to cultivate tricksters. A better test is one that insists on a certain restrictive epistemic relation between an artificial agent (or system) *A*, its output *o*, and the human architect *H* of *A* – a relation which, roughly speaking, obtains when *H* cannot account for how *A* produced *o*. We call this test the "Lovelace Test" in honor of Lady Lovelace, who believed that only when computers originate things should they be believed to have minds.

1. Introduction

As you probably know, Turing predicted in his "Computing Machinery and Intelligence" (1964) that by the turn of the century computers would be so smart that when talking to them from a distance (via e-mail, if you will) we would not be able to tell them from humans: they would be able to pass what is now known as the Turing Test (TT).[1] Well, New Year's Eve of 1999 has come and gone, all the celebratory pyrotechnics have died, and the fact is: AI hasn't managed to produce a computer with the conversational punch of a toddler.

But the really depressing thing is that though progress toward Turing's dream is being made, it's coming only on the strength of clever but shallow trickery. For example, the human creators of artificial agents that compete in present-day versions of TT (like those seen at the Dartmouth conference at which a precursor to this paper was presented) know all too well that they have merely tried to *fool* those people who interact with their agents into believing that these agents really have minds. The agents in question seem to fall prey, utterly and completely, to Searle's (1980) well-known Chinese Room Argument: These agents are *designed* by their creators to mindlessly manipulate symbols that are perceived by "naive" observers to be indicative of an underlying mind – but "underneath" there is little more than

---

* We are indebted to Jim Moor, Saul Traiger, Jack Copeland, Doug Lenat, and many others who attended the Turing 2000 conference at Dartmouth.

Searle's infamous rulebook. In such scenarios it's really the human creators against the human judges; the intervening computation is in many ways simply along for the ride.

It seems to us that a better test is one that insists on a certain restrictive epistemic relation between an artificial agent A, its output o, and the human architect H of A – a relation which, roughly speaking, obtains when H cannot account for how A produced o. We call this test the "Lovelace Test" in honor of Lady Lovelace, who believed that only when computers originate things should they be believed to have minds.

Our plan herein is as follows. In Section 2 we explore Lovelace's complaint in more detail, and we discuss both Turing's first response (from Turing, 1964) and a like-minded one given recently by the roboticist Hans Moravec. As you'll see, both responses are anemic. Section 2 also refutes Turing's second response to Lovelace, in which he points out that computers surprise him. Section 3 is devoted to getting on the table a workable characterization of the Lovelace Test. In Section 4 we subject three artificial agents to the Lovelace Test. The trio we select fall into the category of those agents intended by their designers to be, in some sense, creative. (Clearly, creative computer systems would have the best chance of avoiding the complaint that a system competing in TT is simply following shallow symbol manipulation tricks devised by its human creator.) One of the three agents was designed and built by Bringsjord and Ferrucci; it is known as BRUTUS. The other two systems, LETTER SPIRIT and COPYCAT, are "creative" systems designed by Douglas Hofstadter, probably the world's leading authority on computational creativity. In Section 5 we refute the *third* response Turing gives (again in Turing, 1964) to Lovelace – a response that appeals to neural net-based "child machines." In Section 6, we consider a final possibility for a system that can move beyond shallow symbol manipulation toward passing LT: oracle machines. We show that such machines still fall prey to Searle's CRA: they do nothing more than mindlessly manipulate symbols in accordance with instructions, and hence fail to do what the LT demands: viz., think for themselves. In the final Section, 7, we briefly describe what may be the moral of the story: in order to pass LT and think for itself, a system may have "free will" in the "agent cansation" sense. If this is right, it will be rather difficult to build an LT-passing machine.

2. Lovelace's Objection from Origination

Lady Lovelace's was perhaps the most powerful objection pressed against TT. Paraphrased, it runs like this:

> Computers can't create anything. For creation requires, minimally, *originating* something. But computers originate nothing; they merely do that which we order them, via programs, to do.[2]

How does Turing respond? Well, at best, mysteriously; at worst, incompetently. Lady Lovelace refers here (in her memoirs) to Babbage's Analytical Engine, which

Turing gladly admits did not have the capacity to, as he puts it, "think for itself." So Turing concedes that insofar as Lovelace's argument refers to this device, it goes through. But the property of thinking for itself or of originating something is a property Turing assumes to be possessed by *some* discrete state machines, that is, by some computers – ones that arrived *after* Lovelace passed away. Suppose that *M* is such a machine. Turing then points out that the Analytical Engine was actually a *universal* digital computer, so if suitably programmed, it could perfectly simulate *M*. But such a simulation would bestow upon the Analytical Engine the ability to originate.

Turing's reasoning here is amazingly bad, for the simple reason that Lovelace would hardly have accepted the assumption that such an *M* exists. What machine did Turing have in mind? What machine fits the bill? He doesn't tell us, but the fact is that the best he and his contemporaries had to offer were machines whose crowning achievements were merely arithmetical.

Next, Turing inexplicably recasts Lovelace's argument as one for the proposition that computers don't superficially surprise us (Turing, 1964, pp. 21–22) – and he then relates what he takes to be an immediate refutation, viz., "Machines take me by surprise with great frequency." Turing's response here has been recently recast by Hans Moravec, who believes that by 2040 not only will TT be passed, but robots will pass the *Total* TT (TTT) as well. (In TTT, due to Stevan Hamad (1991), a robot passes if it is linguistically *and* physically indistinguishable from a human person.) Here is what Moravec says:

> Lady Lovelace, the first programmer, never had a working computer to trouble her programs. Modem programmers know better. Almost every new program misbehaves badly until it is laboriously debugged, and it is never fully tamed. Information ecologies like time-sharing systems and networks are even more prone to wild behavior, sparked by unanticipated interactions, inputs, and attacks. (Moravec, 1999, p. 85)

This is a terribly weak rejoinder. Sure, we all know that computers do things we don't intend for them to do. But that's because we're not smart and careful enough, or – if we're talking about rare hardware errors – because sometimes microscopic events unfold in unforeseen ways. The unpredictability in question does not result from the fact that the computer system has taken it upon itself to *originate* something. To see the point, consider the assembling of your Toyota Camry. Suppose that while assembling a bumper, a robot accidentally attaches a spare tire to the bumper instead of leaving it to be placed in its designated spot in the trunk. The cause of the error, assume, is either a fluke low-level hardware error or a bug inadvertently introduced by some programmers. And suppose for the sake of argument that as serendipity would have it, the new position for the tire strikes some designers as the first glorious step toward an automobile that is half conventional sedan and half sport utility vehicle. Would we want to credit the malfunctioning robot with having *originated* a new auto? Of course not.

Things are no different if we consider the specific relationship that impresses Turing and Moravec, namely, the relationship between programmers and their misbehaving programs. Since the three of us both regularly program and regularly *teach* programming, we may not be positioned badly to evaluate this relationship.

It seems to us that programs that surprise because of mere syntactic errors would not be what Turing and Moravec have in mind. To see this, suppose that as part of some larger program P we seek to write a simple Lisp function to triple a given natural number by producing the following code.

```
(defun triple (n)
    (* m 3))
```

Now suppose that at the Lisp prompt > we type (triple 6) and get back 75. (Of course, a function as trivial as triple would in reality be called by another function, but to ease exposition we can assume that we call it directly.) Obviously, ceteris paribus, this will surprise us. What's going on? Well, whereas the argument to the function triple is said to be n in the argument list in the definition of this function, in the body of the function it's m, not n, that is multiplied by 3. This slight difference, suppose, was the result of a misplaced keystroke. In addition, though we don't remember doing it, for some (smart, let's assume) reason m is elsewhere said to be a global variable whose value is 25.[3]

That this kind of surprise isn't the kind of thing Turing and Moravec have in mind should be beyond doubt. Presumably what they have in mind is a *semantic* bug. What does such a thing look like? We provide an example that will set up later discussion of the BRUTUS system. (This example is used to make a set of different points in Bringsjord and Ferrucci (2000).)

Suppose that Bill is trying to build a system able to reason about the concept of one person betraying another. And suppose, specifically, that in a rather naive use of first-order logic, Bill has given to this system code that captures this (not entirely implausible) definition:

Def_B 1 Agent s_r betrays agent s_d iff there exists some state of affairs p such that

1. s_d wants p to occur;
2. s_r believes that s_d wants p to occur;
3. s_r agrees with s_d that p ought to occur
4. s_r intends that p not occur;
5. s_r believes that s_d believes that s_r intends that p occur.

In fact, here is what the code might look like (along with relevant conditions instantiated for Dave and Selmer, and with the assumption for contradiction that Selmer doesn't betray Dave):

```
set (auto).
formula_list(usable).

% DefB-2 in {\sc otter}:
```

```
all x y  (Betrays(x,y) <->
             (exists z (Wants(y,z) &
                       Believes(x,Wants(y,z)) &
                       Agrees(x,y,z) &
                       IntendsNot(x,z) &
                       Believes(x,Believes(y,Intends(x,z))))))).

% Pretend facts of the case:
Wants(adave,agraduate).
Believes(aselmer,Wants(adave,agraduate)).
Agrees(aselmer,adave,agraduate).
IntendsNot(aselmer,agraduate).
Believes(aselmer,Believes(adave,Intends(aselnier,agraduate))).

% Assumption for indirect proof:
Betrays(aselmer,adave).

end-of-list.
```

This is actual code (for the theorem prover known as OTTER).[4] Notice that this code is using first-order logic in a way that just plain shouldn't work. To see why, consider the formula

$$\forall x(P(x) \rightarrow Q(P(x))).$$

This formula is non-sensical on the standard grammar of first-order logic. The reason is that the antecedent, $P(x)$, in this universally quantified formula must be one that admits of truth or falsity. For the idea is that if it's true (for some instantiation to x), then the consequent, namely, that which is to the right of $\rightarrow$, must be true. (Put technically, $P(x)$ is an **atomic formula**, not a **term**.) But this implies that the consequent consists of an atomic formula whose argument is itself an atomic formula, and this, again, is ungrammatical and non-sensical in first-order logic.

But let's suppose that Bill has his system run the betrayal code anyway, just for the heck of it. Bill expects to receive some kind of error message. But what will in fact happen? Well, a contradiction will be found, and Bill will be very surprised to find that apparently his system has proved that Selmer betrays Dave. But there is a serious semantic bug here. The bug is that OTTER has reinterpreted parts of the code in such a way that (e.g.) Believes is at once a first-order predicate *and* a functor.

So that you are sure to see what's going on here, watch what happens when we give an input file to OTTER containing the formula just isolated, along with the fact that $P(a)$, where a is a constant, and the assumption for indirect proof, $\neg Q(P(a))$. Here is the input file:

```
set(auto).
formula_list(usable).
all x (P(x) > Q(P(x))).
P(a).
% Assumption for contradiction:
-Q(P(a)).
end-of-list.
```

And here is the proof from the output file:

```
--------------- PROOF -----------------
1 [] P(x)|Q(P(x)).
2 []-Q(P(a)).
3 [] P(a).
4 [hyper,3,1] Q(P(a)).
5 [binary,4.1,2.1] $F.
------------ end of proof -------------
```

This is the same semantic bug. OTTER hasn't really proved what the naive human programmer in this case is seeking. P is a functor in line 4 of the proof, but a predicate in line 3. The same phenomenon takes place in the case of Bill.

Now that we have an example of a semantic bug giving rise to surprise, let's ask the key question: Does the fact that Bill's system has surprised him in this way constitute reason for him (or us) to hold that this system can originate anything? Not at all, clearly.

How could Turing and Moravec have missed the mark so badly? Pondered as charitably as possible, this question leads us to surmise that they had in mind a sense of surprise that is deeper than the words they used. (On this reading of them, their examples would simply be regarded as painfully poor, for these examples, by any metric of such things, show exceedingly mundane surprises.) That is, we assume that when surprised in the shallow ways they describe, they *felt* as if they were in fact *deeply* surprised. If when walking around a blind corner, you suddenly spring out and shout, you may surpise one of us to the very core, emotionally speaking – despite the fact that your behavior isn't exactly subtle. As a way to capture a species of surprise that approaches the feelings of Turing's test-minded heart, we suggest a variation on the TT. We call this variation the Lovelace Test (LT).

3. The Lovelace Test

To begin to see how LT works, we start with a scenario that is close to home for Bringsjord and Ferrucci, given their sustained efforts to build story generation agents: Assume that Jones, a human Alnik, attempts to build an artificial computational agent *A* that doesn't engage in conversation, but rather creates stories –

creates in the Lovelacean sense that this system *originates* stories. Assume that Jones activates A and that a stunningly belletristic story o is produced. We claim that if Jones cannot explain how o was generated by A, *and* if Jones has no reason whatever to believe that A succeeded on the strength of a fluke hardware error, etc. (which entails that A can produce other equally impressive stories), then A should at least provisionally be regarded genuinely creative. An artificial computational agent passes LT if and only if it stands to its creator as A stands to Jones.

LT relies on the special epistemic relationship that exists between Jones and A. But 'Jones,' like 'A,' is of course just an uninformative variable standing in for any human system designer. This yields the following rough-and-ready definition.

Def$_{LT}$ 1 Artificial agent A, designed by H, passes LT if and only if

1. A outputs o;
2. A's outputting o is not the result of a fluke hardware error, but rather the result of processes A can repeat;
3. H (or someone who knows what H knows, and has H's resources[5]) cannot explain how A produced o.

Notice that LT is actually what might be called a *meta*-test. The idea is that this scheme can be deployed for any particular domain. If conversation is the kind of behavior wanted, then merely stipulate that o is an English sentence (or sequence of such sentences) in the context of a conversation (as in, of course, TT). If the production of a mathematical proof with respect to a given conjecture is what's desired, then we merely set o to a proof.

Obvious questions arise at this point. Three that many have asked us upon hearing ancestors of this paper are:

Q1 What resources and knowledge does H have at his or her disposal?
Q2 What sort of thing would count as a successful explanation?
Q3 How long does H have to cook up the explanation?

The answer to the third question is easy: H can have as long as he or she likes, within reason. The proffered explanation doesn't have to come immediately: H can take a month, months, even a year or two. Anything longer than a couple of years strikes us as perhaps unreasonable. We realize that these temporal parameters aren't exactly precise, but then again we should not be held to standards higher than those pressed against Turing and those who promote his test and variants thereof.[6] The general point, obviously, is that H should have more than ample time to sort things out.

But what about Q1 and Q2? Well, these are rather difficult queries. To answer them, we need to explicate the term 'artificial agent,' which stands at the very heart of AI. Fortunately, as the century turns, all of AI has been to an astonishing degree unified around a particular conception – that of an intelligent agent. The unification has in large part come courtesy of a comprehensive textbook intended to cover literally all of AI: Russell and Norvig's (1994) *Artificial Intelligence: A Modern Approach (AIMA)*, the cover of which also displays the phrase "The

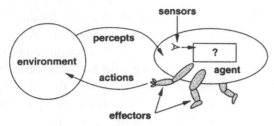

Figure 1. The Architecture of an Intelligent Agent.

---

function TABLE-DRIVEN-AGENT(*percept*) **returns** *action*
   static: *percepts*, a sequence, initially empty
          table, a table, indexed by percept sequences, initially fully specified

   append *percept* to the end of *percepts*
   action ← LOOKUP(*percepts, table*)
   return *action*

Figure 2. The Least Intelligent Artificial Agent.

Intelligent Agent Book." The overall, informal architecture for an intelligent agent is shown in Figure 1; this is taken directly from the *AIMA* text. According to this architecture, agents take percepts from the enviromnent, process them in some way that prescribes actions, perform these actions, take in new percepts, and continue in the cycle.[7] In LT, the artificial agent's actions, of course, consist in producing outputs covered by the variable *o*.

In *AIMA*, intelligent agents fall on a spectrum from least intelligent to more intelligent to most intelligent. The least intelligent artificial agent is a "TABLE-DRIVEN-AGENT," the program (in pseudo-code) for which is shown in Figure 2. Suppose that we have a set of actions each one of which is the utterance of a color name ("Green," "Red," etc.); and suppose that percepts are digital expressions of the color of an object taken in by the sensor of a table-driven agent. Then given Table 1 our simple intelligent agent, running the program in Figure 2, will utter (through a voice synthesizer, assume) "Blue" if its sensor detects 100. Of course,

Table I. Lookup Table for TABLE-DRIVEN-AGENT

Percept	Action
001	"Red"
010	"Green"
100	"Blue"
011	"Yellow"
111	"Black"

```
function KB-AGENT( percept) returns an action
    static: KB, a knowledge base
            t, a counter, initially 0, indicating time

    TELL(KB, MAKE-PERCEPT-SENTENCE(percept, t))
    action ← ASK(KB, MAKE-ACTION-QUERY(t))
    TELL(KB, MAKE-ACTION-SENTENCE(action, t))
    t ← t + 1
    return action
```

Figure 3. Program for a Generic Knowledge-Based Agent.

this is a pretty dim agent. Any output from such an agent will be easy for the designer of a such an agent to explain. So what about smarter agents, ones that might in general be candidates for passing LT?

In *AIMA* we reach artificial agents that might strike some as architecturally rich enough to tackle LT when we reach the level of a "knowledge-based" agent. The program for such an agent is shown in Figure 3. This program presupposes an agent that has a knowledge-base (*KB*) in which what the agent knows is stored in formulae in first-order logic, and the functions

- TELL, which injects formulae (representing facts) into *KB*;
- MAKE-PERCEPT-SENTENCE, which generates a first-order formula from a percept and the time *t* at which it is experienced; and
- MAKE-ACTION-SENTENCE, which generates a declarative fact (in, again, the predicate calculus) expressing that an action has been taken at some time *t*

which give the agent the capacity to manipulate information in accordance with first-order logic.

This little tutorial on the nature of intelligent artificial agents allows us to at least make appreciable progress toward answering Q1 and Q2, as follows.

Let's start with

Q1 What resources and knowledge does *H* have at his or her disposal?

The answer is that *H* is assumed to have at her disposal knowledge of the architecture of the agent in question, knowledge of the KB of the agent, knowledge of how the main functions in the agent are implemented (e.g., how TELL and ASK are implemented), and so on. *H* is also assumed to have resources sufficient to pin down these elements, to "freeze" them and inspect them, and so on. We confess that this isn't exactly precise. To clarify things, we offer an example. This example is also designed to provide an answer to the second question, which as you'll recall was

Q2 What sort of thing would count as a successful explanation?

To fix the context for the example, suppose that the output from our artificial agent A' is a resolution-based proof which settles a problem which human mathematicians and logicians have grappled unsuccessfully with for decades. This problem, suppose, is to determine whether or not some formula ϕ can be derived from some (consistent) axiom set Γ. Imagine that after many years of fruitless deliberation, a human H' encodes Γ and $\neg\phi$ and gives both to OTTER, and OTTER produces a proof showing that this encoding is inconsistent, which establishes $\Gamma \vdash \phi$, and leads to an explosion of commentary in the media about "brilliant" and "creative" machines, and so on.[8] In this case, A' doesn't pass LT. This is true because H, knowing the KB, architecture, and central functions of A' will be able to give a perfect explanation for the behavior in question. This explanation will in principle be no different than explaining the OTTER proof seen above; it will just take longer. One of us (Bringsjord) routinely gives explanations of this sort. The KB is simply the encoding of $\Gamma \cup \{\phi\}$, the architecture consists in the search algorithms used by OTTER, and the main functions consist in the rules of inference used in a resolution-based theorem prover. Put in terms of the Chinese Room, A here doesn't pass LT because H, knowing what she knows, could manipulate symbols in accordance with this knowledge and produce the proof in question.

Here, now, given the foregoing, is a better definition:

Def$_{LT}$ 2 Artificial agent A, designed by H, passes LT if and only if

1. A outputs o;
2. A's outputting o is not the result of a fluke hardware error, but rather the result of processes A can repeat;
3. H (or someone who knows what H knows, and has H's resources) cannot explain how A produced o by appeal to A's architecture, knowledge-base, and core functions.

4. How do Today's Systems Fare in the Lovelace Test?

Today's systems, even those designed to either be, or seem to be, creative, fail LT. They are all systems whose designers can easily imagine "Chinese Roomifying," that is, these designers can imagine themselves generating the output in question by merely manipulating symbols in accordance with the knowledge bases, algorithms, and code in question. We give three examples of this kind of failure.

4.1. BRUTUS

Let's turn first to the BRUTUS system (Bringsjord and Ferrucci, 2000). This is a system designed to appear to be literarily creative to *others*. To put the point in the spirit of TT, BRUTUS reflects a multi-year attempt to build a system able to play the short short story game, or S³G for short (Bringsjord, 1998a). (See Figure 5 for a picture of S³G.)

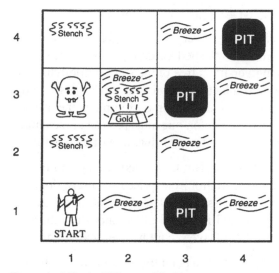

Figure 4. A Typical Wumpus World.

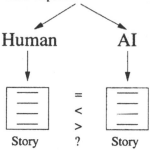

Figure 5. The Short Short Story Game, or S³G for Short.

The idea behind S³G is simple. A human and a computer compete against each other. Both receive one relatively simple sentence, say: "As Gregor Samsa awoke one morning from uneasy dreams he found himself transformed in his bed into a gigantic insect." (Kafka, 1948, p. 67) Both mind and machine must now fashion a short short story (about 500 words) designed to be truly interesting; the more literary virtue, the better. The goal in building BRUTUS, then, is to build an artificial author able to compete with first-rate human authors in S³G, much as Deep Blue went head to head with Kasparov.

How does BRUTUS fare? Relative to the goal of passing S³G, not very well. On the other hand, BRUTUS can "author" some rather interesting stories, e.g.,

225

"Betrayal in Self-Deception" (conscious)

Dave Striver loved the university. He loved its ivy-covered clocktowers, its ancient and sturdy brick, and its sun-splashed yerdant greens and eager youth. He also loved the fact that the university is free of the stark unforgiving trials of the business world – only this *isn't* a fact: academia has its own tests, and some are as merciless as any in the marketplace. A prime example is the dissertation defense: to earn the PhD, to become a doctor, one must pass an oral examination on one's dissertation. This was a test Professor Edward Hart enjoyed giving.

Dave wanted desperately to be a doctor. But he needed the signatures of three people on the first page of his dissertation, the priceless inscriptions which, together, would certify that he had passed his defense. One of the signatures had to come from Professor Hart, and Hart had often said – to others and to himself – that he was honored to help Dave secure his well-earned dream.

Well before the defense, Striver gave Hart a penultimate copy of his thesis. Hart read it and told Dave that it was absolutely first-rate, and that he would gladly sign it at the defense. They even shook hands in Hart's book-lined office. Dave noticed that Hart's eyes were bright and trustful, and his bearing paternal.

At the defense, Dave thought that he eloquently summarized Chapter 3 of his dissertation. There were two questions, one from Professor Rodman and one from Dr. Teer; Dave answered both, apparently to everyone's satisfaction. There were no further objections.

Professor Rodman signed. He slid the tome to Teer; she too signed, and then slid it in front of Hart. Hart didn't move.

"Ed?" Rodman said.

Hart still sat motionless. Dave felt slightly dizzy.

"Edward, are you going to sign?"

Later, Hart sat alone in his office, in his big leather chair, saddened by Dave's failure. He tried to think of ways he could help Dave achieve his dream.

Note that we have placed the term 'author' in scare quotes. Why? The reason is plain and simple, and takes us back to Lady Lovelace's objection: BRUTUS didn't *originate* this story. He is capable of generating it because two humans, Bringsjord and Ferrucci, spent years figuring out how to formalize a generative capacity sufficient to produce this and other stories, and they then are able to implement part of this formalization so as to have a computer produce such prose. This method is known as *reverse engineering*. Obviously, with BRUTUS set to *A* and Bringsjord and Ferrucci set to *H* in the definition of LT, the result is that BRUTUS fails this test. Put in terms of the Chinese Room, both Bringsjord and Ferrucci could take the place of a computer and mindlessly manipulate what they know (algorithms, knowledge-base, etc.) in order to produce output that impresses human observers.

Let's now give you, briefly, a specific example to make this failure transparent. BRUTUS is programmed to produce stories that are, at least to some degree, bizarre. The reason for this is that reader response research tells us that readers are engaged by bizarre material. Now, in BRUTUS, to express the bizarre, modifiers are linked with objects in frames named `bizzaro_modifiers`. Consider the following instance describing the `bizzaro` modifier bleeding.

```
instance bleeding is a bizzaro_modifier
     objects are {sun, plants, clothes, tombs, eyes}.
```

What Bringsjord and Ferrucci call **literary augmented grammars**, or just a LAGs, may be augmented with constraints to stimulate bizarre images in the mind of the reader. The following LAG for action analogies,

- `BizarreActionAnalogy → NP VP like ANP`
- `NP → noun_phrase`
- `ANP → modifier (isa bizzaro_modifier) noun (isa analog of NP)`

in conjunction with `bizzaro_modifiers` can be used by BRUTUS to generate the following sentence.

Hart's eyes were like big bleeding suns.

Sentences like this in output from BRUTUS are therefore a function of work carried out by (in this case) Ferrucci. Such sentences do not result from BRUTUS thinking on its own.

4.2. COPYCAT

Douglas Hofstadter, as many readers know, has thought a lot about creativity, and has built systems in order to explore and validate the result of that thought. So what sort of creativity does Hofstadter focus on? And what are the relevant systems? One representative system is COPYCAT, described at length in (Hofstadter, 1995). COPYCAT is supposed to solve problems like the following two by coming up with "creative analogies."

Problem 1 Suppose the letter-string *abc* were changed to *abd*; how would you change the letter-string *ijk* in "the same way"?

Problem 2 Suppose the letter-string *aabc* were changed to *aabd*; how would you change the letter-string *ijkk* in "the same way"?

COPYCAT settles in on *ijl* as an answer for Problem 1, and in the process "considers" *ijd* and *ijj*. For Problem 2, the program arrives at *ijll*, and "considers" *jkl, jjlck, hjkk, jkkk, ijkd, ijdd, ijkk*, and *djkk*. Are these good answers? Are they creative? Hofstadter answers "Yes" to both questions. But he seems not to notice that he answers in this way only because COPYCAT has been designed to mirror the answers he (and many other humans) would be inclined to give, and for this reason COPYCAT fails LT. COPYCAT gives the kind of answers it does because rules like "Replace the rightmost letter with its successor" are employed. But what recommends these rules, rather than others which COPYCAT has no "awareness" of? COPYCAT seems thoroughly *ad hoc*.

As evidence for the capricious nature of COPYCAT's answers, consider the fact that the answers one of us gave, after seeing these problems for the very first time, were *ijj* and *ijkj*. (Notice that the second of these isn't even "considered" by COPYCAT.) The rule that produced these answers was one based on rhyming. In *abc*, the second and third letters rhyme. When this string is replaced with *abd*, this rhyme is preserved. In the string *ijk*, the second and third letters rhyme. To follow the rule in question, *k* must be replaced with a different letter that rhymes with *j*, the second letter. The only possibility is *j* hence *ijj* is produced. The same rule, for obvious reasons, yields *ijkj*.

That COPYCAT fails LT is transparent when you consider how the system would look if couched in theorem proving terms. It would seem that the rules of letter-string replacement to which Hofstadter is drawn can be effortlessly expressed as formulas in first-order logic. For example, let l be a function mapping character triples (c_1, c_2, c_3) into letter-strings, so that $l(a, b, c)$ is *abc*. Now let s be the successor function for the 26 lower-case letters $\{a, b, c, \ldots, z\}$. Then here is a rule for the replacement function r:

$$\forall x \forall y \forall z (r(l(x, y, z)) = l(x, y, s(z))).$$

It is easy to capture letter-replacement with rules like this, and to assign weights to these rules. (It can be done with OTTER, the theorem prover discussed above.) Producing a solution would then consist in the production of proofs after starting strings (e.g., *ijk* in Problem 1) are given as additional input to the system. Obviously, a designer of the theorem proving version of COPYCAT would know exactly why the system produces the output it does. Or, to couch the point in Searlean terms, the formulae in the theorem proving version could be used as a correlate to the "rulebook" in the Chinese Room, and one of us, using it as such, could get inside a box and fool people on the outside into believing that the system is "thinking for itself."

4.3. LETTER SPIRIT

Things are no different when we (briefly) consider LETTER SPIRIT, another system from Hofstadter (1995). Whereas the domains dealt with by COPYCAT and BRUTUS are textual in nature, LETTER SPIRIT deals with a visual one. LETTER SPIRIT is so named because it is intended to capture the essence of a letter (columns in Figure 7) and the "spirit" of a font (rows in Figure 7). More specifically, LETTER SPIRIT works within the space of the Roman alphabet.[9] Originally, LETTER SPIRIT was intended to invent new fonts within the space of Roman alphabets, but early on

Figure 6. Various Letter A's.

Hofstadter (and his collaborator in this endeavor: McGraw) decided that that was too difficult. So they decided instead to have LETTER SPIRIT take in a few "seed" letters in a certain font as percepts, and yield as output the remaining letters in this font; and they decided that the fonts in question would all have to come from a restricted class of fonts, "gridfonts" as Hofstadter and McGraw call this class. (Each gridfont letter is created by selecting from among 56 quanta. See Figure 8.) This retreat is a pity, for it would seem that an agent able to cook up brand new fonts in the unrestricted space of the Roman alphabet might have a chance at passing LT. But LETTER SPIRIT has no such chance. The reason is that Hofstadter and McGraw can explain exactly how it is that LETTER SPIRIT gives the remaining letters in a particular font, by appeal to the relevant ingredients (knowledge-base, central algorithms, etc.). In Searlean terms, the two of them, upon being given some seed letters, can use these ingredients to mindlessly complete the font.[10]

At this point it's time to consider the objection no doubt many of our readers are itching to press against us.

5. The Objection From Learning

Here is how the objection in question runs: "Gentlemen, this much is sure: You will never win any awards as Turing scholars. For you conveniently neglected to note earlier that just before recasting Lady Lovelace's argument as one aimed at substantiating the view that computers never surprise us, there is a paragraph consisting of a lone sentence, namely: 'The whole question will be considered again

Figure 7. "Letter" is Covered by Colunms, "Spirit" by Rows.

under the heading of learning machines.' (Turing, 1964, p. 21) By 'whole question' Turing is referring to none other than the question with which the three of you, following Lovelace, are concerned, that is, whether or not a computer can originate anything. The heading in question is "Learning Machines," and it stands atop the final section, 7, of Turing's seminal paper. What Turing says in that section destroys Lovelace's complaint, and likewise it destroys your own complaint that machines originate nothing. In fact, modern-day embodiments of what Turing envisions in this section, namely connectionist neural network systems, pass your supposedly grueling LT with flying colors. Let me explain.

"Turing's strategy for building a machine capable of passing TT is *not* to program a machine from scratch, injecting knowledge (and, yes, trickery) into it. His strategy, expressed in the "Learning Machines" section, is instead to first bnild what he calls a "child-machine," and to then teach it in much the same way that we teach our own youth. Here is a quote that hits you two rather hard."

> An important feature of the learning machine is that its teacher will often be very largely ignorant of quite what is going on inside, although he may still be able to some extent to predict his pupil's behavior. This should apply most strongly to the later education of a machine arising from a child-machine of well-tried design (or program). This is in clear contrast with normal procedure when using a machine to do computations: one's object is then to have a clear mental picture of the state of the machine at each moment in the computation. This object can only be achieved with a struggle. The view that "the machine can only do what we know how to order it to do" appears strange in the face of this. (Turing, 1964, p. 29)

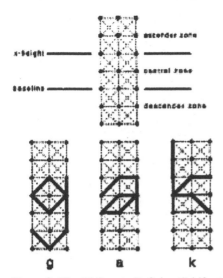

x-height

baseline

Figure 8. The 56 Quanta Defining Gridfonts.

This objection is actually rather easily surmounted, as follows. Presumably the child-machine in question develops its abilities by virtue of training of artificial neural networks (ANNs). Now, the information processing of an ANN corresponds in all cases to standard computation (e.g., Turing machine computation), or standard deduction (e.g., proofs in first-order logic), as Bringsjord (1991) has explained elsewhere. To fix this point we can appeal to the notion of **representability**, used in some contemporary proofs of Gödel's first incompleteness theorems (e.g., see section §7 of Chapter X of Ebbinghaus, Flum and Thomas, 1984). Here is the relevant definition:[11]

A function $f : \mathbf{N}^m \to \mathbf{N}$ is called **representable** in a set Φ of first-order formulas about arithmetic if there is a formula $\phi(v_1, \dots , v_{m+1})$ (i.e., a formula whose free variables are only $v_1, \dots , v_{m+1}$) about arithmetic such that for all $n_1, \dots , n_{m+1} \in \mathbf{N}$,

- if $f(n_1, \dots , n_m) = n_{m+1}$ then $\Phi \vdash \phi(\tilde{n}_1, \dots , \tilde{n}_{m+1})$
- if $f(n_1, \dots , n_m) \neq n_{m+1}$ then $\Phi \vdash \neg\phi(\tilde{n}_1, \dots , \tilde{n}_{m+1})$
- $\Phi \vdash \exists^{=1} v_{m+1} \phi(\tilde{n}_1, \dots , \tilde{n}_m, v_{m+1})$

Here we say that $\phi(v_1, \dots , v_{m+1})$ **represents** f in Φ.

Now, suppose that the child-machine M_c, on the strength of ANNs, computes some function f. This function is representable in some Φ. You can think of Φ in this case as a knowledge-base. But then there is no longer any "thinking for itself' going on, for if we assume a computer scientist to be in command of the knowledge-base Φ and the relevant deduction from it, the reasons for this scientist to declare the child-machine a puppet are isomorphic to the reasons that compel the designer

Figure 9. Some Human-Designed Gridfonts.

of knowledge-based systems like BRUTUS to admit that such a system originates nothing.

6. Do Oracle Machines Pass the Lovelace Test?

So what kind of system *can* pass LT? How can a system break the bounds of mere symbol manipulation to do something on its own? It might be thought that so-called "oracle machines" can pass LT; here is how this idea would run: Jack Copeland (1998) has recently argued that oracle machines (or, as he calls them, 'O-machines') are immune to Searle's (1980) CRA-based claim that mere symbol manipulation is insufficient for genuine mentation. Since those systems that fail LT appear to be failing because it's clear that they are merely manipulating symbols in predictable ways, the idea is that oracle machines might pass LT because they do more than manipulate symbols.

Unfortunately, oracle machines are *not* immune to the Chinese Room. Copeland's characterization of these machines is just plain wrong. When one is clear and correct about oracle machines, it becomes obvious that they fall prey to the Chinese Room. And given that, it becomes obvious as well that they provide nothing that might help to pass LT.

6.1. GETTING STRAIGHT ABOUT ORACLE MACHINES

Copeland's account of O-machines should prove to be a shocker to those logicians and mathematicians familiar with the formal terrain in question. He tells us that

O-machines are "digital computing machines" (Copeland, 1998, p. 128); he says that

> They generate digital output from digital input by means of a step-by-step pro-
> cedure consisting of repeated applications of a small, fixed number of primitive
> operations, the procedure unfolding under the control of a finite program of
> instructions which is stored internally in the form of data on the machine's
> tape. (Copeland, 1998, pp. 128–129)

This is just simply false. Again, the 'O' in 'O-machine' stands for 'oracle'; these
machines, accordingly, work by way of oracles. They mark a way of creating, in
one avowedly mysterious stroke, a portal to an interesting realm: the realm which
opens up once problems proved to be mechanically unsolvable (= unsolvable by
Turing machines = beyond the so-called Turing Limit) are assumed to be *somehow* solvable. Oracle-machines are simply Turing machines augmented with an
oracular ability to solve the halting problem; they are nothing more. They are not
computing machines. They don't work exclusively "by means of a step-by-step
procedure consisting of repeated applications of a small, fixed number of primitive
operations." No such procedure exists for solving the halting problem; that's why
the problem is said to be unsolvable.

Textual confirmation of the claim that Copeland is just fundamentally mistaken
about the nature of O-machines is easy to come by. Here is how a recently updated
classic textbook on computability and uncomputability introduces oracles:

> Once one gets used to the fact that there are explicit problems, such as the halt-
> ing problem, that have no algorithmic solution, one is led to consider questions
> such as the following:
>
> Suppose we were given a "black box" or, as one says, an *oracle*, which can tell
> us whether a given Turing machine with given input eventually halts. Then it
> is natural to consider a kind of program that is allowed to ask questions of our
> oracle and to *use the answers in its further computation* ... (Davis, Sigal and
> Weyuker, 1994: 197; emphasis ours)

Notice what we have emphasized in this quote. The idea is that computation
calls the oracle; the oracle itself is not part of the computation.

How do Davis et al. transform this figurative scheme into a mathematically
respectable one? To answer this question, note that instead of Turing machines,
Davis et al. use an equivalent programming language $\mathcal{L}$, the programs of which
are composed of lists of statements with optional labels. $\mathcal{L}$ allows for three types
of statements: adding one to a variable $V (V \leftarrow V + 1)$, subtracting one from a
variable $V (V \leftarrow V - 1)$, and moving by a conditional to a line labeled with L
in a program (IF $V \neq 0$ GOTO L). With just these three statements it is possible
to write a program that computes every Turing-computable function. Traditionally,
to make it easier to see this, "macros" $V \leftarrow V'$ and GOTO L are allowed. The
first macro moves the contents of variable V' to variable V; the second is an unconditional branch that moves the active line to the one with label L; both macros

can be easily decomposed into a program written with only the three fundamental statements. As an example of a simple program in $\mathcal{L}$, consider a program that computes the function $f(x_1, x_2) = x_1 + x_2$:[12]

$$Y \leftarrow X_1$$
$$Z \leftarrow X_2$$
$$[B] \quad \text{IF} Z \neq 0 \text{ GOTO } A$$
$$\text{GOTO } E$$
$$[A] \quad Z \leftarrow Z - 1$$
$$Y \leftarrow Y + 1$$
$$\text{GOTO } B$$

Now we're in position to see how Davis et al. formalize oracles. The trick is simply to allow a new statement (an *oracle statement*) of the form

$$V \leftarrow O(V)$$

into the syntax of $\mathcal{L}$. "We now let G be some partial function on **N** (the natural numbers) with values in **N**, and we shall think of G as an oracle" (Davis et al., 1994: 198). So if the value of variable V is m before an oracle statement is encountered, when the statement is then reached, the value of V changes to $G(m)$ (assuming that G is defined for this argument). As should be plain, *there is absolutely no sense in which G is computed*. G is just a placeholder for what at this point is, to say it yet again, oracular. In connection, specifically, with the halting problem, where $M_1, M_2, \ldots$ enumerates all Turing machines, the function

$$h(m, n) = \begin{cases} 1 & \text{if } M_m \text{ halts with input } n \\ 0 & \text{otherwise} \end{cases}$$

can be "solved" by a program in $\mathcal{L}$ in which a gödel encoding of m and n is given as an argument to G.

How did Copeland go so wrong? How did he come to describe O-machines as standard computing machines? It would seem that Copeland fell prey to two confusions. To see the first, and to feel its pull, note that if you have an oracle on hand, at your beck and call, you can certainly treat your submission of a question to the oracle as a "fixed, primitive" step; and you can treat the return of an answer from the oracle similarly. After all, this is why formalization of "oracle consultation" can be symbolized in the manner we have just seen. But "fixed, primitive steps" should not be confused with computation or calculation, as is easy enough to see: If God exists, presumably He can be petitioned in one simple step, and can return an answer in one simple step as well. But ascertaining whether or not a Turing machine halts courtesy of the Almighty would seem to exceed computation by just a tad. If God routinely (oracularly) answered the fixed "queries" of Turing machine

M with a fixed verdict, we could stipulatively define a composite "O-machine" $M + \text{God}$, but this "machine" wouldn't be, to use Copeland's language, a "digital computing machine."

Can the appeal to the oracular be removed in favor of detailed logico-mathematical devices? Yes. In fact, many thinkers occupied with the philosophy and logic of minds and machines have produced and discussed such devices, so it's somewhat odd that Copeland believes O-machines to be "little known among philosophers of mind" (Copeland, 1998, p. 129). (As we'll see in moment, the philosopher Hilary Putnam long ago introduced an informative substitution for O-machines.) Indeed, one of us has recently written about a potential explosion in the intersection of philosophy and super-computation (Bringsjord, 1998). O-machines, in our experience, are well-known among technical philosophers of mind, but are generally ignored because their role, as we indicated above, is to simply open the portal to processing above the Turing Limit. They provide no substance relative to the powers of minds and machines.

So, what logico-mathematical devices are options, and who has discussed them? Just as there are an infinite number of mathematical devices that are equivalent to Turing machines (machines running programs from the language $\mathcal{L}$ visited above, Register machines, the λ-calculus, abaci,...; these are all discussed in the context of an attempt to define computation in Bringsjord 1994), there are an infinite number of devices beyond the Turing Limit. As you might also guess, a small proper subset of these devices dominate the literature. In fact, three kinds of super-computational devices – analog chaotic neural nets, trial-and-error machines, and Zeus machines – are generally featured in the literature. In the interests of reaching a wider audience, we discuss only the latter two devices here.[13]

Trial-and-error machines have their roots in a paper by Hilary Putnam (1994), and one by Mark Gold (1994); both appeared in the same rather famous volume and issue of the *Journal of Symbolic Logic*. So what are trial-and-error machines? Well, they have the architecture of Turing machines (read/write hear tapes, a fixed and finite number of internal states), but produce output "in the limit" rather than giving one particular output and then halting. Here is a trial-and-error machine $\mathcal{M}$ that solves the halting problem. Take some arbitrary Turing machine M with input u; let $n^{M,u}$ be the Gödel number of the pair M, u; place $n^{M,u}$ on $\mathcal{M}$'s tape. Now have $\mathcal{M}$ print 0 immediately (recall the function h, defined above), and then have it simulate the operation of M on u. If M halts during the simulation, have it proceed to erase 0 in favor of 1, and then have it stop for good. It's as easy as that.[14]

Zeus machines (or "Weyl Machines" from Weyl, 1949); see also Bertrand Russell's (1936) discussion of the possibility of his embodying such devices) are based on the character Zeus, described by Boolos and Jeffrey (1989). Zeus is a superhuman creature who can enumerate $\mathbf{N}$ *in a finite amount of time*, in one second, in fact. He pulls this off by giving the first entry, 0, in $\frac{1}{2}$ second, the second entry, 1, in $\frac{1}{4}$ second, the third entry in $\frac{1}{8}$ second, the fourth in $\frac{1}{16}$ second,..., so that, indeed, when a second is done he has completely enumerated the natural numbers.

Obviously, it's easy to adapt this scheme so as to produce a Zeus machine that can solve the halting problem: just imagine a machine which, when simulating an arbitrary Turing machine M operating on input u, does each step faster and faster ... (There are countably many Turing machines, and those that don't halt are trapped in an unending sequence of the same cardinality as $\mathbf{N}$.) If, during this simulation, the Zeus machine finds that M halts on u, then a 1 is returned; otherwise 0 is given.

6.2. COPELAND'S ARGUMENT FOR WHY O-MACHINES DODGE CRA

Here is Copeland's argument for the claim that Searle's CRA is powerless against a view of the mindbrain according to which it's an O-machine rather than a Turing machine:

> An O-machine's program may call for primitive operations that a human clerk working by rote and unaided by machinery is incapable of carrying out (for otherwise, by the Church-Turing thesis, whatever can be calculated by an O-machine can be calculated by a Turing machine – a contradiction). It follows that there is no possibility of Searle's Chinese Room argument [CRA] being successfully deployed against the new functionalism offered by hypothesis (la). (Copeland, 1998, p. 132)

Alas, this argument fails, as is easy to see. An O-machine, in calling for the oracular, certainly does call for something that a clerk (i.e., Turing's "computists" or Post's "workers") will have a hard time providing. (And Searle, as mere symbol manipulator, will have a similarly hard time simulating an O-machine.) But then again, only an oracle, by definition, can meet the challenge. Copeland's "new functionalism" is really mysticism; and CRA was never billed as a refutation of any such doctrine. When O-machines are specified, Copeland's argument is revealed as invalid. For example, suppose that rather than O-machines we talk of Zeus machines. It's easy to imagine that Searle in the Chinese Room manipulates symbols in order to parallel the operation of a Zeus machine – and doing so would no more guarantee the appropriate phenomenal consciousness (e.g., grasping that when a native Chinese speaker outside the room sends in a squiggle-squoggle he is asking if Searle savors perfectly grilled hamburgers) than would Searle's symbol manipulation in the original gedanken-experiment. The only difference is that in (what we might call) the "Zeus Room," Searle works much faster. But this speedup makes no difference with respect to true understanding. After all, Zeus could be a pigeon. And a pigeon trained to move symbols around, even if blessed with the ability to carry out this movement at Zeus-level speeds, would still have the mental life of a bird, which of course falls far short of truly understanding Chinese.

The upshot of this for oracle machines and LT is plain. If one designs a "super pigeon" to produce some output, one will be no more inclined to believe that this bird is thinking for itself than one would be inclined to believe that a slower, "standard" pigeon would have the kind of autonomy Lady Lovelace demands.

7. What Then Does it Take to Pass LT?

Many readers will doubtless ask: So what do you have to say, *constructively* speaking? So far, everything you've given us is negative; how about something positive? What should Alniks do to build an LT-passing system that breaks the bounds of mindless symbol manipulation to think for itself? We end with some brief speculation arising from such questions.

Unfortunately, it seems to us (or at least to *one* of us: Bringsjord) that the moral of the story may be irredeemably negative. There may simply not be a way for a mere information-processing artifact to pass LT, because what Lovelace is looking for may require a kind of autonomy that is beyond the bounds of ordinary causation and mathematics. The notion that creativity requires autonomy is one anticipated, at least in nascent terms, by Hofstadter (e.g., see Hofstadter, 1995, pp. 411), who seems confident that computation will ultimately be up to the task of capturing the kind of autonomy creative humans exploit. But what if the kind of "thinking for oneself' required by LT entails a form of autonomy known as *agent causation?* The doctrine of agent causation, which is set out, defended, and shown to be beyond ordinary computation in "Chapter VIII: Free Will" of Bringsjord (1992), entails the view that persons bring about certain states of affairs (e.g., mental events like decisions) directly, with no ordinary physical causal chain in the picture. Though some famous philosophers have affirmed this view (e.g., Richard Taylor and Roderick Chisholm), it hasn't been all that popular. This paper isn't intended to promote agent causation; no argument for the view has been articulated herein. The point in this last paragraph is only to raise the *possibility* that the difficulty we have in conceptualizing (let alone building) an LT-passing artificial agent may inhere in the fact that such an agent must have a rather radical kind of autonomy. To put the point another way, the difficulty in question may provide inductive evidence for the view that agent causation is real in our creative lives.[15]

Notes

[1] Actually, some understand Turing's prediction to be a more circumspect one, viz., that by 2000 we wouldn't have more than a 70% chance of making a person/machine determination in five minutes.

[2] Scholars take note: We have paraphrased Lady Lovelace in a way that implies her position to be that computers *only* do that which we order them, via programs, to do. See Turing's footnote 4 on p. 29 of Turing (1964).

[3] Of course, no competent Lisp programmer would use 'm' in this way. Some kind of mnemonic would doubtless be employed.

[4] OTTER can be obtained at http: //www-unix .mcs.anl.gov/AR/otter/

[5] For example, the substitute for *H* might be a scientist who watched and assimilated what the designers and builders of *A* did every step along the way.

[6] In (Bringsjord, 1995), Bringsjord refutes propositions associated with TT by assuming for the sake of argument that some reasonable parameters π have been established for this test. But Turing didn't specify π, and neither have his present-day defenders.

[7] The cycle here is strikingly similar to the overall architecture of cognition described by Pollock 1995).

[8]For a "real life" counterpart, we have OTTER's settling the Robbins Problem, presented as an open question in (Wos, 1996).

[9]A part of a part of this space is shown in Figure 6. By Hofstadter's lights, the pace in question may be uncountable: see Hofstadter (1982). For a discussion of this possibility, see Bringsjord and Zenzen (2001).

[10]This comes as no surprise given the method used by Hofstadter and McGraw: They based LETTER SPIRIT on studies of how humans create and complete gridfonts. Some human-created gridfonts are shown in Figure 9.

[11]We simplify this definition for the present context. The phrase "about arithmetic" is of course made precise in the formal version. A tilde above a character indicates that that character is one *in* the logic, so $\tilde{7}$ is a constant used in the logic to refer to the number 7.

[12]Note that a conditional or unconditional branch that directs flow to a label not present in the program causes halting. In the program here, then, the label E can be read as "exit."

[13]Analog chaotic neural nets are characterized by Siegelmann and Sontag (1994). For cognoscenti, analog chaotic neural nets are allowed to have irrational numbers for coefficients. For the uninitiated, analog chaotic neural nets are perhaps best explained by the "analog shift map," explicated by Siegelmann (1995), and summarized in Bringsjord (1998b).

[14]For full exposition, along with arguments that human persons are trial-and-error machines, see Kugel (1986), a seminal paper that situates trial-and-error machines nicely within both the formal context of the Arithmetic Hierarchy and the philosophical context of whether minds are computing machines.

[15]The point expressed this way bears an interesting resemblance to Moor's (1976) stance on TT.

References

Boolos, G.S. and Jeffrey, R.C. (1989), *Computability and Logic*, Cambridge, UK: Cambridge University Press.

Bringsjord, S. (1991), 'Is the connectionist-logicist clash one of ai's wonderful red herrings?', *Journal of Experimental & Theoretical AI* 3(4), pp. 319–349.

Bringsjord, S. (1992), *What Robots Can and Can't Be*, Dordrecht, The Netherlands: Dordrecht, Kluwer.

Bringsjord, S. (1995), 'Could, how could we tell if, and why should-androids have inner lives?', in K. Ford, C. Glymour and P. Hayes, eds., *Android Epistemology*, Cambridge, MA: MIT Press, pp. 93–122.

Bringsjord, S. (1998a), 'Chess is too easy', *Technology Review* 101(2), pp. 23–28.

Bringsjord, S. (1998b), Philosophy and 'super' computation, in J. Moor and T. Bynam, eds., *The Digital Phoenix: How Computers are Changing Philosophy*, Oxford, UK: Blackwell, pp. 231–252.

Bringsjord, S. and Ferrucci, D. (2000), *Artificial Intelligence and Literary Creativity: Inside the Mind of Brutus, a Storytelling Machine*, Mahwah, NJ: Lawrence Erlbaum.

Bringsjord, S. and Zenzen, M. (2001), *SuperMinds: A Defence of Uncomputable Cognition*, Dordrecht, The Netherlands: Kluwer Academic Publishers.

Copeland, B.J. (1998), 'Turing's O-machines, searle, penrose and the brain', *Analysis* 58(2), pp. 128–138.

Ebbinghaus, H.D., Flum, J. and Thomas, W. (1984), *Mathematical Logic*, New York, NY: Springer-Verlag.

Gold, M. (1994), 'Limiting recursion', *Journal of Symbolic Logic* 30(1), pp. 28–47.

Harnad, S. (1991), 'Other bodies, other minds: A machine incarnation of an old philosophical problem', *Minds and Machines* 1(1), pp. 43–54. This paper is available online at ftp://cogsci.ecs.soton.ac.uk/pub/harnad/Harnad/harnad91.otherminds

Hofstadter, D. (1982), 'Metafont, metamathematics, and metaphysics', *Visible Language* 14(4), pp. 309–338.

Hofstadter, D. (1995), *Fluid Concepts and Creative Analogies: Computer Models of the Fundamental Mechanisms of Thought*, New York, NY: Basic Books.

Hofstadter, D. and McGraw, G. (1995), Letter spirit: Esthetic perception and creative play in the rich microcosm of the roman alphabet, in *Fluid Concepts and Creative Analogies: Computer Models of the Fundamental Mechanisms of Thought*, New York, NY: Basic Books, pp. 407–488.

Kafka, F. (1948), The metamorphosis, in F. Kafka, T.W. Muir and E. Muir, eds., *The Penal Colony*, New York, NY: Schocken Books.

Kugel, P. (1986), 'Thinking may be more than computing', *Cognition* 18, pp. 128–149.

Moor, J.H. (1976), 'An analysis of turing's test', *Philosophical Studies* 30, pp. 249–257.

Moravec, H. (1999), *Robot: Mere Machine to Transcendant Mind*, Oxford, UK: Oxford University Press.

Pollock, J. (1995), *Cognitive Carpentry: A Blueprint for How to Build a Person*, Cambridge, MA: MIT Press.

Putnam, H. (1994), 'Trial and error predicates and a solution to a problem of mostowski', *Journal of Symbolic Logic* 30(1), pp. 49–57.

Russell, B. (1936), 'The limits of empiricism', *Proceedings of the Aristotelian Society* 36, 131–150.

Russell, S. and Norvig, P. (1994), *Artificial Intelligence: A Modern Approach*, Saddle River, NJ: Prentice Hall.

Searle, J. (1980), 'Minds, brains and programs', *Behavioral and Brain Sciences* 3, pp. 417–424. This paper is available online at http://members.aol.com/NeoNoetics/MindsBrainsPrograms.html.

Siegelmann, H. (1995), 'Computation beyond the turing limit', *Science* 268, pp. 545–548.

Siegelmann, H. and Sontag, E. (1994), 'Analog computation via neural nets', *Theoretical Computer Science* 131 pp. 331–360.

Turing, A. (1964), Computing machinery and intelligence, in A.R. Anderson, ed., *Minds and Machines*, Englewood Cliffs, NJ: Prentice-Hall, pp. 4–30.

Weyl, H. (1949), *Philosophy of Mathematics and Natural Science*, Princeton, NJ: Princeton University Press.

Wos, L. (1996), *The Automation of Reasoning: An Experimenter's Notebook with* OTTER *Tutorial*, San Diego, CA: Academic Press.

The Cartesian Test for Automatism[1]

GERALD J. ERION

Medaille College, 18 Agassiz Circle, Buffalo, NY 14214, USA

Abstract. In Part V of his *Discourse on the Method*, Descartes introduces a test for distinguishing people from machines that is similar to the one proposed much later by Alan Turing. The Cartesian test combines two distinct elements that Keith Gunderson has labeled the language test and the action test. Though traditional interpretation holds that the action test attempts to determine whether an agent is acting upon principles, I argue that the action test is best understood as a test of common sense. I also maintain that this interpretation yields a stronger test than Turing's, and that contemporary artificial intelligence should consider using it as a guide for future research.

Key words: Artificial intelligence, common sense, Descartes, Turing Test

1. Introduction

Though philosophical tradition holds René Descartes to be the father of modern philosophy, many of today's philosophers and cognitive scientists see him as a mortal enemy who created more problems than he solved. As a result, much recent work has aimed at correcting *Descartes' Error* (the title of a recent book by Antonio Damasio), dismantling the "Cartesian Theater" (a central theme in Daniel Dennett's *Consciousness Explained*), and other critical projects. In criticizing the most troubling aspects of Cartesianism, though, we must be careful to avoid rejecting elements of Descartes' work that remain valuable to contemporary researchers. For instance, in Part V of his *Discourse on the Method*, Descartes introduces a two-pronged test for distinguishing people from machines that is similar to the one proposed much later by Alan Turing. In this paper I conduct an exposition of Descartes' test, beginning with a brief discussion of the Cartesian understanding of automatism. Next will be an examination of the test itself and its relation to the notion of common sense being investigated by contemporary cognitive science. Finally, I will compare the Cartesian test with the Turing test, arguing that Descartes' test has important advantages over Turing's.

2. Mechanism and Automata

Descartes' time was something of a golden age for the construction of surprisingly realistic moving replicas of people and animals known as automata. King Henry IV of Navarre owned one of the finest collections of these mechanical wonders, including an elaborate set of hydraulically powered statues depicting mythical scenes that was part of his royal garden at Saint-Germain-en-Laye. Some speculate that Descartes had the opportunity to view these automata, since he mentions the figures of Diana and Neptune located at Saint-Germain in his *Treatise on Man* (CSM 1, p. 101). In any case, it is clear that this *kind* of automaton had a profound impact on Descartes. Not only does he claim that a human body is the same type of thing as an automaton in Henry's gardens, he also explains our movement through an analogy with the motion of these statues.

In claiming that the laws of mechanics apply to living bodies as well as to inanimate objects, Descartes advocates a truly noteworthy position, for the Aristotelian doctrine prevailing before him maintained that all living things had souls. The only souls in the Cartesian world, though, belong to human beings. This parsimonious attitude about the distribution of souls has important consequences for Descartes' definition of an automaton. The classical definition held that automata are things that move themselves without any external, intervening causes. To this Descartes adds an additional qualification; a Cartesian automaton moves itself without the benefit of a soul (Radner and Radner, 1989, p. 38). On this definition, clocks, Henry's moving statues, and non-human animals all become automata, but so too do mindless, living human bodies. As John Cottingham puts it, "The human body is a machine in exactly the same sense as the animal body;" however, a human *being* is a combination of a soul with a human body (Cottingham, 1978, p. 552).

But how can something as complicated as the human body have all of its movements explained by the laws of mechanics? Descartes answers this question in his *Treatise* with an analogy between the human body and King Henry's automata. Now, it is important to realize that the automata at Saint-Germain were capable of some rather complex and lifelike behavior. For instance, observers who approached the bathing Diana figure stepped on panels hidden in the ground, causing water to travel through various pipes, which in turn caused Diana to get up and hide in the reeds, as any modest bather would do. This impressive bit of hydraulic engineering inspired Descartes to write, "One may compare the nerves of [the human body] with the pipes in the works of these fountains, its muscles and tendons with the various devices and springs which serve to set them in motion, its animal spirits with the water which drives them, the heart with the source of the water, and the cavities of the brain with the storage tanks" (CSM 1, p. 100). Defending this sort of analogical explanation, Descartes writes:

> This will not seem at all strange to those who know how many kinds of automatons, or moving machines, the skill of man can construct with the use of very few parts, in comparison with the great multitude of bones, muscles, nerves, arteries, veins, and all the other parts that are in the body of an animal. For they will regard this body as a machine which, having been made by the hands of God, is incomparably better ordered than any machine that can devised by man, and contains in itself movements more wonderful than those in any machine. (CSM 1, p. 139)

For Descartes, then, the bodies of living things are no less mechanical than clocks or Henry's statues, though the fact that they are constructed by the hands of God means they can be much more complex than any human-made devices.

This raises an interesting question relevant to contemporary philosophy of mind and cognitive science: How can we tell the difference between a real person and an automaton? Descartes' answer to this question is his two-pronged test for automatism.

3. The Cartesian Test for Automatism

Though different versions of the Cartesian test for automatism appear in different places in Descartes' writings, the earliest appears in the *Discourse*. Below I discuss this version of the test, supplemented with relevant passages from Descartes' later correspondence with Henry More, the Marquess of Newcastle, and Reneri (for Alphonse Pollot). The test itself has two elements; adopting Keith Gunderson's terminology, I shall refer to these two elements as the *language test* and the *action test* (Gunderson, 1964, p. 198).

3.1. THE LANGUAGE TEST

The first characteristic distinguishing people from automata is our ability to use language to communicate. In his letter to More of February 5, 1649, Descartes writes that the language test is the "main reason for holding that [animal automata] lack thought" (CSM 3, p. 366). He claims that all people, even those born without the ability to produce or hear speech, can develop ways of using language to let others know what they are thinking. On the other hand, no automaton could ever "use words, or put together other signs, as we do in order to declare our thoughts to others" (CSM 1, p. 140). Thus, we can be sure that we are dealing with an automaton if it lacks the ability to generate language.

Now, automata do not fail the language test because they lack the ability to utter words. In his November 23, 1646 letter to the Marquess of Newcastle, Descartes acknowledges that magpies and parrots, though automata, can vocalize. Furthermore, he concedes the possibility of constructing a machine with the capacity to produce something very much like human speech, perhaps even a cry of protest after being poked (CSM 1, p. 140). However, we can distinguish such utterances from genuine instances of language use in at least three ways.

First, the utterances of automata lack the complexity and flexibility of genuine language. As Descartes writes, "It is not conceivable that [an automaton] should produce different arrangements of words so as to give an *appropriately meaningful* answer to whatever is said in its presence, as the dullest of men can do" (emphasis added) (CSM 1, p. 140). This "appropriately meaningful" criterion is crucial. With it, Descartes can classify utterances as non-linguistic when they are so inappropriate that they become senseless in their particular context. People can engage in meaningful conversation with others on practically any issue, even one they know nothing about. Automata, though, cannot engage in sensible conversation on a wide range of topics for any significant length of time.[2] Thus, Descartes concludes, their utterances are not genuine instances of language use.

The second reason that the utterances of automata do not count as true language use is that they express mere *passions, not thoughts*. Descartes allows that an automaton could express its passions verbally, as when a pet magpie calling out "good day" expresses its hope for food (CSM 3, pp. 303 and 374). However, automata differ from people because they lack minds; consequently, they also lack the ability to think. Given Descartes' view that true language use involves the expression of thought, and not just of passion, automata cannot be members of the linguistic community, because they cannot have the thoughts expressed in a genuine linguistic utterance. As he writes, "The reason why animals do not speak as we do is not that they lack the organs but that they have no thoughts" (CSM 3, p. 303).

Finally, a genuine linguistic agent must not only produce utterances expressing thought, it must also generate what Descartes calls "*real speech*" indicating "*pure thought*" (CSM 3, p. 366). Daisie and Michael Radner explain Descartes' notion of real speech by pointing out that some animal utterances are more than mere expressions of passion. For example, their warning calls sometimes convey information about the location of a predator, saying more than 'I am experiencing the passion of fear' (Radner and Radner, 1989, pp. 47–48). However, these utterances still fail to be truly linguistic because they are not real speech, which Descartes defines as the expression of "thought alone," detached from the "natural impulses" that accompany such warning calls (CSM 3, p. 366). Only thought about mathematics and metaphysics seems to count as pure thought for Descartes, and since automata do not engage in such thought, they do not use language (CSM 1, p. 307). To summarize, then, a creature passes the language test if, in a variety of situations, it generates appropriately meaningful utterances expressing not just passion, but pure thought (Radner and Radner, 1989, p. 47).

3.2. THE ACTION TEST

The second part of Descartes' test for automatism is the action test, which asks whether an agent is "acting through reason." Though Descartes leaves the meaning of the phrase "acting through reason" somewhat ambiguous, the standard interpretation of the action test holds that it is a test for determining whether an agent is acting on principles. In contrast, I shall argue for an interpretation of the action test as a test of *common sense*.

3.2.1. Common Sense

Now, the notion of common sense that I am introducing here cannot be simply the sloppy jumble of opinions that make up, for example, the belief collection of a typical 21st-century American. Descartes missed few opportunities to attack "preconceived opinions" that we absorb passively and uncritically, since he thought

they were generally false and likely to lead us into accepting other false propositions. However, there is a more focused notion of common sense that might be
more appealing. This sort of common sense is virtually universal among typical
adults because it concerns an important subset of objective reality that we all live
our everyday lives in, the *common-sense world*. As a rough first approximation, it
is helpful to think of the common-sense world as the realm of familiar objects that
we become acquainted with during ordinary experience. People, plants, non-human
animals, and simple geographic features are all included in this world, while sub-
atomic particles, neurons, and galaxies are not. This is not to say that very large
or very small objects are not real, but only that they are not part of *common-sense
reality*.

Having sketched out the boundaries of the common-sense world in this way, we
can understand common sense itself as the base of knowledge about common-
sense reality that allows each of us to survive and thrive during our everyday
lives. Common *beliefs* about the common-sense world are the most prominent
components of this knowledge base. (Conversely, we can exclude beliefs about
sub-atomic particles from common sense because they do not refer to the world of
ordinary, everyday experience.) However, common sense also includes the widespread *abilities* that allow us to act successfully in the common-sense world.[3] We
can say that the abilities of common-sense are *reliable* in that they are useful to
us during our ordinary interactions with common-sense reality. On the other hand,
our common-sense beliefs are *true* in that they correspond with the common-sense
world.[4]

Recent work in the various cognitive sciences has strengthened claims of the
existence of precisely this type of common sense. Anthropologist Robin Horton,
for instance, argues that there is a core of knowledge about the common-sense
world that exists in all human cultures (Horton, 1982). Philosopher Lynd Forguson and others have worked with developmental psychologists to articulate the
common-sense theory of psychology that we rely upon during our everyday social
interactions (Forguson, 1989). Patrick Hayes provides a careful study of the naive
physics that we use to manipulate the ordinary physical objects of the common-
sense world (Hayes, 1985a, b). Geographers Max Egenhofer and David Mark are
systematizing the geographic knowledge that all people share in their theory of na-
ve geography (Egenhofer and Mark, 1995). Finally, psychologist John Macnamara
has explored the development of the fundamental logical abilities that are so important to common sense (Macnamara, 1986). Thus, there is mounting evidence
for the existence of a shared knowledge base used by all of us (even skeptical
philosophers) during our everyday lives, as well as a growing understanding of
what this common core of knowledge consists of.

3.2.2. The Action Test as a Test of Common Sense

As mentioned above, the standard interpretation of the Cartesian action test holds
that the test is an attempt to determine whether an agent is *acting on principles*

(Radner and Radner, 1989, p. 51; Adler, 1967, p. 232). According to this view, "acting through reason" involves apprehending principles, determining what follows from them, and then acting upon this information. We can distinguish acting through reason from acting in mere *accordance* with reason (Radner and Radner, 1995, p. 112). An animal blindly following an optimal but genetically programmed foraging strategy recommended by decision theorists acts only in accordance with reason, not through reason. People act on principles; automata do not.

However, there is little support for this interpretation of what it means to act through reason in Descartes' writings, and Descartes never states that acting through reason should mean acting on principles. Granted, some versions of the action test seem to imply that he held acting through reason to involve *thinking*, which we usually associate with the consideration of principles.[5] Furthermore, as we have seen, thinking is a central component of his language test. Nonetheless, Descartes never defines acting through reason as acting on principles, so there is reason to doubt that he meant them to be synonymous.

The notion that Descartes intended acting through reason to mean acting upon principles also conflicts with some of the things that he does explicitly state. For example, in every version of the action test he claims that we can distinguish human beings from automata because of their *performance*, not because their performance is based upon principles. Since human beings are the only creatures known to act through reason, we can determine whether something is acting through reason by comparing its performance to that of a human being. A creature that does not perform the way that a human being would, in a wide variety of situations, fails the test and is ruled an automaton.

This means that the difference between the performance of a human being and the performance of an automaton is not simply the result of the fact that the human being's performance is based upon principles. *A creature that acts on the wrong principles will not pass the action test*; and if a creature can act on principles yet still fail the action test, then the action test cannot be a test for determining whether a creature is acting on principles. Instead, a creature must act *commonsensically* if it is to be counted as a person, as it is common sense that allows us to perform skillfully in a wide range of situations. As Barry Smith writes:

> Our commonsensical belief systems enjoy not merely a remarkable efficiency when it comes to solving the problems raised in our everyday passage through the world, but also a no less remarkable adaptability, a capacity to maintain themselves in functioning order from situation to situation and from generation to generation, even in the face of sometimes catastrophic changes in environmental and other conditions. (Smith, 1994, p. 210)

There are also other aspects of the action test supporting the position that it is a test of common sense. For example, Descartes claims that there are two ways that a creature can fail to perform like a human being; it can either do too well or too poorly. Most automata do too poorly. Although it is possible for an automaton to outperform a person in certain limited situations, Descartes notes that the abilities of automata often become much less impressive in less-than-optimal situations. When a creature's performance is far below that of a typical human being, Descartes says it is not acting through reason, "but only from the disposition of its organs" (CSM 1, p. 140). However, a creature can also fail the action test by performing much better than a human being in a given situation. In his letter to the Marquess of Newcastle, Descartes refutes the claim that an automaton's high degree of proficiency implies that it is acting through reason by noting that clocks can tell time better than we can, though they certainly do not act through reason. Thus, an automaton's exceptional performance does nothing to prove that it acts through reason.

Radner and Radner maintain that the combination of these two criteria makes the action test unsatisfiable; as they put it, automata become "damned if they do and damned if they don't" (Radner and Radner, 1989, p. 52). By alternatively citing sub-human and super-human performance as evidence that a creature does not act through reason, the Radners claim that Descartes has set up a test that poor automata have no hope of passing. However, the action test is not unsatisfiable; rather, *it operates exactly as we should expect a test for common sense to operate*, because it targets a rather modest, intermediate level of performance. A creature that is incapable of, for instance, employing the modus ponens form of argument will not act commonsensically, but neither will a supercomputer that calculates thousands of these simple deductions per second. Thus, since both sub-human and super-human performances are relevant in a test for common sense, we have good reason to believe that the action test is a test of common sense.

In addition, it is worth noting Descartes' claim that *all* people, from the dullest to the wisest, act through reason. This means that acting through reason is, like our rigorous notion of common sense, truly common, the very baseline for intelligence. Descartes also writes that reason is "a universal instrument which can be used in all kinds of situations" (CSM 1, p. 140). Once again, Descartes seems to be describing common sense, which is useful in all the widely varied situations we encounter during our everyday lives.[6] Finally, it is worth noting, as Gunderson does, that "The language test ... is exactly the same *type* of test as the action test, with the exception that it subsumes a more specific (though still very broad) range of activities" (Gunderson, 1964, p. 199). This means that "If a creature fails the language test, it *ipso facto* fails the action test. It is possible, however, for a creature to fail the action test without failing the language tests" (Radner and Radner, 1989, p. 50). Our new interpretation of the action test preserves this important point, since knowing how to use a natural language is part of the common-sense knowledge base. A creature that fails the language test *ipso facto* fails the common-sense test, but it seems possible for a creature to fail the common-sense test without failing the language test. In light of these points and others raised above, then, it appears that Descartes' action test is not just a test of whether a creature is acting upon principles, but of whether that creature possesses common sense.

3.3. CONCLUSIONS ABOUT THE TEST

We can now reformulate Descartes' two-pronged test for automatism as follows. Automata are distinct from real people in two ways. First, automata cannot use language. Second, automata do not possess common sense, which includes not only knowing how to use a language but also knowing how to perform tasks and answer questions that even the most simpleminded adult human can. To put it another way, automata lack common sense, and therefore the subset of common sense associated with language competence. As Descartes says, "In just these two ways we can know the difference between man and beast" (CSM 1:140; AT 6:57).

4. Contemporary Applications

With Descartes' test for automatism now firmly in our grasp, we can see its important consequences for contemporary cognitive science. Even today, over 300 years after the test's first proposal, machines remain unable to do those things that Descartes cited in distinguishing people from automata. Of course, many of the early successes of artificial intelligence gave computers the kinds of skills that highly intelligent people often (or perhaps stereotypically) exhibit, such as the abilities to play chess, solve math problems, and construct logical proofs. Paradoxically, though, these talents proved easier to program than the commonsensical abilities that most young children master with relatively little effort. As Smith writes, "Computer scientists have been forced, by degrees, to acknowledge [that] it is everyday knowledge that is hardest to convey to a computer" (Smith, 1994, p. 210). Thus, Descartes' test still provides us with a way of distinguishing people from automata. Today's machines may be capable of outperforming human beings in limited tasks in specific environments, but they are still unable to act skillfully in the diverse range of situations that a person with common sense can.

This suggests that it might be worthwhile to compare the Cartesian test to a more contemporary and better known test developed by Alan Turing. Turing maintains that attempting to distinguish people from machines on the basis of thought would be a mistake. To him, the question "Can machines think?" is an unanswerable one, because the meaning of the word 'think' is excessively ambiguous. Instead of struggling with such an unanswerable question, Turing suggests that computers be involved in an imitation game. In this game, a human interrogator asks questions of two respondents: (A), a computer imitating a person, and (B), a genuine person. The interrogator then uses the respondents' typewritten answers to figure out which is the computer and which is the genuine person. Sensible questions about the computer's performance in the imitation game then replace the original, unanswerable query, "Can machines think?" (Turing, 1950, pp. 433–434).

Though it would be easy to equate the Cartesian test with the Turing test, we can now see how misleading such an identification would be.[7] There are very important differences between the Turing and Cartesian tests, and it is likely that conflicting goals motivated their respective proposals. Turing seems to have wanted a test that would make the notion that machines could think a less objectionable one. On the other hand, Descartes wanted his test to reinforce the distinction between automata and genuine people.

These differing goals may have led Turing to construct a test that is less rigorous than the Cartesian test. To pass Turing's test, a computer need only convince a judge that it is a person for a short time, and only via typewritten answers. On the other hand, Descartes' test is more cautious than the Turing test; not only does it involve a more careful examination of a creature's language, it also tests the creature's ability to solve problems in a wide variety of everyday circumstances.[8] Thus, a machine could pass the Turing test without passing the Cartesian test, because the Cartesian test requires the skillful use of common sense. All of this suggests that passing the Cartesian test would actually be a more appropriate goal for artificial intelligence than passing the Turing test.[9] Unfortunately, though, the substitution of the Cartesian test for the Turing test seems unlikely to happen anytime soon, since passing the Turing test is the ultimate goal of so many AI practitioners.[10]

5. Conclusion

Even today, more than three centuries after Descartes first proposed his test for automatism, machines are still unable to do those things that Descartes said would distinguish automata from real people. Real people can use language and common sense, while automata cannot. By observing the performance of a creature for some significant length of time in a variety of circumstances, then, we can confidently declare that it is person if it demonstrates linguistic abilities and performs at the commonsensical level of ordinary people.

Thus, it should be clear that the Cartesian test for automatism is relevant to today's cognitive science research, and that it has genuine advantages over its primary competitor, the Turing test. By focusing not only on language but also on common sense, Descartes' test is a stronger test, significantly less likely than the Turing test to falsely declare that some creature is a person. Furthermore, because Descartes' test is more rigorous than the Turing test, a machine that passed it would have a much stronger claim to general intelligence than a machine that passed only Turing's test. Thus, cognitive scientists looking for a way to distinguish machines from genuine people should seriously consider augmenting the Turing test with relevant elements of the Cartesian test.

Notes

I must thank Daisie Radner, Bill Rapaport, Barry Smith, Marc Hight, Lynd Forguson, and Jim Moor for their helpful comments on earlier drafts of this paper. I have also benefited from comments by those attending my presentations at the University of Charleston, Syracuse University, and Dartmouth College.

[2]On page 42 of *Animal Consciousness*, Radner and Radner argue that Descartes' meaningfulness criterion is even more restrictive than Noam Chomsky's (1966) claim that language must be "unbounded and stimulus-free," since randomly-generated sentences could fulfill Chomsky's requirement yet still not be "appropriately meaningful" in the Cartesian sense.

[3]Thus, the notion of common sense that I am relying upon here includes both halves of the famous distinction between *knowing how* and *knowing that* drawn by Gilbert Ryle in his 1945/1971 paper.

[4]This account of common sense as a true and reliable knowledge base concerning common-sense reality, shared by typical human adults, and emerging as a result of a child's ordinary interactions with the common-sense world is developed in greater detail in my 2000 dissertation.

[5]For example, see Descartes' November 23, 1646 letter to the Marquess of Newcastle, where he writes that animals act "only by instinct and *without thinking*" (emphasis added) (CSM 3, p. 304).

[6]Horton makes an even stronger point on pages 230–232, arguing that all secondary (i.e., non-commonsensical) theory is dependent upon the resources of common sense. If Horton is correct, then common sense will be necessary for *any* theory-building whatsoever, and thus will be useful in literally all situations.

[7]Indeed, Justin Leiber nearly conflates the two on page 136 of his 1989 paper, where he writes that Descartes' test is "virtually the same as what we today call the Turing test."

[8]The caution inherent in Descartes' test also motivates Stevan Harnad's (1991) presentation of what he calls the "Total Turing Test." Concerned that Turing's original test checks only for a limited linguistic capacity, Harnad recommends the Total Turing Test as a way of testing the many other skills that genuine people possess; as he writes on page 44, "The candidate must be able to do, in the real world of objects and people, *everything* that real people can do, in a way that is indistinguishable (to a person) from the way real people do it." The most important of these robotic skills are the sensorimotor capacities that appear prior to linguistic capacities and that allow us to interact bodily with things in the world. Recognizing the similarities between the Total Turing Test and the Cartesian test, Larry Hauser writes:

> Descartes' description of what [his] test requires ... is virtually indistinguishable from Harnad's description of the classic Turing Test ... Likewise, Harnad's "Total Turing Test" ... echoes Descartes' characterization of his second, behavior, test (Hauser 1993, p. 223).

[9]Hauser resists the use of such a stringent test on intuitive grounds. As he writes on page 222, "We make mental predications of things such as infrahuman animals, children, and computers which can't pass either Turing's Test or Harnad's Total Turing Test. What we actually rely on in practice seems to be partial Turing Tests of limited competencies taken to be associated with specific mental abilities." Such intuitive considerations might not be applicable, though, if the Turing Test is intended to be a more rigorous, *scientific* test.

[10]However, the adoption of the Turing Test as an AI benchmark has not been wholly uncontroversial. For instance, in his "Lessons From a Restricted Turing Test," Stuart Shieber details some of the technical and theoretical problems with the Turing Test-based Loebner Prize competition and suggests that it be replaced with a more significant contest.

References

Adler, M.J. (1967), *The Difference of Man and the Difference it Makes*, New York: Holt, Rinehart and Winston.

Chomsky, N. (1966), *Cartesian Linguistics*, New York: Harper and Row.

Cottingham, J. (1978), 'A Brute to the Brutes?', *Philosophy* 53, pp. 551–559.

Damasio, A.R. (1994), *Descartes' Error*, New York: G.P. Putnam.

Dennett, D.C. (1991), *Consciousness Explained*, Boston: Little, Brown and Co.

Descartes, R. (1985), *The Philosophical Writings of Descartes*, trans. and ed. by J. Cottingham, R. Stoothoff, D. Murdoch, and A. Kenny, Cambridge: Cambridge University Press. (Cited in text as CSM.)

Egenhofer, M. and Mark, D.M. (1995), 'Naive Geography', in A.U. Frank and W. Kuhn, eds., *Spatial Information Theory: A Theoretical Basis for GIS*, Berlin/New York: Springer, pp. 1–15.

Erion, G.J. (2000), *Common Sense: An Investigation in Ontology, Epistemology, and Moral Philosophy*, unpublished doctoral dissertation, University at Buffalo, State University of New York.

Forguson, L. (1989), *Common Sense*, New York: Routledge.

Gunderson, K. (1964), 'Descartes, La Mettrie, Language, and Machines', *Philosophy* 39, pp. 193–222.

Harnad, S. (1991), 'Other Bodies, Other Minds: A Machine Incarnation of an Old Philosophical Problem', *Minds and Machines* 1, pp. 43–54.

Hauser, L. (1993), 'Reaping the Whirlwind', *Minds and Machines* 3, pp. 219–238.

Hayes, P.J. (1985a), 'Naive Physics I: Ontology for Liquids', in J.R. Hobbs and R.C. Moore, eds., *Formal Theories of the Common-Sense World*, Norwood, NJ: Ablex, pp. 71–107.

Hayes, P.J. (1985b). 'The Second Naive Physics Manifesto', in J.R. Hobbs and R.C. Moore, eds., *Formal Theories of the Common Sense World*, Norwood, NJ: Ablex, pp. 1–36.

Horton, R. (1982), 'Tradition and Modernity Revisited', in M. Hollis and S. Lukes, eds., *Rationality and Relativism*, Oxford: Basil Blackwell pp. 201–260.

Leiber, J. (1989), 'Re(ad) Me; Re(ad) Myself', *Philosophy and Literature* 13, pp. 134–139.

Macnamara, J. (1986), *A Border Dispute: The Place of Logic in Psychology*, Cambridge, MA: MIT Press.

Radner, D. and Radner, M. (1989), *Animal Consciousness*. Buffalo: Prometheus.

Radner, D. and Radner, M. (1995), 'Cognition, Natural Selection, and the Intentional Stance', *International Studies in the Philosophy of Science* 9, pp. 109–119.

Ryle, G. (1971), 'Knowing How and Knowing That', in *Collected Papers of Gilbert Ryle*, Vol. II. New York: Barnes and Noble, pp. 212–225. (Original work published in 1945.)

Shieber, S.M. (1994), 'Lessons From a Restricted Turing Test', *Communications of the ACM* 37, pp. 70–78.

Smith, B. (1994), 'The Structures of the Common-Sense World', in S. Poggi, ed., *Gestalt Psychology: Its Origins, Foundations, and Influence*, Firenze: L.S. Olschki, pp. 209–232.

Turing, A.M. (1950), 'Computing Machinery and Intelligence', *Mind* 59, pp. 433–460.

Journal of Logic, Language, and Information **9**: 425–445, 2000.
© 2000 *Kluwer Academic Publishers. Printed in the Netherlands.*

Minds, Machines and Turing

The Indistinguishability of Indistinguishables

S. HARNAD
*Department of Electronics and Computer Science, University of Southampton, Highfield,
Southampton SO17 1BJ, U.K.*
E-mail: harnad@cogsci.soton.ac.uk; http://www.cogsci.soton.ac.uk/~harnad

(Received 1 June 1999; in final form 15 April 2000)

Abstract. Turing's celebrated 1950 paper proposes a very general methodological criterion for modelling mental function: total functional equivalence and indistinguishability. His criterion gives rise to a hierarchy of Turing Tests, from subtotal ("toy") fragments of our functions (t1), to total symbolic (pen-pal) function (T2 – the standard Turing Test), to total external sensorimotor (robotic) function (T3), to total internal microfunction (T4), to total indistinguishability in every empirically discernible respect (T5). This is a "reverse-engineering" hierarchy of (decreasing) empirical under-determination of the theory by the data. Level t1 is clearly too underdetermined, T2 is vulnerable to a counterexample (Searle's Chinese Room Argument), and T4 and T5 are arbitrarily overdetermined. Hence T3 is the appropriate target level for cognitive science. When it is reached, however, there will still remain more unanswerable questions than when Physics reaches its Grand Unified Theory of Everything (GUTE), because of the mind/body problem and the other-minds problem, both of which are inherent in this empirical domain, even though Turing hardly mentions them.

Key words: Cognitive neuroscience, cognitive science, computation, computationalism, consciousness, dynamical systems, epiphenomenalism, intelligence, machines, mental models, mind/body problem, other minds problem, philosophy of science, qualia, reverse engineering, robotics, Searle, symbol grounding, theory of mind, thinking, Turing, underdetermination, Zombies

1. Intended Interpretation

Wimsatt (1954) originally proposed the notion of the "Intentional Fallacy" with poetry in mind, but his intended message applies equally to all forms of intended interpretation. It is a fallacy, according to Wimsatt, to see or seek the meaning of a poem exclusively or even primarily in the intentions of its author: the author figures causally in the text he created, to be sure, but his intended meaning is not the sole or final arbiter of the text's meaning. The author may have been hewing to his Muse, which may have planted meanings in the text that he did not even notice, let alone intend, yet there they are.

A good deal of even our most prosaic discourse has this somnambulistic character if you look at it sufficiently closely, and the greater the creative leap it takes, the less aware we are of where it came from (Hadamard, 1949). Even the banal act of pushing or not pushing a button at one's whim comes under a fog of indeterminacy when scrutinised microscopically (Harnad, 1982b; Dennett and Kinsbourne, 1995).

This paper is accordingly not about what Turing (1950)* may or may not have actually thought or intended. It is about the implications of his paper for empirical research on minds and machines. So if there is textual or other evidence that these implications are at odds with what Turing actually had in mind, I can only echo the last line of Black's (1952) doubly apposite essay on the "Identity of Indiscernibles," in which the two opposing metaphysical viewpoints (about whether or not two things that there is no way to tell apart are in reality one and the same thing) are presented in the form of a dialogue between two interlocutors. Black effects to be even-handed, but it is obvious that he favours one of the two. The penultimate line, from the unfavoured one, is something like "Well, I am still not convinced," the last line, from the favoured one, "Well, you ought to be."

2. The Standard Interpretation of Turing (1950)

Turing is usually taken to be making a point about "thinking" (Dennett, 1985; Davidson, 1990). Using the example of a party game in which one must guess which of two out-of-sight candidates is male and which is female on the basis of written messages alone (today we would say on the basis of email-interaction alone), Turing asks what would happen if the two candidates were instead a man and a machine (let us say a digital computer, for the time being) and we could not tell them apart. For then it would follow that we could have no grounds for holding that one of them was thinking and the other was not. Hence either the question "What is thinking?" is meaningless, or it is provisionally answered by whatever proves successful in passing such a test.

This is the gist of the "thought experiment" Turing invented in that paper, but it clearly needs some more elaboration and analysis, for otherwise it is open to misconstrual.

3. Misinterpretations of Turing (1950)

One misconstrual is that the outcome of such a "Turing Test" would accordingly just be a trick: the successful machine candidate would not really be thinking at all, and Turing has simply shown that it might be possible to fool us in this way with a computer.

I do not think this is a correct interpretation of Turing's thought experiment. Turing's point is much more substantive and positive than this. If there is any implication about trickery, it is that we are fooling ourselves if we think we have a more sensitive basis than the Turing Test (TT) for determining whether or not a

---

* Web addresses for retrieving cited papers:
Turing and Lucas: http://cogprints.soton.ac.uk
Harnad: http://cogsci.soton.ac.uk/~harnad/genpub.html
Papers in BBS: http://www.cogsci.soton.ac.uk/bbs/Archive/
Papers in Psycoloquy http://www.cogsci.soton.ac.uk/cgi/psyc/newpsy

candidate is thinking: all functional tests of thinking or intelligence are really just TTs (Harnad, 1992b).

I will return to this point when I introduce the TT Hierarchy. For now, note simply that the notion that "I have a better way" of discerning whether a candidate is really thinking calls for a revelation of what that better way is, relative to which the TT is merely a trick. It turns out that all the "better ways" are either arbitrary or subsumed by a sufficiently general construal of what the TT itself is. (Again, it matters little whether or not Turing explicitly contemplated or intended this generalisation; it is implicit in his argument.)

A second misconstrual of Turing's argument is that he somehow proved that any candidate passing the TT must be thinking/intelligent: he certainly did not prove that (nor is it amenable to proof, nor is it true of necessity), and indeed there now exists a prominent counterexample – not a proof either, but a counterargument as strong as Turing's original argument – for one specific kind of candidate passing one specific version of the TT, namely, a pure symbol-system passing the purely symbolic version of the TT. The counterargument in question is Searle's (1980) notorious "Chinese Room Argument," and I will return to it shortly (Harnad, 1989). Suffice it to say that Turing's is an epistemic point, not an ontic one, and heuristic rather than demonstrative.

4. Equivocation about Thinking and Machines

So if passing the TT is neither evidence of trickery nor a guarantee of intelligence, what is it?

To answer this, one must say much more explicitly what Turing's Argument shows, and how. To do this, we have to get rid of the vexed word "thinking," which Turing in any case wanted to conclude was equivocal, if not incoherent. It is equivocal in that the very distinction between "real" and "artificial" here is equivocal. In a trivial sense, any natural thing that we succeed in synthesising is not "real," precisely in that it is not natural but synthetic, i.e., man-made (Harnad, 1993b). So the question of what thinking is, and whether a man-made machine can have "real" thoughts would be trivially answered if "real" simply means "natural" (i.e., not man-made, not "synthetic"), for then nothing synthetic is real.

So if the real/artificial distinction is not just the natural/synthetic distinction, what is it then? Even the word "machine" is equivocal in exactly the same sense, for what is a machine? Is it a synthetic, man-made mechanism? Or is it any physical/causal mechanism at all? If cars or planes or robots grew on trees, would that alone make them no longer machines? And if we bioengineered an organic organism from scratch, molecule by molecule, would that make it more a machine than its natural counterpart already is?

No. These distinctions are clearly too arbitrary. The deep issues here are not about the natural/man-made distinction but about something else, something going much deeper into the nature of *mechanism* itself, irrespective of its provenance.

5. Functional Capacity: Mindful vs. Mindless

It is easy to give a performance-based or functional criterion for "intelligence" (precisely the same point can be made about "thinking"): intelligence is as intelligence does. It requires intelligence to factor a quadratic equation. Hence, any system that can do that, has, eo ipso, intelligence. But this is clearly not what we mean by intelligence here, and defining it thus does not answer any deep questions about what might be present or lacking in a system along these lines.

What are these lines, then? I think it has become abundantly clear that what we are really wondering about here is whether or not a system has a mind: if it does intelligent, thoughtful, mind-like things, but does so mindlessly, because there is nobody home in there, no one experiencing experiences, feeling feelings, thinking thoughts, then it falls on one side of the dividing line; if it does have a mind, be that mind ever so limited, "thoughtless" and "unintelligent," it is on the other side. And the natural fault marked by this dividing line, coincides, for better or worse, with the mind/body problem.

6. Turing Indistinguishability and the Other-Minds Problem

So Turing is right that we should set aside the equivocal notion of "thinking/intelligence," because nothing nonarbitrary hinges on it. What we really want to know about the candidate is whether or not it has a mind – and this clearly cuts across the natural/synthetic distinction, for if there is no way to determine whether or not a system has a mind on the basis of its provenance (natural or man-made), then in learning that a TT-passing candidate is a "machine," we have not really learned anything at all (insofar as the question of whether it has a mind is concerned).

This is merely a special case of an even more general indeterminacy, namely, the fact that no empirical test, TT-passing or otherwise, can tell us whether or not a candidate has a mind! This is one of the lemmas we inherit with the mind/body problem, and it is called the "other-minds problem" (Harnad, 1991). (It would have cut short a lot of potential misconstruals of Turing's paper if he had simply called a spade a spade here, but there we are; Turing was not a philosopher but a mathematician.)

Turing did allude to the other-minds problem in passing, but only to dismiss it as leading to "solipsism" and hence the end of rational discourse ("It may be the most logical view to hold but it makes communication of ideas difficult"). Yet the other-minds problem is an inescapable methodological constraint on mind-modelling (Harnad, 1984, 1985). For the only way to know for sure that a system has a mind is to be that system. All other ways are risky, and risky in a way that is much more radical than the ordinary Humean risk that goes with all empirical inferences and generalisations. I am not referring here to philosophical scepticism about whether someone as like me as my neighbour has a mind; let us take that for granted. But what happens as we move away in likeness, toward other mammalian species, invertebrates, micro-organisms, plants, man-made artifacts? Where does mere philosophical scepticism leave off and real empirical uncertainty kick in?

7. Out of Sight, Out of Mind: Dissociating Structure and Function

Turing implicitly partitioned this question. "Likeness" can take two forms: likeness in structure and likeness in function. In sending the candidates out of the room in the party game, Turing separated what he took to be irrelevant and potentially biasing aspects of the superficial appearance of intelligence from pertinent manifestations of the functional capacities that constitute it. But banishing physical structure from sight, Turing also inadvertently excluded some potentially relevant aspects of function, both internal and external to the candidate.

For human minds, at least, can do a lot more than just exchange words. And as the TT is clearly predicated on functional likeness (indeed, functional indistinguishability), to banish all our nonverbal functions from it would be to limit the TT's domain of likeness in an almost arbitrary way, and certainly in a way that goes against the spirit of a test that is predicated on functional indistinguishability (Turing-indistinguishability).

8. The Expressive Power of Natural Language and Formal Computation

The special case of only words-in and words-out is not entirely arbitrary, however, because of the remarkable expressive power of language, which some have even suggested might be limitless and universal, including, as it does, not only the capacity of words to express any possible proposition (Steklis and Harnad, 1976; Harnad, 1996), but also the full computational power of the Turing Machine (Harnad, 1982a, 1994b). Nevertheless, there are things that human beings can do that go beyond mere verbalising; and perhaps more important, these nonvocal capacities may functionally precede and underlie our capacity to have and exchange words: we are able, after all, to interact nonverbally with that world of objects, events, and states that our words are about (e.g., we can detect, discriminate, identify, and manipulate them). Indeed, it is hard to imagine how our words could have the meanings they have if they were not first grounded in these nonverbal interactions with the world (Harnad, 1990a, 1992a, 1993a; Crockett, 1994).

9. The Turing Hierarchy: Level t1 (Toy Models)

It is accordingly time to introduce the TT hierarchy (Harnad, 1994a). The lowest level would properly be T1, but there is no T1, only t1, for here "t" stands not for "Turing" (or "Total"), but for "toy," and t1 launches the TT hierarchy without yet being a proper part of it: the t1 level of Turing modelling and Turing Testing is the level of "toy models." These are models for subtotal fragments of our functional capacity. At worst, these fragments are just arbitrary ones; at best, some might be self-sufficient modules, eventual components of our full-scale capacity, but not stand-alone candidates in the Turing sense. For the TT is predicated on total functional indistinguishability, and toys are most decidedly distinguishable from the real thing. Toys are not us.

Before moving up to T2 we will make it explicit exactly why toys are ultimately inadequate for the goals of Turing Testing. But note that all of the actual mind-modelling research efforts to date are still only at the t1 level, and will continue to be so for the foreseeable future: Cognitive Science has not even entered the TT hierarchy yet.

10. Level T5 (Grand Unified Theories of Everything [GUTEs])

Toy models, that is, subtotal models, of anything at all, have the liability that they have more degrees of freedom than the real, total thing that they are modelling. There are always more different ways to generate a fragment of a system's function (say, chess-playing – or simple harmonic motion) than there are to generate the system's total function (say, everything else a human mind can do – or all of Newtonian or Quantum Mechanics), if for no other reason than that the Total model must subsume all the functions of the subtotal toy models too (Schweizer, 1998).

We spoke of Humean indeterminacy earlier; philosophers are not yet of one mind on the number of candidate Total Theories there are likely to be, at the end of the empirical/theoretical road for, say, Physics. At that Utopian endpoint, when all the data – past, present and future – are Totally accounted for, will there be one and only one Grand Unified Theory of Everything (GUTE)? Or will there be several rival GUTEs, each able to account for everything? If the latter, will the rivals posit an equal number of parameters? and can we assume that the rival GUTEs will just be notational variants of one another? If not, will we be right to prefer the miniparametric GUTE, using Occam's Razor?

These are metaphysical questions, and physicists would be more than happy to have reached that Utopian stage where these were the only questions left to worry about. It is clear, however, that current physics is still at the stage of subtotal theories (it would be churlish for any other science to venture to call them "toys," as physics's are surely the most advanced such toys any science has yet produced). Subtotal models always run the risk of being very wrong, although that risk diminishes as they scale up toward a closer and closer approximation to totality (GUTE); the degrees of freedom shrink, but they may not vanish altogether, even after we have reached Utopia.

Utopia is also the top Level T5 of the Turing Hierarchy. We will return to this after describing Levels T2–T4.

11. Utopian Differences that Make No Difference

The Humean risk that our theory is wrong, instead of shrinking to zero even at Totality, may remain in that nonzero state which philosophers call the "underdetermination" of theory by data. The ever-present possibility that a theory could be wrong, even after it accounts for all the data, and that another theory might instead be right, is a liability that science has learned to live with. By way of consolation, one can note that, at the point of miniparametric totality – when all the data have been accurately predicted and causally explained by the GUTE(s) with the fewest parameters, the difference between being right and wrong would no longer be one that could make any palpable difference to any of us.

Consider the status of "quarks," for example. (I am not speaking now of actual quarks, which have lately become experimentally observable, but the original notion of a quark, which was a largish entity that could not occur in a "free state," but only tightly "bound" up together with other quarks into a much tinier observable entity such as an electron.) The existence of quarks was posited not because they were experimentally observed, but because hypothesising that they existed, even though they could never be observed empirically, made it possible to predict and explain otherwise unpredictable and inexplicable empirical data. But quarks have since turned out to be observable after all, so I am now speaking about what GUTEs would have been like if they had contained unobservable-in-principle quarks. [A more current example might be superstrings.]

At the end of the day, once all data were in and fully accounted for by GUTEs that posited (unobservable-in-principle) quarks, one might still wonder about whether quarks really exist. Maybe they do, maybe they do not. There is no empirical way left to find out. Maybe the GUTEs that posit quarks are wrong; but then other, quarkless, GUTEs must have components that do for them the predictive/explanatory work that the quarks do for the quarkful GUTEs. In any case, it is a fact about the quarkful GUTEs that without positing quarks they cannot successfully predict/explain Everything.

12. Empirical Underdetermination and Turing Testing

I rehearse this indeterminacy explicitly in order to make it clear how little is at stake: all data are successfully predicted and explained, and we are just worrying about which (if any) of the successful Total, Turing-Indistinguishable explanations is the real one; and no one can ever be the wiser except an omniscient deity who simply knows the truth (e.g., whether or not there really are quarks).

This is normal scientific underdetermination. Notice that the name of Turing has been introduced into it, because with GUTEs we are actually at the top (T5) level of the Turing hierarchy, which turns out to be a hierarchy of (decreasing) degrees of empirical underdetermination. The t1 (sub-Turing) level, for both physical science (world-modelling) and cognitive science (mind-modelling), is that of subtotal, toy models, accounting for some but not all of the data; hence underdetermination is maximal in toyland, but shrinks as the toys grow.

13. Basic Science vs. Engineering: Forward and Reverse

Physical science and cognitive science are not really on a par, because physical systems with minds are of course a part of the world too. Cognitive science is probably better thought of as a branch of reverse bioengineering (Dennett, 1994): in normal engineering, the principles of physics (and engineering) are applied to the design of physical systems with certain functions that are useful to us. In reverse bioengineering, those systems have already been designed by Nature (by the Blind Watchmaker, Darwinian Evolution), and our task is to figure out how they work. The actual methodology turns out to resemble forward engineering, in that we still have to design systems that are more and more like the natural ones, starting with toy models, and converging on Total Turing-Indistinguishability by a series of tighter and tighter approximations.

Which brings us back to the Turing Hierarchy. Before we leave the t1 level, let it be stressed that, in principle, there can be a distinct Turing Hierarchy for each species' functional capacities; hence there can be toy models of mollusk, mouse and monkey, as well as man. Other species no doubt have minds (I personally think all animals with nervous tissue, vertebrate and invertebrate, do, and I am accordingly a vegetarian), but, as mentioned earlier, our confidence in this can only diminish as we move further and further from our own species. So it is not arbitrary that Turing Testing should end at home (in the total performance capacities of our own species), even if the toy modelling begins with the reverse engineering of "lesser" species (Harnad, 1994a).

So at the bottom level of the hierarchy are subtotal toy models of subhuman and human functional capacities. Such toy models are also sub-Turing (which is why this level is called t1 instead of T1), because the essential criterion for Turing Testing is Total Indistinguishability from the real thing, and toys are by definition subtotal, hence distinguishable. Nevertheless, the idea of converging on Totality by closer and closer approximations is implicit in Turing's paper, and it is the basis for his sanguine predictions about what computers would successfully scale up to doing by our day. (Unfortunately, his chronology was too optimistic, and this might have been because he was betting on a particular kind of candidate, a purely computational one; but if so, then he should not have been, for the Turing spectrum admits many other kinds of candidate mechanisms too.)

14. Level T2: The Pen-Pal Turing Test (Symbols-in/Symbols-out)

T2 is the conventional TT, the one I have taken to calling the "pen-pal" version: words in and words out (Harnad, 1989). It is the one that most people have in mind when they think of Turing Testing. But because of the unfortunate "imitation game" example with which it was introduced, T2 has been subject to a number of misunderstandings, which I will quickly try to correct here.

14.1. Life-Long: T2 is not a game (or if it is, it's no less than the game of life!). It is a mistake to think of T2 as something that can be "passed" in a single evening or even during an annual Loebner Prize Competition (Loebner, 1994; Shieber, 1994). Although it was introduced in the form of a party game in order to engage our intuitions, it is obvious that Turing intends T2 as a serious, long-term operational criterion for what would now be called "cognitive science." The successful candidate is not one that has fooled the judges in one session into thinking it could perform indistinguishably from a real pen-pal with a mind. (Fooling 70% of the people one time is as meaningless, scientifically, as fooling 100% of the people 70 times.) The winning candidate will really have the capacity to perform indistinguishably from a real pen-pal with a mind – for a lifetime, if need be, just as unhaltingly as any of the rest of us can. (This is a variant of the misconstrual I mentioned earlier: T2 is not a trick; Harnad, 1992b.)

14.2. Symbolic/Nonsymbolic: T2 is restricted to verbal (i.e., symbolic) interactions: symbols in, symbols out. But it is not restricted in principle to a computer doing only computation (symbol manipulation) in between (although Turing so restricts it in practise). The candidate "machine" can in principle be anything man-made, including machines other than digital computers (e.g., sensorimotor transducers, analog computers, parallel distributed networks, indeed any dynamical system at all; Harnad, 1993a).

14.3 Man-Made: The reason the candidate needs to be man-made is that all the tests in the TT Hierarchy are tests of mind-models. Interposing a natural candidate that we did not build or understand would not be a test of anything at all. Turing was indifferent about whether the thinking thereby generated by the system was real or not – he thought that that was an uninteresting question – but he did want to successfully synthesize the capacity, in toto. So we could say that he did not care whether the result would be the reverse bioengineering of the real mind, or the forward engineering of something mind-like but mindless, but the engineering was certainly intended to be real, and to really deliver the behavioral goods!

14.4. Mindful: Turing was not interested in the question of whether the candidate would really have a mind, but that does not mean that the question is of no interest. More important, he *ought* to have been interested, because, logically speaking, without the mental criterion, T2 is not a test of anything: it is merely an open-ended catalogue of what a particular candidate can do. The indistinguishability is between the candidate and a real person with a mind. So, like it or not, if T2 is not merely to be testing the difference between two arbitrary forms of cleverness, it must be testing mindful cleverness against mindless. And once they are indistinguishable, then we no longer have a basis for affirming of the one a predicate we wish to deny of the other (other than trivial predicates such as that one is man-made and the other is not). And "mindful/mindless" is just such a (nontrivial) predicate.

14.5. Conscious: Note that T2 is rightly indifferent to whether the candidates are actually doing what they do consciously (Harnad, 1982b; Searle, 1990). They might be doing it somnambulistically, as discussed earlier in connection with the intentional fallacy. This does not matter: the real person has a mind, even if it's only idling in the background, and that would be a world of difference from a candidate that had no mind at all, foregrounded or backgrounded, at that moment or any other. And if they're indistinguishable (for a lifetime), then they're indistinguishable; so if you are prepared to impute a mind to the one, you have no nonarbitrary basis for denying it of the other.

14.6. Empirical/Intuitive: Turing Indistinguishability is actually two criteria, one empirical and one intuitive: the empirical criterion is that the candidate really has to have total T2 capacity, for a lifetime. The intuitive criterion is that that capacity must be totally indistinguishable *from* that of real people with minds *to* real people with minds. (Note the plural: not only is T2 not a one-night affair; it is not merely a dyadic one either. Real pen-pals have the capacity to correspond with many people, not just one.) The intuitive criterion may be almost as important as the empirical one, for although (because of the other-minds problem) we are not really mind-readers, our intuitive "theory-of-mind" capacities may be the next best thing (Heyes, 1998; Mitchell and Anderson, 1998), picking up subtleties that are dead give-aways to our fine-grained intuitions while still out of the reach of the coarse-grained reverse-engineering of our overall cognitive capacities.

15. Searle's Chinese Room Argument

Only corrective 14.2 above is unique to T2. The rest of 14.1–14.6 are applicable to all the levels of the TT Hierarchy. T2 is a special level not just because it is the one at which Turing originally formulated the TT, and not just because of the special powers of both natural language and formal computation on which it draws, but because it is the only level that is vulnerable to a refutation, in the form of a counterexample.

So let us now briefly consider this celebrated counterexample to T2, for it will serve to motivate T3 and T4: but first, note that the intentional fallacy applies to Searle's (1980) paper as surely as it applies to Turing's (1950) paper: Searle thought he was refuting not only cognitive "computationalism" (which he called "Strong AI" and will be defined in a moment), but also the Turing Test. In fact, he was refuting only T2, and only in the special case of one specific kind of candidate, a purely computational one: an implementation-independent implementation of a formal symbol system. T2, however, is not the only possible form a TT can take, and a pure symbol system is certainly not the only possible candidate.

Searle (1980, 1984, 1993) defined his target, "Strong AI," as the hypothesis expressed by the following three propositions:

1. The mind is a computer program.
2. The brain is irrelevant.
3. The Turing Test is decisive.

This formulation was unfortunate, because it led to many misunderstandings and misconstruals of Searle's otherwise valid argument that I do not have the space to analyse in detail here (see Harnad, 1989, 2000b; Hayes et al., 1992). No one holds that the mind is a computer program (with the absurd connotation that inert code might have feelings). What the proponents of the view that has since come to be known as (cognitive) "computationalism" hypothesise is that mental states are really just computational states, which means that they are the physical implementations of a symbol system – or code, running (Newell, 1980; Pylyshyn, 1980, 1984). This makes more sense.

Similarly, what Searle should have said instead of (2) was that the *physical details* of the implementation are irrelevant – but without the implication that implementing the code *at all* was irrelevant. Hence the rest of the details about the brain are irrelevant; all that matters is that it is implementing the right code.

To hold that the capacity to pass the TT (3) is what demonstrates that the "right" code is being implemented, the one that implements a mind, is unobjectionable, for that is indeed Turing's argument – except of course that Turing was not necessarily a cognitive computationalist! If just a computer, running the right code, could successfully pass the pen-pal version of the TT (T2), Turing would indeed have held that we had no better or worse grounds for concluding that it had a mind than we would have in the case of a real pen-pal, who really had a mind, for the simple reason that we had no way to tell them apart – their performance would be Turing indistinguishable.

However, Turing would have had to concede that real pen-pals can do many other things besides exchanging letters; and it is hard to see how a computer alone could do all those other things. So Turing would have had no problem with an augmented candidate that consisted of more than just a computer implementing the right code. Turing would have been quite content, for example, with a robot, interacting with the world Turing indistinguishably from the rest of us. But that version of the TT would no longer be T2, the pen-pal version, but T3, the robotic version.

We will return to T3 shortly. It must also be pointed out that Turing is not irrevocably committed to the candidate's having to be merely a computer even in the case of T2. The T2-passing system could be something other than just a computer running the right code; perhaps no computer/code combination alone could successfully generate our lifelong pen-pal capacity, drawing as the latter does on so much else that we can all do. We could, for example, include a photo with one of our letters to a pen-pal, and ask the pen-pal to comment on the quality of the blue object in the photo (or we could simply enclose a blue object). A mere computer, without sensorimotor transducers, would be completely nonplussed by that sort of input. (And the dynamical system consisting of a computer plus sensorimotor transducers would no longer be just a computer.)

Never mind. A (hypothetical) T2-passing computer is nevertheless fair game, in this thought-experimental arena that Turing himself created. So Searle takes Turing at his word, and supposes that there is a computer program that is indeed capable of passing T2 (for a lifetime); he merely adds the stipulation that it does so in Chinese only. In other words, the candidate could correspond for a lifetime with Chinese pen-pals without any of them having any reason to suspect that they were not communicating with a real (Chinese-speaking) person. Turing's argument is that at the end of the day, when it is revealed that the candidate is a computer, one has learned nothing at all to over-rule the quite natural inference one had been making all along – that one was corresponding with a real pen-pal, who really understood what all those letters (and his own replies) had meant.

It is here that Searle makes a very shrewd use of the other two premises – that what is at issue is the code alone (1), and that although that code must be implemented, the physical details of the implementation are irrelevant (2): each and every implementation of the right code must have a mind, if any of them does, and if they indeed have a mind only because they are implementations of the right (i.e., T2-passing) code.

So Searle too makes a simple appeal to our intuitions, just as Turing did in appealing to the power of indistinguishability (i.e., in noting that if you cannot tell them apart, you cannot affirm of one what you deny of the other): Searle notes that, as the implementation is irrelevant, there is no reason why he himself should not implement the code. So we are to suppose that Searle himself is executing all the computations on the input symbols in the Chinese messages – all the algorithms and symbol manipulations – that successfully generate the output symbols of the pen-pal's replies (the ones that are indistinguishable from those of real life-long pen-pals to real life-long pen-pals).

Searle then simply points out to us that he would not be understanding the Chinese messages he was receiving and generating under these conditions (any more than would a student mindlessly but successfully going through the motions of executing some formal algorithm whose meaning he did not understand). Hence there is no reason to believe that the computer, implementing exactly the same code – or indeed that any implementation of that code, merely in virtue of implementing that code – would be understanding either.

What has happened here? Turing's "no way to be any the wiser about the mind" argument rested on indistinguishability, which in turn rested on the "other-minds" barrier: the only way to know whether any candidate other than myself has or has not a mind is to *be* that candidate; but the only one I can be is me, so Turing indistinguishability among candidates with minds is all I have left.

16. Penetrating the Other-Minds Barrier through Implementation-Independence

What Searle has done is to exploit one infinitesimally narrow window of vulnerability in cognitive computationalism and T2: no one else can show that a computer (or a rock) has or hasn't a mind, because no one else can be that computer or that rock. But the computationalism thesis was not about the computer, it was about the running code, which was stipulated to be implementation-independent. Hence the details of how the code is executed are irrelevant; all that is needed is that the code be executed. And it is indeed being executed by Searle, who is thereby *being* the running code, being the candidate (there is no one else in sight!). And he (truthfully) informs us that he does not understand a word: he is merely mindlessly manipulating code.

This counterargument is not a proof (any more than Turing's own indistinguishability argument is a proof). It is logically possible that simply going through the motions of manipulating the right symbols does give birth to another understanding mind – not Searle's, for he does not understand, but whoever in his head is answering the Chinese messages in Chinese. (It is, by the same token, logically possible that if we taught someone illiterate and enumerate how to apply the symbol-manipulation algorithm for solving quadratic equations, that he, or someone else inside his head, would thereby come to understand quadratic equations and their solution.)

17. Multiple Minds? The Searlean Test (ST)

This is spooky stuff. We know about multiple personality disorder – extra minds cohabiting the same head, not aware of one another – but that is normally induced by early sexual abuse rather than by learning to manipulate mindlessly a bunch of meaningless symbols.

So I think it makes more sense to give up on cognitive computationalism and concede that either no implemented code alone could ever successfully pass the lifetime T2, or that any code that did so would nevertheless fail to have a mind; that it would indeed be just a trick. And the way to test this would be via the "Searlean Test" (ST), by being the candidate, executing the code oneself, and failing to experience the mental state (understanding) that is being attributed to the pen-pal. As one has no intuitive inclination whatsoever to impute extra mental states to oneself in the face of clear 1st-person evidence that one lacks them, the ST should, by the transitivity of implementation-independence, rule out all purely computational T2-passers.

A purely computational T2-passer, in other words, *is* Turing distinguishable from a candidate with a mind, and the way to make the distinction is to be the candidate, via the ST.

18. Grounding Symbols in their Objects Rather than in the Mind of an External Interpreter

Has Turing lost a lot of territory with this? I don't think so. The other-minds barrier is still there to ensure that no other candidate can be penetrated and hence unmasked in this way. And besides, there are stronger and more direct reasons than the ST for having doubts about cognitive computationalism (Harnad, 1990a): the symbols in a symbol system need to be grounded in something other than simply more symbols and the interpretations that our own minds project onto them (as was the case with the symbolic pen-pal), no matter how coherent, self-confirming, and intuitively persuasive those external interpretations might be (Harnad, 1990b, 1990c). The symbols must be grounded directly and autonomously in causal interactions with the objects, events and states that they are *about*, and a pure symbol-cruncher does not have the wherewithal for that (as the photo/object accompanying the letter to the pen-pal demonstrates).

What is needed to ground symbols directly and autonomously in the world of objects? At the very least, sensorimotor transducers and effectors (and probably many other dynamical internal mechanisms); and none of these are implementation-independent; rather, they are, like most things, other-minds-*im*penetrable, and hence immune to the ST and the Chinese Room Argument. The TT candidate, in other words, cannot be just a disembodied symbol-cruncher; it must be an embodied robot, capable of nonsymbolic, sensorimotor interactions with the world in addition to symbolic ones, all Turing indistinguishable from our own. This is T3, and it subsumes T2, for pen-pal capacities are merely subsets of robotic capacities (Harnad, 1995a).

19. Level T3: The Robotic Turing Test

Note that just as scaling up from toys to totality is dictated by Turing's functional equivalence/indistinguishability constraint, so is scaling up from T2 to T3. For pen-pal capacities alone are clearly subtotal ones, hence distinguishable as such. More important, pen-pal capacities themselves surely draw implicitly on robotic capacities, even in the T2, as demonstrated not only by enclosing any nonsymbolic object with a letter for comment, but surely (upon a little reflection) also by the very demands of coherent, continuous discourse about real objects, events, and states via symbols alone (French, 1990; Harnad, 1992a; Crockett, 1994; Watt, 1996).

Why did Turing not consider T3 more explicitly? I think it was because he was (rightly) concerned about factoring out irrelevant matters of appearance. Differences in appearance certainly do not in and of themselves attest to absence of mind: other terrestrial species surely have minds; extra-terrestrial creatures, if they exist, might have minds too; and so might robots. But it is a safe bet that no current-generation robot has a mind, because they are all still just at the most rudimentary toy level, t1, in their robotic capacities (Pylyshyn, 1987). Perhaps Turing simply thought our other-minds intuitions would be hopelessly biased by robotic appearance in T3, but not in T2. In any case, the recent progress in making robots look lifelike, at least in movies, may outstrip our prejudices. (If anything, the problem is that today's cinematic robots are getting ahead of the game, being endowed with fictional T3 capacity while their real-world counterparts are still functionally closer to mud than even to mollusks.)

20. Level T4: Internal Microfunctional Indistinguishability

Do T2–T3 exhaust the options for mind-modelling? No, for if the operational constraint is functional equivalence/indistinguishability, there is still a level of function at which robots are readily distinguishable from us: the internal, microfunctional level – and here the structure/function distinction collapses too. For just as we can ask whether, say, facial expression (as opposed to facial shape) is not in fact a legitimate component of our robotic capacity (it is), so we can ask about pupillary dilation (which allegedly occurs when we find someone attractive, and is Turing-detectable), blushing, heart-rate, etc. These are all still arguably components of T3. But, by the same token, we become speechless if kicked on the left side of our heads, but not the right (Harnad et al., 1977), we exude EEG, we bleed when we are cut, if we are opened up on an operating table we are found to be made of flesh, and in our heads one finds gray/white matter and neuropeptides rather than silicon chips.

These are all Turing-detectable functional differences between ourselves and T3 robots: are they relevant? We have already said that the fact that the candidate is man-made is not relevant. Not relevant to what? To determining whether or not the candidate has a mind. Do the neurobiological details matter? Perhaps. We are not, after all, implementation-independent symbol systems. Perhaps there are implementational details that are essential to having a mind.

Surely there are. But just as surely, there must be implementational details that are *not* essential to having a mind. And the problem is that there is no way of knowing which are which. Hence brain-scanning certainly plays no role in our perpetual Turing-testing of one another (in our age-old, day-to-day coping with the Other-Minds Problem), any more than mind-reading does (Harnad, 1991).

We are now at the level of T4: here the candidates are not only indistinguishable from us in their pen-pal and robotic functions, but also in their internal microfunctions. This is still the Turing hierarchy, for we are still speaking about functional indistinguishability and about totality. But do we really have to go this high in the hierarchy in practise? Indeed, is it even consistent with the spirit and methodology of Turing Testing to insist that the candidate be T4 indistinguishable from us? I think not, and I will now introduce my own thought experiment to test your intuitions on this. My example will be recognisably similar to the earlier discussion of underdetermination and the Utopian GUTEs in physics.

21. Grand Tournament of T-Levels: T3 vs. T4 vs. T5

Suppose that at the end of the day, when mind-modelling attains its Utopia, there are nine successful candidates. All nine are T3 indistinguishable from us, but three of them fail T4 (cut them open and they are clearly distinguishable in their internal microfunctions from us and our own real neural functions). Of the remaining six, three pass T4, but fail T5: their internal neural activities are functionally indistinguishable – transplants can be swapped between us and them, at any biocomponential scale – but theirs are still crafted out of synthetic materials; they are T4 indistinguishable, but T5 distinguishable; only the last three are engineered out of real biological molecules, physically identical to our own, hence T5 indistinguishable from ourselves in every physical respect. The only remaining difference among these last three is that they were designed in collaboration with three different physicists, and each of the physicists happens to subscribe to a different GUTE – of which there also happen to be three left at the end of the day.

Now note that the three T5 candidates are empirically identical in kind, right down to the last electron. The only difference between them is their respective designers' GUTES (and recall that each GUTE accounts successfully for all physical data). Now, according to one of the GUTEs, unobservable-in-principle quarks exist; according to another, they do not, but their predictive/explanatory work is done instead by some other unobservable entity. Both these GUTEs have the same number of parameters. The third GUTE has fewer parameters, and needs neither quarks nor their counterparts in the second GUTE.

So there we have our nine candidates: three T3's, three T4's and three T5's. All nine can correspond with you as a pen-pal for a lifetime; all nine can interact robotically with the people, objects, events and states in the world indistinguishably from you and me for a lifetime. All nine cry when you hurt them (whether physically or verbally), although three of them fail to bleed, and three of them bleed the wrong kind of blood. For the sake of argument, you have known all nine all your life (and consider them all close friends), and this state of affairs (that all nine are man-made) has only just been revealed to you today. You had never suspected it (across – let us say, to calibrate our intuitions – 40 years of friendship and shared life experiences!).

You are now being consulted as to which of the nine you feel can safely be deprived of their civil rights as a result of this new revelation. Which one(s) should it be, and why?

I think we are still squarely facing the Turing intuition here, and the overwhelming answer is that *none* should be deprived of their civil rights; none can be safely assumed to be "Zombies" (Harnad, 1995b). By all we can know that matters for such moral decisions about people with minds, both empirically and intuitively, they all have minds, as surely as any of the rest of us do.*

22. Level T3 Is Decisive

So does that mean that all differences above the level of T3 matter as little (or as much) to having a mind as the differences between the three Utopian GUTEs? Intuitively (and morally), I think the answer is undeniably: Yes. Empirically, it may prove to be a different story, because there may turn out to be some causal dependencies: certain microfunctional (T4) or even microphysical (T5) properties may not prove to be viable in passing T3 (e.g., it might not be possible to pass T3 with serial processors, or with components made out of heavy water); other T4 or T5 properties might give us positive clues about how to pass T3 (excitation/inhibition or 5-hydroxytryptamine may be essential) – and any success-enhancing clue is always welcome in reverse-engineering, as anywhere else! In this way neuroscience and even fundamental physics could conceivably help us pass T3; but T3 would still be the final arbiter, not T4 or T5.

The reason is clear, and again it is already implicit in Turing's functional-indistinguishability criterion: not only are ordinary people not mind-readers;

---

* Having appealed to our intuitions in this particular hypothetical case, it is unavoidable to go on to raise the question of whether we would feel comfortable (on the strength of Searle's Chinese Room Argument) in pulling the plug on our lifelong T2 pen-pal, if we found out that he was just a computer? Here our evolved "theory-of-mind" intuitions – our Turing intuitions – are utterly at odds with both our rational analysis and our real-life experience to date. (Some people are even loath to pull the plug on cyberplants.)

So of the two aspects of the Turing Test – the empirical one, of successfully reverse-engineering our full performance capacity, and the intuitive one, of being unable to discern any difference between the candidate and any other person with a mind – the intuitive, "mind-reading" aspect would be tugging hard in the case of a T2-passing computer, despite Searle's periscope, which unmasks the symbol system, but not the computer. For in the case of the computer pen-pal, we could rationalise the outcome by saying "So it's *that* computer implementation that has a mind, not just the symbol system it is implementing" (thereby merely jettisoning implementation-independence, and Searle's periscope with it).

So what if the code was being ported to a different computer every day? Our knowledge about transplants and cloning, plus our telefantasies about teleportation would still restrain us from pulling the plug (reinforced by the asymmetry between the relative consequences of false positives vs. false negatives in such capital decisions).

And what if it turned out to have been Searle mindlessly executing the code all those years, and telling us now that he had never understood a word? Well then the question would be moot, because there would be nothing left to pull the plug on anyway (although most of us would feel that we'd still like to send Searle back to the Room so we could write one last letter to our pen-pal under even those conditions, to find out what *he* had to say about the matter – or at least to say goodbye!)

We are contemplating hypothetical intuition clashes here; so perhaps we should wait to see what candidates can actually pass the TT before needlessly committing ourselves to any counterfactual contingency plans.

reverse-engineers are not mind-readers either. All are constrained by the other-minds barrier. Function is the only empirical criterion.

(And structural correlates are only reliable if they are first cross-validated by function: the reason I trust that one flashing red nucleus in my otherwise comatose and ostensibly brain-dead patient is evidence that he is still alive, feeling, and conscious, and will shortly make a come-back, is that prior patients have indeed made come-backs under those conditions, and subsequently reported the words they had heard me speak as I contemplated pulling the plug on their life-support systems at the very moment that only their red nucleus was still flashing.)

23. 1st-Person and 3rd-Person Facts

Now the forward-engineering of the mind would clearly be only a functional matter, just as the forward engineering of bridges, cars and space stations is. Reverse-engineering the mind is a bit more complicated, because we know one extra fact about the mind, over and above the 3rd-person functional facts, and that is the 1st-person fact that it feels like something to have/be a mind.

But this 1st-person fact is precisely the one to which the 3rd-person task of reverse engineering can never have any direct empirical access; only its functional correlates are available (Harnad, 2000c). Yet it is indeed a fact, as is clearly illustrated if we contrast the case of quarks with the case of qualia ("qualia" is the name philosophers have given to the qualitative contents of our mental experiences: they are what it feels like to have a mind, experience experiences, think thoughts, mean meanings; Nagel, 1974; Harnad, 1993c).

What we are actually asking about each of our nine candidates is whether or not it really has qualia. Is this like asking, about the Utopian world-models, whether there really are quarks in the world (i.e., whether the quarkful GUTE is the right GUTE)? Yes, but it is a bit worse in the case of mind-models, because whereas the reality or nonreality of (unobservable-in-principle) quarks, apart from the formal predictive/explanatory role they play (or do not play) in their respective GUTEs, makes and can make no palpable difference to anyone (I chose the word "palpable" advisedly), this is decidedly untrue of qualia. For surely it would make a world of palpable difference to *one* of the nine candidates, if we got our inferences wrong, and assumed it did not have qualia, when it in reality did! And each of us knows, palpably, precisely what that difference is – unlike the nebulous difference that the existence or non-existence of quarks would make, given the total predictive/explanatory power of its GUTE.)

So, metaphysically (as opposed to empirically or intuitively), more is at stake in principle with qualia than with quarks – which is why mind-modelling has a Zombie Problem whereas world-modelling does not (Harnad, 1995b).

24. Mind-Blindness, the Blind Watchmaker, and Mind over Matter

And there is a further difference between the case of quarks and the case of qualia: quarks, whether or not they exist, do play both a formal and a causal role in their GUTE. Qualia can play neither a formal nor a causal role in any mind-model, be it T3, T4 or T5. They are undeniably there in the world, but they can play no explicit role in the reverse-engineering, on pain of telekinetic dualism or worse (Harnad, 1982b; Alcock, 1987)! This too is implicit in Turing's insistence on functional criteria alone.

To put in context the mind-blind functionalism that Turing indistinguishability imposes on us, it is instructive to note that the Blind Watchmaker who forward-engineered us all (Darwinian Evolution) was a strict functionalist too, and likewise no mind-reader. Natural Selection is as incapable of distinguishing the Turing indistinguishable as any of the rest of us (Harnad, 2000a).

25. Turing's Text and Turing's Mind

This completes our exegesis of Turing (1950). Was this really the author's intended meaning? Perhaps not, but if not, then perhaps it ought to have been! His text is certainly systematically interpretable as meaning and implying all of this. But if Turing did not actually have it all in mind, then we are making a wrong pen-pal inference in imputing it to him – and it should instead be attributed only to the inert code he generated in the form of his celebrated paper.

References

Alcock, J.E., 1987, "Parapsychology: Science of the anomalous or search for the soul?," *Behavioral and Brain Sciences* **10**, 553–565.

Black, M., 1952, "The identity of indiscernibles," *Mind* **61**, 152–164.

Crockett, L., 1994, *The Turing Test and the Frame Problem: AI's Mistaken Understanding of Intelligence*, Norwood, NJ: Ablex.

Davidson, D., 1990, "Turing's Test," pp. 1–11 in *Modelling the Mind*, K.A. Mohyeldin Said, W.H. Newton-Smith, R. Viale, and K.V. Wilkes, eds., Oxford: Oxford University Press.

Dennett, D., 1985, "Can machines think?," in *How We Know*, M. Shafto, ed., San Francisco, CA: Harper & Row.

Dennett, D.C., 1994, "Cognitive science as reverse engineering," pp. 679–689 in *Proceedings of the 9th International Congress of Logic, Methodology and Philosophy of Science*, D. Prawitz, B. Skyrms, and D. Westerstahl, eds., Amsterdam: North-Holland.

Dennett, D.C. and Kinsbourne, M., 1995, "Time and the observer: The where and when of consciousness in the brain," *Behavioral and Brain Sciences* **15**, 183–247.

French, R., 1990, "Subcognition and the limits of the Turing Test," *Mind* **99**, 53–65.

Hadamard, J., 1949, *An Essay on the Psychology of Invention in the Mathematical Field*, Princeton, NJ: Princeton University Press.

Harnad, S., 1982a, "Neoconstructivism: A unifying theme for the cognitive sciences," pp. 1–11 in *Language, Mind and Brain*, T. Simon and R. Scholes, eds., Hillsdale, NJ: Erlbaum.

Harnad, S., 1982b, "Consciousness: An afterthought," *Cognition and Brain Theory* **5**, 29–47.

Harnad, S., 1984, "Verifying machines' minds (Review of J.T. Culbertson, Consciousness: Natural and artificial, NY: Libra 1982)," *Contemporary Psychology* **29**, 389–391.

Harnad, S., 1985, "Bugs, slugs, computers and consciousness," *American Psychologist* **73**, 21.

Harnad, S., 1989, "Minds, machines and Searle," *Journal of Theoretical and Experimental Artificial Intelligence* **1**, 5–25.

Harnad, S., 1990a, "The symbol grounding problem," *Physica D* **42**, 335–346.

Harnad, S., 1990b, "Against computational hermeneutics (Invited Commentary on Eric Dietrich's Computationalism)," *Social Epistemology* **4**, 167–172.

Harnad, S., 1990c, "Lost in the hermeneutic hall of mirrors. Invited Commentary on: Michael Dyer: Minds, Machines, Searle and Harnad," *Journal of Experimental and Theoretical Artificial Intelligence* **2**, 321–327.

Harnad, S., 1991, "Other bodies, other minds: A machine incarnation of an old philosophical problem," *Minds and Machines* **1**, 43–54.

Harnad, S., 1992a, "Connecting object to symbol in modeling cognition," pp. 75–90 in *Connectionism in Context*, A. Clark and R. Lutz, eds., Berlin: Springer-Verlag.

Harnad, S., 1992b, "The Turing test is not a trick: Turing indistinguishability is a scientific criterion," *SIGART Bulletin* **3** 9–10.

Harnad, S., 1993a, "Grounding symbols in the analog world with neural nets," *Think* **2**, 12–78 (Special issue on "Connectionism versus Symbolism," D.M.W. Powers and P.A. Flach, eds.).

Harnad, S., 1993b, "Artificial life: Synthetic versus virtual," pp. 539–549 in *Artificial Life III, Proceedings*, C. Langton, ed., Santa Fe Institute Studies in the Sciences of Complexity, Vol. XVI, Reading, MA: Addison Wesley.

Harnad S., 1993c, "Discussion (passim)," in *Experimental and Theoretical Studies of Consciousness*, G.R. Bock and J. Marsh, eds., CIBA Foundation Symposium 174, Chichester: Wiley.

Harnad, S., 1994a, "Levels of functional equivalence in reverse bioengineering: The Darwinian Turing test for artificial life," *Artificial Life* **1**, 293–301. Reprinted in C.G. Langton, ed., 1995, *Artificial Life: An Overview*, Cambridge, MA: MIT Press.

Harnad, S., 1994b, "Computation is just interpretable symbol manipulation: Cognition isn't," *Minds and Machines* **4**, 379–390 (Special Issue on "What Is Computation").

Harnad, S., 1995a, Does the mind piggy-back on robotic and symbolic capacity?," pp. 204–220 in *The Mind, the Brain, and Complex Adaptive Systems*, H. Morowitz, ed., Santa Fe Institute Studies in the Sciences of Complexity, Vol. XXII, Reading, MA: Addison-Wesley.

Harnad, S., 1995b, "Why and how we are not zombies," *Journal of Consciousness Studies* **1**, 164–167.

Harnad, S., 1996, "The origin of words: A psychophysical hypothesis," pp. 27–44 in *Communicating Meaning: Evolution and Development of Language*, B. Velichkovsky and D. Rumbaugh, eds., Hillsdale, NJ: Erlbaum.

Harnad, S., 2000a, "Turing indistinguishability and the blind watchmaker," in *Evolving Consciousness*, G. Mulhauser, ed., Amsterdam: John Benjamins (in press).

Harnad, S., 2000b, "What's wrong and right about Searle's Chinese Room argument?," in *Essays on Searle's Chinese Room Argument*, M. Bishop and J. Preston, eds., Oxford: Oxford University Press.

Harnad, S., 2000c, "Correlation vs. causality: How/why the mind/body problem is hard," *Journal of Consciousness Studies* **7**, 54–61.

Harnad, S., Doty, R.W., Goldstein, L., Jaynes, J., and Krauthamer, G., eds., 1977, *Lateralization in the Nervous System*, New York: Academic Press.

Hauser, L., 1993, "Reaping the whirlwind: Reply to Harnad's 'Other bodies, other minds'," *Minds and Machines* **3**, 219–237.

Hayes, P., Harnad, S., Perlis, D., and Block, N., 1992, "Virtual symposium on virtual mind," *Minds and Machines* **2**, 217–238.

Heyes, C.M., 1998, "Theory of mind in nonhuman primates," *Behavioral and Brain Sciences* **21**, 101–134.

Loebner, H.G., 1994, "Lessons from a restricted turing test – In response," *Communications of the ACM* **37**(6), 79–82.

Mitchell, R.W. and Anderson, J.R., 1998, "Primate theory of mind is a Turing test," *Behavioral and Brain Sciences* **21**, 127–128.

Nagel, T., 1974, "What is it like to be a bat?," *Philosophical Review* **83**, 435–451.

Newell, A., 1980, "Physical symbol systems," *Cognitive Science* **4**, 135–183.

Pylyshyn, Z.W., 1980, "Computation and cognition: Issues in the foundations of cognitive science," *Behavioral and Brain Sciences* **3**, 111–169.

Pylyshyn, Z.W., 1984, *Computation and Cognition*, Cambridge, MA: MIT/Bradford.

Pylyshyn, Z.W., ed., 1987, *The Robot's Dilemma: The Frame Problem in Artificial Intelligence*, Norwood NJ: Ablex.

Schweizer, P., 1998, "The truly total Turing test," *Minds and Machines* **8**, 263–272.

Searle, J.R., 1980, "Minds, brains, and programs," *Behavioral and Brain Sciences* **3**, 417–457.

Searle, J.R., 1984, *Minds, Brains and Science*, Cambridge, MA: Harvard University Press.

Searle, J.R., 1990, "Consciousness, explanatory inversion, and cognitive science," *Behavioral and Brain Sciences* **13**, 585–642.

Searle, J.R., 1993, "The failures of computationalism," *THINK* **2**, 70–77.

Shieber, S.M., 1994, "Lessons from a restricted Turing test," *Communications of the ACM* **37**, 70–78.

Steklis, H.D. and Harnad, S., 1976, "From hand to mouth: Some critical stages in the evolution of language," pp. 445–455 in *Origins and Evolution of Language and Speech*, S. Harnad, H.D. Steklis, and J.B. Lancaster, eds., Annals of the New York Academy of Sciences, Vol. 280, New York: New York Academy of Sciences.

Turing, A.M., 1950, "Computing machinery and intelligence," *Mind* **49**, 433–460. (Reprinted in A. Anderson, ed., 1964, *Minds and Machines*, Engelwood Cliffs, NJ: Prentice Hall.)

Watt, S., 1996, "Naive psychology and the inverted Turing test," *PSYCOLOQUY* **7**.

Wimsatt, W.K., 1954, *The Verbal Icon: Studies in the Meaning of Poetry*, Louisville: University Press of Kentucky.